DAVI~
UMPI~
DABC/H~

M000250891

REC 9-7-04

BEGIN: 10/28/04   0153 HRS.

END: 11/17/04   0352 HRS

Everything Happens in Chillicothe

RICHMOND ROOSTERS LEAVING FRONTIER
LEAGUE TO TRAVERSE CITY, MI
FOLLOWING 2005 SEASON.

ALSO BY MIKE SHANNON

*The Day Satchel Paige and the Pittsburgh Crawfords
Came to Hertford, N.C.: Baseball Stories and Poems*
(McFarland, 1992)

*Diamond Classics: Essays on 100 of the
Best Baseball Books Ever Published*
(McFarland, 1989; paperback 2003)

Everything Happens in Chillicothe

in Chillicothe

*A Summer in the Frontier
League with Max McLeary,
the One-Eyed Umpire*

M<small>IKE</small> S<small>HANNON</small>

McFarland & Company, Inc., Publishers
Jefferson, North Carolina, and London

LIBRARY OF CONGRESS CATALOGUING-IN-PUBLICATION DATA

Shannon, Mike.
    Everything happens in Chillicothe : a summer in the Frontier League
with Max McLeary, the one-eyed umpire / Mike Shannon.
       p.   cm.
    Includes index.

    ISBN 0-7864-1694-7 (softcover : 50# alkaline paper) ∞

    1. McLeary, Max.   2. Baseball umpires—United States—Biography.
3. Frontier League—History.   4. Minor league baseball—United
States—Anecdotes.   I. Title.
GV865.M314S53   2004
796.357'092—dc22   2003022656

British Library cataloguing data are available

©2004 Mike Shannon. All rights reserved

*No part of this book may be reproduced or transmitted in any form
or by any means, electronic or mechanical, including photocopying
or recording, or by any information storage and retrieval system,
without permission in writing from the publisher.*

Cover photograph: Umpire Max McLeary

Manufactured in the United States of America

McFarland & Company, Inc., Publishers
  Box 611, Jefferson, North Carolina 28640
   www.mcfarlandpub.com

To Jeanne and Wilson; "Here we go again."
—Max, #9

For Meg, Casey, Mickey, Babe, Nolan,
and, most of all, Derms.
—Mike

In memory of
Roger W. Hanners:
March 4, 1931–January 24, 2002

Acknowledgments

IN WORKING ON THIS BOOK I received the generous cooperation of hundreds of people. I am grateful to them all, including everyone mentioned by name in the text proper. My thanks also go to the following: Matt Andrews, the radio voice of the Chillicothe Paints; David Arch of the Cook County Cheetahs; Scott Brumfield of the Richmond Roosters; Sara Coblentz, "the baseball wife"; Jim Crowley; Joyce Crull of the Indiana Football Hall of Fame; Danielle DeGroodt of the River City Rascals; Tom Eckel; Dustin Egan of the *Chillicothe Gazette*; Chad Epperson; Rodney Fender, aka Chief Crazy Horse; Bill Felix of The Candy Store in Johnstown, PA; Christina Foster of the Chillicothe-Ross Chamber of Commerce; Scott Graham of Adelphia Cable; Andy Furman of WLW radio in Cincinnati; Noah Hanners; Greg Heffernan; Lonnie Herman; Amir Kanji; Marie Knecht; Dr. Michael Leadbetter; Annie Lightle; Sister Francis Margaret Maag, CDP; John Masson; Ricardo Mathison; Pat McAllister; Bill McGill, Managing Editor of *Spitball: The Literary Baseball Magazine*; Mary McMahon; Bob Nelson of the Chillicothe Tree Commission; Scott Osborne of the *Chillicothe Gazette*; Todd Porter of the *Canton Repository*; Shawn Robinson; Greg Rhodes; Mike Scherr; Mark Schraf; Joshua Smith of the *Richmond Paladium-Item*; Dee Taylor of the *Chillicothe Gazette*; John Westover; Jason Swegman, Marty DeRemer, Roger Bingle, Ronald Williams, Garrett Stevenson, and Chris Lovins of the Krispy Kreme Doughnut Corporation; and Tom and Jo Ann White.

Special thanks, as always, go to my parents, John Hubert and Willie Mae Shannon; to my sisters and brothers, Laura Smiley, Susie Klemmt, Johnny Shannon, and Tim Shannon; and to their husbands, wives, and children: Jeff and Andrew Smiley; Lyle and Evan Klemmt; Janice, Rachel, John, and Laura Shannon; and Carla, Riley, and Claire Shannon.

Contents

1

Boswell Meets His Johnson

BEFORE I MET MAX MCLEARY I knew exactly where his place of business was, near the corner of Harrison and Queen City Avenues, just past the viaduct which carries traffic over Cincinnati's rail yards and into the city's lower West End. While delivering Krispy Kreme doughnuts, I'd driven past his shop many times, and it's pretty hard to miss a building with the back half of a pink '57 Chevy sticking out of the roof at a jaunty angle as if it were some kind of automotive lawn dart.

The car was originally black, but about two months after Max and nine or ten of his closest friends had hoisted it onto the roof with block and tackle and braced it into place, he painted it pink, using a two-inch roller, so that the car would attract the attention of more potential customers to his automotive reupholstering business.

One of the first people to notice Max's nifty paint job was a City of Cincinnati building inspector. "How long has that ... that thing been up there?" he asked.

"You mean the car?" said Max. The man definitely meant the car. "Oh, a couple of months."

"Like hell," said the inspector peevishly. "This is my territory, and I've never seen that thing before. There's no way I've missed it for two months." Max assured the inspector that, as much as it looked like it had, the Chevy had not fallen out of the sky just five minutes earlier.

The next day Max went downtown with his checkbook as he had been ordered to. "I want to apply for a building permit," he said to the man at the counter.

1

"What's the permit for?" asked the clerk.

"I was told it would be classified as a sign," said Max.

"What kind of sign is it?"

"A '57 Chevy."

"Well, well," said the bemused clerk, "You must be Max McLeary."

I drove over to Max's on Friday morning, May 26, hoping to get a few good baseball stories for a new book of baseball anecdotes that would follow *Tales from the Dugout* and *Tales from the Ballpark*. In fact, I knew for certain that I'd get some good stories because I'd already heard second-hand versions of them from Jerry Hazelbaker, a mutual friend of mine and Max's. For years Jerry owned and managed a popular Cincinnati sports bar called Crosley's, and he had been invaluable in putting me in touch with people with funny baseball stories in their repertoire.

Jerry and Max had gotten to know each other through their participation in an over-forty baseball league known as Roy Hobbs Baseball; Jerry as a player, Max as an umpire. Jerry had once told me, "I love it when Max umpires one of our games. I know he's not going to ring me up on a questionable pitch on the corner, so the pitchers have to give me something to swing at. When I get to the ballpark and see Max, I go 'All right!'"

If Max had become infamous overnight to the employees in the Cincinnati Building Inspection Department, his legend in baseball circles had grown slowly, like the rings in a giant redwood. Max had been umpiring for over thirty years, and in that time he had worked hundreds of minor league games, in addition to thousands of games on the collegiate, high school, and a variety of amateur non-scholastic levels. And he had done so with only one good eye.

An umpire with a glass eye. It sounded like a red-necked witticism, along the order of the one-legged man in an ass-kicking contest. Or like something out of a Franz Kafka novel. Indeed, familiar with the abuse fans often heap on expert baseball arbiters who have all their faculties intact, many reasonable people might conclude that it would be preferable to wake up one day to the nightmare of having been inexplicably transformed into a human-sized cock roach rather than a one-eyed umpire. But Max McLeary was neither the living embodiment of the stereotypical umpire joke—"Hey, ump, you're blind in one eye and can't see out of the other"—nor a figment of the imagination of a literary genius. He was, rather, the truth that is stranger than fiction and a man of some exceptional talents to have survived for so long in such a publicly scrutinized and unforgiving profession as umpiring. These things about Max I knew intuitively. How good an umpire he actually was I had no way of knowing, and I really wasn't all that concerned about it, since all I wanted was a few good stories.

One thing about Max I knew for sure was that he was about as well-adjusted to his disability, if you want to call it that, as anyone could be. For instance, Jerry had already told me about Max's "baseball eye." Every so often, because of slight changes to his good eye, Max requires an optometric artist to paint him a new glass eye so that it matches his good eye. A few years ago Max had the artist paint one of the old glass eyes completely white and then add red baseball stitches to it. Before a college game one spring, Max put in his baseball eye, donned a pair of sunglasses, and walked out to home plate for the groundrules. After Max, his partner, and the two coaches had just about concluded their meeting, Max removed his sun glasses as he got to the end of the following benediction, "Gentlemen, I know we're going to have a fine game today because I can see it in your eyes, as I know you can see it in mine."

Another time while having a few post-game beers with friends, he amused the men and horrified the women at the table by removing his glass eye and plopping it like an antacid tablet into the drink of one of the ladies. Max once even used his eye to shut up an obnoxious high school coach. After he'd heard all the complaining he wanted to hear, Max took his eye out of the socket and handed it to the stunned coach, saying, "You want to umpire this game? Here, be my guest."

Max greeted me warmly a few moments after I walked through the big wooden doors of his shop, which used to house an auto repair garage, and I immediately felt at ease around him. He thanked me for coming by to see him before I could thank him for agreeing to talk to me. Max showed me into his office, a slice of a room off to the right outfitted to look like a soda fountain from the 1950s. I sat down on one of the four padded bar stools on one side of the counter that split the room, and Max took a seat behind the counter. Before we could really get started, the phone rang and Max excused himself to attend to some business in the main part of the shop. I used the interruption to study Max's self-made environment.

The focal point of the back wall of the office behind the counter I was sitting at was supposed to be a neon clock advertising WZIP, the call letters of a Cincinnati radio station that years ago had been changed to WSAI. However, even if the clock had not been running about two hours slow, it would still have been vastly overshadowed by the two University of Georgia gymnastics team posters hanging beneath it. Known as "Gymdogs" instead of Bulldogs and dressed in sparkling tight-fitting one-piece suits, the beaming Georgia coeds pictured in the posters pro-

Max (age 12) shaking hands with Don Hoak at Pittsburgh's Forbes Field.

jected enormous athletic and sexual vigor. Since the posters had been autographed, I wondered if one of the Gymdogs was related to Max. As it turned out, it was another umpire and a friend of Max's who was the father of one of the Gymdogs. He'd given Max the posters in order to brighten up the office. They did that and more. "My umpire buddies drool all over themselves when they see those posters," Max said later.

On the same wall as the clock and the Gymdogs posters hung a framed 8 × 10 which Max treasured. It was a photo of a twelve-year-old Max shaking hands with Pittsburgh Pirates third baseman Don Hoak at Forbes Field in 1960, as a few of Max's Little League teammates and his dad look on. Hoak had been brought over to the box seats by coach Frank Oceak, a native of Johnstown, Pennsylvania, who was an old friend of Max's dad.

Mementos of Max's family were to be found elsewhere in the shop. A decades-old newspaper photo of a football game hung so inconspicuously in a small frame on the wall behind me next to the office door that I didn't even notice it for a good while. The photo captured Penn State running back Franco Harris crossing the goal line for a touchdown in Happy Valley. I later learned that Max is a big Penn State fan because he'd grown up in Johnstown, Pennsylvania. The significance of this particular photo went well beyond one more Nittany Lion TD though. "The referee in the photo signaling 'touchdown' was my dad, Wilson," said Max with pride and reverence. "Officiating is in my blood, and it comes from my dad."

With Max still on the phone, I stepped out of the office and back into the large "garage" area. On the wall directly in front of me hung a bulletin board to which were tacked snapshots, newspaper clippings, pennants, schedules, postcards of baseball stadiums, and lineup cards from games past; all related to baseball or Max's umpiring. One newspaper clipping in particular caught my attention, the one which completed the McLeary generational connection to sports. It was a spring training game report and box score which recorded the game in which Marty McLeary made his pitching debut with the Boston Red Sox.

As soon as Max got off the phone, we got down to business, and I could see after five minutes that he was going to be the easiest interview I'd ever conducted. Delivered in the gravelly voice of the longtime heavy cigarette smoker that he is, the stories flowed out of him ceaselessly and unbidden, like springtime melt water rushing down a mountain gully. Everything Max brought up seemed to be either a prelude or a segue to a new story, and he told each tale with the same passion and desire to please that Scheherazade must have felt in narrating *The Arabian Nights' Entertainments.*

"I'm very superstitious," he said. "I have certain rituals I follow before, during, and after every game. For instance, I never go on the field without my three rocks or my two dollar coin I got in London last year while doing the playoffs." I didn't understand the reference to London but knew I could ask about it later.

"Lemme tell you how I got my rocks," he continued. "I was doing the plate for a big Conference USA game here in Cincinnati between Memphis State and UC. One of the Memphis State hitters took a strike, and I rang him up: 'STREEE!!!' Except that it wasn't the third strike. As soon as I did it, I knew I'd screwed up. Nobody in the stands cheered, none of the players reacted. You talk about the worst feeling in the world! Oh boy. Well, I recovered as fast as I could ... 'Two and two!' ... 'Two and two!' When the inning was over, the Memphis State coach walked down from the third base coach's box. He put three small rocks in my hand and said, 'Here, Max. See if you can keep these straight.'

"I've carried those rocks with me ever since, never walk on the field without 'em."

Max paused just long enough to light another cigarette and then was off again. "The one thing I've never done as an umpire is work the plate for a no-hitter," he said. "I've been on the bases for four or five of them but never behind the dish. Not in pro ball, college, or even high school.

"Last spring I was scheduled to work the plate for an important high school game in Cincinnati between Moeller and Sycamore near the end of the season. Moeller is a sports powerhouse in the Greater Catholic League—as everybody knows Moeller is where Ken Griffey, Jr. went to high school—and Sycamore is a big public school. And since they're geographically so close together, they're big rivals.

"The day before the big game the Sycamore coach calls me up and says, 'Max, I just want to warn you, it's gonna be "pitch and duck" out there tomorrow. All my front line pitching is either injured or worn out, so I'm down to my number five starter. It could get real ugly.' Okay, fine, I thought, we'll all just have to do the best we can.

"So the game starts, there's a huge crowd, and we're rolling. The Sycamore kid is pitching a great game. He's got good stuff and great control, around the plate with every pitch. It's beautiful the way we're rolling through this game. Come to find out later on, not only is the kid inexperienced, but it's also his first high school start ever. Nevertheless, Sycamore is up 5–0 and this kid is just breezing through the game.

"When the Sycamore catcher comes out to start the seventh inning, he turns his back to the mound and says, 'Hey, Max, do you know what that stupid shortstop of ours just did in the dugout? He went up to our pitcher and asked him if he knew he was throwing a no-hitter!' Aw, crap, I thought. That dumb S.O.B., now he's done it.

"I hadn't even been aware that the kid had a no-hitter going. I knew now though that Moeller was going to be bunting. Even being behind 5–0 they didn't want to be no-hit, so I knew they'd do anything they could to break it up. I waved at the Sycamore third baseman to play in, but he ignored me. And sure enough, the leadoff Moeller batter bunted the first pitch of the inning down third. It rolled about half way down the line, and the third baseman was so far back he didn't even make a play on it. I ran out from behind the plate and could see that the third baseman wasn't going to get it, so I was hoping for a big gust of wind to push it foul or an earthquake or anything, but it stopped right on the line. Had no choice but to signal: … fair.

"Well, the Moeller dugout was hooping and hollering, there was a lot of noise and commotion in the stands, and it took a little while for everything to settle down. I went back behind the plate but just before I got ready to signal to the pitcher to throw, I called time. I looked over at the Sycamore dugout and yelled to the coach that the time out was not going to be charged to him. 'It's on me, this one's on me,' I said.

An umpire can do that in certain situations, like if he can tell that a pitcher has hurt himself and isn't throwing right.

"I walked out to the mound, the Sycamore coach came out, and then I called the whole infield in for a conference. When all the kids were there, I looked right at the shortstop and said, "Fellas, there's two things no pitcher ever, ever wants to hear. One is 'Honey, I'm pregnant.' And the other is 'Duh, gee ... YOU'RE PITCHIN' A NO-HITTER!'

"The coach almost fell down laughing, and the word obviously got around later after the game because the next day I got a call from the Moeller coach, Mike Cameron. Mike told me, 'Max, I've been teaching and coaching for thirty years, and today four teachers who haven't spoken to me in ten years came up to me in the halls and asked me if the umpire really said what they'd heard he said. And this morning to conclude our devotions and announcements over the PA, the question of the day was, 'What are the two things a pitcher never wants to hear?'"

Max's glass eye made me a little nervous. Because I was afraid I might stare at it, I made a special effort to look only into his good eye. However, as his stories went on and on, I was able to relax more and more and I soon forgot all about his glass eye.

Max's cropped silver hair and the lines in his pleasant, swarthy face made him look older than he was—I was surprised to learn later that he was only 52—but they also gave him a distinguished appearance like that of an ancient Roman senator perhaps that was perfectly suited for his work as an authority figure among contesting athletic men in the prime of their lives.

As if to add a moral to his story about his near no-hit game, Max said, "I didn't plan on saying something like that. It just came to me, and I went with it. But you have to pick your spots for things like that—and that game was 5–0 in the last inning—because you don't ever want to do anything to compromise the integrity of the game. But players and coaches and managers have come to expect just about anything from me. And things just pop out of my mouth sometimes.

"Like the time I was doing an NCAA Division III tournament game between Wooster and Wittenberg. The game was at Ohio Wesleyan University in Delaware (OH), and both teams were bearing down on every pitch because they were both trying to advance to the college world series. Wooster was batting with a man on first when there was a ground ball to second. The runner coming from first took out the Wittenberg shortstop and he wasn't able to get the double play, but it was totally legal because the shortstop was coming into the basepath.

"Well, both coaches came flying onto the field. I started going one-on-one face-to-face with one guy when the other guy moved in and all of a sudden I was going one-on-one with him. Then they both got face-to-face with me, one on either side. That's when I stepped back and said, 'Gentlemen, I'm not going to handle two things at the same time. I haven't been able to deal with two things at once since the Pink Floyd concert in 1992.'

"And that just floored them both. They stood there quietly a few seconds, then Tim Pettorini, the Wooster coach, shook his head and said, 'Max, you're fucked up.' Then he turned to the other coach, Rick Willis of Wittenberg, and said, 'There's no use you arguing with 'im either.' And with that they both walked off the field and we got on with the game. They both knew me and probably expected something bizarre."

During the telling of the "Pink Floyd" story, Max's friend and fellow umpire Tim Johnson walked in. Tim had just gotten off work from the Keebler Cookie Company and was still wearing his company uniform shirt embroidered with the Keebler logo. Clearly one of Max's biggest fans, Tim had chuckled gleefully throughout Max's rendition of the story. When it was over, he added his own coda to it. "What makes Max such a good umpire is his people skills," he said. "And that's why Max and Jim Schaly make such a good combination. Schaly, who's something of a hot head, is the complete opposite of Max. As Schaly says, 'Max, you kill 'em with kindness, and I kill 'em with a size nine up the ass!' And then Tim laughed uproarishly at his own Maxy anecdote.

"That's right," said Max. "I will not swear or raise my voice. Sometimes you're tempted to, but there's usually a better way to handle the situation.

"One time I was doing a Frontier League game in Chillicothe, Ohio, between the Richmond Roosters and the Chillicothe Paints," he began another story to illustrate the point, "and the base ump—I can't remember who it was—had left the game for some reason. I don't know why but for whatever reason he was gone. We used to have three man crews, but the League went to two man crews three years ago to save money. Anyway, Chillicothe was in the field, and the batter took a checked swing. The Chillicothe catcher, as catchers always do in that situation, asked me to check with the base umpire, who supposedly has a better view of whether or not the batter actually swung at the pitch. Well, when I took off my mask and looked down to first to ask the base ump for his help, there was nobody there.

"Rogers Hanners, the Chillicothe manager, started out of the dugout, so I knew I had to do something fast. I turned around, looked up into the stands, and asked the fans, 'DID HE GO?' Like a church congregation answering the preacher they shouted back in unison, 'NO, HE DIDN'T GO!'

At Chillicothe, versus Richmond.

"I looked at Roger and said, 'Is that good enough for you?' And, of course, he said, 'Yeah, that's good enough.' What else could he say since it was his team's hometown fans who had rendered the verdict?"

I was beginning to realize that Max officiated baseball games as if he'd graduated *summa cum laude* from the Bill Veeck ("As in Wreck") Academy of Umpiring. Of course, Veeck, the owner who once sent a midget to bat for the St. Louis Browns in an official American League game, had never run such a school, but if baseball's ultimate maverick and showman had done so, the school undoubtedly would have turned out graduates like Max, who umpired enthusiastically, resourcefully, and, when the occasion demanded it, unorthodoxically.

It also finally dawned on me that Max was still umpiring professionally. For some reason I had thought that his professional career was all in the past. I recalled Max's earlier allusion to London … London, Ontario, as it turned out, which I now surmised correctly was a member of the Frontier League.

I knew that the Frontier League was an independent minor league, which means that while its members are professional baseball organizations, they are not affiliated with (nor supported by) major league teams, as are the teams in the standard "affiliated" minor leagues. But that was about all I knew. My own experience with the Frontier League was limited to a single game I'd attended in 1996. Because of that game I knew one more thing about the League: it made baseball fun in a way the major leagues, with their greedy owners, spoiled players, and inflated prices, rarely did anymore.

At the time, I was still playing fast pitch softball, that wonderful game, the men's version of which is dying because pitchers who have taken the time to master the art of the underhanded windmill delivery at the heart of the sport are harder to find than a good deal on a used car lot.

It was the weekend of August 10 and 11, and we were playing in a national qualifying tournament in Zanesville, a small Ohio town about 100 miles east of Columbus that is skirted by Interstate 70 as it stretches towards Wheeling, West Virginia. By early afternoon the Hamilton (OH) Merchants team I played first base for had won our first two games, so we had the luxury of being able to look forward to enjoying the evening's entertainment—whatever it might prove to be—full of the relief, confidence, and exuberance felt by a team still in the winner's bracket after the first day of competition. The evening's diversion turned out to be a Frontier League game between the hometown Zanesville Greys and the Johnstown (PA) Steal.

After we'd showered and changed into our party clothes, we discovered that we weren't the only ball team staying at the Best Western on N. Seventh Street in downtown Zanesville. It wasn't another fast-pitch softball team we ran into but the Steal, as they were getting dressed and were waiting to board two Greyhound buses idling in the front parking lot. I went looking for center fielder Matt Wynn and third baseman Steve Morgan, the two ringleaders of the Merchants' social club (motto: "If there's a good time out there, we'll find it"), and I located them on the walkway running along the second level on the backside of the motel, talking to a Steal's relief pitcher by the name of Brett McAdams. Both in their late twenties, Wynn and Morgan represented youth by Merchants' standards, but McAdams—about 22 years old—truly was young, just a kid really. "I'm here because I love the game, " he said. "We all do. We're trying to play well enough to impress somebody so that we get signed by a major league organization. All we want is a shot." Maybe the kid had a college degree and maybe he didn't, but it would have been pretty hard to sum up any better the mission statement of the Frontier League from a player's perspective.

McAdams offered to collect enough players' tickets from his teammates so that our team would be able to pass into the Greys–Steal game that night. A voice came from the walkway above us: "We're wearing the gray hats tonight. Gray hats." We thanked McAdams, then headed

ZANESVILLE Greys (GANT
MUNICIPAL)
STADIUM

for the Zanesville Ponderosa with its all-you-can-eat buffet, where we did some serious damage to the restaurant's profit margin for the month. As a parting joke Morgan said, "We'll leave you guys some passes to our fastpitch game tomorrow morning."

10/29/94

Gant Municipal Stadium, which was the home of the Greys, isn't hard to find. You go west out Main Street a couple of miles, then bear left as you cross Zanesville's famous Y Bridge. After another mile or so, light stanchions, towering over the houses still ahead on the right, come into view. I rode over to Gant with our catcher-DH Bill Kintner, in real life a cigar-smoking, vitamin-binging traveling salesman, who is also a college basketball junkie and a huge Rush Limbaugh fan. We walked up to the lone ticket window and told the ticket lady that one of the Johnstown players was supposed to have left tickets for us. "Your buddies are already inside," she said as she slid us two $3 General Admission tickets.

As we walked through the gate around eight o'clock, we passed a little girl seated in a folding chair. She'd probably tripped while running up and down the grandstands, and her skinned knee and elbow were being attended to by medical personnel. I walked forward and up a wide ramp. When I emerged into the fading sunlight I found myself on the left field line in a sparsely populated grandstands that seated about 2,000. It was prime seating for the high school football games played there—a white goal post loomed over the left field wall—but a quick look to the right made it obvious that plenty of better baseball seats were available in the grandstands between the dugouts. Kintner and I joined the other Merchants, including our 57 year old pitcher Larry "Skinman" Skinner, in the top half of Section 2 behind the visitor's dugout on the first base side.

For the next couple of hours we had a blast, talking about fastpitch softball and our crabby but lovable manager Murel J. Phillips, a legend in fastpitch circles who was too sick from cancer to travel with us; drinking in the cheap beer and the minor league-small town ambience; and watching the Greys and Steal go at it. A couple of banners proclaimed that Gant Stadium would be the site of the upcoming American Legion State Tourney, and an elderly female fan rang a cow bell to celebrate every good play made by the Greys. At one point a goateed Steal player, the bill of his cap curved downwards as if he'd tried to pinch the sides together, stood up next to the dugout and looked into the stands. Three giggly pre-pubescent girls were sitting near us. The boldest of them stood up and shouted at him, "Will you take us out to dinner after the game?" He nodded, then spit. The girl smiled at her friends, then asked, "Will you pay for it?" He nodded again.

On the field the play was decidedly minor league but exciting

JOHNSTOWN STEAL

nonetheless. Although we saw quite a few screaming line drives hit, the batters all seemed to have warning track power at best (the field had rather modest dimensions). The fielding seemed fine and we even saw a couple of super plays, but the pitching looked suspect. Both managers trotted out a succession of pitchers, and as far as I know, Zanesville pulled it out 9–8, the score when we left in the top of the ninth. The highlight of the game came when Johnstown had the bases loaded and almost scored all three runners on the same wild pitch. The runner on third scored easily. The runner on second scored when the Zanesville catcher threw wildly to the pitcher covering home. The runner on first came all the way around and sped for home plate too as the Zanesville short-stop slipped and fell, the ball rolling past him and into left field. It looked to us as if the Steal runner from first beat the left fielder's throw, but the ump called him out. We all jumped up and booed heartily (we were pulling for our Johnstown cohorts of course), while the rest of the stadium cheered the putout.

I was curious about the Greys and the league they played in and amazed that we had found professional baseball so far out in the boonies. Hoping to find a little information about both, I bought a program for a dollar. Sure enough, it informed me that Zanesville had a professional baseball history that dated back to 1884. Ad Gumbert, Jim Thorpe, Tommy Henrich, and Clay Bryant had all played pro ball for one Zanes-ville minor league team or another before moving on to the big leagues, and over the years Zanesville had had franchises in the Ohio League, the Tri-State League, the Ohio and West Virginia League, the Pennsyl-vania, Ohio, and Maryland League, the Central League, the Middle Atlantic League, and the Ohio-Indiana League.

The program also said that the Frontier League had begun three years earlier, in 1993, and had been founded by Bud Bickel under the premise that "undrafted players could play in smaller markets to hone their skills and impress major league talent scouts." Zanesville, I read, was one of three original members still in the league. In addition to Zanesville and Johnstown, league membership was made up of the Chil-licothe (OH) Paints, Evansville (IN) Otters, Kalamazoo (MI) Kodiaks, Ohio Valley (Parkersburg, W VA) Redcoats, Richmond (IN) Roosters, and Springfield (IL) Capitals.

While I was looking through the program, one of the promotions run throughout the game took place. "Fans, check your program, and if your program has the signature of a Zanesville Greys player or coach, you are the lucky winner of a $10 gift certificate from Steak'n Stein," said the P.A. announcer. I turned the pages of my program to the Steak'n Stein ad, and there I saw the signature in gold ink of pitcher/coach Tom Crowley, #4.

I headed for the Courtesy Booth out in the picnic area farther down the right field line to claim my prize, but when I got there the woman manning the booth realized there was a problem. I had the winning program all right, but somehow the Steak'n Stein GC had already been given away. The assistant GM said they'd have to give me a substitute prize. I said I'd be happy to have a Greys tee shirt from the nearby souvenir stand, but he said no, he didn't think he could do that. Okay, fine, I thought, whatever. I was resigned to getting something like a Greys bumper sticker or a coupon for a discount at a local hair salon and was flabbergasted when he brought me a Cooper bat autographed by the entire Zanesville team. The bat had been cracked—aluminum bats, of course, are not allowed in pro ball—and none of the Merchants had heard of any of the players who'd signed the bat, but they agreed with me that the assistant GM had been thoughtful and generous in substituting the bat for the GC.

Towards the end of the night I tracked down the Greys General Manager, David L. Maloney. His picture was in the program, and his beard and tinted glasses made him easy to spot. He told me about his previous experience in professional baseball—he'd worked 17 years for the San Diego Padres in various capacities—gave me a brief history of the Zanesville franchise and the Frontier League; and said with confidence that it was just a matter of time before a player would graduate from the Frontier League to the majors, just as Philadelphia Phillies pitcher Mike Mims was the first player to make it to the big leagues after playing in the Frontier League's counterpart and model, the independent Northern League which had been started by *Baseball America* publisher Miles Wolff. Maloney also admitted that while six of the eight Frontier League franchises were doing very well, Zanesville was one of the two franchises that were not. "The selling season, which is key for minor league baseball, is in the fall. Because of a change in ownership last year, we missed that opportunity and it's really hurt us," he said. "Attendance is up this year, but we are still going to lose money because we didn't sell enough advertising in the fall." Gee, I thought, maybe we should have paid for our tickets, just to help the Greys out. As if he'd read my mind, Maloney said, "In the minors you don't make money off ticket sales. You make it on advertising and also on concessions and souvenir sales." No problem there, I thought. The Merchants have kept the concession workers busy all night.

The phone rang in the Greys' business office, and Maloney had to take it. Morgan came over to tell me the Merchants were heading back to the motel. We played at ten the next morning and needed some rest. Maloney's call must have been from home because I heard him say, "The game's almost over. See you soon. ... I love you too."

KINTNER THE SHANNON'S CATCHER FOR TEAM, PC 11

As I walked across the main aisle that ran between the dugouts, headed out of the stadium, I was hit by a balled-up napkin. I didn't even look up, figuring it had been thrown by a Zanesville park rat. Then he called out to me: "Shannon!" It was Kintner, who'd supposedly left an hour earlier to return to Cincinnati so that he could catch an early morning flight to San Diego to attend the Republican National Convention. He was sitting with the female fastpitch umpire who'd worked the bases during our second game. Altogether she'd worked three games that day but loved baseball enough to be at Gant Stadium that night. At the Greys game she had probably been watching the umpiring as much as the ball playing, maybe doing a little dreaming just like the youngsters in the stands. Bill wanted me to join him and the lady ump, but I told him I had to go or I was going to be left behind by the rest of the team.

I walked out of Gant Stadium, and there was Matt Wynn, using my autographed Greys bat to practice his beautiful left-handed swing underneath a lamp post in the parking lot. Mentally, I wished the Greys good luck and hoped that the citizens of Zanesville and Muskingum County would do whatever was necessary to keep the Greys alive because the last thing Maloney had told me was that the survival of the Greys was "up in the air."

As the Frontier League became the main topic of conversation between Max and me, my experience with the League, as limited as it was, began to create a bond between us.

In describing my Zanesville Greys experience to Max, I'd only told him that the game would be forever memorable to me for two things. The first thing was the play which had almost allowed three runs to score on the same wild pitch. Even zanier was something which we hadn't even been aware of when it happened. I learned about it later by reading the local Sunday newspaper.

Johnstown pitcher Jamie Irving had entered Saturday night's game in relief and had pitched lefthanded. The night before, on Friday, he had also pitched in relief, but the ambidextrous hurler had pitched righthanded then!

Before I could finish telling this story, Max began nodding his head in recognition and could hardly wait for me to spit it out so that he could begin his own story. "I had that same kid," he said excitedly. Max seemed to know personally every player, manager, and coach he talked about, but for once he didn't know a player's name.

"This kid was a lefthander, and for five innings he pitched a real nice game for the Johnnies," he said. "That's the same Johnstown team you were just talking about. For years the Johnstown minor league team

At Chillicothe.

was called the Johnnies. When they first got a franchise in the Frontier League they called the team the Steal, but a few years ago they changed the name back to the Johnnies. Anyway, this lefthanded kid had a nice little curve. He kept dinking it right on the outside corner, and for four innings the other team didn't touch him. In the fifth inning they started hitting 'im. They still didn't score, but some of the outs were hit pretty hard.

"Where was this?" I asked.

"This was in Chillicothe," he said. "So Johnstown's batting in the top of the sixth, and I notice they've got a righthander warming up in their bullpen. I guess they didn't like the way Chillicothe hit the ball in the fifth inning, and they're thinking they want to get the kid out of there before he gets into real trouble.

"After Johnstown goes out, here comes the righthander in from the Johnstown bullpen to start the bottom of the sixth. So I turn around, look up at the press box, and point over my shoulder at the mound, which is what we do to officially wave a new pitcher into the game. Until we do that, he's not official. But as I'm doing this, I can see the press box guys are cracking up about something. And John Wend, the public address announcer, is trying to signal me. He's making a pitching motion with his left arm, then one with his right arm, and then he points out at the mound. I turn around, look out at the mound, and then it hits me: it's the same kid that started the game! Only now he's warming up righthanded and throwing the ball much harder. Well, he finishes the game, blowing his good fastball by the hitters, and if I'm not mistaken he wound up pitching a shutout. He pitched the whole game, the first five innings lefthanded, and the last four righthanded."

Once I knew that Max was indeed still umpiring professionally, and for the Frontier League at that, my perspective had started to change. Now I was certain that things were headed in a different direction than before. "Max, I didn't know it when I came over here this morning, but you are a lot more than a couple of funny stories. I think you and the Frontier League are a book," I said. I let that sink in for a moment, then I asked him, "Could you stand to have me follow you around all summer?"

"I'd love it," he said, "and I'll do everything I can to help you." And just like that we were partners, ready to spend an entire summer together, riding like barnstormers up and down monotonous interstates and lonesome country two-lanes in search of nothing more than the good times and fond memories we knew would be the inheritance of anyone willing to give a season of his life to independent professional baseball.

Max was going to umpire in Richmond, Indiana, on Opening Day. He told me that it was a tradition for him to open the Frontier League season there. It couldn't be a very old tradition, I thought, but I liked the notion anyway.

With our sights now set firmly on Opening Day less than a week away, Max began to drop in my lap the names of people he suspected a writer interested in the Richmond Roosters would want to meet and talk to. There was John Cate, the Roosters manager who'd made the jump from high school coaching to professional managing; Cate's girlfriend, Cindy, "a real sweetheart who busts her ass doing a fantastic job" as the Roosters' head groundskeeper; Duke Ward, the affable Director of Business Operations, who would, Max was sure, help me in any way that he could; Big John, the clubhouse manager who had helped salvage for Max as a souvenir a big block of granite that had been part of McBride Stadium, home of the Roosters, before it underwent a facelift; David Knight, the Roosters' official scorer, as well as Earlham College's Sports Information Director and a close personal friend of Max's; a big Roosters fan known to Max simply as "Doc" who'd fashioned a handmade poster proclaiming "Max For President"; and Max's regular postgame drinking buddy, Tom, a box seat season ticket holder who, Max said, never sits in the box seats, preferring to stand out in the beer garden where he leans over the railing near the visiting dugout so that he's

BOOK OF ENT. 'OPENIN' DAY' 2004 SEASON (RICHMOND IND)

*I MET DUKE THROUGH, TOM 8/2004 SEASON.

1. Boswell Meets His Johnson

sure his comments will be heard by the players, managers, and umpires
he directs them at.

Max had made Richmond sound like a wonderful place for minor
league baseball and I couldn't wait to go there and get the 2000 Frontier League season started. We were both tiring, but before I left that
day I had to get one more story straight from the horse's mouth. It was
the story I'd come for more than for any other story. It was the most
famous of all Max stories. It was the one called "The Mask Story."

"One of my drinking buddies, a guy named Bob Hughes, went with
me to the game that day—I'll give you his phone number—and he can
tell you this story too," Max began.

"This was the night before the end of the season, and it was about
the fifth inning."

"Where was this, Max?" I asked.

"This happened in Chillicothe too," he replied. "Damn! Everything
happens to me in Chillicothe! Anyway, the batter fouled one back, and
the catcher didn't even get his glove on it. It came straight back and went
through the bars of my mask!

"Actually, the ball got stuck in my mask. And I mean it was stuck!
Nobody could pull the ball out of my mask with their hands, and it took
two of the strongest players on the Paints to hammer the ball loose with
a bat. We figured out later that the ball had to have been tipped perfectly
with the bat and that it had to have hit the mask dead-on perfectly. It
was just a freak accident.

"Of course, when the ball went through my mask, it hit me in the
face. I went down like a shot. My nose was broken, there was blood all
over my face, I had a concussion … the whole nine yards. I remember
the Chillicothe catcher standing over me, and I remember him saying,
'Max is bleeding!' He said that to the Paints' trainer and the team doctor because they were on their way out to the field in seconds after it
happened. They knew right away that I was hurt. And then I passed out.

"Well, my buddy Bob Hughes was coming back from the concession
stands when this happened. At first he thought a player had gotten
plunked, then he realized that it was me on the ground being attended
to. The medical people were really worried. They didn't think I was
going to make it there for a while. There's no trauma center out there
in Ross County, so they called Columbus and had an emergency heli-
copter on standby.

"The trainer took out one of those small flashlights, and when he
shined it in my eye, he didn't get the reaction he was looking for. He
said, 'We're losing him! His eye is glassing over!'

"And Bob Hughes, who's standing behind the backstop with a Pepsi

TALE?

I SAW 1ST FRONTIER
GAME 1998 THEN FL ALLSTAR
GAME FOLLOWING, 1998

in one hand and a bag of popcorn in the other ... he shouts: 'CHECK HIS OTHER EYE!'

"They let Bob ride over to the hospital with me in the ambulance. And would you believe that it just happened to be biker weekend in Chillicothe? Every summer for one weekend thousands of bikers, most of them Harley-Davidson owners, invade Chillicothe and practically take over the town, and it was on that weekend that this happened. All the emergency rooms in every hospital in town were packed with motorcycle guys who had been hurt in accidents or fights.

"On the way over Bob said, 'Hell, give him a beer and a cigarette and he'll go back and finish the game.' It was the first time in 29 years that I hadn't finished a game, and I did hate to leave.

"I made a full recovery, but for a while I really scared 'em. They thought I was dead. Of course, I wasn't ... they just picked the wrong eye to start with."

2

10/29/04
2007

Taking Richmond by Storm

THE MAJOR LEAGUE BASEBALL season was already two months old when the Frontier League began its 2000 schedule on Wednesday, May 31. Such a late start was not anything extraordinary for minor league baseball, but it was definitely more in keeping with the commencement dates of affiliated rookie leagues and "short-season Class A" leagues than those of the Class A affiliated leagues which the Frontier League bills itself as being comparable to.

One look at the schedule also made it obvious that the Frontier League season would be more of a sprint than a marathon. The entire 84-game slate was going to be neatly crammed into the summer vacation period of the American educational establishment; with a total allotment of four off days for all of June, July, and August (not including the two travel days sandwiched around the All-Star Game set for mid–July). Despite this relative brevity, I had a feeling that both Max and I would be considerably winded after our race around the bases of the Frontier League season.

Around ten o'clock Wednesday morning I called Max to get directions to his home in eastern Indiana, just across the Ohio border.

"Then you're really going through with this?" he asked.

"Heck, yeah. I'm more excited about it now than I was last Friday, and I can't wait to get started," I said.

"Atta baby!" said Max.

After a few more mutual reassurances, Max gave me directions, right up to the end of his driveway. "You'll know it's the right place when you see my mailbox. I've got wooden baseball bats nailed to both sides of the post the mail box sits on top of."

"This just keeps getting better and better, Max!" I said.

Max's place could hardly have been easier to find. I drove west from Cincinnati on I-74 towards Indianapolis for some twenty miles and took the second exit in Indiana. Off the exit I turned north onto a two-lane road called Route 1. Two miles down this pike on the right I passed St. Leon, a town of less than 500 residents; then I went another two miles to come upon Southgate, Indiana, where Max lives. Max tells people that he lives in St. Leon because nobody has ever heard of Southgate, Indiana. Actually, St. Leon is so small and devoid of the businesses and municipal buildings one expects to find in even the smallest towns that it is easy to pass by it without even realizing it, and the town has achieved the recognition it enjoys in the public consciousness primarily because it shares the large exit signs on I-74 with Lawrenceburg. As for Southgate, even once you've been there, it is difficult to think of it as an actual community. From what I could tell it's not much more than a crossroads.

Max's domicile was a mobile home, a single-wide, set back about thirty yards off the road. Max had told me that the trailer was serving as temporary quarters until he and his wife, Patty, finished renovating an old brick one-room school house, situated on the same piece of property, that would become their permanent home. The lawn stretched out in front of the trailer was as smooth and green as the top of a billiards table and was bounded on the left by a row of five fecund apples trees standing in front of a corn field. On the right and at the far end of Max's black-topped driveway sat a recently built three-car garage, the three doors facing not the road but Max's svelte lawn and the corn field beyond. A curved walk of large flat stones, set in crushed brick and spaced about a foot apart, connected the driveway to a covered wooden porch that defined and protected the entrance to the trailer. Although it was an obvious victim of age and neglect, the school house stood proudly some twenty feet to the right of the garage and, understandably, much closer to the road, since its original function had been public in nature. With its bell tower and arched, six-over-six windows—three on each side and a pair flanking the main entrance—it might have been easily mistaken for a former church instead of a former school building. And despite its still shabby appearance and gutted interior, the little school house's architectural charm and, especially, the new green metal roof it sported projected a sense of hope and renewal, rather than one of abandonment and decay.

I pulled into Max's driveway and parked my '93 Nissan Quest, a mini van in need of some brake work, next to a bright red Toyota pickup parked at the end of the blacktop on the left. I knew the Toyota was Max's vehicle because more than a dozen umpire shirts and pants hung on a clothes rod stretched from side to side of the cab behind the seats.

The sound of my approaching car had set off Max's house alarm— two dogs barking—and the two canine sentinels came bounding outdoors with Max to confront me. Max was wearing navy Bermuda shorts, penny loafers, and no shirt—his typical lawn mowing attire, as I would later learn. He had just finished mowing, in fact, and the sweat still glistened on his face and upper body. With his shirt off, I noticed for the first time the rich bronze tone of his skin which was apparently natural and so even over his entire body as to give him what sun bathers would describe as the perfect tan.

Max introduced me to the dogs in order to settle them down. Both dogs had come to the McLeary's as strays. Mostly collie with some golden retriever mixed in, FM had simply showed up one day at Max's shop on Harrison Avenue. "He was just a pup then," says Max, "about the size of two fists. I have no idea where he came from. He walked off the street, through the front door, right past me and a couple of friends who were visiting me at the shop, and into the bathroom. How'd he get the name 'FM'? Well, there was a metal shelving unit in that bathroom against one of the walls, and the bottom shelf which was just above the floor was full of cassette tapes. When I walked into the bathroom to see what had happened to the dog, there he was laying in the middle of those tapes. All you could see was his head sticking out. And right then I said, 'This dog likes rock 'n roll! He's definitely not an AM dog. We're gonna call you FM, little buddy.'"

Jo Pa had also moved in uninvited on the McLeary's years before, when they had been renting a farmhouse not far from their present address in Southgate. He was even more of a mutt than FM. According to Max, "He has some beagle in him but also half the neighborhood and two counties. His mother was a lover." Max named him after his favorite college football coach, the legendary Joe Paterno of Penn State.

I asked Max if it was okay for me to leave my van where I'd parked it. "Thank you for asking," said Max. "That's Patty's spot, and she'll be home any time now. I'd really appreciate it if you'd leave that space for her."

I backed down the driveway past the garage and then pulled off to the right and into the grass, a spot which became my regular parking place for the rest of the summer whenever Max and I rode up to Richmond together. Minutes later, Patty turned her Ford Tempo into the driveway and pulled into the spot I'd just vacated.

As the dogs had been (and still were) wary of me, so I was a little wary of Max's better half. I was convinced by now that Max was behind our project 100%, but would Patty be? From past experience I knew that wives are sometimes jealous of their husbands' friends and diversions—of anything actually that directs the husbands' attention away from themselves or impinges on the time the wives and husbands have to spend together—and so it occurred to me in a vague way that Patty might not be all that thrilled to have a writer, whom Max didn't even know a week before, move into their lives, lock, stock, and tape recorder. At the very least, I didn't want to get off on the wrong foot with Patty.

Happily, I needn't have worried. Patty greeted me with neither resentment nor false effusion but with sincerity and courtesy. She also spared us both the awkwardness that sometimes occurs when two people who have just met feel obligated to make small talk by immediately turning her attention towards Max.

"Larry, do you want me to fix you something to eat before you leave? Why don't you let me fix you a grilled cheese sandwich? You need something to eat before you leave."

Larry, aka Max, did not want to eat. It was Opening Day of the 2000 Frontier League season, and he was already too nervous to even think about food. "If I can just get that first pitch right ..." he said softly, the unspoken conclusion of his proposition remaining suspended in the heat like an "Out!" call everyone knows is coming as soon as the umpire determines that the catcher has held onto the ball after slapping a tag on a runner sliding into home.

Max kept popping into the kitchen/dining room, either to ask Patty where she had put something or other he needed or to check, probably for the one hundredth time that day, the weather channel on the big television against the wall to my right. Now I had played and coached enough baseball and fast pitch softball to know the number one rule regarding baseball and rain. Which is, that even if it's raining hard enough to lift your house off its foundation and float it down the street, you don't *assume* that even one drop of rain has fallen on the ball diamond your game is scheduled to be played on, even if that diamond is a mere two blocks away. This is the rule. I had always lived by it, and it had never let me down. Today though wasn't a day for this rule but for its corollary.

It had been a muggy, sunny day in Cincinnati, and it was still sunny in Southgate, Indiana; but Richmond was an hour north of us (and an hour behind us on Central, not Eastern, Standard Time). It was quite possible, I realized from Max's fretting, that the Richmond Roosters and London Werewolves might be looking at a rainout.

"Are you worried about rain, Max?" I asked to make conversation.

"I've been watching it all morning, and it's definitely coming our way," said Max.

"Can you call them in Richmond to see if it's raining there?" asked Patty.

Staring vacantly at the TV, Max ignored his wife's question. I was almost certain that Max and I would be driving over to Richmond, regardless of the current weather conditions there. Patty wasn't offended or irritated in the slightest at Max's failure to respond to her query, but it made me a bit uncomfortable. "Max, can the umpire call a rainout before the game even begins?" I tried.

"No," he said. "Once the lineup cards are exchanged at home plate, the game becomes the umpires' responsibility, but up till then it's the GM's call." When Max was finally ready to go, Patty sent him off with a kiss and made him promise he'd call her on his cell phone when we were on our way home.

[handwritten margin note: DON'T STAY? OVER!]

If we'd been riding a city bus, we would have needed several transfers to get from Southgate to Richmond. Three miles north of Max's, Route 1 turns left and merges with U.S. 52. According to the map, this intersection marks the location of a community called Cedar Grove, but it is so small and inconspicuous that only the most alert of drivers would notice it (in other words, Cedar Grove is another Southgate). We drove up 1/52 in a northwestern direction for six miles into Brookville, then picked up State Route 101 which runs directly north for eighteen miles into Liberty. There, on the west side of town, 101 makes a seamless connection to US 27 which took us the rest of the way into Richmond.

U.S. 52 requires a driver's full attention because it is a winding, hilly, two-lane road. For several stretches, the Whitewater River snakes alongside the western shoulder of 52, but in the summer, when the foliage of the Indiana countryside is in full bloom, one can safely catch only glimpses of its waters while driving. The road is all the more dangerous because it is also heavily traveled. Route 1 joins 52 just past a bridge over the Whitewater. As Max slowed his truck to come to a stop at this intersection, something tugged at my memory. "Why does 52 sound familiar to me?" I wondered out loud.

Pointing towards a rectangular, two-story farmhouse of white siding with red shutters and a long porch across its front, about 30 yards to our right, Max said, "That's where those kids from LaSalle High School got killed last year."

The tragedy, every parent's worst nightmare, had been big news in Cincinnati for several weeks. LaSalle is a well known all-male Catholic high school, and a carload of LaSalle students had gotten lost on their way to a graduation party. They pulled into the driveway of the house on our right in order to turn around. For some reason, the driver of the car backed onto 52 into the path of a semi passing by; some say the truck was "speeding" by. Two young men were killed instantly, and a third died of his injuries days later. A fourth became a paralytic invalid and died in the hospital, choking on a grape fed to him by his father.

Although none of my own kids attend LaSalle, we live about a mile from the school. The Catholic grade school my youngest kids attend is a feeder school for LaSalle, and my daughter Casey's steady boyfriend, Keith Schneider, is a recent LaSalle graduate. In fact, Keith had been best friends with one of the boys killed in the accident. All this was more than enough to send a shiver down my spine as I gazed towards the conjunction of that fateful driveway and that busy road which disappeared around the bend into a sinister line of trees. Death had not directly struck my family there, but it had come close enough.

Max and I were still getting to know each other, and there was obviously a lot about him I didn't know.

"Larry, huh," I said. "Why does Patty call you that?"

"Because that's my name."

"Well, where does 'Max' come from then?" I resumed in an attempt to get to the point.

"Well, when I was growing up my dad was known as 'Mac,' and at some point people started calling me 'Mac' too. The phone would ring and my mom would say: 'Do you want Big Mac or Little Mac?' When I first started my customizing business in Cincinnati in 1976, I named it MaxTrux, sort of a pun after my nickname. People thought Max was my name, started calling me that, and I've been using it ever since."

"Does anybody else call you 'Larry'?"

"No. Nobody but Patty."

"Not even your brothers or sisters?" I asked, realizing as I asked the question that I didn't even know if Max had any living siblings.

"No. I'm an only child."

"How about your parents?"

"Mom and Dad are both gone."

"So Patty's the only one?"

"Yep. Nobody else even knows my real name is Larry. Well, nobody except for people like you and Jim Schaly, my partner you're gonna meet, who hear Patty call me Larry. But nobody calls me Larry. Except for Patty." It was obvious that that's the way Max liked it, and to be sure, the name—uncommon, catchy, manly—suited him perfectly.

Brookville, population 2529, came up quickly, and Max immediately turned off Route 1/U.S. 52, which becomes the main drag as it runs through Brookville, to take a zig-zagging detour through the town's main residential neighborhood of modest, working class homes. This detour allowed us to bypass five or six traffic lights. It also helped us avoid the notice of the two or three-car Brookville police force, a diversionary maneuver that would become more important on our way home after Frontier League games.

As we left Brookville on Route 101 the road straightened out quite a bit but surprisingly never leveled out for long. Brookville Lake, one of the biggest lakes in all of Indiana, stretched north and south on our left the entire 18 mile distance between Brookville and Liberty. Although the Lake remained completely out of view, we were reminded of its existence by the bait and boat shops and turnoff signs we passed. *[handwritten: I DROVE THERE FOR BRINKS']*

Max began to talk about Richmond and all the people associated with the team he wanted to introduce me to. He would go on about a particular person for a while and then invariably conclude with an advisory which became a refrain: "I'll introduce you, but then you're on your own." As he talked, he kept a cigarette constantly lit and did so without ever looking away from the road in front of us. I was glad of that because, the truth be told, I was a little nervous riding with him. One-eyed umpiring was one thing, but now he had my life in his hands. Eventually, I realized that Max is an excellent driver, and I was able to completely relax as his passenger, but at that moment I was still a little leery. Closing my right eye, I peered through the truck windshield to experience driving as Max does for a few moments. Opening my eye, I said a few prayers for our safety and checked my seatbelt.

Max went on to explain that one of the reasons Richmond is a special place for him is that it was the Roosters who arranged for his mom to see the only game she ever saw Max umpire. The Roosters hosted Mrs. McLeary, who was ill with cancer, during the 1998 season. "After the game, I asked her, 'Whadya think, Mom?'" said Max. *[handwritten: MY 1st GAMES 1998]*

"She said, 'Well, from my vantage point, I thought you did a good job high and low, but I couldn't tell how you were inside and out.'

"'Atta baby, Mom!' I said. We went to the Wheel, the bar in Richmond I've been telling you about, and stayed there talking about the game until the place closed at two or three in the morning. That night meant a lot to me because three weeks later Mom was dead."

By the time we pulled onto Route 27 for the last leg of our trip, a roiling canopy of low gray clouds had completely obliterated the sun. There was a palpable drop in the temperature, and raindrops began to fall on my elbow sticking out the window. As we rolled ever closer to Richmond, Max began to feel butterflies again. "Richmond's pitcher better throw the first pitch down the middle. I know I can't miss that one. ... This league's been so good to me I don't want to do anything to embarrass the kids or myself," he said. "If I do, that'll be the time to quit."

"You know my buddy in the beer gardens, Tom, he dubbed me Doug Harvey," Max said.

"You mean 'god'?" I said, referring to the monicker that had been bestowed upon Harvey because of his near-flawless and absolutely authoritative umpiring and handling of players.

"That's right," said Max. "And I admire Harvey too. Not just because he was such a good umpire, but also because of the way he left the game. See, nowadays they use a rotation system in the major leagues for All-Star Games and the World Series. Everybody gets a turn. In the old days though, they did it by merit. They picked the best umpires, so some guys never got a shot at the big games. Well, when Harvey was at the end of his career, it was automatic that he was going to work the World Series, but he said, 'No, I'm not going to do it. It's time for some of the younger guys to have a chance.' And he didn't work the Series. It was his last shot at the spotlight, but he wanted to take care of the younger umpires. And that's how I want to go out. I want to quit when I can still do the job, and I want to quit to give some younger guy a chance to work the All-Star Game and the playoffs. I just hope I know when it's time for me to hang 'em up."

It was unsettling to hear Max talk about retiring right before the start of a new Frontier League season and before I'd even seen him make a single call, but then I realized that it was only the same discomforting feeling we get whenever we contemplate the transient nature of all things in this world. And, as usual, recognizing this feeling for what it was was the first step in my being able to overcome the discomfort it caused.

We rounded one final bend and suddenly, with the city's sprawling power plant on our left and the widening of the road into four lanes, we were in Richmond, Indiana. "Man, I've got to get that first pitch right tonight. It doesn't matter what I did last year," said Max.

Unpretentious, well-kept, and aging gracefully, McBride Stadium is a lot like the city of Richmond. Built in 1936 with WPA funds, the ballpark received a major renovation in 1999 which modernized it for fans, players, and front office personnel alike; yet it retained the original structure which gives it most of its character, the main concrete grandstand with its wooden bench seating and the steel columns that support its roof. The presence of view-obstructing support columns has been used as an excuse to demolish classic major league ballparks, such as Comiskey Park and Tiger Stadium, but the columns at McBride are not a problem because the ballpark is never sold out and nobody ever has to sit behind them. Roosters fans, if they give McBride's columns any thought at all, consider them to be as harmless and as inconspicuous a part of the setting as the bird's nests in the rafters.

Paid for with a combination of Build Indiana funds (secured with major support from State Senator Allen Paul) and money from the Richmond Park Department, the renovation cost just under $400,000; a justifiable sum to spend not only because such an amount is a pittance compared to the cost of building new, but also because McBride is a communal ballpark. In addition to the Roosters, the Earlham College, Richmond High School, and local American Legion baseball teams all play their home games at McBride, and it is not unusual for the Stadium to host scholastic and amateur baseball tournaments as well. Richmond definitely gets its money's worth out of the place.

Age and appearance are not the only things that link McBride to classic ballparks of the past. Like its forerunners that were usually crammed into dense urban landscapes, McBride inspired the construction of a "renegade bleacher" structure, built by enterprising fans averse to paying the Roosters' modest $3 ticket price. The renegade bleacher was actually only a wooden platform with railing added to the roof of a small cape cod located across the street on the third base side of the Stadium. A long section of pvc pipe ran from the roof down the side of the house: a chute to dispose of empty beer cans. Although nobody I talked to knew why, the house was empty, and the roof top box seats went unused all season.

Not surprisingly, McBride was originally called Municipal Stadium, and its purpose was not to host professional baseball but to accommodate the recreational activities of the ordinary citizens of Richmond. That's why to this day McBride is still considered by city officials to be part of the Clear Creek Park complex, which surrounds McBride on three sides with softball fields, the city tennis courts, and a 50-meter, outdoor Olympic style swimming pool. The first professional baseball team to call McBride home did not move in until 1946, ten years after the Stadium was built.

Richmond's first, largely-forgotten experiments with professional baseball came in 1908 and 1917 when teams named the Richmond Quakers played single seasons, first in the Class D Indiana-Ohio League and then in the Class B Central League. Both teams were undoubtedly named after Quakers John Smith and Jeremiah Cox, who founded Richmond after leaving the South in opposition to slavery. While these Quaker nines faded into peaceful oblivion, the nickname has been kept alive by the intercollegiate athletic teams of Earlham College, located only a few city blocks away from McBride.

McBride's first professional baseball tenants, the Richmond Roses, played two years in the old Class D Ohio State League, then shifted into the Ohio-Indiana League for the 1948 season after the former circuit folded. The Roses were an affiliate of the Braves, of Boston, not Atlanta.

[handwritten margin note, right side: McBride Stadium 1936 — McBride old Stadium 2005]

[handwritten note at bottom: My 1st 4(2) college umpiring jobs were at Earlham + at McBride Stadium]

When the franchise switched its affiliation to Detroit, the team was renamed the Tigers, the name the Richmond boys played under for the next three years, from 1949 through 1951, after which the franchise disbanded, again, along with the league itself. Richmond old-timers remember that two Richmond Tigers pitchers, Jim Bunning and Billy Hoeft, climbed to the top of the ladder. Hoeft put together one twenty-win season in the big leagues; Bunning put together a career that was belatedly recognized as worthy of the Hall of Fame. Nevertheless, it was Hoeft, not Bunning, whose youthful impressions of Richmond were recorded for posterity. After being given the celebrity tour of the town, the young, newly arrived pitcher was asked by a Richmond newspaperman what he thought of Richmond and its ballpark. Apparently as conservative of his words as his pitches, Hoeft answered, "Nice." After the Tigers went out of business, Richmond did not have professional baseball again until the Roosters came to town in 1995, two years after the Frontier League got off the ground.

By the time Max and I turned right onto N.W. 13th Street about an hour and a half before game time, we could see the Opening Day tail gate party beginning to unfold in the unpaved, grassy parking lot between the first base side of McBride Stadium and the softball field that takes up the corner of West Main and 13th. We could see that it had rained a little in Richmond but certainly not enough to even delay the start of the game. Better news yet, while the sky remained overcast and the air dank, it appeared that we were probably going to be spared a deluge.

Max's parking spot was underneath a huge Sycamore tree by Clear Creek which runs behind McBride's right-center field wall. To get to it we went down a short gravel roadway between the small paved lot reserved for the players, Roosters employees, and the visiting team bus adjacent to McBride on our left and the grassy field on our right that served as the main parking lot, where the tailgate party was taking place. Before we went down this gravel drive, Max stopped the pickup for a moment and said, "There it is. Looking good."

"There's what, Max?" I said.

"Mom's tree," he said. I had forgotten about it, but Max had told me that he and Patty had bought a maple tree at a nursery and presented it to the Roosters' groundskeeper, Cindy Blunk. Max had said, "You've had your hands in the dirt all year, so here's a little present to say 'thank you' for all your hard work." Max had also intended the tree to serve as a memorial to his mother. Cindy had planted the sapling near the beginning of the sidewalk that leads up to the main entrance of McBride. It had taken firm root in the Richmond soil and, oblivious to the Opening Day pressure felt by Max, was clearly doing fine.

Driving past the picnic Max spotted a couple of fans he recognized, so as soon as we parked, we walked over towards them. The fans turned out to be a retired doctor, Alan Glock, and Ken Voshell, the father of one of the Roosters' players, second baseman Key Voshell. They were as glad to see Max as Max was to see them.

When Dr. Glock asked Max how he was doing, he was making a real inquiry, not just saying "hello." Max admitted his Opening Day jitters. "I'm sicker than a dog shitting bones," he said.

The friendly and vigorous doctor, who shook hands as if his bear paw of a hand were a can crusher, took me under his wing, and I felt welcome to address him the same way Max did, simply as "Doc." Max couldn't have addressed him as Dr. Glock because he didn't know Doc's last name. Babe Ruth met so many people, he gave up trying to remember anybody's name and wound up calling practically everybody "kid." Casey Stengel knew everybody's name, but his mind was always such a whirlwind of activity he couldn't be bothered trying to pronounce the names correctly. Max didn't learn the last names of many people he was fond of simply because the only thing important to him were the people themselves. With most people, one graduates in the relationship to first-name status; with Max, there is a good chance you will begin, and remain, on a first-name basis *only*.

As the formal introductions were concluded, Max said for my benefit, "Doc's the one who made that sign, 'MAX FOR PRESIDENT!'" I nodded, remembering the hand-lettered poster that Max had saved and hung up in his shop.

"And I meant it, too," said Dr. Glock. "That ought to tell you how much we think of Max. The fans don't feel that way about every umpire, you know."

We all laughed at the understatement, and then Max and I were invited to join the picnic. Max declined and excused himself in order to take his gear into the Stadium and to attend to his pre-game duties, but I readily accepted the invitation. After all, I had a lot less to be nervous about than Max.

The food was plentiful and delicious, and since I didn't want to hurt any of the cooks' feelings, I sampled as much of it as possible. Doc insisted that I try something he and his wife Carolyn had brought: some creamy yogurt packed with chunks of fresh strawberries that was so good it couldn't have been much less fattening than the brownies and cookies brought by other fans.

I was impressed with the presence of a player's parent at Opening Day, but as it turned out, Mr. Voshell lived in Milford, Ohio, a small town just east of Cincinnati; and so he hadn't traveled much farther than I had. Ken, I learned, had been the baseball coach at Milford High School, where both Key and Key's younger brother Chase, a shortstop, had played for him. Chase had recently made his pro debut, in affiliated ball, having been drafted in the third round of the 2000 amateur draft out of Wake Forest University by the St. Louis Cardinals. With Key, Mr. Voshell would receive double the pleasure, in watching both his son and a former player perform. \10\13\01\04\

As the native Richmonder, it was up to Doc to tell me something about the city. Doc mentioned some of Richmond's important industries and companies of the present and the past—a number of automobiles were made at one time in Richmond, including the Pilot, Westcott, Richmond, Rodefeld, Davis, and Crosley—as well as several firsts the city is proud of, such as being the birth place of recorded jazz. This claim stems from the fact that in 1923 Hoagy Carmichael recorded his famous tune "Star Dust" at Richmond's Gennett Recording Studios in the old Starr Piano building, and I remembered seeing on our way to the ballpark a mural on the side of a downtown building that commemorates the event. More than anything else, however, Doc took a great man approach to Richmond history and, big sports fan that he is, put famous native Richmond sports figures at the top of his list, particularly a trio of NFL greats: Weeb Ewbank, Paul Flatley, and Lamar Lundy. Doc named Andy Brown, a former number one draft pick in the entire country currently playing Double A ball in the New York Yankees system, as the most accomplished baseball player to hail from Richmond, but once baseball became the topic it was inevitable that Morgan Burkhart, Richmond's favorite adopted son, would dominate the conversation, just as he had dominated Frontier League pitching during his Roosters career.

What little Max had told me about Morgan Burkhart was not easy to forget. Burkhart had played four years for the Roosters before "aging out" of the league after the 1998 season (in order to maintain its credibility as a league for prospects, the Frontier League enforces an eligibility rule that stipulates that "No player may turn 27 years of age prior to June 1st of that season"). Morgan was named the MVP of the league the last three years he played and in his final season won the Triple Crown, batting .404 with 36 home runs and 98 RBI over an 80-game schedule. At the end of Burkhart's last season in the league, Commissioner Bill Lee called him "the Michael Jordan of the Frontier League," and Richmond manager John Cate, who knew him better than anybody else as a player, said, "I don't know if there will ever be another Morgan Burkhart in this league again. That's a big statement to say 'never,' but with the numbers he's put up for four years, it might be true." Burkhart was so feared as a hitter that he was walked intentionally with the bases loaded ... and more than once! Cate later told me about one of the occasions when this happened. "It was our last game of the season, and Andy McCauley, who was managing Kalamazoo, at the time, walked Morgan intentionally with the bases loaded," he said. "They finished in last place, but Andy was still trying to win the game, which is what he was supposed to do. The walk to Morgan forced in a run, of course, but they got out of the inning with no more runs scoring, and they won the game. The loss cost us a spot in the playoffs."

More dumbfounding than Burkhart's performance was the fact that, for the longest time, no major league team would sign him. The knock on him was that he was supposedly too slow ... and too short for a first baseman. The Boston Red Sox finally signed Burkhart after his Frontier League career was officially over.

Doc told me that Burkhart had actually been his patient. According to Doc, the Roosters had misdiagnosed him. "They thought he had shin splints," said Doc. "He didn't. He had periontinitis—inflammation of the muscles—and I treated him for what he had. His legs quit hurting, and he started running a little faster."

Doc had kept up with Burkhart and was able to tell me that Morgan had kept on hitting for the Red Sox's Single A and Double A teams in Sarasota and Trenton in 1999. He had also just finished playing winter ball in Mexico, where he had been named MVP of that league. He had started the 2000 season at Triple A Pawtucket, and Doc and Carolyn were planning to take a bunch of Rooster fans,—"as many as we can fit into our RV"—to Indianapolis on June 26 to see Morgan play.

It was time for me to go to work. As I started making my thank-you's, Doc had one more thing to tell me. "I had this cheer I'd say when Morgan came to bat. 'Sic 'em, Morgan!' I'd yell. And more times than not, he would. His last time at bat for the Roosters, I got the whole section to holler it." Going into their second season without Morgan Burkhart, Richmond Roosters fans were still trying to wean themselves of the biggest sports hero to ever have worn the name of the city across his chest. Burkhart would never return to suit up in a Roosters uniform again, but it was already clear to me that, in a sense, he was not gone and never would be.

The most conspicuous and most expensive part of McBride's recent renovation had been the construction of an 80 × 40-foot building located on the first base side of the grandstands. The Roosters' new offices occupied the upper level of this building, while the lower level housed new locker rooms for both the Roosters and visiting teams, storage areas, and the umpires' dressing quarters. A 40 × 40-foot observation deck, where front office staff, interns, and young concession workers sometimes paused to watch the game, connected the new building to the walkway running behind the original grandstand. The existence of the umpires' locker room was something of a miracle, as the umpires have often not been given much consideration in ballpark architectural plans of the past; and, as the season wore on I would see first hand several examples of the needs of the umps having been forgotten altogether during the design and construction phases. There was nothing hanging on the cinder block walls of the umps' dressing room at McBride except for a large poster copy of the Frontier League groundrules and a smaller sign, which said:

> *The big league manager dreamed he was in heaven. Everywhere he looked he saw a Hall of Fame player. So he formed a team. The phone rang. It was the devil.*
>
> *"I have a team that can beat your team," said Satan.*
> *"Impossible," bellowed the manager, "I've got the greatest players of all time."*
> *"Yeah," replied the devil, "but I've got all the umpires."*

The little story is a tribute to the importance of umpires to the game of baseball, but the joke cuts both ways: after all, according to the story, umpires are fiends, not saints.

I walked into McBride through the players' gate on the corner of this new building, past the first base dugout about ten yards to my right, then up the steps of the aisle on the corner of the first base grandstand, and across the observation deck to reach the Roosters' offices. It was easy for me to see who was in the Roosters' offices because in actuality the "offices" were one large room. There were three desks, of sufficient size and quality to stroke the egos of most executives, along the lefthand, diamond side of the room. I assumed that two of these desks belonged to Deanna Beaman, the General Manager, and Duke Ward, the Director of Business Operations, but I would never see either person ever sit at the desks. Both Ward and Beaman would always be too busy to sit down. Everyone else, if they needed a work space, had to sit in the middle of the room where a couple of long tables and chairs were positioned. Beaman, several teen-aged vendors, and a couple of Rooster Chicks, mostly college-aged cheerleaders dressed in Roosters T-shirts and skimpy orange shorts, were in the room, but not Mark Hadley, the person I needed to see. The goateed Hadley was about to graduate from the University of Dayton's Sports Management program. He was serving his internship in the Roosters' front office, and he was being given a lot of responsibility. Mark was the one holding my Roosters press pass. Deanna tracked him down over their walkie-talkies, so after I finished looking around the office a bit, I went outside to wait for him on the observation deck.

As I leaned over the railing at the corner of the deck, I could look down and see almost directly below me a tall concrete extension of the building that formed a right angle and served as both a retaining wall and the entrance to the passageway leading to the door of the home team's clubhouse. Seated on a bar stool in the corner of this right angle and wearing an orange Roosters cap was Big John, the clubhouse man, guarding the entrance to the players' sanctuary. I stood there a while watching Roosters players come and go. A few minutes later, Max stepped out of his dressing room. He had changed into this umpiring uniform, and he stood there on the sidewalk, facing Big John and absorbing the scene, just as I was doing. In the next instant I saw John Cate, the Roosters' manager, walk out of the Roosters' clubhouse. As he made the right turn at Big John's outpost, the short and stocky Cate put on the brakes like a baserunner caught in a rundown when he saw Max directly in front of him down the sidewalk. Eschewing a welcome-back handshake in favor of some good-natured mockery, Cate stretched out both arms and made exaggerated bowing motions of homage towards Max. Replying in kind, Max grabbed his crotch in a universal jock culture gesture of disdain.

As Max and his partner Rod Rollins walked from the first base dugout towards home plate for their pre-game meeting, Max looked in the direction of the third base dugout and made a sweeping circular motion with his right arm. This wasn't a loosening-up exercise but Max's sign language for "I'm going to the Wheel after the game. Will you meet me there?" Standing by the far end of the London dugout, leaning over the fence that made the out-of-play area there the Roosters' left field beer garden, Max's buddy Tom made the same sweeping circular motion. It was sign language for "Hell, yes, I'll meet you there, at the Wheel!"

One by one, the Roosters in the starting lineup took the field to the playing of "Sirus," the Alan Parsons Project song made famous as sporting event introductory music by the Michael Jordan–era Chicago Bulls. As each Rooster ran onto the field towards his position, he was accompanied by an excited youngster from a local Little League team, who got to stand next to his hero during the playing of the National Anthem. I would see this sweet touch employed around the league all season long.

A righthander named Phill Kojack had been given the honor of being named the Opening Day starter for the Roosters, and as he threw his final warm-up pitches from the mound, Max took his stance behind catcher Keith Fout and got in a little practice himself. Up until the early 1970s, American League umpires used to use outside chest protectors, big cloth-covered pieces of hard foam with shoulder straps and hand grips. When an umpire wore an outside chest protector, he would bend his knees slightly and lean a little forward but pretty much remain standing upright. The inside chest protector, which all umpires use now, requires the umpire to hide more behind the catcher, to use the catcher's body as a shield. In the past, umpires using the inside protector stance basically squatted or bent over awkwardly while peering over the catcher's shoulder. Since both positions were uncomfortable and especially tiring, umpires eventually found a better stance, a variation of the half kneeling position batters take in the on-deck circle. In this new-and-improved stance, the umpire leans forward over his bent left knee, but instead of resting his weight on his right knee bent into the ground, he keeps his right leg fairly straight and thrust out behind him as a brace. This is the stance that Max was using.

When Warren Zevon wrote the song, he never imagined that "Werewolves of London" would one day supply a Canadian city with the perfect nickname for their professional baseball team, but that is exactly what happened. The Werewolves were actually descendants of the Newark (OH) Bisons, a franchise put together for the Frontier League's second year of operation in 1994. The Bisons lasted two years, before a group of investors from Michigan purchased the franchise and moved it to Kalamazoo (MI). In their three years of existence the Kalamazoo Kodiaks compiled a horrendous 85–150 record, the all-time record for futility in the Frontier League, so after the 1998 season, the franchise was sold again and moved to London, Ontario, thus making the Frontier League an international circuit. Under the leadership of manager Andy McCauley, the Werewolves made a complete turnaround in their inaugural season north of the border in 1999. They first put together the best overall record in the League at 54–30, then beat Johnstown in the first round of the playoffs 2–0, and finished off a great year by sweeping Chillicothe 2–0 in the finals. They thus opened the 2000 season in Richmond as the defending Frontier League champions.

Right before the game started Max looked up to the heavens and remembered his parents, as he did before the start of every game he umpired. "Here we go, Jeanne. Here we go, Wilson," he said to himself. Center fielder Jason Borghese batted first for the Werewolves, and Kojack started him off with a fastball. The first pitch of the 2000 Frontier League season was on the outside corner, not right down the middle, but it looked good to Max, who, dramatically pointing rightwards with his right index and little fingers extended, bellowed, "STREEEE!"

Kojack missed with a high curve ball, then picked up a second called strike on another fastball on the outside corner. After Borghese fouled the fourth pitch straight back, Kojack got him to reach for a low

THE FUCKIN' SCISSORS" WHICH HAS A PISS POOR BALANCE!. '0|30|04 breaking ball, which resulted in a four-hopper to second baseman Key Voshell. It couldn't have been a more routine play, but Max ran halfway down to first anyway.

Dyterious Edwards, the speedy London shortstop, dropped a bunt single down third and a few pitches later stole second base. Rick Nadeau, whose .348 batting average had been the sixth best in the league the previous year, then hit a high chopper to the left of the mound. For a moment it looked as if Kojack would snatch it and trap Edwards between second and third, but Kojack couldn't quite reach the ball. Charging hard behind Kojack, shortstop Jason Guynn did field the ball and, throwing on the run, nipped Nadeau at first. Kojack seemed to be struggling to get his breaking pitches over the plate, but after cleanup hitter Dan Swift ran the count to 2–2, Kojack threw him a changeup for a called strike three to end the inning with Edwards stranded at third. During Swift's at bat, the sun reappeared and, as it began to expire for the day, flooded the horizon past the left field wall with orange light as bright as the Roosters' jerseys, caps, and socks. Despite this good omen and the good starts by Kojack and Max, it would not turn out to be a successful Opening Day for Richmond.

The one area that had not received much attention in McBride's renovation was the press box, which could be described as having been done in Early Home Depot Display style. The structure atop the edge of McBride's roof was literally not much more than a rectangular plywood box with windows, divided into two rooms, but it served its purpose. It only took a second to grasp the layout. The smaller room on the right was for the official scorer (David Knight) and the visiting team's broadcaster (or, on occasion, broadcasting duo); while the main room, situated more directly behind home plate, provided seats on the left for the public address announcer and the scoreboard operator and the Roosters' play-by-play radio broadcaster, Gary Kitchel, on the right. There was room in between these two stations for two or three other chairs, and this is where I would sit whenever I watched a game from the press box.

I sat down next to a very composed older guy holding a radio microphone on Kitchel's left. I estimated that he was nearing retirement age, but his snappy crew cut, wry expression, and the ever-present gleam in his eyes made him seem much younger. He looked as if he might have been a farmer or a veteran high school gym teacher. His comments though showed him to be knowledgeable about baseball, as well as Richmond, and because he was so comfortable on the air and familiar with Kitchel, I assumed that he was Kitchel's Joe Nuxhall (the regular partner of Cincinnati Reds' broadcaster Marty Brennaman). He wasn't. He

I MET
JAN THRU TOM
KINDA - STANDOFF ISH "!.

was Jan Clark, the sports editor of the Richmond daily newspaper, the
Palladium-Item. Even though he wasn't Kitchel's regular side kick, Jan
turned out to be the most frequent of Gary's many guest color com-
mentators. When Kitchel mentioned that Roosters third baseman Ryan
Anholt hailed from Moose Jaw, Saskatchewan, Clark said, "You just love
saying that name ... 'Sas-kat-che-wan' ... don't you, Gary!"

"And, by the way," he added, "Anholt came to the Roosters via the
same scout who recommended Morgan Burkhart."

The P.A. announcer was a local radio personality named Troy Derengowski who sounded exactly like Ryan Stiles, the actor who plays the
character of Lewis on the *Drew Carey Show.* About thirty-five years old,
the red-headed Derengowski wore a St. Louis Cardinals cap and a T-shirt
that exposed big biceps. He had his hands full trying to execute his
multi-faceted duties. In addition to playing the correct musical batting
intros selected by each Roosters player, Derengowski was required to
read numerous advertising and public service messages and to introduce and run, in conjunction with a miked, on-field promotions coordinator, a series of contests and give-aways that occurred every half
inning. When a foul ball arched back high over the press box and completely out of McBride Stadium, Derengowski cued the sound of a window shattering loudly, then said, "Fans, if that was your car, you need
to call RMD Patti Insurance and Financial Services ..." It was the kind
of thing that's funny the first one hundred times you hear it.

Kojack and the London starter, Scott Connor, traded goose eggs
for three innings, but then the Werewolves got to Kojack for a single
run in the fourth. That run would be all that Connor and two London
relievers would need as they went on to shut out the Roosters 3–0 on
four hits.

In the middle of the fourth inning Jan Clark left the press box for
a few minutes. When he returned, he announced, on the air, that the
Opening Day crowd was pretty good, probably over 2,000. "And you
should see the lines at the concession stand," he said.

This guess at the game's attendance caused Derengowski to say,
"My first year here there'd be 300 fans in the stands, and they'd tell me
attendance was 1,600. I'd say, 'What? You want me to announce what?'"
"No one in the press box was surprised at this admission, and in fact
the consensus seemed to be that in years past every Frontier League
team had probably padded their attendance figures at one time or
another when they'd struggled at the gate.

There was also consensus that the pitcher's duel we were witness-
ing was a most un–Frontier League type of baseball game. According
to the banter in the McBride Stadium press box, more typical of the
Frontier League would be a 13–12 slugfest, lasting four to four and a half

hours and featuring 15 hits and five or six errors, by each team! The other guys in the press box had seen a lot more Frontier League games than I had, so I listened to their opinions with respect, but I also realized that they were exaggerating some too, in affecting the cynicism that is supposed to be the mark of seasoned sports media professionals. Atypical or not, the game moved along briskly, was well played—neither team committed an error—and was a pleasure to watch. Only one thing concerned me: the umpiring, at home plate.

What worried me was Max's strike zone. As far as players and managers are concerned, competence in calling balls and strikes is the most important aspect of any umpire's game. Related to this fact, is a saying so widespread in baseball at all levels that it has become a cliché: "I don't care how the ump calls balls and strikes, as long as he is consistent." Max's strike zone seemed to be fairly consistent, but from where I was sitting in the press box, it still appeared to be something of a problem because it was so wide. As the game went on there seemed to be an inordinate number of called strikes and called strike three's on outside pitches. Two things were certain about the situation: first, there were a lot of strikeouts in the game, 27 all together. The three London pitchers combined for 13 strikeouts, while Kojack racked up 13 himself in his seven and a third innings of work. And second, Max's strike zone definitely drew some unwanted attention to his performance. When Max rang up Key Voshell on an outside pitch in the fourth inning, Kitchel told his listeners, "Voshell didn't like it, and neither did I." Two innings later after another Richmond batter took a called strike, there were audible groans from the Richmond dugout, and third base coach Woody Sorrell came half way down the line to ask, "Was it a swinging or called strike?" Sorrell knew that the pitch had been called a strike, but since arguing balls and strikes is not allowed, asking the question was a backhanded way of letting Max know that he and the rest of the Roosters disagreed with the call. The same pitch prompted Kitchel to say, "That's a very generous outside corner by home plate umpire Max McLeary." Something else about Max's performance was clear, and it was important to note: Max's generosity went both ways. When London's designated hitter Chris Gavriel was called out on strikes in the seventh, Kitchel said, "He didn't like the call, but quite frankly it was too close to take with two strikes." Jan Clark added the salient point: "Well, Max has been calling that outside pitch all night, so by now the hitters ought to know his strike zone."

Despite the loss by the home team, the fireworks show celebrating Opening Day went off as planned, with orange and green Roosters colors predominating. All lights in the ballpark were turned off, even in the press box, so Kitchel had to keep his cigarette lighter lit in order to see his notes and scorebook. In the dark and under the barrage of noise caused by the exploding fireworks, he recapped the game flawlessly, one of the more impressive performances of the evening.

Max had described The Wheel as a "biker bar," and I found the place to be pretty much as advertised. Located conveniently across the street from the Richmond junk yard on South L Street, it had pin ball machines, dart boards, and pool tables in a back room on the left, a good juke box, a large color TV always turned to ESPN, an autographed Pete Rose photo behind the bar, and an assortment of beer signs and posters and Nascar and Indiana Hoosier basketball schedules hanging on the walls; in other words, there was very little to distract the patrons from the main activity of the place: drinking. There were also ribald reminders that The Wheel was a place where people on the make could meet without apology or pretension. A sign over the dart boards said, "Your place or mine? Or the pool table? (If the pool table is full, use the alley)." Over the front door hung a piece of cardboard to which had been taped a three-page photo from a porno magazine, showing the rear ends of 50 naked female cyclists bending over their bicycles.

I soon realized that Max loved the place for several practical reasons: the beer was cheap, the service attentive, the famous Wheelburger big and tasty, and the music never so loud as to impede the conversation. The Wheel also stocked Max's favorite beer, Coors Light, and it was obviously the kind of working-man's watering hole where guys like Max and Max's buddy Tom feel comfortable hanging out. And hanging out in a bar was more than part of Max's routine; it was at the core of the philosophy he had absorbed from his father, who'd taught him that "You work hard, and you play hard." For Max, an integral part of the latter was dancing. He loved to dance, and over the course of the summer I'd see him give many a friend's wife or girlfriend a harmless twirl around the dance floor.

We parked across the street in front of the tall, white-washed board fence surrounding the junk yard (which euphemistically calls itself a "Recycling Center"); stepped around a big Harley parked in the street in front of The Wheel; and walked inside past a bar stool on the sidewalk propping open the front door. Max, Rod Rollins, David Knight, and I took up at a table in The Wheel's main room located between the game room in the rear and the bar by the front door. When Max wanted the waitress to bring another round of beers, he'd circle a finger overhead and tell her to "Sprinkle the infield." After the first two rounds I'd started making "No More for Me" signs to the waitress.

Naturally, there was a lot of discussion about the game Max and Rod had just worked. Most of it centered around the play that had generated the biggest protest from either team. The controversy had happened when Roosters' reliever Jamie Blaesing picked a London runner off first base to end the top of the eighth inning. London thought that Blaesing balked on the play, and both Werewolves' base coaches briefly argued the "non-call." After the ornery Rollins had delivered his low opinion of the London protest at The Wheel, Max let us in on the conversation that had finally put the matter to rest.

London had capped the scoring in the game when first baseman Dan Swift led off the ninth with a home run. In the bottom of the ninth, Werewolves' manager Andy McCauley made a visit to the mound, presumably to talk to his pitcher, reliever Jeff Wools. In actuality, he wanted an opportunity to gripe one more time about Blaesing's supposed balk. As he walked back to the dugout, he said to Max, "Look, you two guys need to get your heads out of your asses."

"Hey, you're up 3–0. ... You want me to take it out *now*?" said Max.

"No, never mind," McCauley said. "On second thought, leave it there."

Max's buddy Tom was more than just a loyal Roosters fan. He was as much of a fixture at McBride as the bases and as integral to the entire operation as any employee. Tom and his buddies liked to hang out around two picnic tables in the beer gardens, which over the years had become their turf. One time a Roosters front office employee who did not appreciate Tom's importance wanted the picnic tables moved to the plaza outside the office so that they could be used by the guests of local companies sponsoring a day at the ballpark for their employees. Asserting his squatter's rights, Tom told the front office butt-in-ski that he could have one of the tables but not both of them. When both tables were moved nevertheless, Tom went on strike and without any fanfare began a boycott of Roosters' games. Richmond manager John Cate noticed Tom's absence by the second night of the boycott, and when he found out what had happened he blew his stack, pleaded with Tom to return, and made Tom promise that if anything similar happened in the future he would come directly to John about it immediately.

Tom had beaten us to The Wheel, but he didn't join us until the friends he'd come with were ready to call it a night. Tom was an average-sized guy, but his fu-man-chu, penetrating stare, and loud, deliberate way of speaking could make him an imposing presence nevertheless. And he did have a major league set of lungs. As he engaged in conversation at our table, he realized that he was talking extra loud, even for him, and that he was beginning to slur his words. His apology for his tipsiness was rebuffed with laughter, which was redoubled when he gave as his excuse the fact that he'd been celebrating his birthday. Tom told me that his last name was Arnett and that he worked as a cabinet maker. Max, of course, had not known Tom's last name, but he had known that Opening Day was Tom's birthday. Between innings Max had sent a birthday beer over to Tom in the beer garden. I wanted to hear in Tom's own words what he felt his role with the Roosters was, and he came through beautifully. Without the slightest trace of facetiousness, he said, "I'm the official heckler." Later, he told me that he'd recently called Morgan Burkhart to say that he'd see Morgan when the Pawtucket Red Sox visited Indianapolis to play the Indians. "So Morgan knows you by name, huh?" I asked.

"No. He knows me by voice," said Tom, again without irony.

Right before we left The Wheel, Max bought a six-pack of Coors Light for the ride home. It was my job to fish a can out of the bag, pop the top, and hand it to Max, who watched the road and, particularly, the dark driveways and side roads where a state patrolman or little town cop might have been hiding. When he was on his second beer, Max told me a story about the time he was caught red-handed, drinking and driving on the way home from Richmond in his other vehicle, a four-door Buick Regal.

"We'd had a double-header that night in Richmond," he said. "I'd had time for only one at The Wheel, so I got two for the road: one to get me to Liberty, and the other one to get me the rest of the way home. I was talking to Patty on my cell phone to let her know I was on the way, and I had the first beer which I'd just opened between my legs on the front seat. I'd taken just two sips of the beer so far. Well, this state trooper passed me going the other way. I didn't see him at first because he was behind a semi. When I'm driving down US 1 at night, I always check the rear view mirror to see if the tail lights on a passing car come on. If they do, I know it's a cop, and I know he's stopping so he can turn around and come after me. I looked in the mirror, and sure enough I saw those tail lights come on. Now, obviously, I didn't want to get caught with an open container in the car, so I said goodbye to Patty, hung up the phone, rolled down the driver's side window, and threw the can out the window. The only problem is that I rolled the window *up* instead down. The can bounced off the window, then hit the windshield and sprayed beer all over the door, the dashboard, the front seat, and me.

"I pulled over, and the first thing the state trooper asked me when he walked up beside my car was, 'Have you been drinking tonight?'

"There was no way I was going to be able to deny that. My shirt and the front of my pants were both soaked, and the car reeked of beer. I even had some beer still dripping off my eyebrows. So I made up a story, and I was very polite to the guy. 'Officer, I'm a professional baseball umpire in the Frontier League, and I just got finished doing a doubleheader for the Richmond Roosters. It was a long, hot night, and my partner and I were dying of thirst after the game. Like we usually do, we decided to have a beer in the parking lot and discuss the game. Well, my partner thought he'd be a comedian, so he shook up my beer when I wasn't looking. Naturally, when I popped the top, the beer sprayed all over me. … I only had the one beer—really, it was less than that since half of it got wasted—and my judgment is not impaired at all. Believe me, sir, I've got more beer *on* me than *in* me, and all I'm trying to do is get home to my wife who has supper waiting for me on the table."

"Well, he basically bought the story. I guess in the dark he didn't notice the beer still dripping down the inside of the windshield. And maybe he figured the beer on my face was sweat—it was a hot night—I don't know. He did ask me if I'd be willing to take a breath-a-lyzer test. I said, 'Sure,' and added, 'You're going to have one heck of a story to tell the guys back at headquarters.'

"I blew nothing—passed the test with no trouble—and he let me go. He said, 'You're right: I am going to have a helluva story to tell. Now get out of here.'

"Looking back on it, I was pretty lucky he let me go. But I did do some pretty fast thinking and some pretty fast talking too. And, you know, I still have the trophy, the chip in the car window from where the beer can hit it. I never got it fixed and never will."

3

Big Bad Jim Schaly, the Canton Crocodiles, and Good Ol' Joe Charboneau

"YOU KNOW, MAX, I've been thinking about the mask you were wearing when you got hit in the face," I said as we drove through the sun-drenched streets of Richmond. "Did it have solid bars or that real thick wire? And was it so old that it had rusted in a bad spot or was it defective somehow? I just can't imagine a baseball squeezing through a metal mask like that unless something was wrong with it."

"It's not a metal mask," Max said.

Aha! I thought. That explains it. Max's revelation actually didn't explain anything, but it confirmed my suspicion that there was more to the story, which Max proceeded to tell me.

"It's plastic, real hard plastic ... well, not plastic exactly ... what do you call it? ... Resin! That's it," he said. "I was probably the first umpire in Cincinnati to use the mask. See, I always like to try new things, new equipment, and Koch's Sporting Goods in downtown Cincinnati knows this. They take real good care of me down there. When this new mask first came on the market in 1998, Koch's called me and told me about it. I tried it out and absolutely loved it. Because it's so light. If you hold this mask in one hand and a baseball cap in the other, you can't tell any difference in their weights. And that's important when you work

42

over 300 games a year. Besides, contrary to your assumption, metal masks do wear out ... they start to cave in because of the pounding they take, whether they have bars or wire.

"Within two months, the factory issued a recall on it. I took it in to Koch's, and they gave me a metal mask made by the same company to use. A couple of weeks after that they called back and said, 'Max, we just got the mask back. It's okay now. You can come get it.'

"After I got hit in the face in Chillicothe, I called Koch's to let them know about it. I wasn't blaming them. I just needed somebody to talk to. They gave me the 800 number of the company which makes the mask, and I called them, but they never got back to me. Everybody told me I should sue the manufacturer of the mask, but I'm not like that. ... And I love their product, what can I say."

A thought occurred to me and I started to dismiss it, but then I decided that I shouldn't assume anything. "Max, what mask are you using now?" I asked.

"The same one," he said. "I've never had a problem with it since that night in Chillicothe. It was just a freak accident, a one-in-a-million shot, that's all."

Five or six blocks from McBride we turned into the parking lot of the Village Pantry, a convenience store on Main Street. We had stopped there the day before on Opening Day; we would stop there tomorrow right before the final game of the series with London, and we would stop there before every game Max umpired in Richmond. Umpires, like ballplayers, observe a lot of rituals, and stopping at the Village Pantry was one of Max's. Max would usually buy cigarettes; sometimes he would pick up an oddball item such as breath mints or antacid tablets; and he would always purchase a copy of the *Palladium-Item.* He would never look at the newspaper though until he was back home, unwinding after the game. He would fold it up and put it in the back seat or hand it to me to read if I cared to. He said it was bad luck to read the paper before a game. Besides, if something critical had been written about the umpiring the day before, he didn't want to know about it an hour before he had to go out and work a new game.

My goal for the day was to talk to the previous day's starting pitchers. I was in luck because I immediately found Phill Kojack without having to venture into the Roosters' clubhouse, which I did not yet feel comfortable entering. Kojack was sitting in a chair on the observation deck being interviewed by somebody from a local radio station. He had on sunglasses, and around his neck hung a gold cross and chain. He looked very relaxed and could afford to be that way knowing that he'd pitched well the night before and that he wouldn't have to pitch again for three more days.

I stood nearby, not so close as to intrude on the radio guy's interview but close enough to establish a posture of my being "next."

"Hey, Mike," I heard from below. Looking down, I saw Max on the sidewalk standing next to Mike Zerbe, the Roosters' beefy first baseman with the Ron Swoboda sideburns who had just come off the diamond. "Talk to Zerbe," Max hollered, and before I could say a word, Zerbe was bounding up the steps towards the observation deck.

When Zerbe introduced himself, he shook my hand in a peculiar way, keeping his index finger extended, as if it were bruised and needed protecting. Zerbe was thick in the neck, the arms, the legs, ... and he had a thick torso too; with the result that his uniform looked as if it had been spray-painted on. He let me know that he was at my disposal, saying, "Any friend of Max's is a friend of mine." I studied him closely and found no trace of ego or condescension in his face or in his voice. I thanked him and told him I did want to talk to him. Then, as much as I hated to have to do it, I told him that now was not the right time for us to talk. "No problem," he said. "Just let me know when you want to do it."

In a span of two minutes Mike Zerbe had really shown me something, and it had nothing to do with the way he swung the bat or fielded his position. Ballplayers seldom go out of their way to accommodate reporters or writers, and they rarely treat them as equals. At best, they tolerate as necessary evils those whom Ted Williams sarcastically referred to as the "knights of the keyboard." What is completely unheard of is a player *volunteering* to talk to a writer, but that is exactly what Zerbe had done. Such courtesy and thoughtfulness is against the unwritten code that players live by, and Zerbe would definitely have been setting himself up for some grief had his conduct been witnessed by the wrong teammates. Even more amazing than Zerbe's having made the first move was his gracious reaction to being told he'd have to wait his turn. He hadn't been insulted in the least, nor had he shown the slightest irritation. Amazing.

Moments after Zerbe and I parted, Kojack completed his first interview and stood up to stretch as the radio guy hustled away carrying his tape recorder. Phill looked my way, and I started to speak to him when my place in the Kojack interview line was stolen by an interloper. A distinguished-looking, well-dressed man had appeared out of nowhere to accost Kojack with a request that Phill give some pitching pointers to the man's Little League–aged son. Delivered with an air of expectation that it would unquestionably be granted, the request was really a demand.

Nevertheless, Kojack, like Zerbe, responded graciously. After Kojack, and presumably the boy too, had satisfied the man, Kojack turned his attention to me and apologized unnecessarily for the man's behavior.

Getting right to the point, I asked him, "What did you think of the umpiring last night?"

"You mean by Max?" he replied. Yes, I meant the umpiring by Max. "Max did a great job last night. He always does," he said.

"Well, what about his strike zone?"

"Max has a good zone," said Kojack. "One of the best in the league. He was giving me the outside corner, but he established what his zone was going to be in the first inning, and he stayed with it all night. I don't know if you happened to notice, but once Keith and I realized that Max was going to give us the outside corner we tried to use it to our advantage all night."

"So you're saying he was consistent?"

"Yeah, he was. And for both teams, I might add. Scott Connor got the same calls on the outside corner that I did. I don't know exactly how many he had, but I think Scott had quite a few strikeouts too."

"Connor had eight, and the London relievers had five more. All together there were 27 strikeouts in the game," I said.

"That many? Hmm. That was a lot."

"So would you say that Max is a pitcher's umpire, with him having such a wide strike zone?"

"No, not at all. What you have to understand is that Max may have widened the strike zone, but he also lowered it too. He wasn't calling any high strikes ... or, to put it another way, you could say he wasn't calling strikes on pitches that were a little up in the normal strike zone. So he was giving the pitchers something, but then he was also taking something away from us. He had a legitimate zone though last night. I think if you talk to Scott Connor he'll tell you pretty much the same thing. ... Now the hitters may not have liked Max's strike zone last night, they may have done some complaining about it, but they usually do whenever the pitchers get a lot of strikeouts."

I was just about convinced but wanted to ask one more question. "How would you compare Max to the other umpires in the league?"

"He's one of the best in the league; there's no doubt about that. I always enjoy pitching when Max is behind the plate. Like I said, he calls a good game, and you know that he really cares about what he's doing. ... The other thing about Max is that he's not perfect—nobody is—but when he makes a bad call, he doesn't make excuses or get defensive. He admits his mistakes. He'll say, 'I blew that one, but hang with me. I'll get the next one right.' And although he knows he's not perfect, he is a perfectionist. He wants to do everything properly. Like when he throws me a new ball: if he doesn't make a good throw, he'll apologize and make a face like he's disgusted with himself. I think you have to respect somebody like that."

I asked Kojack about the two "l"s in his first name. "No, it's not a typo," he said. "When I was a little kid, I asked my mother why "Phil" only had one "l" in it when my full name had two. She said that's just the way everybody always shortened the name. I told her, 'Maybe so, but "Phillip" has two "l"s, and I want "Phill" to have two "l"s too.' She said okay, and I've spelled my name that way ever since."

I reached out for a thank you-and-see you later handshake. "Phill, I really enjoyed watching you pitch last night," I said. "You pitched good enough to win."

"Thank you," he replied. "I was pretty nervous in the beginning, but I said a prayer on the mound and asked the Lord to relax me. He did and I became a different pitcher. The credit goes to Him. ... By the way, I hear you're writing a book or something. ... What's the book going to be about?"

"It's going to be about Max and the whole Frontier League," I said. "But mainly about Max. He's such a great character. Really, he's an almost unbelievable character. I mean, a one-eyed professional umpire, come on!"

"Max only has one eye! I didn't know that," Kojack said.

Another baseball cliché is the saying that an umpire has done his job well when no one notices he was there. After talking to Kojack I asked myself rhetorically: "How good a job is an umpire doing when most people, including the players, don't even notice that he's literally blind in one eye?"

It didn't take long for me to realize that perhaps the wags in the McBride Stadium press box had a valid point after all. In contrast to the artful pitching performances I'd witnessed Opening Day, the Roosters' second Frontier League game of the season was as sloppy as an unsupervised kindergarten finger painting class. The Roosters gave London four runs in the top of the first by committing three errors, then got their act together and gradually built a comfortable lead. When Richmond's left fielder, the short but powerfully built Aaron Sledd, hit a grand slam in the bottom of the sixth to make it 12–5, the lead looked insurmountable. Hardly.

Takanori Mizuno started the seventh in relief of Roosters starter Rich Jelovcic, and all six Werewolves batters who faced him reached base (three via base hits and three via free passes) and eventually scored. Alejandro Bracho came on and got one out but then needed relief himself after walking the next two batters. Before Jamie Blaesing could put out the fire, London had scored eight times to take a 13–12 lead. It was a breathtaking dissipation of prosperity. Richmond rallied once again though, and closer Bobby Chandler shut out London over the last inning and 2/3s to get the save. Still, Richmond's 14–13 win barely felt like a victory. Roosters manager John Cate said, "We're just going to turn the scoreboard off and get out of here and regroup. It just wasn't good baseball." No one was inclined to argue with Cate, not with the four-hour slug-&-boot fest having produced 27 runs, 10 errors, and 17 bases on balls, not to mention three HBPs.

At least the Roosters' bats had come alive. Richmond knocked out 16 hits, including home runs by third baseman Ryan Anholt and DH Mark Tomse, in addition to Sledd's grand salami. Although you wouldn't know it from the score of the game, the Roosters had also gotten good starting pitching again. Jelovcic, a 6′ 3″, 220-pound righthander with good stuff from Queens, New York, gave up five runs in his six-inning stint, but none of the runs were earned. In essence, the Roosters had already wasted two quality starts in as many games. Heading into the rubber game of the first series of the year, Roosters fans had plenty of reasons for optimism and pessimism both.

Before the game I'd finally gotten a chance to "officially" interview Mike Zerbe. We met at his locker in the Roosters' clubhouse, and Zerbe, dressed like a college kid, was right on time; another courtesy almost unheard-of among pro athletes. He had on jeans, a brown T-shirt, and a Nike ball cap. Over his T-shirt he wore a short-sleeved collared sport shirt which he left unbuttoned, a style favored by most of his team-mates. Unlike the other Roosters, Zerbe smoked cigars, and I noticed a pair of them standing in the pocket of his shirt. In the off-season Mike worked as a bartender, and I assumed that that's how he'd picked up the habit.

Nothing sensational came out of the interview, but it was still a pleasure to get the basic Mike Zerbe story. Zerbe had played college ball in his hometown of Tampa, Florida, for the University of Tampa, and he had gone right into the Frontier League when he was overlooked in the draft. In college and when he'd started out in the Frontier League with Kalamazoo, he'd been a catcher. In fact, that's how he and Max had gotten to be such good friends. Zerbe had been one of the human backstops that squatted behind the plate, protecting Max from foul balls, during Max's rookie Frontier League year in 1996.

Mike knew his pro career was about over and with it his dream of ever playing in the big leagues, but feeling sorry for himself was the farthest thing from his mind. "Hey, even if this is my last year, I can't complain. I've had a great time, and it's been an incredible experience. I've been a professional baseball player which is what I always wanted to be. I've been paid to play this game; I haven't been paid much, but I have been paid. Not many people ever get a chance to play pro baseball, even at this level. Whether it's affiliated ball or not affiliated ball, who gives a shit? I've had four years of professional experience, and that's four years more than most people get. It's a long shot to make it to the big leagues—we all know that. Look at Morgan Burkhart: he was here for four years. But we're still playing; that tells you something about how much the guys in this league love the game. If somebody in affiliated ball picks me up, great. If not, I'll have no regrets. It's been a great run."

After the game Werewolves manager Andy McCauley had more on his mind than the loss to Richmond. He was worried about getting his team back to Canada for their home opener. Something was wrong with the Werewolves' bus, and it would go no faster than 10 mph. Talking to Max outside the umpires' dressing room at McBride, McCauley said, "My shortstop was late and missed the bus today when we left the motel for the ballpark. He started running after us and we were going so slow, he caught the bus before we'd gone two blocks."

It really wasn't all that funny to the Werewolves, but we laughed at the idea of their bus chugging along at 10 mph all the way up to London, Ontario.

The Roosters dropped the rubber game of their series with London 11–8 in ten innings on Friday, June 2. Key Voshell, who went 4–6 with a pair of doubles, was probably the star of the game for the Roosters; but it was Tim Still, the only black player on the team, whose triple, double, and three RBI amounted to the most personally meaningful performance of the night. As one of seven outfielders on the Roosters' Opening Day roster, along with Ryan Peavey, Shannon Rushing, Sledd, Shap Stiles, Tomse, and Dan Wydner, Still desperately needed to produce as soon as he was given a chance. He had come through in his first start of the season, and presumably he now stood out a little from the crowd vying for playing time in the Roosters' outfield for something other than his skin color.

In contrast to Still, Venezuelan righthander Tomas Medina pitched poorly in his first start, allowing nine hits and five earned runs in five and a third innings. Worse, the Roosters' bullpen continued to perform like a millstone tied around the neck of a drowning man. The season was only three games old, but it was obvious nevertheless that the Roosters' pitching staff and defense were going to have to find a way to significantly reduce the nine runs allowed per game average they had lavished on London.

Max's next series was in Canton, Ohio, between the Evansville Otters and the hometown Crocodiles. I missed the first game on Saturday night, but on Sunday morning after Mass I decided that I was going to join Max in Canton. "I'm dreading the long drive up I-71," I told my long-suffering wife Kathy, trying to emphasize the concept that this was work I was engaged in, "but I feel like I have to go." Kathy, who stood at the kitchen sink washing the breakfast dishes, was used to me leaving home for days at a time either to play ball or to watch somebody else play, but that didn't mean that she liked it when I left. She turned and gave me a do-what-you-have-to-do look of resignation. As I left the kitchen to begin packing in the bedroom, I tried to reinforce my argument. "I'm afraid I'll miss something important if I don't go," I said.

On the way up to Canton in my Quest I had the radio tuned to the Reds–Twins game on the Reds flagship station, Cincinnati's 700 WLW, the behemoth of the AM airwaves that likes to brag that its signal can be heard in 35 states. I've never doubted the claim as I've picked up the radio voices of home while driving through a number of distant states such as New York, North Carolina, Florida, Alabama, and Missouri.

The broadcaster doing the play-by-play, of course, was Marty Brennaman, who was scheduled to be honored later in the summer by the National Baseball Hall of Fame, along with a trio of other Reds: manager Sparky Anderson, clutch hitter Tony Perez of the Big Red Machine, and 19th century stalwart, Bid McPhee, a second baseman who was the last major leaguer to play without a fielder's glove. Brennaman, who would be inducted into the broadcaster's wing of the Hall of Fame, was every bit as worthy of his honor as the other Reds were of theirs.

For more than two decades Reds fans across the Midwest had enjoyed Brennaman's "good old boy" style, his true friendship with his partner Joe Nuxhall, and his penchant for coining colorful terms and sayings. For instance, Brennaman would often say that so-and-so had just hit, not a three-run homer, but a "three-run Johnson"; somebody who was miffed about something had, according to Brennaman, a bad case of the "goo-goos"; and after congratulating Mr. & Mrs. Reds Fans on 30 years of marital bliss, he would pause long enough to allow everyone in the booth to join him in adding the benediction, "Ain't love grand!" He played extended jokes that other broadcasters would not have dared try or been able to pull off with equal panache, like making the radio booth a veritable shrine to Elvis Presley with photos and pieces of Elvis memorabilia he'd invited his listeners to send in. He was never afraid to stray momentarily onto discussions of other sports and non-sport topics; he bantered nightly with Nuxhall and off-the-air members of the broadcasting crew; and he never hesitated to criticize players, umpires, or anyone else he felt deserved it. Reds fans loved Brennaman and his partner so much that it became a tradition while watching a Reds television broadcast to turn down the sound on the tube and listen to "Marty and Joe" on the radio. Above all, and without ever being a "homer," Brennaman made rooting for the Reds fun, and he made his signature punctuation mark on every Reds' victory something to be repeatedly savored: "And this one belongs to the Reds!"

Somewhere between Cincinnati and Canton, my mind drifted away from the Reds–Twins game on the radio. Marty brought it back when I heard him begin to talk about something that had just happened in the Frontier League.

On Friday night, June 3, in London's home opener against the Chillicothe Paints, the Werewolves' Brett Gray had struck out 25 batters in a nine-inning complete game victory, reported Brennaman. "He's not a prospect because he's thirty-three years old," said Marty. It took me a few seconds, but I realized that Brennaman was misinformed about Gray's age. Since the Frontier League has an age limit of 27, I knew that Gray wasn't anywhere near 33. Despite his ignorance of Frontier League rules, Brennaman instinctively expressed a proper appreciation of Gray's performance in his own inimitable style: "I don't care if you're thirteen or thirty-three, that's getting the job done!"

I found Thurman Munson Memorial Stadium right off Interstate 77, set in a fairly wooded industrial park, not far from downtown Canton. The Stadium's spacious gravel parking recalled Canton's former days as a Cleveland Indians farm team in the Class Double A Eastern League. Max had told me that Canton and nearby Akron were keeping a Hatfield vs. McCoy–type feud going over professional baseball. According to Max, the former owner of the Canton Indians had complained like a spoiled brat until Canton spent a lot of money to fix up Thurman Munson. All the while he was wooing Akron to build him a brand new ballpark. When the Indians moved to Akron and changed their name to the Aeros, the Frontier League rushed in where accountants would have feared to tread. The Crocodiles immediately won the league championship in 1997, but the perceived treachery of the Indians had soured Canton on professional baseball. Announced attendance at Crocodile games had dropped every year—from 75,000 in the championship inaugural season to 64,000 in 1998 to 50,000 in 1999—and the actual numbers may have been even worse. The Canton Frontier League franchise had some things in its favor—a good ballpark and a new GM who knew what he was doing—but it was not going to be easy to win back the trust of the aggrieved Canton political establishment, business community, and populace.

The Crocodiles had opened the season in Chillicothe, losing the first two games of the series by wide margins before salvaging the get-away game 6–3. They had won their home opener Saturday night against Evansville 8–3, behind the four-hit, complete game pitching of Ron Deubel ... and in front of 1,064 diehards. That was a disappointing number, to be sure, considering the fact that Canton's Opening Day attendance was less than what every other Frontier League team was averaging. What made such a paltry attendance worse was the spaciousness of Thurman Munson, the second biggest ballpark in the Frontier League with a seating capacity of 5,700. Ironically, in Canton's situation such capacity was a problem, not an asset. The fans sat spread out as if each were being quarantined for having had a contagious disease. Every problem is an opportunity for somebody to demonstrate ingenuity, and the Crocodiles' new GM, Alfredo Portela, had an interesting idea about how to solve this one. As he would tell me later, Alfredo was considering covering up the seats in large areas of the stadium down both foul lines so that the fans would be squeezed in closer together behind home plate, thus creating an intimacy the ballpark woefully lacked.

With its all-metal seats and flooring, Thurman Munson was also the noisiest place in the world to play ball. It was especially noisy for the players and umpires who labored on a field that performed acoustically like an echo chamber since the last row of the grandstands was about six feet above the playing surface. There wasn't much that Alfredo, the aspiring Christo of Baseball, could do about the noise problems of "The Erector Set," as Max called Thurman Munson, unless he could convince the fans that a "Shoeless Joe Jackson Imitation Day" at the ballpark would be a lot of fun. Thankfully, one promotion Alfredo never considered running was "Bat Day."

Whereas the offices and clubhouses were housed in a building separate from the grandstands at McBride Stadium, at Thurman Munson everything was neatly tucked away underneath the grandstands. Both dugouts were directly connected to the clubhouses, making movement between them both private and convenient; and the Crocodile offices, located just to the first base side of home plate, offered through their wide plate glass windows a spectacular just-below field level view of the game. The umpires' dressing room was also behind home plate but a little to the third base side of it. The room was as spartan as the typical umpires' quarters, containing nothing more than a couple of lockers and chairs, a wash basin, and a shower and toilet, neither of which offered the slightest privacy. The room was also nondescript, with nothing in it to offer a clue as to who used it, besides the umpiring gear that had been left behind the night before and a stack of four boxes, each containing

JIM'S DAD
HEAD BASEBALL
COACH AT DIV III
MARIETTA COLLEGE!

a dozen official Frontier League baseballs. I sat down and waited for Max and Jim Schaly who were due to arrive soon.

I had gotten only bits and pieces of information about Jim Schaly from Max. And that was fine with me because I didn't want to pre-judge the man. Especially since Max and others had insinuated that there was a negative side to knowing and working with Schaly, who seemed to constantly flirt with trouble. I had already heard Max say more than once, "Sometimes I have to be Jim's daddy."

Of course, Max wasn't Jim's daddy, even if Max did on occasion treat Schaly as a wayward son. Jim's actual father was a famous college baseball coach, Don Schaly, who was getting close to having coached baseball at Marietta (Ohio) College for four decades. Back in 1993 he had become the first Division III coach to ever reach 1,000 wins. The Schaly-led Pioneers of Marietta had won national championships in 1982, 1983, and 1986; and Schaly's teams, while having won more than 1,200 games by the end of the 2000 college season, had still not lost their 300th. Don Schaly's astounding .800+ winning percentage was the best ever recorded by the coach of a major college program. Successful major league pitchers Kent Tekulve and Terry Mulholland had both played for Schaly at Marietta. In a brief 1993 article saluting Schaly's milestone 1,000th win, *Baseball America* included comments by Mulholland about how his coach's work ethic had rubbed off on him: "Coach Schaly always felt that we weren't working hard enough. And if we didn't work hard enough, someone else was working harder. You know, I've been in professional baseball for eight years now, and I have yet to run across someone who knows as much about the game of baseball as Don Schaly."

Some of Don Schaly's philosophy had obviously rubbed off on his son too, as Jim had risen to the top of the umpiring profession, the major leagues. Jim's career in the majors had been short and was tainted in the eyes of some people because he had umpired as a scab during the umpires' strike of 1995, but he had made it to the top. Given these circumstances, the question that naturally occurred about Jim Schaly was "What was he doing in the Frontier League?" The possibility that the answers to the question might be unpleasant, if not tragic, made the prospect of meeting and getting to know Jim Schaly all the more intriguing, as well as a little forbidding.

When Max and Schaly walked into the room, the first thing I did was comment on their attire. They were wearing dress pants, collared shirts, and loafers, and Max, of course, had on his sunglasses. We all shook hands, Max formally introducing Jim and me, and then I said, "Planning to hit the town tonight after the ballgame, are we?" That was exactly the plan, and they told me that they'd just been arguing over where to go. Max wanted to visit a place around the corner in Canton, while Jim favored getting the drive back to Marietta out of the way first. Whenever Max and Schaly umpired together in Canton, they would spend the night at Jim's apartment in Marietta, about two hours south of Canton, on the Ohio-West Virginia border. Reciprocally, when they partnered for games in Richmond, they would spend the night at Max's.

In response to my comment, Jim said, "Mike, you'll find that the umpires in this league dress with a lot more class than the ballplayers. The players are slobs for the most part. ... And when you're trying to get laid, every advantage helps."

As Max and I laughed, Schaly added, "Women don't throw themselves at umpires like they do ballplayers, you know."

I had always heard that size in an umpire is an advantage, just as it is for ballplayers, especially pitchers. The thinking is that umpires are less likely to become intimidated when they are as physically imposing, if not more so, as the managers and ballplayers who are screaming in their faces. Short umps, it is feared, might also have a tendency towards trying to prove their toughness in an effort to compensate for their lack of stature, thus making an already tough job more difficult. I'd thought about these things when I'd met Rodney Rollins, Max's partner for the series in Richmond. Rodney was short, and I thought I'd detected a little "Don't mess with me; I'm tougher than I look" bravura in him. But that could have just been my imagination, because Rodney had had a good series, and nobody that I was aware of had challenged him in the least.

Schaly certainly was not deficient in this regard. He looked to be a good 6' 2"—he might even have been closer to 6' 3"—and he weighed about 220. He didn't have a weightroom physique, but he was a very solid specimen. The absence of a gut, normally standard equipment for big umpires, meant that Jim also watched what he ate. Schaly had a somewhat fleshy, but pleasant and boyish face, with a flush in his cheeks and not much evidence that he ever needed to shave.

As Max and Schaly settled in and began undressing and carefully hanging up their civilian clothes, they talked shop and I listened. Max smoked greedily, one cigarette after another, as if he were building up a reserve to cover the upcoming three-hour period on the diamond when he would be unable to light up. Occasionally, I would ask a question, but more often they would keep me involved in the conversation themselves by identifying people being discussed they knew I didn't know and by pausing to give explanations necessary for me to understand what they were talking about.

I took the lid off the top box of baseballs stacked in the middle of the room and, for the first time, studied an official Frontier League base-ball. I saw that it was made by Wilson and that each ball was stamped with the facsimile signature of Bill Lee, the Frontier League commissioner, and the Frontier League logo, a smiling baseball head wearing a Daniel Boone–type coonskin cap. As neither Max nor Schaly had made a move towards the four dozen baseballs that needed rubbing up, I asked, "Who's got the dish tonight?"

"Me," said Max. "I'm strapping. ... And it ain't no 'dish.'"

"What is it then, Max?" asked Schaly, who grinned in my direction. I knew by that grin that Jim was in a better mood than Max because Jim would not be behind the plate.

"It's a Flaming Pie," said Max, who, I learned later, had borrowed the phrase from a Paul McCartney album of the same name. "Yeah, you better believe it. When you're in a one-run ballgame, last of the ninth, and you have the home team's base runner sliding into home, and you call him out, and you get the call *right*, it ain't no plate or dish—it's a Flaming Pie!"

As the home plate umpire, or the umpire working the Flaming Pie, Max, then, had the responsibility of rubbing up the baseballs. First, Max got the baseballs in each box ready to rub, a box at a time. He tossed away the cardboard separators in each box and ripped each ball out of its plastic bag. Then he started rubbing, returning all twelve rubbed balls to its box before moving on to the next box. Max would hold a new ball in his left hand, while he dipped his right index and middle fingers into the mud. He would smudge two fingerprints of mud onto each of the four "crescents" of the ball and then rub the ball with both hands. He used a twisting motion as he rubbed and often spit into his hands to keep them moist. From the grandstands baseballs always appear to be white as snow, but Max's rubbed up Wilsons looked decidedly dingy compared to those still unrubbed.

I noticed that Max's mud was in a small square Tupperware container. "Max, does the League supply you with mud, or do you have to get your own? And is that the famous mud from the Delaware River that the major leagues use?" I said.

"No, the League doesn't supply us, but this is the stuff they use in the majors," he said.

"Where'd you get it then?"

"I got this from Ohio State. I was doing a game in the finals of the high school state tournament at Bill Davis Stadium. They had a couple of cans of the stuff, so I scooped out about three handfuls, just enough to get me through the rest of the season. ... I'm a thief with honor."

Max had done this so many times, it didn't take him long at all to rub up the four dozen balls. When he was finished, he dumped them, box by box, into a canvas baseball satchel. Except for the six balls he kept to start the game with. They would go into the two ball pockets attached to his belt, one on each hip, three balls in each pocket. It was up to Schaly, the base ump, to carry the bag onto the field and into the home team's dugout. As Max finished rubbing up the baseballs, Schaly began polishing his shoes. I wouldn't have paid much attention to that, except that Jim was spraying his shoes with Pledge, not shoe polish. He seemed delighted that someone would actually be interested in hearing him explain why umpires use furniture polish on their shoes. "Before you can use Pledge, you have to use this stuff called Leather Luster," he said. "We borrowed it from the guys in the military. It's what they all use to get that great shine on their shoes.

"The first thing you do is take a brand new pair of shoes and strip 'em down. You scrub all the black off the shoes. They give you a special brush with the Leather Luster to do this. I spent about 30 hours stripping these shoes down. The leather actually gets green when you get all the black off them. When you're down to the leather, you put a coat of Leather Luster on the shoes, and then set the shoes out in the sun to let them dry. The first coat takes a long time to dry.

"When the first coat is dry, you take some steel wool and rub the shoes down lightly—you barely touch 'em. After this you can add as many new coats of Leather Luster as you want to—it doesn't take as long for them to dry as the first coat. I probably have eight coats on these shoes. Once you get the Leather Luster on your shoes, all you have to do is spray Pledge on 'em and wipe 'em off, and they shine like glass." Schaly's shoes did look fantastic, and they would surely have passed inspection in any branch of the service.

"Let me show you what the stuff looks like," said Schaly, as he began rummaging through his equipment bag.

"Son of a bitch!" he said. "Max, that damn Yonto got me again." Schaly pulled a large flat chocolate bar in a beat-up red wrapper out of his bag and held it up to show Max. Schaly knew I wanted to hear the story behind the candy bar, and so he began by asking me about a movie. "Mike, have you ever seen *Rudy*?" he said.

I told him that although I'd never seen the movie, I knew what it was about: a scrawny kid on the Notre Dame football team who never got into a game until the last play of the last game of his senior year.

"That's right," said Schaly. "And it's a true story. You gotta see the movie. Anyway, Max and I umpire with Joe Yonto, and Joe's dad coached football at Notre Dame for twenty years. Joe's dad was the one who convinced them to keep Rudy on the team.

"Naturally, Joe is a big Notre Dame football fan. I can't stand Notre Dame because I'm a big Ohio State fan, and we're always arguing about which school has the better football program. Well, one day when we were umpiring together, Joe gave me a candy bar he'd bought at Notre Dame. He said, 'Here, I got this for you.'

"'I don't want it,' I said. 'First of all, I don't eat candy. I don't like it. And second, I don't want anything that has the name and colors of a second-rate football team like Notre Dame on it.'

"I thought that was the end of it, but when I wasn't looking, Joe put the candy bar in my equipment bag. I found it later after I got home. I saved it until the next time we umpired together. Then I slipped it into his equipment bag, and he didn't find it until he got home. After that, it kept going back and forth, back and forth. Eventually, it got so beat up I had to throw it away. So what I did then was I bought the same kind of extra-large fund-raising candy bar at Ohio State—that's why this one has a red and white wrapper—and we started passing this one back and forth. Besides my equipment bag, Yonto's hid this thing in my suitcase, my clothes bag, my car, my shoes, my plate coat ... and probably some other places I can't remember right off hand. And this one's about worn out now. It's so flat and stretched out and hard, it's more like petrified taffy than a chocolate bar."

Schaly's story tickled me, particularly because I had, second-hand, a similar story to share with him. My wife, Kathy, and her college roommate had also played this adult version of the game of tag. The object my wife and her roommate passed back and forth was a plastic boob, a health aid normally used to help women learn how to perform breast self-examinations. Twenty years later Kathy was still at it, with Mary Cox, a co-worker in the Cincinnati Recreation Commission. This time the object was a miniature, ceramic cherry pie that somebody with no taste had actually given as a thank-you gift to a third party in the office. Ironically, this testament to tackiness had wound up providing Kathy and Mary with a lot of amusement, as they repeatedly attempted to one-up each other in their game of "Gotcha Last!" Kathy's proudest moment had come when Mary went on a vacation to California to visit relatives. Mary wasn't there more than a day or two when a package with no return address arrived for her at her sister's house in Los Angeles. Mary's curiosity and anticipation turned to disbelief when she opened the package and found ... an all-too-familiar, ugly, ceramic cherry pie.

Max took one last drag on his final cigarette, and Jim stuffed a big wad of Red Man Golden Blend into his mouth—"We're allowed to chew in this league," he said, "on the bases." As they headed out the door, I said to them what I would say to them all summer: "Good luck, guys." They thanked me, sincerely, for appreciating the fact that they were walking into an unpredictable collision of events and personalities that could become on any given pitch what umpires call "a shit house."

It was not necessary for me to climb onto the roof, as in Richmond, since the need for a press box at Thurman Munson had been anticipated from the beginning. The press box in Canton sat at the back of the grandstand, under the roof, and was part of a complex of media booths and private boxes that were connected by a walkway curving around the back of the Stadium. The Crocodiles' radio booth was empty because the team had no radio contract—a startling indication of the disarray the franchise was in. Alfredo would tell me later that he had been brought on board too late to negotiate a new radio deal, but he guaranteed that the Crocs would have a radio contract for the 2001 season.

The press boxes in Richmond and Canton were different in another way too. In Richmond a minimum professional decorum was maintained at all times—David Knight saw to that—but the atmosphere was hardly staid. The McBride press box was often as chatty as a coffee shop, and the only thing appreciated more than a great play on the field was a witty putdown or outrageous pun. In contrast, the Canton press box was as subdued as a classroom during a final exam. And in a way, that's exactly what it was, a sort of learning lab where the members of the Crocodiles' young front office staff could receive much of their on-the-job training.

There was no doubt about Alfredo's role in this environment. He was a drill instructor barking orders that were carried out swiftly and unquestioningly. He was also a critic of how his staff was running things: the music was too loud, one promotion was taking too long, another promotion was done in the wrong place, the scoreboard was too slow, the timing of the P.A. announcements was bad, and on and on. Alfredo's minions needed to get up to speed in a hurry, or the Frontier League's brief season was going to seem like an eternity for them.

With Alfredo's staff scurrying to meet his demands and the official scorer and the local Crocodiles beat writer as inexplicably reticent as jury members under a gag order, I settled into an expectation of watching the game in near silence. Before I turned my attention to the game on the field, I read a faxed press release from the London Werewolves that the Crocodile front office had made available. The press release was about Brett Gray's astounding strikeout performance, and it pointed out several things about the feat I hadn't known. It said, for instance, that Gray struck out four batters in an inning on two separate occasions. This meant two things to me: that Gray had gotten a couple of extra chances for strikeouts, and that his pitches had probably been as difficult to catch as they were to hit. Gray also did not come close to pitching a no-hitter or even a shutout, as one of the three hits he allowed (along with one walk) was a seventh-inning home run by the Chillicothe shortstop, Mike Cervenak. None of these facts diminished his accomplishment; they were just interesting to note. According to the press release, Gray also had 24 strikeouts through eight innings. This meant that he had at that late juncture a chance to tie the all-time record for strikeouts in a nine-inning professional game (27), set by Ron Necciai in a 1952 Appalachian League game. However, Gray was able to add only one more K in the ninth, as two Paints batters made out on fly balls. Still, his final total of 25 was likely the second most in pro baseball history and was definitely the most since Necciai's 27.

I found the concluding statement in the press release the most interesting of all: "Gray, who has failed to hook on with affiliated teams due to his lack of size (6' 0"), set a Frontier League single season strikeout mark last season (129) and is now just 56 K's away from the all-time league mark." The reference to baseball's prejudice against short pitchers was akin to editorializing, something press releases normally don't do, at least not those emanating from the offices of baseball teams. In this case though, it was highly understandable as the press release undoubtedly was meant to serve as a sales pitch to the scouting departments of all the major league clubs that received it. Implicit in the editorializing was the question: "Though he may be a couple of inches shorter than he supposedly needs to be, what else does Brett Gray have to do to earn a shot in affiliated ball?"

Brett Gray certainly wasn't the only short ballplayer in the Frontier League. Phill Kojack was short, and I had wondered back in Richmond if his lack of height was hurting him in the eyes of scouts as much as Morgan Burkhart's lack of height had hurt him. Not surprisingly, the Crocodiles and Otters both had their share of short players too. Canton had six players on its roster listed as standing under 6' 0" (including a first baseman with the unforgettable name of Macky Waguespack, who was definitely shorter than the 5' 10" height he was listed at), while Evansville had nine. The Otters even had a shortstop, Paul Bartolucci (officially listed as 5' 7"), who was only a close haircut away from being a clone of the Royals' former shortstop, Freddie Patek, who was the shortest player in the majors during his career. Of course, as Patek and Burkhart had proven, a lack of height is not necessarily fatal to a ballplayer's dream of making the major leagues; however, as the Frontier League was clearly demonstrating, it does make the road to Kansas City and to Boston and to every other major league baseball city that much harder to travel.

The knock on Canton's starting pitcher, Nate Buttenfield—if there was one—was definitely not his height. At 6' 8" and 230 pounds, Buttenfield had the size to play in the NBA. And for somebody built like a power forward, he pitched a fairly good game. Although he walked in Evansville's first two runs in the second inning, Buttenfield worked into the ninth, trailing only 3–1. After the seventh inning I left the press box to watch the rest of the game from underneath the grandstands, directly behind home plate. The area I moved to was the grounds crew's hangout. There was no where to sit besides on top of a waist-high concrete wall, but the bunker-like view was unbeatable. When the ninth inning started, it seemed as if the Crocodiles' failure to score in the first inning with the bases loaded and no outs loomed as a haunting explanation for Canton's impending defeat; but a six-run Evansville rally made that lost opportunity academic. My vantage point under the grandstands was so close to the action at home plate, it seemed almost voyeuristic. Canton reliever Kurt Umbarger had a rough outing, and I could see that it was primarily because he had trouble getting his breaking ball over the plate. Sitting on Umbarger's fastball, the Otters either worked him for a walk or hit the ball hard. With the score 9–1 going into the bottom of the ninth, finishing the game was not much more than a formality. The Crocodiles did plate one run when right fielder Willie Carter singled home second baseman Cary Zamilski, but Carter's hit came with two outs and only delayed the inevitable. Evansville reliever Cliff Brand, who had come on in the seventh, wanted to waste no more time or effort and quickly got ahead of Canton third baseman John Poss 0–2. The Crocodiles were down to their last strike. Brand hardly paused to check Carter at first, then fired a high fastball towards the plate.

In *The Science of Hitting* Ted Williams pointed out that a batter facing a 90 mph fastball has only 0.4 seconds to react to the pitch. That's less than a half second of reaction time when the ball is traveling about sixty feet. When you think about it, it is astounding that hitters can actually do what they do: pick up sight of the ball; recognize the pitch as to its speed, location, and movement; decide whether or not to swing; and then execute a successful, often perfect, swing, all done in that flicker of a moment. When the distance a baseball travels is only four or five feet, from the batter to the umpire, a 90 mph fastball can not be reacted to. It is humanly impossible to do so.

John Poss swung at Cliff Brand's fastball, and the next thing I knew ... the next thing anybody in the ballpark knew ... Max was down, on his back, having collapsed in the grass behind home plate. Poss' foul tip had skipped over the mitt of Evansville catcher Michael Waugh and had hit Max squarely, somewhere, despite all the protective gear he was wearing.

In seconds Max was surrounded by a ring of coaches and players, who quickly gave way to team trainers and to a couple of paramedics, who had been stationed at the game. The absolute silence of the stunned crowd made palpable their fear that they had perhaps just witnessed the worst thing they could imagine seeing on a baseball field.

For agonizing moments this fear lingered, as Max made not the slightest movement while the paramedics administered to him.

Finally, after what seemed like fifteen minutes but in reality was more like five, Max slowly sat up, and the relieved crowd issued some halting applause. Max had been hit in the collarbone, and he was in serious pain. With the paramedics and trainers hovering over him, Max managed while grimacing to get to one knee. "Jim, where's my mask?" he said.

"Right here, Max," said Schaly, as he handed the mask over.

"You don't need that," said one of the paramedics. "You're not gonna finish this game."

Max struggled to his feet and stood bent over, his hands on his knees. "I can do it," he said. "Just give me a minute."

Since it was now obvious that there was not a dead umpire on the field, Brand began tossing with the first baseman Derrick Levingston to keep his arm loose. Schaly tried to distract Max from his pain. "Max, you staggered, you staggered, and then you fell down in the grass. You found the grass. You didn't get dirty one bit! Great job!" said Schaly. Max didn't laugh, but a policeman standing nearby did. Max and the cop had met a couple of months earlier, in the spring when Max had been in Canton to umpire a college baseball tournament for the North Coast Athletic Conference. Max recognized the officer and, as bad as he felt, had to say hello. "How ya doing!" he said.

The paramedic was insistent. "Listen to me: you are not finishing this game. You're hurt. You have no business being out here now. Besides, an ambulance is already on its way."

"I've been umpiring for thirty years," said Max, "and there's only been one game I didn't finish. I should have finished that one too. This one I know I can finish."

The paramedic started to protest again but was interrupted by the cop. "Aw, let him go. He can finish the game. He's a tough monkey," he said. Encouragement and "You okay, Max?" inquiries came from all sides now. Standing upright, Max nodded affirmatively and pulled his mask on. Reluctantly, the paramedic started to walk away. "I'm against this," he said. "I don't recommend that you continue. ... And you're taking a ride to the hospital as soon as this game's over."

As Max settled in behind the Evansville catcher, Canton's manager Dan Massarelli gave John Poss a little advice. "If I were you, I'd be swinging at that next pitch coming in," he said.

Poss, a Frontier League veteran who'd been in the Baltimore Orioles organization the year before, had enough confidence in Max to ignore Massarelli's advice. He took Brand's second 0–2 pitch, a curveball down and away. It was close, but Max called it a ball. The next pitch, another curveball, was not even close, and the count ran to 2–2. Brand came in with the sixth pitch of the extended at-bat, a fastball, and Poss swung at it, lifting a high fly ball to medium center field. Max didn't wait for the catch. As soon as he saw Otter center fielder Jose Colon camped underneath the ball, he started walking off the field.

When I walked into the umpires' dressing room, Max had his outside shirt off, and Schaly was tightening the straps on Max's chest protector. Schaly was making the point that Max had been vulnerable to Poss's foul tip because he had allowed the straps of his chest protector to become loose, which caused the protector to sag just enough to expose his collarbone. Max had already lit a cigarette and in between drags on it, he was gulping a beer. Max couldn't raise his right arm, so Schaly helped him take off the chest protector. I wanted a look at the injury, so Max pulled down his sweat-drenched gray undershirt a tad to show me. He had a golf ball-sized knot on his collarbone, and on the knot I could see the impression of baseball stitches.

"Two outs and two strikes, bottom of the ninth … all we needed was one more strike, and we were out of there!" grumbled Max, wearily. … "That fuckin' Poss, wait until I get him again. He'd better be swinging because everything's going to be a strike."

Schaly and I both laughed at Max's idle threat. We knew that Max was just blowing off steam in his misery and that he didn't hold Poss responsible for the play which resulted in his injury. If anybody were to blame, it was the Evansville catcher, Waugh, who didn't get his glove up in time to stop the ball. But we all knew that Waugh wasn't really to blame either. It was a fatalistic baseball truth for which you could make a bumper sticker: UNCAUGHT FOUL TIPS HAPPEN. Max picked on Poss because he was the initiator of the foul tip and also because he knew Johnnie Poss. Waugh was a rookie and not yet part of Max's huge unofficial baseball family.

"Max, you scared the hell out of me," I said. Like Schaly, I was joking about the injury in an effort to take Max's mind off his pain. "The first thing that went through my mind was 'Max is dead. … Aw crap, there goes the book!' Or, maybe it was the other way around: 'Damn! There goes the book! … Oh, yeah, Max is dead.'"

"Mike, you should have been here last night," said Schaly, with a big grin on his face. "Max was in the middle of the infield around second base, and he got hit in the leg with a line drive. It was hit so hard he couldn't get out of the way!"

"That's right!" said Max. "I'd forgotten about that. Son of a bitch!"

"We call that a magnet," laughed Schaly. "That's two in a row, Max. What are you going to do for an encore tomorrow night?"

"Fuck you," said Max. "You better be happy if I show up at all."

The paramedics came into the room and immediately told Max to quit drinking beer. They wanted to give him some medication, and he wasn't supposed to have any alcohol in his system. Max tried to argue with them—one beer wasn't going to hurt anybody, and, besides, he *deserved* at least one beer—but they were adamant, and he acquiesced. He quit drinking … in front of them. Every time they turned around or went outside for a moment, he sneaked another sip.

There wasn't much for me to do, so I found out which hospital they were going to take Max to and headed over there. There was no sign of Max or Schaly at Aultman Hospital, only a couple of miles from downtown Canton, so I asked a nurse at the Emergency Room desk to let them know I was there. I sat down in the waiting room and began watching the Los Angeles Lakers and Portland Trailblazers duke it out in the seventh game of the Western Conference Finals.

Going into the fourth quarter, the Lakers trailed by 13. They outscored Portland 31–13 in the fourth and wound up winning by five. It was a great comeback by the Lakers or a big choke by the Blazers—they shot 22 percent (5–27) in the fourth quarter after hitting 50 percent through the first three quarters—depending on how you wanted to look at it. Schaly joined me for the last few minutes of the game while Max was getting x-rayed. By his comments I surmised that Schaly probably did some basketball officiating, as well as umpiring. I asked him about that, and he told me that, yes, he officiated basketball—high school and small college—and football too. When I asked him what he did for a living, Schaly told me that he taught grade school. That was true, but it wasn't the whole story. Max had told me that because umpiring always seemed to interrupt Schaly's studies it had taken Jim nearly twenty years to get his college degree. When Schaly admitted that he was a substitute, not a full time, grade school teacher, I started to realize how important umpiring was to him. In short, everything in Jim Schaly's life was secondary to umpiring. He arranged his life around his umpiring schedule and even sacrificed his teaching career to his umpiring. He doubtlessly enjoyed officiating football and basketball games, but he almost had to do so, out of financial necessity, since his earning power was hampered by his devotion to umpiring. The $75 per game that Schaly earned for each Frontier League game he worked may not have added up to enough money over the length of the season for the position to be realistically considered his profession, but there was no question in my mind that umpiring was Jim Schaly's vocation. Just as it was Max's vocation too.

As soon as the game was over, Jim and I headed for Max's room. On the way there I got Jim talking about his abbreviated career as a major league umpire. When I found out that one of the series he'd worked was between the Seattle Mariners and Detroit Tigers, I asked him if he had any stories to tell me about one of my favorite players, Cecil Fielder, the Tigers' huge first baseman at the time. Jim did have a story about an encounter with Fielder, an encounter that didn't exactly endear him to Schaly.

"Seattle was up, and one of their hitters beat out an infield hit," said Schaly. "After the batter ran past first, he turned towards the outfield on his way back to the bag. Fielder walked down the line to meet him, reached down, and tagged him on the leg. And then he looked over at me with a big expectant look on his face, like he wanted me to call him out. I ignored him at first, but he started crying, 'What is he, ump? He's out, right? He turned the wrong way. Is he out?' Finally, just to shut him up, I went: safe." As he said this, Schaly made the slightest of safe signals, mimicking the disdainful way he'd done it for Fielder.

"When I did that, Fielder said, 'Man, you don't even know the rules. He turned the wrong way, so he's supposed to be out.' I said, 'He's not out because he didn't make any attempt to advance to second. Unless he does that, he can turn any way he wants to.' And then Fielder said, 'Well, I still can't wait until the real umps come back.'"

"What did you say to that?" I asked.

"The only thing I could say: 'Fuck you, Cecil.'"

The doctor was just leaving as Schaly and I reached Max's room. Max was sitting on a cushioned examination bench, the kind that has a paper sheet pulled across it for each new patient; and his arm was in a sling. The x-ray showed that Max's collarbone was cracked, not broken. "Since you're not going to be getting any flowers, let's get the hell out of here," Schaly said to Max. Max and I were as anxious to get going as Schaly was. As we walked down the corridor on our way out of the hospital, Max and Schaly talked about medical insurance. The Frontier League, I learned, did not provide any coverage for its umpires, who were regarded as independent contractors. Max did have some coverage on his own though. In Ohio every high school umpire is insured under a group policy, and the coverage of this policy extends to any game umpired, not just high school games. Max was also entitled to some medical benefits through Patty's position at St. Lawrence, the Catholic grade school she taught at. Still, the League's lack of medical insurance for its umpires was regarded by the umpires themselves as a galling lack of respect, and Max and Schaly grumbled about their situation all the way to Jim's van in the parking lot.

Max and Schaly were heading back to Jim's apartment in Marietta, but not empty-handed. They were going to stop for beer at "the first neon sign" they came to. Max, who had been given some pain killers in the ambulance, wasn't the least bit worried about mixing alcohol and the medication. Nor did he accept the doctor's prognosis. The doctor had told Max that he'd be out of commission for two to three months and that he needed to rest his arm in the sling for that period of time. "Yeah, right," Max had thought. I knew that, if it were humanly possible, Max would be on the field tomorrow for the finale of the Canton–Evansville series. Before Schaly started the engine, Max took off the sling and tossed it over his cracked collarbone into the back seat of the van.

The next morning, under gray skies and a steady drizzle, I checked out of the Days Inn and headed to the Pro Football Hall of Fame. I'd never been to the museum, and this was my chance to see it. I wanted to enjoy my visit unprejudicially, but it was difficult for me not to compare the Pro Football Hall of Fame with the Baseball Hall of Fame at every turn. I'd been to Cooperstown for Induction Weekend every summer since 1986. I immediately fell in love with the town, and throughout the following years the mere thought of Cooperstown in summer was enough to chase away any blues brought on by winter's cold and lack of sunshine. Matching Cooperstown, I knew, would be a tough, nigh impossible, order for any other sports museum.

Right off the bat, so to speak, the Pro Football Hall of Fame comes up way short of Cooperstown in terms of setting. While Cooperstown completely envelopes the visitor in an intoxicating ambience of Rockwellian charm without even trying, the Pro Football Hall of Fame is located right next to an interstate highway. The Pro Football Hall of Fame has a spacious parking lot, true, but even this amenity points up the difference I'm getting at. The Baseball Hall of Fame has no parking lot at all, since its building, like a classic antique ballpark wedged into a surrounding neighborhood, is merely one landlocked component of Cooperstown's small town Main Street landscape, laid out and built many years ago, before the automobile had even been invented. On the other hand, with its relatively central location in Northern Ohio, Canton and its Hall of Fame are convenient and easily accessible by several transcontinental highways; appropriately modern virtues perhaps for a sport which has for decades traded on its image as the chic sport of action, affluence, and hipness.

Canton does have one advantage over Cooperstown though: Canton does not continually have to live down a somewhat embarrassing inception myth as Cooperstown does. That's because Canton doesn't claim to be the place where football was invented. Canton only claims to be the birthplace of the National Football League, and it's a claim that Canton and the Pro Football Hall of Fame can back up; unlike Cooperstown's inability to substantiate its debunked "birthplace of baseball" claim. It's a little surprising then that a couple of worded panels on the wall to the left of the main entrance, explaining why the Pro Football Hall of Fame is in Canton, pretty much represent the Hall's whole low-key approach to the matter. And, as the panels make clear, it was actually the American Professional Football Association, the direct forerunner of the NFL, that was founded on September 17, 1920, in the showroom of a local auto dealer, Ralph Hay, who also owned the Canton Bulldogs. There are no sacred founding artifacts or treasured pieces of birthplace memorabilia, nor is there a big display of any kind; only a reproduction of a 1961 United Features Syndicate cartoon by Erwin Hess that explains the NFL's humble origins, identifies the League's inaugural members, and recreates the founding scene. The humor of the cartoon comes from a "ballooned" statement made by one of the founding owners: "There's a pretty good team in Green Bay, Wisconsin … started playing last year … called the 'Packers.' They're not in this league. Maybe they didn't have fifty bucks for a franchise!"

Content in the knowledge that the connection between the Pro Football Hall of Fame and its site was entirely legitimate, I spent the rest of the morning and the early part of the afternoon moving slowly through the Hall of Fame's six main exhibition areas and absorbing all sorts of fascinating information about the game of professional football. For instance, I learned that NFL footballs are made of cowhide; a circumstance which makes the use of the term "pigskin" as quaintly archaic as the baseball term "horsehide." I also found out how the Super Bowl got its name. In joint meetings between the National and American Football Leagues, Kansas City Chiefs owner Lamar Hunt had been referring to the first edition of the then-unnamed championship game between the two leagues as "The Final Game." Each of Hunt's three children had recently been playing with a popular toy of the time, a very hard rubber ball that bounced extremely high. Hunt was subconsciously thinking of his kids' Super Balls, when he simply blurted out "Super Bowl." Obviously, the name stuck.

My two favorite exhibits were the Enshrinement Gallery and the Visa Hall of Fans exhibit. The latter honored the NFL's best fans, one per team. With photos, brief bios, and quotes from the honored fans themselves, the exhibit demonstrated just how loyal and how crazy NFL fans can be about their favorite team. Case in point: dressed as a bishop and wearing a mitre (a bishop's tall hat that comes to a point at the top) with Vince Lombardi's picture glued to the front of it, Green Bay fan

John O'Neill went to the 1997 Super Bowl as "Saint Vince Lombardi back from heaven to see his beloved Packers in another Super Bowl!"

When I was a kid back in Jacksonville, Florida, I collected what are known in the baseball memorabilia hobby as Hall of Fame Busts, little three dimensional busts of Hall of Fame players made of white plastic. Naturally, I assumed that these plastic busts were miniature replicas of the actual marble busts that existed in the Baseball Hall of Fame, but I was mistaken. The walls of the Hall of Fame Gallery in Cooperstown are adorned with bronze plaques, although their bas relief sculpting gives them a three dimensional quality. Life-sized bronze busts of Hall of Famers do exist in Canton. I saw them, over 200 of them, lining the halls of two "A"-shaped wings of the museum; and I thought that if Canton has any edge over Cooperstown in any way, shape, or form, that edge comes in the Hellenic grandeur of its Enshrinement Gallery.

When I walked into the Crocodiles' manager's office, everybody was there—the manager Dan Massarelli, who was only 29 years old; his three coaches, Joe Charboneau, Doc Schaedler, and Ben Biery; and Alfredo. It was obvious that they all wondered who the hell I was. Luckily, I had two icebreakers. First, I was one of the few people in Canton, Ohio, who knew where Erskine, South Carolina, is. That's because I'd played basketball and baseball against Erskine College 30 years earlier when I'd been a student at Belmont Abbey College. This experience connected me to Massarelli who'd played baseball at Erskine and then coached there for six years before coming home and signing on to manage the Crocodiles. Second, when I told "Mazz" what I was doing in Canton, my name suddenly rang a bell with Biery, sitting on an old sofa against the wall on the righthand side of the room. "I've heard of you," he said. "I've got your book, *Tales from the Dugout*." That recognition gave me instant credibility, and I could feel the occupants of the room relax their guard against me. Somebody asked how Max was doing, and I told them what I knew. Massarelli told me that the trainer had been very worried because Max had had trouble breathing. "The trainer asked Max if he was dizzy," said Mazz, "and Max said, 'I was born dizzy. And the Pink Floyd concert in '92 didn't help.'"

I took a seat on the couch next to Biery and tried to catch up with, without intruding on, the conversation that had been going on when I came in. They had been discussing personnel, often referring to a depth chart outlined on a large white bulletin board hanging on the wall opposite the door. The names of all the Crocodile players were listed on the board by position, and their all-important status as rookies, first-year players, second-year players, or veterans was indicated by different colors of markers. (By rule, each Frontier League club was limited to three veterans, two players with two years of experience, and seven players with one year of experience; insuring that between 10 and 12 roster spots were filled by rookies.) The bulletin board was the kind that erases with a quick wipe of a paper towel, and that was the point. At that moment, and even though the season was only a few games old, nothing seemed as insecure as a roster spot on a Frontier League baseball team.

One of Alfredo's young charges, public relations specialist, David Skozcen, popped in moments later to check with Alfredo on the status of the game. Alfredo and Massarelli were keeping an eye on the weather channel via the computer on Mazz's desk. Skozcen was immediately accosted with complaints about a lack of hot water at Thurman Munson. Unable to take hot showers, Evansville had left the ballpark in their uniforms after the previous night's game. Skozcen tried to explain and defend himself at the same time: "I asked the guy if we'd have hot water by the start of the season, and he said yes, that he was just waiting on a new hot water heater to get here from North Carolina. I reminded him that we had a professional team coming in on Friday. ... What a great way to represent the city of Canton!"

Joe Charboneau said, "I predict we'll have hot water by the All-Star break." Joe was standing in front of the lockers against the wall to the left of the couch, changing into his Crocs uniform. Everybody else was still in his civilian clothes and in no hurry to change out of them, with the game that night in serious danger of being rained out. I was anxious to talk to Joe Charboneau, the legend.

Charboneau had had one good year in the major leagues. Fortunately for him, it came in his first year and won him the 1980 American League Rookie of the Year Award. That was enough to endear him forever to Indians fans in Cleveland and all over Northeastern Ohio, coming as it did during the Indians' long malaise of mediocrity. But there was also Joe's wildman image as portrayed in his as-told-to autobiography, *Super Joe! The Life and Legend of Joe Charboneau.* From that book and other sources fans learned that Joe did nutty things, like open beer bottles with his eye socket, drink through his nose, and even cut out a bad tooth himself instead of going to see a dentist. My friend John Skurkay once told me a Charboneau story. "Charboneau was in a bar one day minding his own business when this huge guy came up to him and started calling him a 'pussy.' The guy knew that Joe had a reputation as a tough guy, and he was trying to pick a fight with him. Joe *was* tough. He used to fist fight, no gloves, for money in box cars, and you don't do that if you're a pussy. Joe told the guy, 'Look, I don't want any trouble. Why don't you just leave me alone?' But the guy wouldn't back off, so Joe finally went out side with him."

"What happened?" I asked.

"Joe beat the living shit out of the guy."

Now, Skurkay, a pretty big guy himself, is a great baseball fan, the kind of fan who lives to dream up trivia questions nobody else knows the answer to. Such fans have been known to exaggerate or to pass on apocryphal stories as the truth if they are interesting enough, so I thought it prudent to ask, "How do you this story is true, John?"

"I was there! I saw it myself," he said.

The discussion of players was brutally frank. Maurice Washington, an outfielder who had been in the Pirates' organization the year before at Williamsport (PA) seemed to be in trouble. "He's got great bat speed, but that's all he's got, and he's not showing it," said Massarelli. Alfredo began talking about a player from Rancho Cucamonga he could get, a good hitter, that the Crocodiles' brain trust felt they desperately needed.

"He hit .300 in the California League," said Alfredo.

"If he hit .300 in the California League, he can hit," said Joe.

"That was in 144 at bats," said Alfredo.

"That's all he'll get here," pointed out Joe.

"He can come when we get hot water," said Massarelli.

"We'll get hot water when we go over .500," rejoined Alfredo.

Everybody laughed and feigned being vicariously intimidated by Alfredo's challenge. Instead of a comeback, Massarelli took a vote. "Doc, what do you say?" he said

"I say, 'Come on.'"

"Joe?"

"Let's get him."

"Ben?"

"Yes."

"That's three of the four. I'm the fourth," said Mazz, "and I say, 'Get 'em,' so that's four out of four. It's unanimous."

They returned to the board to see who could be released. Several players were discussed, including a pitcher, who was definitely doomed. Massarelli had heard that the pitcher had said he was "milking it." I asked Mazz what that meant exactly, and he said, "It means he doesn't really want the ball." In the end, they decided that they could add the new guy from California without releasing Washington.

With the Crocodiles' roster settled, for the moment, Alfredo and Mazz turned their attention to the game. Alfredo was in favor of cancelling it. Mazz wanted to play. "If we bang it, we can make it up later as a doubleheader because we have another series at home with these guys," said Alfredo. "If we open the door, there's only nine people who are gonna show up, and we'll lose a ton of money. And it'll be a miserable night out there for the players and the fans."

"I know it," said Massarelli, "but my brother's in town. He's off because of the draft." Mazz's brother John was in affiliated ball and managed a team in the New York-Penn League.

"We play in the rain because your brother is here?" asked Alfredo.

"No. It's just too early to call it," said Mazz.

"I know it," said Alfredo. "I'm just preparing you for when I decide to bang it."

"What'll we do about those nine people who are coming out?"

"We can get the word out to them on radio."

Alfredo and Mazz continued to discuss the situation as Alfredo headed out of the office, so I began to talk to Charboneau. Joe may have been a tough guy, but he didn't particularly look like one. He looked instead like one of the happiest and friendliest people in the world. He had a serenity in his face that a person gets when he knows exactly who he is and when he is completely satisfied with his place in life. The Canton Crocodiles were a long way from the major leagues, but that didn't seem to bother Joe Charboneau one bit. I asked Joe to tell me a couple of stories for the book.

He gave me a big smile and said, "I don't have any stories ... besides, they're all in my book! ... Have you heard of my book?"

I assured him that I had. "My book goes for a lot of money, did you know that?" he said. "Last time I looked it was going for about $60 on the Internet." Yes, I also knew that his book was hard to find and somewhat pricey.

I still thought I might get him to talk if I perhaps got the ball rolling myself. "Joe, I heard that one time in the minor leagues you took batting practice naked. Is that true?"

"Nah, nah," he said, shaking his head. And then with a sly grin: "... maybe in a jock strap."

I laughed and said, "Okay, that's close enough. Come on, tell me about that."

"No. Really, I don't have any stories. Ask Mazz. He can tell you some stories."

"Well, there's a story about this kid who came to our tryout in spring training wearing jeans," said Massarelli. "He said, 'I'm good. I can strike anybody out.'

"'Oh, yeah? Who you been pitching for?' I said.

"'I haven't pitched since 11th grade,' he said.

"I told him, 'Go down to the bullpen, and I'll talk to the pitching coach.'

"I forgot all about him, but we ran out of pitchers and needed one more guy to throw to the last group of hitters we were trying out. I remembered this guy and called him over. 'Okay,' I said, 'go with Doc, warm up, pay your $25, and you can show us what you got.'

"He said, 'Oh, it costs $25?'

"'Yeah.'

"He said he had his money in his car. He walked over to his car, got in, and drove off, and we never saw him again."

"Mazz, you shoulda waived the $25," said Joe, "I wanted to see the guy pitch in his jeans."

Mazz rolled his eyes at Charboneau's comment and began a second story. "I took over last year with about 35 games left in the season. I was trying to dot all my i's and cross all my t's, but I still made some rookie managing mistakes, such as the time I left a relief pitcher off the lineup card.

"When I was the head coach at Erskine College, I had an All-American pitcher named Josh Meurer. He was so good I never had to take him out, and this got me into trouble when I had Josh in pro ball. In one of my first games last year with Canton, I went out to the mound to relieve Meurer. My reliever was walking in from the bullpen, and when I told the umpire who he was, he said, 'You can't bring him in. He's not on the lineup card.' I said, 'Ah, crap!' I ran back into the clubhouse and told Meurer, 'You've got to get dressed again and go back out there to pitch. Don't ask me why. Just hurry!' He went out and got the last two outs of the inning. Then I took him out. I told him, 'Okay, that's it. I'm relieving you.' He said, 'Are you sure?'"

Pitching coach Doc Schaedler didn't have a story, so I asked him what he thought the reason was for the prejudice against short pitchers. "It's a durability thing," he said. "Major league organizations like to take chances on big bodies because they think big pitchers last longer and have fewer injuries. Plus, short guys have to push off the mound, while tall guys can drive off it. This doesn't mean short guys can never make it, but if you're 5' 10" or 5' 11" you'd better be lighting up the radar gun."

Alfredo came back into the office and announced "We're playing."

"Really? You made fun of me earlier when I suggested that," said Massarelli.

"I'm always gonna do that," said Alfredo. "The groundskeeper says we'll get it in. The field is fine. We're gonna start at 7:05. A second cell will probably come through around 8:00, but if we start on time we'll get it in."

Alfredo left the office again but returned fifteen minutes later. "That's it. I'm banging it," he said. "The groundskeeper and I have been looking at instantaneous weather reports on the computer, and we're about to get hammered."

"Good," said Massarelli, "I'd rather have my one, two, and three ready for London." Alfredo got on the phone and started giving directions to his staff on how to spread the word that the game had been cancelled.

As Doc started to gather his belongings, he said, "Joe's going home in the daytime? His wife won't know him. She'll call the cops."

"Her boyfriend's climbing out the window as we speak," said Massarelli.

As if he were speaking about a another person, Charboneau said, "Hey, Joe's the smartest guy in the world. He called ahead and let his wife know he's coming home." Then, with a big grin and all the confidence in the world, he added, "I'll never have to see some other guy's car in my driveway."

I shook hands with everybody left in the office, and as I walked towards the door, Charboneau pointed to the press pass hanging around my neck and said while again flashing that sly smile, "Hey, make sure you hang onto that Frontier League press pass. It'll be a collector's item someday."

"Yeah, I will," I said, "even though I know it'll never be as big as *Super Joe!*"

4

Chillicothe, Ohio: A Perfect Place for Minor League Baseball

THE NEXT MORNING I CALLED Max to see how he was doing. He was still in a lot of pain but definitely going to Chillicothe for the start of a three-game series between the Paints and Richmond. "Atta baby!" I encouraged him, using his own expression. In typically Maxy fashion, he thought it necessary to apologize to me. "I'm sorry you went all the way up to Canton for only the one game, but, I've got to be honest with you ... I've never been so thankful for a rainout in my life!"

After telling him for the hundredth time already that I thought he was crazy, I said I'd meet him at the ballpark that night. I wanted to get to Chillicothe early so I'd have some time to look around.

Before I left for Chillicothe, I drove over to Blockbuster Video and rented *Rudy*. It was a heartwarming, inspiring film. I thought the most memorable statement of the movie was uttered by Rudy's well-meaning but discouraging blue-collar father. It comes as Rudy, still determined to play football for the Fighting Irish of Notre Dame despite the skepticism of everyone around him, is boarding a bus for South Bend, Indiana. "Chasing a stupid dream causes nothing but heartache for you and everyone around you," Mr. Rutiger says.

Chillicothe is located in the Scioto River valley of south central Ohio in the middle of Ross county, 45 miles dead south of Columbus and

72

about 90 miles slightly northeast of Cincinnati. Any experienced traveler can take one look at a road map and see that the faster of the two ways to get to Chillicothe from Cincinnati is to drive up I-71, in a northeasternly direction for about an hour, past Chillicothe, and then take Route 35, heading back down in a southeasternly direction, into the northwestern side of town. That's the way to go if you are late for a Frontier League game or a dentist's appointment with Dr. Chris Hanners, the owner of the Chillicothe team, who maintains a dental practice in nearby Piketon, Ohio. If you can afford to take your time and enjoy the scenery though, you might be tempted, as I was, to head out east from the beginning on Route 50 which takes you—with the exception of a last-leg, 15-mile northernly jog—on a pretty straight course into Chillicothe. When you take the back roads, you will always run into a surprise or two: like the John Harris Dental Museum in Bainbridge, 19 miles from Chillicothe. The Museum, maintained in its original structure by the Ohio Dental Association, preserves Dr. Harris' dental school, the first in the world, which operated from 1825 to 1830. The mere thought of a dentist's appointment makes me break into a cold sweat, and there was no way I was going to stop and actually spend time gawking at the primitive instruments of torture Dr. Harris and his students used more than a century and a half ago. (In fact, I sped up and broke the speed limit trying to get out of the little town as fast as possible.) But it was a genuine Fodor's moment, I told myself, for me to see exactly where all the professional drilling, extractions, and root canaling began.

Chillicothe has neither Bunker Hill nor the Liberty Bell, yet it does have a rich early American history of its own, one that is closely tied to the fate of Native Americans. Actually, Paleo Indians lived in the area long before our country was founded, during the Prehistoric Stone Age as early as 11,000 years ago. The Adena and Hopewell, two tribes known as Moundbuilders, developed advanced civilizations and left large ceremonial and burial earthworks which are preserved to this day. By the time whites began to move into the area, the Shawnee were dominant. Indians resisted white expansion for decades, but they lost the decisive battle of Fallen Timbers in 1796 and were forced to sign the Treaty of Greenville which opened Ohio for settlement. The memory of south-central Ohio's Indian wars is kept vividly alive by the outdoor drama *Tecumseh!*, which celebrates the exploits of the Shawnee chief who attempted to unite the area's tribes against the white man's encroachments. The play is staged six nights a week every summer in an amphitheater on Sugarloaf Mountain, just outside Chillicothe.

Out of respect for this Native American heritage, founder Nathaniel Massie chose in "Chillicothe" a name derived from the Shawnee word meaning "principal town." Fortunately, for the peace of mind of every-

Max calls a strike.

one connected to the franchise, Chillicothe's professional baseball team was named, not directly after the area's heroic native warriors, but after the strong and spirited horses they preferred to use in battle. "Paints" was a serendipitous choice because it alludes to the Indians who once lived in the area but can hardly be objected to as being culturally insensitive. In this respect, at least, the Paints are superior to both the Cleveland Indians and the Atlanta Braves, not to mention the especially beleaguered Washington Redskins.

As 50 brings you into the outskirts of town, you pass a sign proudly proclaiming that Chillicothe was the first capitol of the state of Ohio. A quarter of a mile further on around the next bend you see the city, or a fair section of it, below. Imagining that the Paint Street address listed in the Frontier League media guide meant that the ballpark was located in the city proper, I began looking for light towers. I spotted some, but they led me only to a schoolboy football field in the middle of a residential neighborhood. I had gotten enough of a view from 50 to know in which direction downtown lay, so I decided to head that way and worry about finding the ballpark later.

Like many small-to-medium cities all over the country, Chillicothe has a postcard-pretty downtown with wide streets and a large stock of old brick buildings. What sets Chillicothe apart though is that its downtown is still a bustling center of commercial and civic activity, not a symbolic relic of erstwhile vitality characterized by empty storefronts and repeating business failures. I puttered up and down the streets, doing as much exploring and sightseeing as searching; and before I knew it I was on the corner of 2nd and North Paint Streets, right in front of "Paints Corner," the team's gift shop and administrative/ticket office. I realized then that the team's offices and the ballpark were in different locations.

You can tell a lot about a team by studying their gift shop. I already knew that the Paints were special to Chillicothe, but the wide array of Paints' souvenirs and apparel in the shop indicated an impressive level of support. You just don't make that much stuff unless you know you can sell it, and you don't sell that much stuff unless a lot of people love your team. And Paints fans love their team. With a population of 22,000, Chillicothe is one of the smallest markets in professional baseball, yet the Paints are always, relatively, one of the strongest draws in the league. The year before, in 1999, Chillicothe drew 61,249 fans to the ballpark, good for fourth best in the league. Sixty-one thousand over a 42-game home schedule might not sound like much, but it is equivalent to the Cincinnati Reds drawing three million.

In addition to the great fan support they enjoyed, the Paints had a reputation for being the best run franchise in the Frontier League. I didn't want to read too much into it, but the Chillicothe organizational page in the Frontier League media guide seemed to bear out this reputation. The Paints' roster of personnel was longer than any other team, and there were no "TBA's" listed, as there were for most teams in the league.

As I finished browsing through the trove of Paints souvenirs and items of clothing, a couple who appeared to be in their fifties stood at the counter, talking to John Wend, the Paints' friendly Director of Sales and Marketing. Wend was balding, wore glasses, and was fighting a losing battle with his waist line. He had an earnest and direct manner without being overbearing, but the most conspicuous thing about him by far was his voice, a rich, deep instrument which, I learned later, he used to great effect as the Paints' public address announcer. The couple at the counter revealed that they were the parents of Eric Frodsham, a rookie relief pitcher out of tiny Friends University in Wichita, Kansas, and said that they'd been having trouble getting the Paints' website to come up on their computer back home in Kansas. After giving the Frodshams a hearty welcome, Wend told them that the website had been down for updating but would soon return and be better than ever.

After the Frodshams completed their purchases and left the shop, I introduced myself to Wend and to Office Manager Aaron Lemaster. In his mid-thirties, Aaron was younger than John and wore a fu-man-chu that seemed to be perpetually coming in. Like Wend, Lemaster did double duty for the ballclub, serving during games as the team's music coordinator and the official scorer. After we chatted for a while, John loaded me down with a Paints yearbook and current and past editions of the *Stable Report*, a fat promotional newspaper that the Paints give away annually to their fans; told me how to get to the Chillicothe ballpark out on State Route 104; and promised to try to make room for me in the crowded press box at VA Memorial Stadium. The last was a bigger favor than I realized.

    Both the Ross County Fairgrounds and the Ross County Airport are on State Route 104, which runs from the north side of Chillicothe all the way into Pickaway County. The Paints' ballpark, located on the grounds of a large Veterans Administration Medical Center complex south of the airport and Fairgrounds, is only about four miles north of town up Route 104; but there is plenty to see as you make the drive. Namely, two sprawling state prisons on either side of the road: the Chillicothe Correctional Institute on the right, and the Ross Correctional Institute on the left. A third, smaller facility, the Ross Correctional Camp sits adjacent to the latter. Manned guard towers and concertina wire make it clear that these "correctional" facilities are not minimum-security "time-out" corners for celebrity or privileged offenders who've been given a slap on the wrist. Other prisons in Ohio have endured extremely violent riots that resulted in deaths to both inmates and prison guards, but Chillicothe has been spared such calamities. Despite their forbidding appearances, Chillicothe's prisons have not damaged the city or its image in the slightest. The main effect of their presence seems to be a positive one: the nearly 1,000 jobs the prisons supply to local residents.

    A National Historical Park devoted to the preservation of earthen mounds built many centuries ago by Hopewell Indians is located on the right just past the Chillicothe Correctional Institute; while on the left, the VA's nine-hole golf course runs parallel to 104 for several holes, all the way to Hines Boulevard, the road which leads into the VA complex. A road sign marking the boundary of the VA's property promulgates a statement about the sacrifice made by disabled American war veterans: "The cost of freedom is evident here." I couldn't help but think that the sign applies equally well, albeit ironically, to the prisons nearby.

    VA Memorial Stadium is the most unique ballpark in professional baseball, as it is the only ballpark used by a pro team which is owned by the Federal Government. Built in 1954 by the "Blue Star Mothers of America," an organization of the mothers of Navy servicemen, the

Stadium was the key to Chillicothe's entry into professional baseball. As beloved as the Paints are, the city would not have built a ballpark just to attract a Frontier League franchise. Because of the existence of VA Memorial, the city didn't have to. After the Paints poured a lot of owner Chris Hanners' money and the sweat-equity of many volunteers into the refurbishment of the ballpark, it was a more than adequate facility for the Frontier League, especially during the League's infancy when some teams played their home games on high school-grade municipal diamonds.

Because of its setting, VA Memorial Stadium is also one of the prettiest ballparks you will ever see. Huge, sprawling trees, looming high above the outfield walls, are the signature of the ballpark. The massive greenery of these trees contrasts sharply with the jumble of colors on the ad-plastered outfield walls and provides a natural transition to the sky above, whether it is the fragile blue color of fine Irish china or a bruised purple signaling an impending thunderstorm. In the late innings' darkness the hovering trees seem like misshapen monsters waiting for a chance to intrude upon the game. This is not a completely far-fetched image, as branches on the trees beyond the left field wall actually hang over the wall and extend ten-to-twelve feet into the field of play. And then there are the trees located inside the park itself! Believe it or not, three giant trees, a black walnut, a hackberry, and a burr oak, stand down the left field line between the uncovered metal bleachers and a picnic pavilion. During afternoon games, this trio of trees provides some welcome shade for players and fans, but they also block out at all times the press box view of the bullpen pitcher's mounds in foul ground, a small price to pay, me thinks, for the privilege of watching baseball in a veritable arboretum.

[handwritten margin note: Umpire's nightmare]

There is a single entrance to VA Memorial Stadium, and it is on the third base corner of the single red-brick grandstand that is the heart of the Stadium. I arrived pretty early, but the gate was already being manned by young interns who were organizing boxes of Barry Larkin Bamm Beano bears, which would be given away to young Paints fans. After walking through the gate, I turned left and saw immediately on my right the entrance to the visitors' clubhouse, tucked underneath the grandstand. Straight ahead, not more than 20 feet away, was the field. Richmond was in town, and green-capped Roosters involved in various aspects of BP were spread all over the diamond. The field itself, the province of groundskeeper Jim Miner, looked impeccable. The grass had a brilliant sheen, there were no bald spots in the turf anywhere, and the infield dirt shimmered like a Sahara sand dune in the fierce sunlight.

[handwritten: CHILLICOTHE]

As I stood there surveying the scene, a Rooster came out of the dugout, headed off the field towards the Richmond clubhouse. It was Phill Kojack. "I guess Max is coming if you're here," he said. We shook hands, and then I told him about Max, beginning, "You won't believe what happened in Canton ..." Phill told me that the Roosters had split their first two games in Johnstown and been rained out in the third. The rainout had been Phill's start, so he was getting the ball for the opener in Chillicothe. When he said he hoped that Max would be behind the plate, I told him, "I don't know if Max has the plate tonight or not, but if his partner has a heart, he won't."

Thwack! ... Thwack! ... Thwack! That was the timeless, rhythmic sound of batting practice being performed as only professionals do it, with half-speed fastballs being hammered by a wooden bat. It echoed around the empty ballpark, unmuffled by the din of rock 'n roll streaming from the P.A. speakers, and gave me a familiar sense of baseball euphoria.

The Paints are a good neighbor to the VA medical facility and let the patients and residents there into the games free of charge. Everyone knows that the first row of the third base grandstand and the aisle in front of it are reserved for the veterans in their wheelchairs and walkers. The vets are always among the first fans in the ballpark, and several of them were already staking out their spots.

The only other early fan I could see was a man standing near me behind the backstop screen intently watching batting practice. He had a gruff, authoritative demeanor as if he were used to giving orders. It was obvious that he didn't work for the Paints, but that didn't stop him from barking at groundskeeper Jimmy Miner, walking past on the field, to stop goofing around and to get to work. The rotund Miner had a way of shuffling around slowly, but he was hard-working and did a beautiful job, almost single-handedly, on the field, and it was not necessary for anyone to prod him.

I struck up a conversation with this fellow who turned out to be Pete Dunkel, a retired school superintendent who'd been born and raised in the Ross County area. He had also been an umpire for over thirty years, had worked numerous important games in the state playoffs, and had been elected to the Ohio High Schools Athletic Association Hall of Fame.

When I asked him what he thought of Frontier League baseball, he gave me a reply that was so articulate it seemed as if he'd been waiting for someone to ask his opinion. "It's a social event for 75–80 percent of the people who come to these games, but I don't come out for the socializing or the beanie baby give-aways or the half-priced beer or any of that bullshit. I come out to watch the games because I love baseball. I come to every game I can get to when I'm not umpiring.

"It took me a while to come out here. I was a little apprehensive at first, but I eventually came out and it didn't take me long to appreciate the talent that they get here. It definitely takes some talent to play in this league. The caliber of ball is much better than most people realize. There are kids who play four years of Division I ball ... they don't get drafted, they don't get signed, so they come here to try out, and they don't make it. That right there shows you that this is a good caliber of ball.

"The ones that do make it play hard too, all the time. They have to. They know they're on the edge. They can be let go tonight. There's new guys trying out all year long, and you're not assured of nothing."

Dunkel asked me if I'd ever heard of Gator McBride. I certainly had. McBride, Scott Pinoni, and Mitch House were the three biggest sluggers in Paints' history and the only Paints to have had their numbers retired. The squat, powerfully-built Pinoni was the team career leader in home runs (58), runs (187), RBI (237), hits (302), doubles (49), and at bats (850), but it was McBride who was a legend in Chillicothe. He was, in fact, for Paints' fans, the equivalent of Morgan Burkhart, and the paths of McBride and Burkhart had certainly crossed, more than once.

McBride came to the Paints from the Atlanta Braves, who thought very highly of his abilities but had come to believe that chronic leg injuries would prevent him from ever reaching his full potential. In 1998 McBride hit .403 and lost the Frontier League batting title by one point on the last day of the season to Morgan Burkhart. McBride was given a second chance in affiliated ball, and like Burkhart, he was signed by the Boston Red Sox. He did well in the Red Sox minor league system and then played winter ball in Mexico with Burkhart, losing a second batting championship on the last day of the season, again to Burkhart. Like Morgan, Gator had been slated to open the 2000 season in Pawtucket, but a car accident tore up his knee and put his career in jeopardy.

"As soon as I saw Gator McBride, I knew he could play," said Dunkel appreciatively. "That kid was a great hitter. When Gator was here, you could tell with your back turned to the infield that he was hitting batting practice ... by the *sound*. It was a real shame that he got hurt in that accident, but if it's possible, he'll be back. He's a real warrior, that kid."

Like Max, Dunkel had been around baseball a long time. He shared a number of good stories with me, including one about the Hall of Famer many people consider to have been the greatest third baseman of all-time, the Phillies' Mike Schmidt. "Mike Schmidt played college baseball for Bob Wren at Ohio University in Athens, not far from here.

Wren coached at OU forever. Schmidt was not a player when Wren recruited him out of high school, but by the time Schmidt was a senior at OU he was an All-American.

"Although the Phillies moved Schmidt to third, he played short-stop in college. One day during Mike's senior year, the other team hit one in the gap and Schmidt had to go out for the relay. Now Wren had everything down to a science, including how far the shortstop was to go for the throw from the outfield.

"Well, Schmidt went about three feet too far. He took the throw, turned, and threw it home. The throw came up short, bounced, and got by the catcher. Of course, the run scored. Wren was pissed, so he went out on the field and talked to Schmidt. He said, 'When you came here, you weren't worth a dime. Now you're worth $100,000 in the draft'—that was a lot of money back then. 'Now, you worked hard, so you're responsible for $50,000, but I helped turn you into a ballplayer, so I claim $50,000' worth of the credit. You've been here four years. You know our system.' Wren then took his foot and dragged it across the grass to show Schmidt exactly how far he was supposed to go out for the relays. He said, 'If you go past this line on the next relay, your ass'll be sitting next to me on the bench.'

"Sure enough, the next guy hit one in the gap. Schmidt went exactly to the spot Wren had showed him, took the throw from the outfielder, threw a strike to the catcher, and nailed the runner.

"Schmidt came running into the dugout all puffed up like he was proud of having done something great, looking for Wren. Wren moved down to the end of the bench and wouldn't even look in Schmidt's direction, didn't want to give him any satisfaction. After the game, Schmidt thought he'd razz Wren, so he came up to him and said, 'Hey, Coach, how'd you like that second throw?'

"And Wren told him, 'Great throw, Mike. But if you'd done it right the first time, the second one wouldn't have been necessary.'"

In the Frontier League media guide Steve Dawes, a Chillicothe native, was listed as a Paints assistant coach. I'd met Steve two decades earlier when he was a shortstop at Xavier University and I worked one fall season for the team as an assistant coach. I asked Dunkel about Dawes, and sure enough Pete had a story about him too. "Steve was a helluva shortstop, but for some reason he wasn't highly recruited coming out of high school," Dunkel said. "The Xavier coach recognized his talent though and offered Steve a scholarship. Steve gave the coach a verbal commitment, but then a week or two later the coach at Ohio State saw him playing in a tournament, and he offered him a scholarship too. Steve wanted to take the second guy's offer and go to Ohio State. When he told his dad that's what he was thinking about doing, his dad said, 'Well, I'll tell you one thing: you're not doing anything until you call the coach at Xavier and talk to him.' So Steve called the Xavier coach. The guy said, 'Steve, I know Ohio State is the big time, but I saw you first and I believed in you first and I still want you to come to Xavier to play for me; but you do what you think is the right thing to do.' As you know, he decided to go to Xavier."

Dunkel told me that Dawes, now a certified public accountant, never coached for the Paints until August of each year, when his son's youth baseball league season ended. I would eventually get tired of waiting for that point in the summer to come around, and one day in July I visited him at his office in downtown Chillicothe. Although Steve is not, and never was, a big talker, we had a pleasant little chat, catching up on each other's lives. When I told him how much I liked Chillicothe and longed to live in such a place, he said, "Everybody thinks Chillicothe is a dull place and a dead end when they're in high school, and they can't wait to leave. But later on when they realize what a great place it really is to live and raise a family, they all wind up coming back."

Finishing my reconnoitering of the Paints' ballpark, I strolled along the walkway that followed the backstop fence from the end of the third base dugout to the far end of the first base dugout. Turning right, I saw, as I'd suspected, that the Paints' clubhouse was also tucked underneath the grandstand, with the entrance on the side of the grandstand wall. Again, the distance between the door to the clubhouse and the gate to the field was very short. And as the walkway connecting the clubhouse and this gate was open public space, there were undoubtedly many opportunities every game for interaction between players and fans that simply don't exist in affiliated ball.

I continued walking past the Paints' clubhouse, turned right again, and took up a position directly behind the Stadium in a courtyard containing picnic benches, a booth for selling programs, a large souvenir shed, and a bricked Paints Wall of Fame. From there I grasped the entire simple layout of the original Stadium. The grandstands was a three-part structure, with the visitors' clubhouse and the men's restroom underneath the left wing; the home team clubhouse and the ladies' restroom underneath the right wing; and the concession stand, flanked by two wide runways leading to the first rows of seats, underneath the middle section. The only thing I hadn't located was the umpires' clubhouse.

Eventually, I stopped a Paints employee carrying a stack of towels I thought might be the clubhouse manager and asked him where the umpires dressed. Aaron Queen was his name. He was stocky, about 5' 10", and dressed in shorts and a yellow Paints T-shirt. He had a pinch of tobacco between his bottom lip and gums, and he squinted at me suspiciously from under the pulled-down red bill of his navy blue Paints cap. "Why do you want to know that?" he said.

"I'm a friend of one of the umpires, Max McLeary," I explained. "I thought I'd wait for him there."

"Over here," Aaron said as he led the way towards the righthand corner of the underside of the grandstands. There, just to the left of the women's restroom, was the door I'd been looking for. Aaron turned the handle and pushed the door open slightly. "I guess you can wait in there, but don't touch nothing," he said. There wasn't much to touch in the room, containing as it did nothing but an old table, three chairs, and a waist high chest of drawers by the door. The long and narrow space (20' × 5') was more of a hallway than a room, and, in fact, it continued through a door at the far end into the Paints' clubhouse. The door to the Paints' clubhouse was half open, and I could see a long row of open-faced locker stalls filled with uniforms, towels, bats, gloves, and all sorts of baseball gear and personal items belonging to the players. As I waited for Max, somebody closed and locked the door from the Paints' side of the room.

Max had a spring in his step as he turned the far corner by the men's restroom, walked past the souvenir shed, and headed across the court-yard towards his dressing room. He hesitated by the popcorn machine in front of the concession stand but then continued on his way when he saw no one nearby. He'd barely set down his bag and hung up several shirts and pairs of pants before he poked his head out of the door in the direction of the concession stand. "Hold on a minute, Mike," he said. "There's something I've got to do." He walked back towards the concession area and shook hands warmly with the man he'd looked for on his way in. Back in the umpires' dressing room, he said, "I always say 'hi' to the popcorn man. It's the first thing I do when I walk in the ballpark here. I make sure I say 'hello' because I want him to know that he's just as important as I am or the players or anybody else. We're all in this together. And that's what this whole thing is all about."

Max and I made some small talk while he began his preparations. All of Max's umpire shirts had a number 9 on the sleeve, Max's way of paying homage to his boyhood hero, Bill Mazeroski, the former Pittsburgh Pirate considered by many to be the best fielding second baseman to have ever played the game. Max had been wearing number 9 all his life, even on his basketball jerseys. "Man, the officials used to hate me for that," he said.

The numerals, of course, were sewn onto the shirts. What wasn't sewn on any of his shirts were the circular Frontier League patches that he pulled out of his equipment bag. He spread a shirt on the table and spent a couple of minutes trying to press one of the sticky-backed patches onto the left breast of the shirt in just the right place. That's when I noticed the large championship sports ring on his finger. I'd seen enough of that kind of ring to know that that's what he was wearing.

As usual, there was a story that went with his explanation of where the ring had come from. "When I was in affiliated ball, I got a ring for umpiring the finals of the New York-Penn League, and I did something really stupid with it. … I gave it to my girlfriend. Not Patty. This was my old high school sweetheart, somebody I knew before I met Patty or my first wife. Of course, when I lost my girlfriend, I lost the ring.

"I've really missed that ring, and I thought I'd never get another one. Then, last year after Jim and I did the finals for the Frontier League, I told Bill Lee, the Commissioner of the league, to keep the money the league owed me for assigning umpires for the three cities I took care of and make me a ring instead. Well, London just got their rings before their home opener. Bill was up there to hand 'em out.

"Here's the thing though: when Bill was on his way up to London, his two daughters were in a car accident. One of the daughters swerved to avoid another car, went off the road, and hit a tree. The crash wasn't that bad, and the car wasn't even damaged much; but the air bags exploded right in their faces. The air bags really did a number on those poor girls, especially Meghan. Her eye was injured, and they're afraid it might be permanently damaged.

"Bill had been planning to stay for the whole series, but as soon as the first game in London ended, he got in his car and drove back to Zanesville, where he lives and keeps his office, so he could be with Meghan. When I heard about the accident, I knew I had to visit Meghan so I could cheer her up, telling her a bunch of one-eyed umpire jokes. So Jim and I drove over to the hospital in Zanesville on our way up to Canton on Sunday afternoon, and that's when Bill gave me the ring."

The snarling werewolf logo and "London Werewolves" were carved into one shank of the ring; while "UMP," Max's name, and a baseball with "1999" inscribed on the sweet spot were carved into the other. The garnet stone, encircled by the words "Frontier League Champions," was not precious, but I knew, without him having to say so, that the ring was Max's most prized possession. "Wow. Am I jealous of that!" I said, handing the ring back to Max.

"Hey, Byrd!" Max cried. The visitor was Stephen Byrd, a freckle-faced Paints starting pitcher from Rainbow City, Alabama, who, according to the *Stable Report*, insisted on being called by his last name. Although he stood only 5' 11" and weighed but 175 pounds, Byrd was a cocky young man, and with good reason. The previous year he had made the All-Star team and been named the Most Valuable Pitcher on the Paints' staff while posting a 9–4 record with a 3.60 ERA. That ERA doesn't sound impressive, but it was eighth best in the hitting-happy Frontier League, which boasted 28 .300+ hitters for the season.

Max and Byrd compared notes on the season so far, Byrd informing us that he'd won his first start by throwing five shutout innings against Canton. He was going to make his second start in about an hour against Kojack. Max related how he'd been clobbered in Canton and ended the story with a lesson he supposedly had learned from his most recent ordeal: "Instead of the bars in all these towns, I ought to find out where all the hospitals are. I know where half of 'em are already."

Byrd had some Frontier League news too: London pitcher Brett Gray had already been picked up by the Cincinnati Reds and assigned to their Double A team in Dayton, Ohio. "Yeah, we finally got him out of this league," he said. "Max, you know we don't never chirp about balls and strikes …"

"Yeah, right!" laughed Max.

"… but, Max, the umpire's strike zone was this big!" Byrd held his hands far apart as if he were sizing up a whopper of a fish he'd caught. "Some of the strikes the ump was calling were so far outside, their catcher was like this." Byrd bent down towards the floor in imitation of a sprinter's starting position. When he stood up, he concluded his mixed account of Gray's unforgettable performance: "He's a great pitcher … but he did get a lot of help."

The press box at VA Memorial Stadium sits at the top of the center section of grandstands and is as cramped as the "closet" the umpires dress in. As promised, John Wend made room for me, but I realized that he was able to do so only because other people with more claim to the space than I was entitled to had opted to perform their duties elsewhere. People such as Phil Gray, the sports editor of the *Chillicothe Gazette*, Kevin Rouch, the play-by-play man for Paints radio broadcasts; and Doug Kimsey, a reporter for the *Ross County Advertiser* and the author of the award-winning "Kimsey's Korner" segment of the Paints' first-class Internet website.

Max's partner, Matt Neader, did have a heart and was behind the plate when Byrd delivered the first pitch of the game to the Richmond center fielder Shap Stiles. A protégé of Jim Schaly, Neader was another short, stocky umpire. He was young—only 26 years old—but experienced—he had already been umpiring in the Frontier League for five years. He lived in Marietta, Ohio, where he ran his own carpet cleaning business and helped out one of the high schools as an assistant football coach.

After Byrd retired the side, stranding Key Voshell who'd singled sharply to left, Gary Kitchel, sitting to our left in the two-man visiting team's radio booth, leaned back in his chair and asked if I'd be willing to go on the air with him at the start of the fourth inning.

My five and a half innings on the air with Kitchel were humbling and eye-opening. I don't think I caused anybody back in Richmond to turn off his radio, but suffice it to say that anybody even half listening could tell that it wasn't exactly Vin Scully who'd joined Gary. To be blunt, the main problem was that I'm a windbag. If somebody asks me a question, especially about something I'm deeply interested in (like a book I'm working on) I can go on for hours, without pausing for a breath or a drink of water. And, naturally, Gary asked about the book in order to let people know why I was on the air with him.

It didn't take me long to realize that it was "sound bites" I was called upon to add to the broadcast, not a dissertation defense, but it was still difficult to formulate *brief* answers to Gary's questions and then get them out completely before it was necessary for Gary to resume the play-by-play. If you want to know what being rushed feels like, imagine being in the midst of an explanation you know all of a sudden is too long while a pitcher is coming to the plate.

After Gary finished interviewing me, I relaxed a little, and as the innings went by I began to function as his "color man." Or at least that's what I attempted to do. I remembered how natural Jan Clark was behind the mike back in Richmond, and I tried to pattern myself after him.

The problem was I didn't have Jan's experience or his sense of timing. On several occasions I started talking when I thought, mistakenly, that Gary had finished. Even though you can apologize for this miscue—and I did—it's still as embarrassing and frustrating as stepping on a pretty girl's toes while dancing. I also didn't have sufficient knowledge of the players or their names or their positions. There were times when I had a pithy comment all ready to go, I waited cagily for just the right moment to make it, and then I realized that I didn't know who had just tried to score from second and got thrown out at home. And you can't say, "You know, I thought *that guy* who was on second base might have scored if ...blah, blah, blah." That doesn't work.

I found out in a hurry that broadcasting a baseball game is definitely not as easy as it looks. Actually, I knew that already from having read Ken Levine's *It's Gone! ... No, Wait a Minute...*, his hysterical account of his education as a professional baseball radio announcer. I didn't make any boners as egregious as the one referred to in Ken's title, and I like to think that I'd actually improved a little by the end of the game; but, as they say, there was no place but up for me to go as a broadcaster.

Max in Chillicothe. The Paints' bullpen is down the first baseline.

When I thought about it later, I realized how nice Kitchel had been through the whole thing. Not once did he correct me or tell me how the pros do it. He let me figure things out for myself, and, when my debut on the air was over, even said he wanted me to work with him again. That's when I knew for sure that there was something seriously wrong with the man.

Phill Kojack pitched fairly well, but the Roosters were again shut out, just as they had been in his first start of the season. Chillicothe scored a total of four runs—one in the first, two in the fourth, and one in the seventh—all off Kojack. Meanwhile, Byrd pitched four-hit ball over six innings to pick up his second win; sensational Matt Buirley made the Roosters look helpless as he struck out the side in the seventh and the eighth; and Kurt "Woody" Fullenkamp, the Paints' designated closer, pitched the ninth, surrendering only a harmless single to Aaron Sledd.

Buirley and Fullenkamp put on quite a show, but their pitching was actually their second performance of the evening. Their first number came in the bottom of the third, when John Wend said in his booming voice: "Ladies and gentlemen, we direct your attention to the right field line and the Paints' bullpen!" As John made this announcement, the polka popularly known as the "Chicken Dance" song came over the P.A. system.

All six of the Paints' bullpenners began doing in unison the Chicken Dance movements so familiar to American wedding goers. Remaining seated on the bullpen bench which was turned perpendicular to the foul line fence to facilitate the view of the fans in the grandstands, the players made shoulder-high biting beaks with their fingers, flap-flapped their wings, shimmy-shimmied the twist, and then clapped, clapped, clapped! as the entire ballpark clapped along with them. They went through this whole sequence four times, and then when the song changed from a polka into a waltz, they bolted off the bench, split up into pairs, hooked arms, and doe-see-doed around the bullpen like giddy school girls showing off in front of the boys.

The song started over, and the six sat down and went through a second round of the biting beaks-flapping-shimmying-clapping sequences; but this time, when the waltz came around, Fullenkamp and Buirley eschewed the doe-see-doe routine for some individual fancy-step dancing. And then, to punctuate the end of the song, Fullenkamp did a series of cartwheels and a split, and Buirley did a couple of backflips! As the crowd roared its approval, Wend said, "Ladies and gentlemen, a Chillicothe bullpen tradition! ... How about a hand for Woody Fullenkamp and Matt Buirley!" Of course, the crowd roared again.

After the game we headed to The Dock at Water, located on Water Street in downtown Chillicothe, not far from Yoctangee Park which is the center of recreational activities for the city. The bar, which bills itself as "The Official Post-Game Gathering Place of the Chillicothe Paints," is popular with everybody, not just Paints fans, and everyone refers to it simply as The Dock. With its attractive entrance—the oval windows in the large wooden doors are adorned with gold foil lettering—tasteful paneling, antique-style patterned tin ceiling, and brass railings, The Dock is definitely a cut above The Wheel. The Dock appeals to a wide range of ages and classes of people—you're just as likely to find a pair of big choppers parked in front of The Dock as you are The Wheel— but in the summer, when the Paints are in town, the crowds there turn decidedly youngish. In short, the place is a gold mine.

The Dock has a large rectangular bar on the left; and after Max and owner Mary White hugged each other, we took up positions on the near side of the bar where we had a good view of everybody coming in. Players from both teams were already there, sitting at tables around the dart boards area in back, and other players were still coming in. Moments after we arrived, Roosters Mike Zerbe, Aaron Sledd, and Bobby Chandler dropped in, and they all stopped by to say hello to Max. I asked Max if there were any anti-fraternization rules regarding umpires and players away from the ballpark. He said, "Yes and no. There's no written rules about it, but there are some things you do and some things you know not to do. For instance, last year Chillicothe had a team party at the end of the year, and they invited me and Jim, but we couldn't go. It was just one team, and that's where we draw the line. But we'll go into a bar like this where players on both teams hang out. And the main thing is that the veterans know we'll ring 'em up regardless of friendship or having a few beers together or whatever."

Joe Colameco, the Paints' left-handed hitting right fielder who had played with Chillicothe the year before, came in and walked over to us. A Canadian himself, Colameco also had the recent fortunes of the ex–London Werewolf Brett Gray on his mind. And like Byrd, Colameco had a little griping about the umpiring to do too: "One time our first baseman Chance Melvin, who struck out four times, made a little motion to start his swing, but he really didn't move his wrists at all. Their catcher said, 'Check it.' The plate ump checked with the base ump, and the base ump made the sign for 'Strike.' I went nuts. I yelled, 'Why don't you give 'im a strike out before we even walk up there!'"

"What are you, Melvin's agent?" laughed Max between sips of his beer.

"Fuck you, Max," said Colameco.

"So what are you saying, Joe?" I asked. "Did Gray deserve to get signed or not?"

"Oh, yeah. He deserved it," he said. "He shouldn't have been in this league in the first place. … I was three for three in that game myself … strikeouts, not hits."

One reason so many young men can afford to play independent professional baseball in the Frontier League is that the teams arrange for the players to live rent-free with baseball-loving members of the community. This arrangement not only saves the teams money by allowing them to pay the players less than they would otherwise, but it also creates strong bonds between the players and their host families as well as between players who room together with the same family. Woody Fullenkamp and Byrd, being hosted for the summer of 2000 by Cliff and Bea Beeks, were best friends and roommates.

Woody was one of the most sociable and most popular of Paints players. And most recognizable. He had the height (6' 4") scouts like in pitchers and out on the diamond looked taller than he was because of the old-fashioned way he wore his pants, rolled up to the knees. His ears stuck out a little; and while the rest of the team wore dark shoes, he wore his old Ohio State red spikes, providing a burst of color during his nimble dancing that was reminiscent of Dorothy's ruby slippers in the *Wizard of Oz*. Woody may have been the comic ringleader of the

Paints' bullpen, but his pitching was no joke. The year before he had been the league's premier closer, fashioning a 1.16 ERA and holding opposing hitters to a .190 batting average. When he came over to pay his respects to Max, I told him how much I'd enjoyed the Chicken Dance. "Thanks," he said. "The bigger idiots we make of ourselves, the more the fans love it."

The Braves had signed him following the 1999 season, but he hadn't been able to stick with them in spring training. When I asked him about that, he said, "This spring I was with the Braves in their minor league camp for 22 days, but they let me go. Now I'm back here, doing the Chicken Dance. ... I don't care. It's all politics anyway. Besides, it's more fun here." When he said "here," Woody meant Chillicothe in general, but The Dock was definitely a big part of the equation. Paints players are celebrities all over town, but no where more so than in The Dock. Proprietor Mary White is a huge fan and treats the players like family, often buying them pizza and charging them half price for their beer. Woody would be a regular at The Dock all season long, and even after he hung up his spikes, his presence in the place would be assured. The Dock displayed his framed Ohio State baseball jersey on the left hand wall, past the bar, as proudly as it displayed the jerseys of big-time major league baseball and football players. Only Woody's jersey was inscribed. It read: "To 'The Dock,' Thanks for Everything!!! Woody Fullenkamp #37."

By this time I had confidence in Max's ability as an umpire, but that didn't mean I thought he'd always be right. In fact, I was certain he'd missed a call on the bases in the game just played.

In the bottom of the eighth with one out and catcher Ben Gerkin on first, the Paints' second baseman Mike Horning hit a ground ball to third. Richmond third baseman Ryan Anholt went to second for the force on Gerkin. The Roosters' second baseman Key Voshell caught the throw, pivoted, and relayed the ball to first, but not in time to double up Horning. The problem was that when Voshell caught Anholt's throw he had already crossed the bag. Max called Gerkin out, but Voshell was definitely not in contact with the bag when he caught the throw from third. I was sure of it. And I'd said so on the air. "Gary, I think the Roosters got away with one there," I'd said, prior to explaining that I thought the base ump had missed the call.

"Max, I think you might have made a bad call tonight," I said.

Silently, he waited, fixing me with the gaze of a patient professor, full of confidence that he had the right answers and that his student had just provided him with a made-to-order teaching moment.

"On that force play late in the game, Voshell never touched second,"

I continued. "Well, he did step on the bag, but when he did he didn't have the ball yet. By the time he caught the ball, he was two yards away from second base."

"You're right about that," said Max, "but I was right too. See, here's the deal: if you wanted to freeze frame that play, the runner was safer than a dog. I knew that. But it was a 4–0 game, and you don't ask a player to risk injury on a play like that in that situation. Key gave it a good effort, he made a nice play, and so my job was to protect him. What's the point of making the second baseman stand on the bag in that situation just so the runner can cream him?"

"Okay. I understand your reasoning," I said, "but I still can't believe the Paints didn't raise hell about it."

"Nope, Hanners didn't argue, and you know why? ... Because he knows he's gonna get the same call. Nobody said a word about it. ... Except for some fan hollering behind the Paints' dugout."

"Yeah? What did he say?"

"He said, 'Hey ump, whattaya trying to do ... get out of here early? You got a date tonight?' I said, 'Yeah, I do have a date tonight ... AND IT'S WITH YOUR WIFE!' Boy, the Paints loved that one, and it shut that guy up real good."

On our way out of town Max picked up a six-pack at the Dairy Mart on High Street. Moments later, as we headed north up 35, the yellow flood lights of the Ross Correctional Institute were visible on our left. If you looked harder you could also see, about two miles past the prison, a more comforting sight, empty VA Memorial Stadium, still shining in the darkness like a giant bedside nite lite.

"Barkeep, ... ," Max said. I reached into the paper bag on the floor between my feet for a beer, popped the top, and handed it to Max. We were on our way home, unwinding like a coverless baseball rolling down hill.

The next day I found the white-haired Roger Hanners sitting by himself in the sun-baked first base grandstands, watching his Paints take batting practice. He not had changed into uniform yet and wore dark slacks and a white polo shirt with the Paints logo, "a horse with 'painted' markings and war feathers flowing from the horse's mane" inside a navy blue "C," embroidered on the left breast. There was plenty of shade in the grandstands on the third base side, but I guess Roger felt more comfortable, despite the stifling heat, sitting behind the Paints' dugout.

Roger's uniform number was 50, which was exactly the number of years ago that he had started his career in professional baseball as a pitcher. He had been signed by the New York Yankees in 1950 and spent six years in their farm system, rising as high as Triple A before an arm injury ended his playing career. Though he never made it to the big leagues, he and the entire Paints family were proud of the fact that he had played with Mickey Mantle in the minors.

When I'd first begun to get my bearings in the Frontier League and heard about the father-son Hanners team which ran the Chillicothe franchise, I made the same mistaken assumption that everybody else did: that the old man was the team owner and the son the field manager. It seemed like an odd reversal, but both men, I learned, were perfectly suited for their roles.

There were many factors that had contributed to the success of the Chillicothe franchise both on and off the field, but none more important, I was certain, than the contributions of Roger and Chris Hanners; both of whom were extending league longevity records. Chris was the only original owner still left in the league, and Roger was the only manager the Paints had ever known, except for the first 25 games of the inaugural season in 1993.

Roger shook my hand firmly and listened to my questions attentively, although he also kept an eye on batting practice. When he spoke, he did so in a soft, gentle voice. One thing I was curious about was the peculiar situation independent teams find themselves in. They obviously want the best players they can find, but there is an irony in that: namely, the better the player, the greater the chance he will be snatched away by a major league club. I wondered how much losing key players to affiliated signings had hurt the Paints over the years. Chillicothe had never won a Frontier League championship, but they had come oh-so-close, losing in the finals in both 1998 and 1999. The loss in 1998 had been especially hard to take. In the best-of-three championship round, the Paints won the opener in Springfield, Illinois, but then lost games two and three against the Capitals at home in Chillicothe.

"In the past three years we've had players signed into affiliated ball 15 times," said Roger. "It always hurts the team, but you still want the best ballplayer you can get, even if you get to keep him for only one year, or even half a year. I work well with the Braves. When I call them and say, 'I've got a player for you, they sign him.' And when a major league club signs a player, I've done my job. The Chillicothe policy is to let players go as soon as a major league club wants them, the ones who are capable of moving on. We would never stand in a player's way of getting into affiliated ball because that's why they're here, for that chance of getting signed.

"And, no, there's no compensation from the big league clubs. Oh, sometimes I'll say we need a dozen bats, more to be funny than anything else; but when I say that, they do send us the bats.

"This doesn't happen in reverse. In other words, we don't get players sent down to us by major league clubs. They will let us know they've released a kid, but they don't actually send him to us. Their scouts will call me and say, 'We've got a pretty good-looking boy here, but he's not ready yet.' The problem with that is if he isn't ready for their single A clubs, then he usually can't make our club either. You see, we have to win, more so than minor league teams. They can take two or three years to develop a player, but we can't. In the Frontier League you have to win, because if you don't win, you're not gonna draw. And so we have to have players who can produce right now."

It was no big secret that independent minor league baseball teams were risky ventures, and I knew that the Frontier League had seen its share of instability. Two of its eight original teams did not finish the inaugural season in 1993. In fact, they didn't even last a full two weeks before packing it in. The Tri-State Tomahawks of Ashland, Kentucky, folded with a 5–6 record; while the West Virginia Coal Sox of Wayne County, West Virginia, faded into oblivion after winning just three of ten games. There was never another instance of a team not finishing a season, but there were numerous instances of a franchise moving from one city to another; so many, in fact, that the Chillicothe Paints were the only original Frontier League team still playing in its city of origin. I was a little uncomfortable prying into the Paints' financial situation—I didn't represent the *Wall Street Journal*, after all—but Roger had opened the door with his reference to the team's need to draw, and so I asked him how the franchise was doing financially.

"If it wasn't for the sponsors, we couldn't do it," he said. "The sponsors are very, very important to us.

"It costs us $11,000 to put on one game. We're drawing 1,000 fans a game, and you figure they spend about $5 a head. That's not even half." Actually, the Paints were averaging about 1,400 a game, but Roger's point was still well-taken.

"If we break even," he said, "we're happy."

I wondered if the Paints might actually be in a little trouble. When the league first started, Chillicothe was one of its bigger cities. As the years went by though, the league kept going into bigger and bigger markets, so that the trend had clearly become for the league to set up shop in the suburbs of some of the country's biggest cities. The Cook County Cheetahs, for instance, played in Crestwood, Illinois, a suburb of Chicago; and O'Fallon, Missouri, the home of the River City Rascals, was not only a suburb of St. Louis, it was the fastest growing suburb in America! In their first year of existence in 1999 the Rascals had shattered the league attendance record with a total gate of 151,661 and an average of 3,900 per game. Was Chillicothe in danger of being left behind by these new kids on the block?

11/1/04

CHILLICOTHE ORIGINAL
TEAM WHEN FL STARTED IN
1993

$11,000 TO PUT
ON A GAME AT
CHILLICOTHE IN 2000

"Everybody in the league is in the same boat," said Roger. "Even the bigger cities like Chicago, St. Louis, and Evansville. They have to draw to survive too. It's a struggle for everybody.

"We do have one advantage here in Chillicothe over everybody else. With just the one owner, my son Chris, we don't have to satisfy four or five different people. Having multiple owners who can't agree on anything is one thing that has been the downfall of many teams.

"My son is a good businessman too. He treats everybody right. He's also been realistic about this thing from the beginning. The other franchises wanted their money back the first year. Chris said, 'Dad, this is a long term investment.' He was right. The original franchise fee was $5,000. It quickly went up to $125,000, now it's $500,000 or more, and you need another $500,000 operating capital. Chris is the only individual owner left in the league, and I doubt we'll ever get another one because nobody who would be interested in owning a team can afford to do it on his own anymore."

I knew my time with Roger was running out, but before he had to head down to the clubhouse, I asked him why the Paints had wanted to build a new ballpark in downtown Chillicothe. "Well, the government could say at anytime, 'We need this land.' This facility doesn't belong to us, and so we don't ultimately control it. That's why we wanted to build our own park downtown," he said. "Yoctangee Park, where we wanted to locate a new ballpark, is half dilapidated. We wanted to refurbish the whole thing and make new recreational facilities for everybody in the city to use, not just build a new home for the Paints. It would have benefited everybody, but some people were very much against it. I think their feeling was that they didn't want anybody from the outside coming in and making money on their park. Chris thought he would be doing the city a favor, but he backed off because he didn't want to divide the community over the issue."

I also wanted to get Roger's impressions of Mickey Mantle. "Mickey was always a step ahead of me in the Yankees' organization," he said, "but I did play against him in spring training intra-squad games. The first time I faced him, he hit a shot that got past the center fielder. He only got to second, and I thought he was loafing. Then in the locker room when he got undressed after the game, I saw that his legs were taped up from his knees to his waist.

"He was the best athlete and the fastest man I've ever seen. Without the injuries he would have been the greatest ever ... I don't care how much drinking he did."

"One more thing, Roger. What do you think of Max?"

"Oh, Max, ... Max is one of the good guys. He's not a hot head, doesn't have a chip on his shoulder like some umpires do. You can argue with him, as long as you don't cross that line, and he's not gonna argue back with you. He'll let you make your point, let you get out your frustrations, and you'll wind up saying, 'Oh, alright.' He's just a helluva nice guy. ... And he doesn't do any cussing out there, which is highly unusual."

And why didn't Roger argue the call when Voshell made the phantom force out at second? "On that play second basemen hit the bag, and they're gone. The fans don't understand that stuff, but it's an automatic out. We just hope we get the same call. And with Max we know we will."

Max and Jim Schaly were re-united for the second game of the series, with Max going behind the plate first. From my perch in the press box, I could see the fans steadily streaming into the Stadium, and I figured the Paints were giving away another trinket or souvenir to everybody who walked through the gate. "No, that's not it," said John Wend. "It's 'Winning Wednesday.' One of the local dealerships is going to give away two used cars, and we always have a big crowd for this promotion. We draw six Lucky Numbers for each car, and each person gets a key. One key opens the trunk of the car, and the person with that key wins the car."

"The cars are complete junkers, right? The winners probably have to have the cars towed."

"No. They always look pretty nice from here, and they're driven on and off the field."

I was tempted to buy a scorecard and get a Lucky Number that would give me a chance at winning one of the cars. My daughter Casey, a high school senior, reminded me and her mother every day how unfair it was that she didn't yet have her own car while all her friends had already been given cars by their parents; and my oldest son, Mickey, a high school sophomore, had also been recently bitten with the driving bug. One way or another, the Shannon driveway was bound to get cluttered in the near future, and I was all in favor of doing it as cheaply as possible. In the end, some vague notion of the need for me to maintain my professional decorum won out over my family's need for additional wheels, and I held off buying the scorecard which would have put me (actually Casey and/or Mickey) in the running.

Later, when I saw the cars given away by the Nourse Family of Dealerships, a Ford Tempo and an Olds 98, I changed my mind. Either vehicle would have made a nice first car for one of the hubcap-eyed teenagers in my house, and I decided that next time I was going to take a shot at the cars, professional decorum be damned.

1991

Josh White, a stocky righthander from Mt. Vernon, Ohio, started for the Paints. White had a good fastball, and the previous year, his rookie year in pro ball, he'd averaged a strikeout per inning with the Paints.

White pitched seven innings and gave up four runs, but none of them were earned. He gave up only two hits and struck out eight; still he was lucky to get out of the game with a no-decision.

The Roosters scored three runs in the top of the first off him, all set up by Chris Dickerson's error on leadoff man Ryan Peavey's groundball. After Dickerson's error, the Roosters loaded the bases on a walk to Anholt and a single to left by Voshell. Aaron Sledd's sacrifice fly to center scored the first Richmond run, and after Mike Zerbe struck out, DH Shannon Rushing tripled to bring in two more runs. The Paints got one run back in the bottom of the first on center fielder Greg Strickland's single and stolen base, followed by Mick Celli's single to center.

Rich Jelovcic and reliever John Boker held Chillicothe in check until the seventh when the Paints had a chance to get back in the game. With one out, Celli at second, and Chance Melvin at first, DH Jason Baker blasted one off the left field wall. Celli scored easily to make the score 4–2, and third base coach Jamie Keefe, playing aggressively, waved Melvin home from first. Unfortunately for Chillicothe, the Roosters handled the relays—Sledd to shortstop Jason Guynn to catcher Keith Fout—perfectly. The ball and Melvin arrived at home plate at almost the same exact instant. Melvin slammed into Fout, valiantly guarding home plate, and knocked him six or seven feet through the air and onto his ass. Max walked calmly over to where Fout lay, peered down towards the fallen catcher, and signaled OUT! when Fout held the ball up in his glove.

After sitting in with Kitchel during the middle innings, I joined Charles Frodsham in the grandstands, behind home plate about twenty rows below the press box. His son Eric, the Paints' rookie reliever, intrigued me. Tall and skinny with long red hair, and lacking the broad shoulders, powerful legs, and muscular rump that characterized most of the Paints' pitchers, Frodsham was an Icabod Crane in spikes. His submarine delivery set him apart from the other Paints pitchers as much as his physique did, yet it was possible that that same unorthodox delivery would be his ticket to the affiliated minor leagues and possibly even the big leagues, should he master it.

Eric, his father told me, didn't play high school baseball for the simple reason that Beloit (Kansas) High didn't have a baseball program when Eric was there. Eric got some experience playing American Legion ball for Beloit, but as a hitter and outfielder, not as a pitcher. Frodsham wasn't much of a hitter and got cut from the baseball team at Garden City Community College. Undaunted, he finagled a tryout at Friends University, an NAIA Division II school in Wichita, but was told by the coach, Derik Dukes, that if he made the team, he'd have to make it as a pitcher. He'd never pitched before in his life and wasn't impressing the Dukes until he suddenly threw a pitch side-armed. "That's it," said Dukes. "Drop down more." Frodsham dropped his arm angle some more, and Dukes said, "Lower, lower." Frodsham kept going lower until he finally threw one from so low an arm slot it caused him to fall on his face. "That's it!" shouted Dukes. "Keep throwing like that."

In one fell swoop, so to speak, Frodsham became not only a pitcher, but a pitcher with a specialty: the submarine delivery that had enabled some previously-mediocre pitchers to make a nice living in the major leagues; pitchers such as Ted Abernathy, Kent Tekulve, and Dan Quisenberry.

Of course, discovering a new pitch is a lot like finding a bicycle in a box under the Christmas tree: you still have to put it together to have any fun with it. Frodsham realized this and went about the task of transforming himself into a pitcher with the passion of Pygmalion. His coach at Friends University, Mark Carvalho, said, "He's the hardest-working kid I've ever had, and he's one of the hardest-working kids I've ever seen." The submarine delivery, which causes the ball to sink and results in a lot of ground balls, makes it almost mandatory for the practitioner to work out of the bullpen, and Frodsham became Friends' best reliever, earning all-conference honors his junior and senior years. He also turned out to have a rubber arm and wound up setting school records for single-season and career appearances and saves in a single season.

After his senior year of college, Frodsham attended a Northern League tryout in Ft. Lauderdale, Florida. He wasn't signed by any Northern League team but did receive an invitation to attend the Frontier League tryout held in Chillicothe, where he was picked up by the Paints. "Eric loves it here," said his father. "Finally, he's in an atmosphere where they take baseball seriously. In college he wondered why he had to take academic courses in addition to playing baseball. He told me, 'Dad, my new teammates are awesome. They're totally into baseball!'

"Eric is pretty much self-taught, you know, but he tries to learn from anybody he thinks can help him. Like Kent Tekulve. Eric got to meet him and talk to him a little bit here in Chillicothe. Tekulve was here because his son, a first baseman, also tried out for the Paints. Eric was hoping the son would make the team so he'd get to talk to Tekulve some more about submarine pitching, but the son didn't stick."

Eric had been warming up in the bullpen as we talked. Mr. Frodsham concluded his recapitulation of his son's career as the Paints' seventh-inning rally fizzled out. Then, as if on cue, Roger brought Eric on to start the eighth. Eric's strange way of throwing a baseball definitely made him interesting to watch, but his professional debut in front of his father went about as well for the Paints as the top of the first had gone.

Frodsham struck out the side, but also gave up three hits, including doubles by Mike Zerbe and Keith Fout. The hits, coupled with a passed ball and throwing errors by Colameco and Frodsham himself, let in two more runs the Paints could ill afford to surrender.

It was then that something happened which is rarely seen at VA Memorial Stadium: Paints fans started leaving the ballgame early. On his way towards the exit, a man walking past home plate shouted, "Ump, you suck!" A woman, presumably his wife, who was carrying seat cushions and a jacket, turned to fans still sitting in the first row of the grandstand, and said, "Well, he does."

The frustration of the fans was understandable but not their criticism of the umpiring. Four Paints errors had led to five unearned Richmond runs, and so it was the Paints' sloppy play, not the umpiring, which was to blame for Chillicothe being on the short end of the 6–2 score with only an inning and a half left to play. Maybe, I thought, the couple grumbling about the umpiring were actually sore they hadn't won one of the used cars given away.

The fans who left early missed a great comeback, the kind of comeback that unfolds with a harrowing sense of inevitability when it happens against the team you play for, coach, or root for.

The first six Paints to come up in the bottom of the eighth all reached base, and the first five of them scored. Chad Sosebee hit Dave Masterson in the shoulder, then walked Gerkin and Mike Horning. Jamie Blaesing, traded from the Paints to Richmond for Matt Buirley before the start of the season, came on in relief of Sosebee and promptly gave up base hits to leadoff man Greg Strickland and Mick Celli. With the game slipping from his grasp, Roosters manager John Cate went to his bullpen again and called on his ace, closer Bobby Chandler, to dowse the fire. Former All-Big Ten third baseman at the University of Michigan, Mike Cervenak had other ideas. He lined a single into right field to score Horning and the speedy Strickland, representing the tying run. The Roosters finally got the first out of the inning when Chandler induced Chance Melvin to hit a towering pop foul down the first base line. Mike Zerbe made a nice twisting catch on the ball with his back to the plate, but he was in no position to make a strong throw to the plate, and so Celli was able to tag and score the go-ahead run. It turned out to be the winning run after the Roosters failed to score in the top of the ninth against Matt Buirley, who picked up the save.

Even though he gave up two runs in his one inning of work, Eric Frodsham got credit for the win, his first in professional baseball.

After the game, I said goodbye to the Frodshams, walked down to the field level concourse, and headed towards the umpires' clubhouse against the traffic slowly exiting the ballpark. Before I made the right turn to go under the grandstands, I practically bumped into Max. He'd had time only to shed his top shirt and chest protector, light up a cigarette, and grab one of the beers Aaron Queen had left for him and Schaly. "Max, where are you going?" I said.

"The Paints' games are shown on tape delay. There's a lady who tapes all the TV games, and I want to ask her to make a copy of the tape for me. ... Over a season you build up bad habits, and I like to see myself on video so that I can correct the things I'm doing wrong. I'll be back in a few minutes."

Max was not a perfect umpire, and at his age and with his handicap, he was not going any farther than the Frontier League. But he was still trying to improve, and after thirty years of umpiring he was still trying to learn. If I could have said something to the fan who'd criticized Max earlier on his way out of the ballpark, I would have said in my best Brooklyn Dodgers fan accent: "Mister, you got noive ... noive like a toothache!"

The largest crowd of the series, 1,832, showed up Thursday night looking for the Paints to sweep the Roosters. Chillicothe settled the issue immediately by scoring seven times in the first three innings to knock out starter Thomas Medina. Catcher Chris Poulsen, with three RBI, and center fielder Greg Strickland were the offensive stars for Chillicothe. The left-handed batting Strickland singled, stole second, and scored in the first; homered to lead off the second; walked to lead off the fourth; and doubled to knock in the Paints' final run in the eighth.

The Paints could easily have scored even more runs had not Mike Horning hit into a triple play in the third inning. With runners on first and second, Horning hit a scorching line drive up the middle. The ball was hit so hard that Max, standing between the mound and second base, had to dive out of its way to avoid getting hit by it. Roosters' shortstop Jason Guynn caught the ball, stepped on second, and threw to first before the runners could even begin to put on the brakes. Max called the runners trapped off second and first out while sitting on his rear in the infield grass.

Given the Roosters' anemic offense, the contest was over after three innings; however, the game's drama was far from finished.

After Paints starter Andy Lee put the Roosters down 1-2-3 in the fifth inning, Kitchel and I had to begin to take seriously his bid for a no-hitter. When the top of the sixth started, I said, "Gary, if the listeners back in Richmond have been paying attention, they know that this game is beginning to get really interesting because of something that hasn't happened yet. I can't say what it is because baseball tradition holds that it is bad luck to do so."

"Well then, let me be the one to come right out and say that Andy Lee is pitching a no-hitter, and I don't care if I jinx him or not," said Kitchel.

With the taboo against saying the word "no-hitter" broken, Gary and I talked freely for the rest of the game about no-hitters in general and the no-hitter in progress. At one point I mentioned that I'd never seen a no-hitter in a professional game in person. Gary offered that he had witnessed one no-hitter before: the only no-hitter in Frontier League history which had been turned in exactly three years earlier by Richmond's Christian Hess against the Kalamazoo Kodiaks.

There's an old unwritten rule of baseball which stipulates that there is to be "No Cheering in the Press Box." Hall of Fame sportswriter Jerome Holtzman used the phrase as the title of one of his books, and I actually heard it used as a reprimand in the Tiger Stadium press box during the 1984 World Series. You won't hear the phrase though in Frontier League press boxes where rooting for the home team is considered as natural as putting condiments on a hot dog. I was grateful for that relaxation of the rules, because I found it impossible not to root for Andy Lee; even though I was helping with the Roosters' radio broadcast.

Gary, on the other hand, was completely professional. He rooted neither for nor against the no-hitter, nor did he get carried away by the moment. However, after Lee made it safely though the eighth and the Paints went out in the bottom of the inning, he told his producers, "Let's keep it right here instead of going to commercials."

Ryan Anholt lead off the ninth for the Roosters and hit a routine *1 out* fly ball to center on the first pitch. Jeremy Sassanella pinch-hitting for *2 outs* Kevin Moore worked the count to 3–2 but then struck out swinging, for Lee's 13th strikeout of the game.

That brought up the toughest Rooster out, Key Voshell, whose .433 batting average coming into the game was seventh best in the league.

The crowd were now on their feet and clapping continuously. The first pitch to Voshell was low for a ball, and some boos were directed at Schaly. Voshell fouled the second pitch straight back, and Gary said, "Chillicothe pitcher Andy Lee is two strikes away from a no-hitter."

Voshell swung at the next pitch and hit a pop up in fair territory a little behind first base. As Jason Baker settled under the ball, I almost drowned out Gary's description of the play, shouting, "HE DID IT! HE

DID IT!" It was the sort of thing that Joe Nuxhall pulls on Marty Brennaman all the time. I don't know about Marty, but it always bugs me when Joe starts screaming something like "GET OUT OF HERE, BALL! GET OUT OF HERE!!" so that Marty's home run call can barely be heard. Although my outburst had been completely involuntary, I realized that I had pulled a Nuxhall and sounded, to the fans back in Richmond, like a highly partisan turncoat to boot. Contritely, I shut up, put my microphone down, and let Gary finish the broadcast in peace.

While the crowd gave Lee a long standing ovation, his teammates lifted him off the ground and carried him on their shoulders across the field towards the Paints' dugout; behind the umpires, who'd already hurried off the field, as they always do, in an effort to make their departure as inconspicuous as their role in a well-officiated game.

In the umpire's clubhouse Schaly was more animated than usual, as he had every right to be. I congratulated him and, conscious of how much Max wanted to call a no-hitter before he retired, asked him if it were his first no-hitter. "No, it's my second, in the minor leagues," he said. "I've called several others in college and amateur ball."

Jim was also aware that Max had yet to be behind the plate for a no-hitter, and he couldn't resist inserting the needle. "Hey, Max," he said, "how many no-hitters have you called in the minors?"

"Only two fewer than you, you son of a bitch," said Max.

Schaly had been in the middle of his recap when I walked in, and after laughing at Max's comeback, he picked up where he'd left off. "Max, I told Chillicothe's bench, 'Watch this strike zone. If he loses it in the ninth, it's gonna be nobody's fault but his own.'"

I knew Jim was exaggerating and that he hadn't changed a thing to help Andy Lee. He was just excited and, as always, cocky and full of himself, and proud of the job he'd just done. Max had told me many times that Jim was a great umpire and that he was especially great calling balls and strikes, the most difficult and most important thing any umpire has to do. I knew that Jim's comment did not mean that he had expanded his strike zone—Jim had too much integrity to do that—only that he became determined to bear down his hardest and that he was going to give any pitches that could go either way to the pitcher. There was nothing wrong with that, and I thought any reasonable professional player would have agreed with the philosophy. The Roosters had just been no-hit, and they had not argued with one single ball-strike call. That was a tribute to both Lee and Schaly.

Moments later, Schaly made a confession that confirmed my interpretation. "The first four innings I wasn't very good. I didn't feel like being out there, but then I looked up and saw all those zeroes on the scoreboard. I told myself I better get my head out of my ass and get to work."

I asked about Andy Lee's pitching. What, if anything in particular, had made him unhittable? "To tell you the truth, I don't know," Schaly said. "Early in the game he was behind in the count a lot, but Richmond just didn't hit the ball. They swung at a lot of bad pitches too. ... Let's put it this way: I've seen Andy throw better."

I pointed out that the game had been doubly rare because it had also included a triple play. "Yeah, that's right!" said Jim. "I wonder if that's ever happened before. Hey, guess what Horning said when he came up to bat in the fifth inning with two outs and a couple of guys on base. ... 'The good news is that I can't hit into a triple play again.' I thought that was pretty funny."

By this time Schaly had undressed and put a towel around his waist. He stood up and said, "I'm going to take a shower. I worked hard tonight."

"Yeah, yeah, you piece of crap," grumbled Max.

"*Mister* Piece of Crap, to you," said Schaly.

"Okay. I'll give you that one," said Max.

I rushed over to the Paints' clubhouse but could have taken my time. Sports editor Phil Gray and reporter Derek McCord, both of the *Chillicothe Gazette,* and Doug Kimsey of the *Ross County Advertiser* were all standing around waiting for Andy Lee. The Paints were keeping the Budweiser beer wagon open later than usual, and a few Paints players still mingled outside the clubhouse with the fans, who were reluctant to close the book on the historic evening at VA Memorial.

John Wend, who also served as the Paints' official Director of Media and Public Relations, came around the corner, saw the pride of scribes gathered, and said, "Has anybody seen Andy?"

"Uh-oh, that's not a good sign," said McCord.

"I can't imagine that he could escape this crowd of paparazzi," said Gray. We laughed at Phil's little joke which reflected on us as well as on the star of the moment, Andy Lee, but it also referred to our real fear that Lee might well have ducked out on us. Promising to locate Andy and make him available for our questions, John went into the Paints' clubhouse. A few minutes later he came out to inform us that Andy was in the shower and that he'd be coming out soon.

"I just saw Roger," John said, "and I asked him, 'What have you got to say about *that*!?' He said, 'Nothing. Except I'll never forgive Andy for walking those two batters.'"

Actually, Andy had walked only one batter; he hit one and another Rooster had reached on an error by Jason Baker. But we still laughed at Roger's disappointment that Andy had not thrown a perfect game.

When Andy came out, his short dark hair still a little wet, he was dressed in jeans and a red Ohio State polo shirt. Andy seemed like a serious young man. Although we were all beaming, he had a look more of contentment than excitement on his face.

We all congratulated him at the same time, and then I jumped right in with the first question: "Andy, when Don Larsen pitched his perfect game in the 1956 World Series, a reporter asked him one of the dumbest questions ever asked of a ballplayer. I'd like to ask you the same question: 'Was this your best game ever?'"

Andy brightened a little and giggled, "Yeah, I'm pretty sure it was."

Somebody asked him when he started thinking about throwing a no-hitter, and he said, "In the sixth inning I noticed that nobody was sitting next to me in the dugout or saying anything to me anymore. Poulsen was still talking to me, but he was talking about anything but baseball. I knew that they didn't have any hits yet, but it wasn't until the eighth that I said to myself, 'Okay, I've got a no-hitter going.' That's when I really started concentrating as much as possible to get each hitter out. I'd look at a hitter and try to remember what he'd swung at earlier in the game."

The reference to catcher Chris Poulsen brought on questions about his contributions to Lee's performance, and Andy had high praise for his catcher. "I have to give a lot of credit to Chris Poulsen," he said. "He did a great job. It was only the second time I've thrown to him, but we worked great together. He knew exactly what needed to be thrown, and he made me hit spots and keep the ball down."

Phil Gray asked Lee if he ever shook Poulsen off during the game. "Only when he told me to shake him off," he said. "He makes you throw the right pitch on the right count. If you make a mistake, it's not his fault."

"The no-hitter you just threw is only the second one in Frontier League history," said Doug Kimsey, "how does that make you feel?"

"It hasn't even sunk in yet," said Lee. "I know it's something not many people do, and I'm sure it's something I'll be proud of when I'm not playing anymore and I look back on it, but right now I'm just happy that I pitched a good game and that we won."

Andy's dad and girlfriend were standing by patiently and proudly, waiting for us to release their hero so that they could all go out to celebrate, so we wrapped it up. "Andy, what are you going to do for an encore?" I asked.

He chuckled again and then threw us the best change-up he'd delivered all night. "Well, tomorrow morning I'm graduating from Ohio State."

I had brought a couple of traveling companions with me to the game: my eleven-year-old son Nolan Ryan and one of his best buddies, Steven Walsh. They both played sports year-round, and I'd been coaching their CYO basketball team since third grade. Steven was a smart kid, a great speller, and an intense competitor. He, Nolan, and Ben Valentine, another talented, hard-working, and coachable kid, gave me, as their basketball coach, a nucleus of three horses who absolutely hated to be outrun.

I tried to beg off going to The Dock, but Max and Jim wouldn't hear of it. "C'mon, sack it up!" Max said. "You gotta go over to The Dock. We're just gonna have one."

"Yeah, you say that, but 'one' usually means one barrel, not one beer."

"Ah, Mike, c'mon. You gotta come with us. We're gonna celebrate Andy Lee's no-hitter," said Jim.

I got out-voted four to one, so it was off to The Dock we went.

There was another good crowd at The Dock but no Roosters. They were already on the way back to Richmond, where they would start a series with the River City Rascals the next day. Max, Schaly, and I joined Cliff and Bea Beeks at one table, while Nolan and Steve sipped Shirley Temples at the next one.

Everyone was still thrilled at having witnessed Andy Lee's no-hitter, which finally took the spotlight off Brett Gray's 25 strikeouts; but Schaly, still running on adrenaline, was the one holding court.

"We had a good crowd tonight, and they were really into the game," he said. "Chillicothe is really a baseball town in the summer. And there are never any assholes on the ballclub either. Roger Hanners doesn't allow any."

"There's some," said Bea. "but we overlook 'em."

"I saw Andy Lee in the shower," Schaly said, "and I said, 'Great job, Andy.'

"He said, 'Thanks, Jim.'

"'I hope you realize you only get one third of the credit tonight,' I said. 'Chris Poulsen gets a third, and I get a third.'

"'You! Why should you get any credit?'

"'Did you like the strike zone the last three innings?'

"'Yes, I did.'

"'Alright, then.'

"Just wait 'til I get him again when I have the plate. Let's see how many strikes he throws with Mr. No Credit umpiring!

"Oh, yeah! I'm not doing the plate any more this year. Max, you got it the rest of the season. ... I called a no-hitter. I'm selling my gear."

"Oh, geez," said Max, "Jim, you're as full of shit as a Christmas turkey." Max turned to me and said, "That's a 'Wilson'": which meant that the expression he had just used to put down Jim was one that Max had learned from his deceased father, Wilson McLeary. I was learning a new 'Wilson' almost daily, and every time one came out of Max's mouth, I could see in his face and hear in his voice the love he felt for his father.

We talked some more about the game, and after a while the discussion got around to a play which had occurred in the bottom of the seventh: with two outs, Roosters pitcher Alejandro Bracho had picked Joe Colameco off first base. "Colameco was so safe it was criminal," said Jim. "When Jamie Keefe, the Paints' third base coach was walking past me back to the dugout, I said, 'Hey, Jamie, last night you came all the way across the diamond to complain to me about my call on a pickoff play, and at least mine was close.' And he said, 'Well, I like Max.'"

"Max, did you miss that call?" I said.

"Hey, he was walking back to the bag and he was standing up, so I figured we'd get an out!"

"You didn't answer his question," said Schaly.

"Yes, I missed it," Max said.

Woody Fullenkamp walked over to the table to say hello, and I decided to have a little fun with him. "Hey, Woody, how come you guys didn't do the Chicken Dance tonight?" I said.

"Oh, I dunno. Sometimes we just don't feel like it," he said.

"I see. Well, I'd like to tell you a little story," I said. "Oh, by the way, you see those two good-looking boys over there ... that's my son Nolan Ryan and his buddy Steven. They came all the way from Cincinnati just to watch you guys tonight, and they were really excited about it because I told them how much fun a Paints game is."

Woody looked over at the boys and gave them a little wave.

"This is a story about Joe DiMaggio, the great Yankee Clipper," I said. "One day DiMaggio was hurt, and his teammates knew that he would not be in the lineup. When they got to the clubhouse though to suit up for the game, there was DiMaggio, sitting in front of his locker, getting dressed. Now, DiMaggio's teammates were very concerned when they saw this because they not only admired the hell out of him, they truly loved him.

"'Joe, you're hurt. You can't play,' one of his teammates said.

"'Yeah, Joe. Stay out. This game don't mean nothing. We can win without you,' said another.

"'I have to play,' said DiMaggio.

"'Why, Joe? Why do you have to play, even though you are hurt?'

"And DiMaggio said, 'I have to play because in the crowd today there is going to be a father ... and his son ... who have driven a long way, maybe 500 miles or more, to see me play. ...'"

The light of recognition broke across Woody's face, and he said, "Uh, oh, I can see where this is going."

"'And I can't disappoint them. I have to go out there and play for that father and son,' that's what the great DiMaggio said. AND IF THE GREAT DIMAGGIO CAN PLAY WHEN HE'S HURT JUST TO MAKE SOME KID HAPPY," I continued, "THEN SURELY THE CHILLICOTHE PAINTS BULLPEN CAN PERFORM, EVEN WHEN THEY DON'T FEEL LIKE IT, FOR A COUPLE OF KIDS WHO TRAVELED ALL THE WAY FROM CINCINNATI JUST TO SEE THE FAMOUS CHICKEN DANCE!!!"

Everybody laughed and laughed at the story, but before I'd even finished, Woody had walked over and sat down with the boys to apologize and promise to do the Chicken Dance the next time they came to a Paints game.

5

The Hardest Working Act in Baseball Show Business: The Bluuueeesss Brothers!!!

ON FRIDAY, JUNE 9, I placed a call to the National Baseball Hall of Fame and Museum. I was pretty sure that a no-hitter and a triple play had never occurred in the same game in the major leagues. I wasn't so sure about the minor leagues. Here's what researcher Eric Enders was able to tell me: "It's an impossible thing to know. We don't know how many minor league no-hitters have been thrown. We just don't have those records. Nobody does. In fact, we don't even have a list of no-hitters thrown in the minors last year.

"Personally, I think a no-hitter and a triple play in the same game had to have happened before, especially in the heyday of the minor leagues when there were teams and leagues all over the place."

I was a little surprised at first that the Hall of Fame couldn't definitively answer my question; but after thinking about it, I had to agree with Enders. Still, I felt certain that the combination of a no-hitter and a triple play hadn't happened very often, and for a baseball trivia and history nut like me, it's occurrence in Chillicothe made Andy Lee's gem all the more unforgettable.

Max was not scheduled to work in the Frontier League until Canton

Max and Patty at the shop, Max Interior Design.

marched on Richmond for a three-game series June 13, 14, and 15. I took
advantage of the break to visit Patty McLeary at the Cincinnati Catholic
grade school she had taught at for the past thirty years.

St. Lawrence parish was founded in 1868. The church which serves
the parish to this day was built in 1894. A massive stone structure of
gothic design with two towering spires, it is an impressive edifice with
an unquestionable purpose. Located on Warsaw Avenue in a declining
neighborhood known as Lower Price Hill, the church is doubly inspi-
rational when one contemplates the sacrifices of the faithful that were
required to raise such a structure.

I found the school behind the church and parked next to Max's
red Toyota pickup. Patty waved to me from Room 309, her classroom,
and came down to let me into the building.

Patty gave me a tour of her domain; though brief, it made it obvious that a lot went on in her classroom. There were bulletin boards on
every wall and hanging plants in front of every window. A listening center was located against one wall—"They have to listen to stories on tape
and then answer questions; it develops their listening skills," said Patty—
and a library of 1,600 age-appropriate books, mostly bought with Patty's
own money, took up one corner in the back of the room. Behind the front
wall were three closets. Originally, there had been only one, but Patty
had built two more because she needed them to contain all the stuff she'd

accumulated during her long career: teaching manuals, text books, audio-visual aids.

The room also contained a standard issue teacher's desk, but it was supplanted by Patty's secret weapon: her podium on wheels!

I did a double-take when I saw it, a chest-high wooden podium with a fiberglass front shield painted blue and accentuated with lightening bolts. Attached to the front was a Plexiglas sign that said "THE BOSS." And, of course, the darned thing had wheels.

"I wanted a podium, but the school wouldn't provide one," said Patty, "so I gave Larry the measurements and asked him to make me one. I had no idea he was going to make something so elaborate.

"Today, our business, Max Interior Design, is mostly an auto reup-holstering business; but back in 1980 when Larry made the podium it was called MaxTrux because we customized a lot of vans. When I saw the podium for the first time, I knew it was something that Larry had made in the shop. 'It looks like a car!' I told him.

"Once Larry made it for me, I never sat at my desk to teach again. With my podium I move all around the room. When I see a problem, I roll right over and teach from there. In the beginning of the year it always freaks the kids out."

There was one other unusual thing about Patty's classroom: the large crucifix hanging on the wall opposite the door to the room. There was nothing unique about the presence of the crucifix in the classroom. What was extraordinary was that the Christ figure on its cross had no arms.

"Every week a different class is responsible for helping prepare the liturgy for the school Mass," said Patty. "About eight years ago, when it was my class' turn, we decided that we would build the procession into church around the song "One Bread, One Body" and that one of my students would walk in holding the loaf of bread that Father would use for communion and another student would walk in holding that cruci-fix. We practiced, and the kids did great at Mass. When we got back into the classroom after Mass though, we didn't hang the crucifix back on the wall. The boy who'd carried it laid it on top of a bookcase that was underneath the crucifix's space on the wall. Well, shortly thereafter, one of the kids was reaching for a dictionary on the top shelf of that bookcase, and the crucifix got knocked off. It fell on the floor, and both arms were shattered.

"I felt terrible about it, and I didn't know what to do. The crucifix is probably as old as the school itself, and it was certainly very expen-sive and well-made. With it broken, we could see all this very thin, intri-cate wiring that held the plaster together for the arms and the hands and the fingers. As you can see, it's still very beautiful.

"I told Father Dressman about it and asked him if we could still use it and hang it back up on the wall. He said we could. Then I asked him what I should tell the kids because I knew they would want to know why we were keeping a broken crucifix.

"And Father said, 'Teach the children that they will have to be Christ's arms and hands.'

"So I put it back up, and every year my new students ask me, 'What happened to the arms on the crucifix?' I tell them what happened, and then I say, 'You have to be Jesus' arms and hands.'"

Patty and I sat down in student desks facing each other, and as we talked she organized some files.

She told me that she was a local girl all the way. She'd been born in a Cincinnati neighborhood called Delhi and attended Cincinnati Catholic schools all her life: St. Williams grade school, Seton High School, The College of Mount St. Joseph, and Xavier University. She met Max right after her mother Alvina died in June of 1974. Max was working for the Reserve Life Insurance Company and came down from Dayton, Ohio, to settle her mother's life insurance claim. She laughed when I asked her what her first impression of Max was and said, "I can't tell you that." Then she said, "Larry was very polite and very nice. And I thought he was good looking. My friend Joan thought he looked like Omar Shariff because he had dark hair and a mustache. And he weighed considerably more than he does now. He was also very athletic. He ran four miles a day."

Despite the good impression Max made, it took him six months to get a date with Patty. "Max didn't exactly sweep you off your feet then, did he?" I kidded her.

Patty laughed again sheepishly and said, "Well, I was going out with other people. I had a large circle of friends, and we had our rituals where we'd go out to certain places every Friday and Saturday night. He'd call me and ask me to go to a ballgame, but I was always busy. I didn't have time. And I guess I was independent too."

About six months later, Patty broke up with her boyfriend, and Max finally got his chance. "He was a lot of fun; we had a good time together," said Patty. They got engaged in 1979—Max gave her a ring for Christmas—and two years later got married.

"Cincinnati never gets much snow, but in the winter of 1977 we got hit with what everybody calls The Blizzard," said Patty. "Cincinnatians are not used to a lot of snow, and it practically shut the city down. One Sunday night in January of that year Larry was at our family house. We were still dating at the time; we weren't even engaged. My sister was dating a friend of his, and we were all at our family house on Jamestown Street.

"We got cabin fever and decided to go out and mess around in the snow. I had on a pair of those stylish '70s-era boots with the sharp pointed toes. That was the style back then.

"Anyway, Larry picked me up to throw me into a snow bank, but he realized I was going to land on the sidewalk where there was no snow.

"When I started to fall he grabbed me and that caused my foot to come up and kick him dead center in the middle of his right eye with the toe of my boot.

"Of course, it hurt him, so we looked at his eye and tried to assess the damage. His eye did look very red, but it didn't seem to be that bad. However, he couldn't see, so we decided to take him to the emergency room at St. Francis Hospital down on Queen City Avenue. My sister, her boyfriend, Larry, and I all piled into the car, and we drove him down there.

"And they made him sit there for four hours. Why? I don't know. There was nobody else there. After we'd been there for a while, they brought in this man who'd run into a tree while sled riding, and he was in serious condition, so they took care of him right away. But we sat there and waited for four hours, that's no lie. It really upset me for Larry to sit there all that time. We kept telling the people at the hospital that Larry was in a lot of pain and that it was getting worse, but he sat there for four hours. That's a long time.

"What happened was that when my foot hit his eye, the back of his eyeball exploded, and it was losing pressure. And the longer it was without pressure, the less chance there was of his recovering his eyesight.

"Finally, a doctor examined him, and he said I needed to take Larry to see a specialist, Dr. Powers, first thing the next morning. Dr. Powers took one look at Larry's eye and immediately sent him to Good Samaritan Hospital where he removed the eye. Just like that his eye was gone.

"I couldn't believe it was happening. I didn't go in to teach school for several days because I never left the hospital. Finally, a nun came to the hospital and said to me, 'Your principal called me and said that you haven't left this hospital. I want you to go home, shower, and change your clothes. How can you support him if you're here in these clothes you've had on for days?'

"I was so upset, but I had to be there because he couldn't see at all. The right eye was gone, and they had the left one bandaged. They had the good eye bandaged because they were afraid the strain of trying to make up for the lost eye would cause damage to the good eye. It had to be a gradual thing for them to take the bandage off. Well, when he left the hospital, he couldn't go home, so I talked to my two sisters whom I lived with, and they agreed we had to bring him home to live with us. We put him in the bedroom upstairs and took care of him because he couldn't see to walk down the stairs. I'd get him all set up in the morning, then go to school. I'd come home at lunchtime and take care of him and then go back to school. Then after school I'd come home for the day and take care of him that evening.

"Eventually, he was able to take the bandage off, and that very day he went to a car show and was there all day working and looking around at all the cars with his eye patch off. He was supposed to rest so many hours every day, and I tried to get him to do it—'You're going to ruin your good eye!' I'd say—but he didn't listen to me.

"It was truly a shame, and I've always wondered if they'd taken care of him right away, if maybe they would have been able to save at least a little bit of his eyesight.

"I was really distraught over the operation, but Larry told me, 'Look, if you can't handle this, how am I going to handle it?'

"So I had to get my act together. You know what I did before I brought him home from the hospital? I drove around with a patch over my right eye and I worked for days that way so I'd know what he was going through. And one of my sisters did the same thing because she was curious about it. And it is hard if you think about it.

"One of the things I felt so bad about was that he was a good ball-player before the accident, but afterwards he wouldn't even try to play ball again. He was only 27 when it happened. He played a lot of softball—that's all there was to play at the time—and he was very very good, and teams sought him out to play for them. He played for a real good Knights of Columbus team in Cincinnati. They knew he wasn't Catholic, but they wanted him to play because he was so good and because they liked him. There was a Catholic church down the street from his house in Johnstown, and his dad was good friends with the priest there, so Larry claimed that he belonged to that parish. But after he lost his eye, he never picked up a glove or a baseball bat again."

"He's really handled it beautifully though, don't you think," I said.

"Oh, yes. Yes, he has. If he does feel sorry for himself, he certainly hides it well," she said. "And he's never, ever made me feel to blame. He's never done that. This was a very traumatic thing for us both, the kind of thing that could make or break a relationship. I was really guilt-ridden about it, but he's the one who said, 'If you can't deal with it, how can I?' I learned to deal with it, and we made it through. We just handled it."

Patty went on to tell me about their life after the accident: how Max had to give up the insurance business because he couldn't see to drive at night when he needed to make most of his calls; how he took advantage of his design and craftsman skills by starting an automobile and van customizing business called MaxTrux; and how he became more and more involved in umpiring once he realized his playing days were over.

"I have just one criticism of you as a wife," I said. "How come you've never been able to convert Max to Catholicism?"

I was just kidding, but she answered the question seriously. "I never tried," she said. "I think he was raised Methodist, and one time when we first started going out, he started criticizing the Catholic Church for certain things and telling me that some of the things I believed were wrong. I told him, 'Look, don't tell me what to believe. You believe what you want to believe, and I'll believe what I want to believe.' He never said another word about it. ... After Larry lost his eye, he said something about it being God's fault, but I told him that God didn't have anything to do with it, that it was just a freak accident; and I think he knew that because he never brought up that idea again."

"What about baseball?" I asked to change the subject. "Are you a fan in general, apart from Max's umpiring?"

"Oh, I enjoy watching a game, but I never go to a game unless Larry invites me to a game he's going to be umpiring. ... He used to invite me to go with him all the time, but he almost never does anymore."

"What about the Frontier League? How do you feel about Max umpiring in the Frontier League?"

"I hate it that he travels the way he does, and the umpiring takes away from our business—it's not nearly as lucrative as it used to be. But I'm happy for him that he is able to do something that he enjoys doing so much.

"He's happy, and I guess that's what you have to do: you have to do what makes you happy. Otherwise, you're miserable, and you make everybody else around you miserable."

"You just said that Max used to invite you to go along with him all the time but that he doesn't anymore. When did he stop inviting you?"

"When he started umpiring in the Frontier League."

"Why then?"

"I don't know," she said, "unless it's that he feels like he wouldn't be able to stay out after the games as late as he can when he's by himself."

"Well, I guess I wouldn't be telling you anything you don't already know if I were to say that it's mandatory that we stop for beer after every game."

"Heaven's no," Patty said.

"I guess Max has always been a drinker, ever since you first met him, right?"

"Oh, no. He hardly drank at all before he started umpiring in the

Frontier League. That's what I really don't like about the league. For some reason, he started drinking when he got into the league. I worry about him every night he umpires. I can't sleep until he gets home, and I pray that he'll make it back home without getting into an accident. You have no idea how many rosaries have gotten him home safely."

After Patty had walked me downstairs and out of the building, we stood by our vehicles for a few minutes before going our separate ways home. I was still thinking about all the rosaries she'd said for Max's safety, and I told her that I wished I had the spiritual dedication to say the rosary as frequently as she did. "Well, you can always pray the Sacred Heart Beads," she said. "That doesn't take nearly as long as it does to say a rosary." She pulled a string of plastic red beads out of her pocket and explained the difference between the two devotions. Whereas a regular 59-bead rosary has five decades, requiring one to say five sets of ten Hail Marys (plus nine other prayers); a Sacred Heart rosary has only 33 beads, and the same brief prayer is said for each bead: "Sacred Heart of Jesus, I trust in Your love."

I asked Patty if her sisters were as devout as she was. She said they were and then told me a story about them that my question had reminded her of. "St. Anthony, as you probably know, is officially the patron saint of the poor; but people traditionally have asked him for help in finding favorite lost possessions. There's a little prayer that you say:

'Tony, Tony,
Look around;
Something's lost
And must be found.'

"Well, one day in 1986 my sisters were coming to my house for a cookout. We stopped at the grocery store to pick up some things we needed for the cookout, and I decided to buy a lottery ticket. After I put a dollar in the machine, I grabbed my sisters by their hands, and I got them to put their arms around the machine with me. Then I said that little prayer to St. Anthony, except that I changed it a little:

'Tony, Tony,
Look around;
Bills have to be paid
And money must be found.'

"They were completely horrified and snatched their hands away from me. Susanne said, 'You are sacrilegious!' Barbara said, 'God's gonna punish you! You're gonna go to hell for that!!' I started laughing because I'd only been kidding, but that only made it worse as far as they were concerned. They hurried out of the store, and as they were leaving they told all the checkout girls and the bag boys, 'We don't know her. We're not related to her.'"

\\-2-04

On Tuesday, June 13, Max, Whit Hickman, and I headed up to Richmond for the first game of a series between Canton and the Roosters. Whit was yet another short umpire, but he was also well built, young and very handsome. He looked a lot like Tom Cruise and had a perpetual smile on his face. Max told me that the ladies were constantly coming on to him, which is perhaps why he was in no hurry to marry his longtime girlfriend.

Whit had begun umpiring in the Frontier League in 1996, doing games in Zanesville and Chillicothe so he was no rookie; however, this was his Opening Night in the 2000 Frontier League season, and he was feeling some jitters, just as Max had earlier. "I wasn't nervous at all for college ball this year," he said, "but, to be honest, the Frontier League still makes me nervous. I've got so much energy in my system that I can't get to sleep when I get home after a game."

"That's why going to the Wheel tastes so good," said Max.

Some of Whit's jitters were undoubtedly also due to the fact that he was going to see John Cate. "Witt threw John out twice in the first series he ever did in Richmond," explained Max. "He threw him out in the first game, and then threw him out again during the home plate meeting before the second game!"

Witt, who was sitting in the front seat with Max, said, "We don't talk about that, but we both know it's there."

"Man, it would really be nice if we had three-man crews in the Frontier League," he continued. I knew that the league's two-man crews were an issue with Max too. Nobody thought it was a good idea to use two-man crews; the owners of the league simply felt that it was an economic necessity to do so. There was no doubt in the umpires' minds that two-man crews were a foolish parsimony and contributed to missed calls and arguments that could have been avoided. "It would help a lot if they'd weed out the bad umps," said Whit. "But even when you get good umps, two-man crews are tough. Two guys can handle it, but they just can't get everything at this level. The game is too quick."

Another issue for the umpires was the low pay: $75 per game with no additional expense money. The home teams always provided some cold concession food after the games, but paying for gas could take a big chunk out of the $75. What made the pay seem almost insulting to the umpires was that it didn't compare favorably to what they earned doing amateur, scholastic, and collegiate games. Seventy-five dollars, for instance, was the same pay Max got for doing games in the Great Lakes wooden bat league, a high-level summer collegiate league.

Max himself made out a little better than all of his buddies in blue, not only because he umpired so many games (about 300) each year but also because he made some extra money from several assigning jobs. In addition to assigning the umpires for the Frontier League games in Richmond, Max assigned umpires for 15 Cincinnati high schools, 27 colleges, and two of the teams in the Great Lakes summer collegiate league. Max also picked up some extra dough by running umpiring clinics and certification courses.

I was already getting used to hearing the umpires gripe, and they griped not only about the pay but also about how interminable Frontier League games could be. "How many times do you get to the sixth inning in a Frontier League game, and the wheels fall off?" said Whit. "You do the first six in an hour and a half, and you just pray there's nobody warming up in the bullpen."

"No kidding. And when you work nine or ten Frontier League games in a row and then do a Great Lakes doubleheader, two sevens, you're in the sixth inning before you know it," agreed Max.

As we drove closer and closer to Richmond, Max kept looking at the overcast sky and making comments about the probability of rain. "Will you look at those clouds," he said. "They're trouble."

"Max, relax," said Whit, "those aren't rain clouds."

"Oh, yeah? What kind of clouds are they?"

"They're poofy clouds," said Whit, turning in his seat to give me a wink. "They're as dry as cotton balls." Max wasn't buying Whit's assessment of the impending weather, and he continued to fret.

Even though the Roosters had salvaged the last of three against the River City Rascals on Sunday afternoon to break a six-game losing streak, their record stood at 3–8. They were in last place in the East Division; already the front office was making changes to the roster; and the players still on the team were feeling the pressure to perform before they too were sent packing. "There'll be some tight assholes out there tonight," said Witt, "some real puckering."

I thought of Mike Zerbe and hoped he was still with the team. I was pretty sure that he would be, but I knew that there were no guaranteed contracts in the Frontier League. I also knew that the Roosters were counting heavily on Zerbe. Before the season started John Cate had been quoted by *Palladium-Item* sportswriter Don Tincher as saying, "A lot is expected of Mike. Your veterans have to carry you. He's going to have an opportunity to knock in a lot of runs. He's got to have a great year for us."

In Chillicothe I had mentioned to Gary Kitchel, off the air, that I

thought Zerbe was a genuinely good guy. Kitchel said, "He's a great kid.
But I'm not a fan of his out there."

"Why not?" I asked.

"Because he doesn't hit in the clutch. Last year Key Voshell with a
lot fewer at bats had only one fewer RBI than Zerbe, who left a ton of
runners on base. In that respect, Zerbe is the nicest worst ballplayer
I've ever seen. ... The Roosters are going to have to come up with a
couple of hitters who can hit with runners on base."

Standing on the concrete deck outside the Roosters' office, I scoured
the field as players on both teams, assembled on their respective foul
lines in the outfield, stretched, played catch, swung bats, and ran half-
speed sprints into shallow center field. I did not see Mike Zerbe among
the Roosters. Looking towards the third base grandstands I noticed
huge muddy clouds coming from the West and headed straight for us.

Mark Hadley, the recent University of Dayton grad who was intern-
ing as the Roosters' acting director of media relations came by and gave
me press releases covering the River City series I'd missed, plus a press
release about Andy Lee's no-hitter. The latter stated that the game was
the first time since the mid 1980s that a no-hitter and a triple play had
occurred in the same game. Now we're getting somewhere, I told myself;
but Mark couldn't provide me with any details about the reference to
the 1980s game, nor, strangely, could he even remember where he'd
gotten the reference to the game.

I was also encouraged to see that Zerbe had hit his first home run
of the year and driven in two runs in the series opener against River
City, which Richmond lost 10–3; but also a little worried that it might
have been too little too late for Mike.

Moments later I was relieved to see him, hatless, come out of the
dugout and walk off the field towards the clubhouse. He waved at me
as he went by.

Although Zerbe was still around, a revolving door had definitely been
installed in the Roosters' clubhouse. Catcher-first baseman Jeremy Sassanella and center fielder Shap Stiles, victims of log jams at their positions,
had both been released; while pitcher Takanori Mizuno had gotten home
sick and left the club on his own. I was particularly disappointed with
Mizuno's departure. I had been looking forward to talking to him through
his interpreter, the Japanese teacher at Richmond High School, Gerald
Brooks, who had also been the father in the family that hosted Mizuno.
Even though Mizuno's one outing for the Roosters had been a disastrous
one, Cate too was sorry to see Mizuno go. "I'm kind of hurt that he's left
us," he said, "and I still had confidence in him. He threw 88–92 mph and
had a great curveball. He came highly recommended by the scouts."

In the meantime, the Roosters had added a center fielder and a pair of pitchers. The pitchers were both lefties: Kory Hartman, who had pitched, ineffectively, for Richmond the year before; and Steve Carver, a rookie with impressive credentials out of Brewton Parker College. The center fielder was Dan Wydner, whose nine-game trial with the New Jersey Jackals of the Northern League in 1999 had not been enough to cost him his rookie status. Wydner had immediately produced, going 6–13 (.462) in his first three games as a Rooster against River City.

The Roosters had also signed the slender, speedy Freddy Flores. Though nominally an outfielder, the fundamentally sound Flores could play just about any position on the field. He had been cut by the Roosters right before Opening Day, but Cate had made him a coach. Intelligent and personable, Flores was already a professional coach, of the Western New Mexico University women's fast pitch softball team in Silver City, New Mexico, his hometown. Frontier League players make the transition from player to coach all the time, and Flores was more qualified than usual; but his appointment was also a way for the Roosters to be able to keep him around as insurance, in case a playing job opened up. You could have made book on that happening, and Freddy, no dummy, knew that changes were inevitable, especially if the team got off to a bad start.

Flores was especially cognizant of the tenuousness of minor league baseball jobs and of the helter-skelter way Frontier League teams add to and subtract from their rosters because of the way he had originally hooked up with the Roosters. In 1999 he had been cut from the Chillicothe Paints towards the end of spring training. On his drive back home to Mexico, he stopped in Richmond to say hello to old friends, was invited by Cate to join the Roosters' workouts, and wound up making the team.

It was Flores, the re-tread, who had been the star of the game Sunday evening in his first appearance of the 2000 season. With two outs in the bottom of the eleventh and Key Voshell at second, River City elected to walk the dangerous Aaron Sledd to get to Freddy, who had entered the game as a pinch runner for Mike Zerbe in the eighth. Flores punched a single into right field to drive in Voshell with the winning run.

The Roosters took their time again, but they won the opener against Canton 5–4. For the second time in a row, the game went eleven innings, and this time the opposing team had to pitch to Sledd in the clutch. With two outs and the bases loaded, Sledd drove a Brian Zima fastball over the head of Canton center fielder Matt Griswold to send 732 Roosters fans home happy. Mike Zerbe also had a hand in the victory with his second home run of the season, a towering fly ball in the eighth inning that barely cleared the left field fence. The moon shot by Zerbe came on a 3–2 count after Mike had fouled off several pitches, and it tied the game 4–4.

The best line of the night in the McBride Stadium press box came during a discussion of Bobby Knight, Indiana University's legendary basketball coach who was under fire for the one millionth time and, for the first time, in serious jeopardy of losing his job in Bloomington. The University had recently put Knight on notice after having conducted an investigation into the latest allegations that Knight had mistreated some of his players. Trying to mess with Jan Clark who'd been talking about Knight's problems, Troy Derengowski said, "I heard that Bob Knight doesn't like sportswriters."

"I don't know any sportswriters who are on 'Zero Tolerance,'" said Jan.

From an umpiring standpoint, the game was routine except for one play which came in the bottom of the third. With one out and runners on first and second, the Roosters' Ryan Anholt hit a chopper wide of first, which resulted in a race to the bag between Anholt and Canton pitcher Justin Wallace. It looked to me as if Anholt clearly beat Wallace to the bag—Wallace's attempt to tag Anholt at the last second seemed to me to be a confirmation of this judgment—but Whit Hickman called Anholt out. The call elicited strong disapproval from the Richmond dugout.

After the game, I asked Whit about the play and was surprised to hear the Roosters' take on it. Whit said that Richmond didn't argue about who got to the bag first; they argued that the pitcher missed the bag. You can't prove a negative ("There is no intelligent life in the universe except on earth"), but Whit obviously subscribed to the theory that an umpire can't call what he doesn't see; and he said that he definitely did not see Wallace miss the bag. Furthermore, he said he was positive that he did see Wallace beat Anholt to the bag.

Whether Whit got the call right or not, there was no question that Max did his job correctly. As soon as the call was made, Cate and third base coach Woody Sorrell streaked after Whit like heat-seeking missiles. Max intercepted Woody near the pitcher's mound. He put his arm around Woody and started walking him back off the field, to leave Whit to deal with Cate one-on-one. I could just imagine the conversation: "Hey, Woody, did I ever tell you about the time …"

At the Wheel Max related part of the conversation he'd had with Canton manager Dan Massarelli during the exchange of lineup cards at home plate. "Massarelli asked me how my collar bone was doing," Max said, "so I told him, 'You know what my dad, Wilson, always used to say

... "Do you know where *sympathy* is in the dictionary? Between *shit* and *syphilis*, that's where."'" That was Max's way of saying he was okay.

"Then I said, 'Hey, Mazz, I want to get Johnny Poss to sign my sling.' Mazz told me, 'You're too late, Max. Poss retired on his own terms today, right before the bus left Canton. He's got family problems. I understand where he was coming from. I'll say this for him: he went out in a blaze of glory. He went 6–7 in his last two games.'

"Poss is good people," said Max, as he indicated to the barmaid that it was time to sprinkle the infield again. "He's what this league is all about. He'd get in your shit once in a while, but that was just his competitiveness. He told me at the end of last season that he had a little girl he wasn't seeing. He showed me a picture of her. He told me, 'Max, I've got a wife and little girl back in Iowa.' I'm gonna get his phone number and give him a call."

We toasted Poss with our nearly empty beer cans and then were regaled with tales of Tom Arnett's recent heckling episodes during the River City series. Tom had just been trying to have fun with Rod Rollins, but he managed to get under Rod's skin anyway. One time right after Rollins had finished brushing off the plate, Tom yelled, "Good job, Blue; do you do windows too?" Rollins walked down the left field line towards the beer garden, pointed at Tom, and said, "I've had about enough of you!"

In the third game of the series, Tom had hit the lottery, heckler-style: he ragged an opposing player so effectively that the player lost his composure and ragged him back. Tom's heckling of the Rascals second baseman for making the error that led to extra innings bothered him so much, that the second baseman gave Tom the finger as he ran towards the River City dugout at the end of the inning. The second baseman then stuck his head out of the dugout and shouted: "You married your sister!"

Tom answered: "At least I wasn't on Springer last week!"

Even though the sun was shining brightly the next afternoon, Max was even more worried about rain than he had been the day before. "By the way," he said, "forty miles north of us two Great Lakes League games were rained out, so I knew what I was talking about. Whit wasn't scheduled to umpire anywhere tonight, so I called him this morning and said, 'Hey, Mr. Poofy Clouds, you want to do those games in Lima, Ohio, that got rained out last night by the storm that just missed us in Richmond?'"

When we got to McBride, there were Rooster people all over the field like ants on an unattended picnic spread. It was obvious that Richmond had gotten hit hard with rain after we'd left town, and everyone who was physically capable was on the field trying to get it into shape for the upcoming game.

For once, Max's partner wasn't short. Oh no, Deron Brown was a good 6' 2" and built like an NFL linebacker. "Chiseled" was the word Max had used. In real life Deron was a chemistry teacher and the Offensive Coordinator for the varsity football team at the public high school in Piqua, Ohio. Despite his physique, Deron, according to Max, had the temperament of "a big old teddy bear."

Max was concerned about even more rain coming through town, so he walked over to John Cate's office in the Roosters' clubhouse to get a radar update on the weather off John's computer. I stayed in the umpires' dressing room and talked to Deron.

When I mentioned the Mask Story, in explaining why I was following Max around the Frontier League, Deron told me that he had his own story about umpiring in a game when Max took a beating.

"First of all, to appreciate the story, you have to know about the five dollar rule, which is really nothing but an inside joke among umpires," said Deron. "Supposedly, when you have the plate, you always call the first pitch of a game a strike, no matter where it is, even if it's in the dirt or over the backstop. By doing that you set the tone for the whole game; you show both teams that you're going to call the game aggressively. And if you don't call that first pitch a strike, then each base ump holds up a hand, which means 'You owe me five dollars.' Nobody ever pays or collects the money though; as I said, it's really just a joke.

"Well, Max and I were doing a game at Wittenberg University, and Max had the plate. He was using his old chest protector, the one he used before he got the one he uses now, and it wasn't very good. It didn't have nearly enough padding. The Wittenberg pitcher threw the first pitch of the game, and it was a fastball low and inside. It was no where near the plate, but Max called it a strike anyway. I thought, 'Hmm, I haven't seen Max miss that bad in a while.'

"Anyway, one of the Wittenberg kids swung at a high fastball and fouled it straight back. It hit Max right over the heart. It really stunned him and knocked him down to one knee. I was very concerned about him because it was obvious he was in a lot of pain.

"Two innings later, we had the same batter, the same pitch, and the same result. The ball hit Max in exactly the same place, right over the heart, and this time it hurt him so bad he actually had tears in his eyes. I said, 'Max, you need to come out of this game. Let me get my gear out of the car and strap, and I can call a local guy to come do the bases. He can be here in 15 minutes.'

"Of course, Max wouldn't hear of it. He said, 'I've never not finished a game. I've got to finish this one. I'll be okay in a couple of minutes. Just let me know if I get wicky-wacky and start missing pitches.'

"I said okay, and the game resumed. At the end of the inning I came in and asked him how he was doing. He said, 'Okay. Did I miss any pitches?'

"And I said, 'No, you're doing fine. The only pitch you've missed so far was the first pitch of the game.'

"And he said, 'No, sir. I didn't miss that pitch. That was a strike … and I don't owe you five dollars!'"

The Blues Brothers were scheduled to perform, and I was anxious to see their act. Duke Ward, the Roosters' Director of Business Operations and a part owner of the team, had called them "the hardest working act in professional baseball show business."

"The Blues Brothers work their butts off to deliver a funny, family-oriented act we're proud to be associated with," he'd said. "The fans are familiar with the movie the act is based on, but the Blues Brothers put their own personalities into it and update the act every year so it stays fresh. Our fans love them. Every winter as soon as we release our promotional schedule for the new season, our fans call the office to find out when the Blue Brothers are coming to town so they can circle those dates on their calendar."

After dropping off my gear in the press box, I headed towards the Roosters' business office. Peering beyond the deck into the parking lot below I saw the Blues Brothers' huge "bus," for lack of a better term. As I copied down the toll-free telephone number that was on the side of the vehicle, I saw a chunky fellow who had to be none other than Joliet Jake Blues walking towards the bus. He was dressed in a black suit and hat and wore sunglasses. "Hey, I'm writing a book about the Frontier League," I hollered. "If I call that 800 number will you give me an interview?"

"Come on down and we can talk right now," yelled Jake.

"I don't want to get in the way while you're preparing for the show," I said.

"Come onnnn!" he insisted.

Parked next to the big bus was the Blues Brothers car. It was such an authentic reproduction of the cop car that Elwood bought at the Mt. Prospect police auction while Jake was in prison that it should have been on display in the Smithsonian or some museum of great Hollywood props. It was a decommissioned black & white Dodge police cruiser with Illinois tags and a NOV '79 sticker. The motto "To Serve and Protect" on the front fenders and faded sheriff's badges on the doors were left over from its constabulary days, and the car's license number was "BDR529," just like in the movie. On the shelf behind the back seats lay a City of Chicago Police Department Missing Person report with Jake's photo on it. It obviously had been filed by Jake's jilted girlfriend (played by Carrie Fisher in the movie) because it listed "Cause of absence" as "breach of promise." The front dashboard was plastered with crap related to the Blues Brothers and their big adventure: an old, obviously unpaid parking ticket; an Illinois road map; a pack of Lucky Strikes; a marble memo pad which served as the "Blues Car Logbook"; and a flyer from Ray's Music Exchange and Pawn Shop in Calumet City. "Come in & See Ray for the Best Buys & Exchanges & Maybe a Little Xtra Cash for Those Unwanted Items," it read. The only things missing from the car were the things that were supposed to be missing: the antenna, the hub caps, and the cigarette lighter that Jake throws out the window while taking his first ride in the car after being released from prison.

It couldn't have looked more like the movie version, although it probably did not have the same performance equipment as the proto-type. In the movie, Elwood tells Jake that he traded the original Blues Brothers Cadillac for a microphone. ("A microphone! ... I can see that," says Jake.) When Jake makes it clear he doesn't like the replacement, Elwood tries to change Jake's mind by making a possible-only-in-the-movies jump over an opening drawbridge. After they rocket over the yawning opening and land on the other side of the bridge, Elwood points out, "It's got a cop motor on a 440 cubic inch plant. It's got cop tires, cop suspension, and cop shocks. It's a model made before catalytic converters so it'll run good on regular gas. ... Whattaya say: Is it the new Bluesmobile or what?"

"Yeah, I guess so," says Jake. "Just get the cigarette lighter fixed."

The Blues Brothers "bus" turned out to be a customized combina-tion of RV and Freightliner tractor trailer, with a Caterpillar semi engine providing the power to move the thing down the highway. Located between the cab in front and a garage in the back that housed the Blues Brothers car was the combo living room/kitchen. The bus also contained four beds; two in the front above the cab and two in the rear above the garage. It was an amazing vehicle and must have cost a small fortune to build.

Jake Blues turned out to be a comic named Greg Walters. Greg was a graduate of the Players of the Second City, the same Chicago comedy school, he told me proudly, that John Belushi had come out of. Greg's partner, the much taller Bob Masewicz, played Elwood. The act, which had been playing around the country since 1984, had been Bob's idea. Bob told me that they were on the road for 160–180 days a year and averaged 150 shows annually. In addition to baseball games, they worked basketball and hockey games and, of course, blues concerts.

In addition to Greg and Bob, the Blues Brothers entourage included Dave Carter, a black comic whom Bob had hired to film a documentary about the act and minor league baseball; Chris Barton, a ten-year-old kid who played the role of Buster Blues from the sequel *The Blues Brothers 2000*; and Ezra Firkins, the behind-the-scenes guy who directed the music for the show and coordinated things with the hosts. When I'd been in the press box earlier, I heard Ezra giving instructions to a Roosters employee via walkie-talkie. "If the Roosters' mascot or any other Roosters employee tries to go out and dance with the Blues Brothers, stop him ... tackle him, shoot him, do whatever you have to do, but keep him out of the way and keep the spotlight on the Blues Brothers."

Like Greg, Bob was already in costume when I entered the bus. The costumes, along with their physiques, really made them resemble the John Belushi and Dan Aykroyd Blues Brothers. They certainly tried their hardest to be as authentic with their persons as they were with the Blues Brothers car. Naturally, they both had long sideburns, but they also went to the trouble of penning their names on their knuckles, one letter per knuckle, just as Jake and Elwood do in the movie, even though nobody in the crowds they played to could ever notice such a small detail.

Although he was friendly and quite witty, Bob was reticent and pre-occupied with reviewing last-minute plans for the upcoming show. While Bob conversed via walkie-talkie with Ezra Firkins, stationed in the McBride Stadium press box, the ebullient Walters answered my questions and entertained me with a stream of stories and wise cracks. Even out of character, Greg was always on, responding to an inner challenge to constantly improve his already-impressive improvisational skills.

The fourth person to play the role of Jake, Greg had made a five-hour Amtrak train trip from Chicago to Bob's home in LaCrosse, Wisconsin, to audition for the job. "Bob made us sing and dance for three days," said Greg. "When it was over, he asked me to stick around for a few days for his upcoming engagement party, so I did. I guess he liked me because he told me to drive his car back to Chicago, pick up my clothes, and come back. I did and when I got back I went to work for him."

I was sitting on the couch in the bus' "living room." Across from me lay a yellow Labrador retriever named Fez who was contentedly gnawing on a baseball. "Fez looks kind of hungry," I said.

"Ah, he's okay," said Greg. "We don't even buy him dog food. We just let him forage around the ballpark." I marveled at the versatility and completeness of the Blues Brothers home-(office-and-garage)-away-from-home. Greg pointed out that the bus was equipped with a 25-inch TV, a satellite dish, a DVD player, four cell phones, and five computers. "We're wired way beyond what we should be," he said.

I asked why they needed so many computers. "We do a lot of stuff on them," he said. "We make hotel reservations, map trips, do some of the contracts, ... and procure road bitches. They're for Bob, based on his 16 years of dedicated service."

Posted on the wall near the door to the bus was a copy of Bob's "Rules of the Road" and the "Word of the Day." Greg told me that everybody paid attention to the "Word of the Day" because Bob actually gave a graded vocabulary test at the end of each week. "Dags" or demerits were the penalty for wrong answers. Dags were also incurred for other offenses, Greg explained, such as being late for "roll time" or for inviting chicks who were deemed to be too heavy or ugly to participate in the show. Once somebody in the group racked up 50 dags, he had to take everybody else out for lunch.

Assuming that things didn't always go as planned, I asked Greg to tell me about some of the mishaps he'd been involved in during his time with the act.

"Well, there was the time my pants fell down, and the crowd made fun of the size of my penis," he said. "No. I'm just kidding. Actually, they couldn't believe how huge I am. No, just kidding again. Let's see ... I've gone down in the stands a few times. We do a lot of crazy dancing during the show, and I'm not as graceful as Bob.

"There was the time we were in Knoxville, Tennessee, and I was up in the press box getting a bottle of water. I made a wrong turn and found myself outside the stadium. I was trying to get back into the ballpark, when I heard over the P.A. system, 'And, here they are again, the Blues Brothers!' By the time I got out there, I was so out of breath and rattled I could hardly sing or do the dance moves."

It had started raining, and Firkins came over the walkie-talkie to tell Bob that the start of the game was being delayed. The rain delay wound up lasting 12 minutes.

"Who are you going after tonight, one of the umps or the first base coach?" Bob said to Greg.

"I don't know. Whoever I can coax into the car," said Greg.

"Hey, do you want to ride in the car?" Bob asked me.

It was a very very tempting invitation, but I declined. "This book is about Max and everybody else in the Frontier League," I said, "so I don't want to inject myself into the story any more than necessary." I went on to mention how I already had misgivings about having let Gary Kitchel lure me into pretending to be a color man on the Rooster radio broadcasts.

"Remember that *Seinfeld* episode when George fakes being a marine biologist to impress his girlfriend?" said Bob. "And then George winds up saving the beached whale by pulling a golf ball out of its blow hole?" Sure, I remembered.

"Do you remember what George says? He says, 'For that moment, I *was* a marine biologist.' Well, for that moment, you *were* a baseball radio broadcaster.

"You won't be in our way. We let people ride in the back seat all the time."

"Well …," I said weakening.

"Come onnnnn! It'll be good for the book! Do it for Max!" said Greg.

"Okay. What the hell," I said. "I'd be honored."

Rumble, rumble, rumble rumble. I could hardly believe it, but I was sitting in the back seat of the Blues Brothers car, idling noisily outside the gate in the right field corner, waiting for the moment when we would make our grand entrance.

It was the bottom of the second inning, and Firkins, as he had done since the start of the game, was keeping Bob apprised of how many outs remained before it was time to reeve up the Bluesmobile and tear onto the field. "Two outs to go, two outs to go," he said over the walkie-talkie.

Bob got out of the car and did some stretching exercises to loosen up his legs. Then he did some of the exaggerated, high-stepping, clodhopper dance moves that Aykroyd's Elwood does so hilariously in the movie.

"Oh, yeah. I remember something else that happened," said Greg. "This was in Toledo about five years ago during the seventh inning stretch. I was getting the crowd all worked up to shout out 'Wuz Up!' before leading them in the singing of 'Take Me Out to the Ballgame.' I ran over to the first base side and got them to shout it: Wuz Up! Then I ran over to the third base side and got them to shout it: Wuz Up! Then I got the whole stadium to do it together. It had been threatening rain all game, but nothing had happened yet. So, I get the whole crowd to shout at the top of their lungs: WUZ UP!!! And at that exact moment a bolt of lightening came down and hit a transformer and knocked out the lights. There was nothing but stunned silence. The players ran off the field, and then the rain came down in buckets. I took a deep bow, and the crowd laughed like crazy."

Back in the driver's seat Bob double-checked with Ezra about the date of the Blues Brothers return to Richmond later in the summer.

"Hey, Greg. I've got a tip for you," I said. "Max's day job is reupholstering ragged-out seats, just like these. If you ask him, he'll probably give you a good deal." I was only trying to make a joke, as I knew the ratty seats were part of the whole Blues Brothers schtick.

"Are you kidding? This car is a chick magnet! We don't need to do a thing to it," he said.

There was only one out to go. Bob took off his black hat, and Greg followed suit. Then Bob began to pray: "Heavenly Father, thank you for this glorious day and for all the many blessings you have bestowed on us. Thank you for the talents you have given us, and help us to perform up to our abilities. Keep us safe during our work and during our travels, and please watch over our loved ones back home. Help us to put on a show that is enjoyed by this crowd in Richmond, but most of all help us to know your will and to do it so that you, above all others, will be pleased by our actions. We ask this in the name of your son, our Lord Jesus Christ, Amen."

I said "Amen" right behind Bob and Greg and joined in when Bob led us in the Lord's Prayer.

Moments later, the Roosters were out in the bottom of the second, and it was show time! As "Peter Gunn" with its pulse-quickening beat blared over the P.A. system, Bob pealed off and we were through the gate and flying around the warning track. As we sped past the Crocodiles' bullpen, Greg climbed halfway out of the car and shouted, "WUZ UP!" Bob ran the car right through the middle of a big puddle in front of the third base grandstand, splashing muddy water towards three women who shrieked in horror. "We SOAKED 'em!" laughed Greg. Bob circled behind home plate and skidded the car to a halt in front of the Roosters' dugout. He and Greg jumped out and ran towards the grassy area behind home plate where their microphones and stands were suddenly waiting for them. With the Bluesmobile still rumbling in PARK, I watched them do their number through the back window of the car. Bob, that is Elwood, unhandcuffed himself from his brief case, opened the brief case, then removed his harmonica with a flourish. They sang and did some funky dancing and mike stand dipping to Sam and Dave's song "Soul Man." Towards the end of the number as Elwood played the harmonica, Jake ran over to the first base coaching box, swapped hats with pitcher J.T. Engstrom, and pushed J.T. into the car next to me.

When the number ended, Jake lingered to promise the crowd that he and Elwood would be back out for another song later in the game. The car was already pulling away, so Jake had to run to catch up with us. "ELWOOD, WAIT FOR ME!" he shouted, before he dove through the window into the moving car. The crowd ate it all up. To the alluringly sinister music of "Peter Gunn" again, we circled the ballpark in triumph before exiting through the gate in the right field corner. Elwood kept his left index finger high in the air the whole time, and Jake pounded on the side of the car like a maniac. When we passed the Rooster bull-pen the second time on our way off the field, J.T.'s teammates there pointed towards their comrade and howled with laughter. "This is so cool!" shouted a beaming J.T. Indeed, it was.

After my joy ride with Jake and Elwood, I reclaimed my seat in the McBride Stadium press box, where Don Tincher, a frizzy-haired former high school and college basketball coach, caught me up.

Although Don was essentially the beat man for the *Palladium-Item*, I hadn't met him until the night before. That's because Don often watched the game, not in the press box, but in the stands, just as the scribes in Chillicothe did; however, such informality was no reflection on the job turned in either by Don or his paper. Tincher took his work seriously, did it professionally, and was respected by everybody; and the *Palladium-Item* gave the Roosters great coverage. If the Richmond franchise ever failed, no one would be able to blame the failure on a lack of support from the local press.

I could see by the scoreboard that the Roosters were still hot and led 4–0 going into the bottom of the third. Tincher informed me that Mike Zerbe, DH-ing because of a bad hamstring, had staked Richmond to a 2–0 lead in the first by hitting his third dinger of the season; and that Jeremy Robinson, who'd started the game by whiffing five straight Crocodiles, was having no trouble making the lead hold up.

Off in the distance lightening periodically cracked the sky. One of the Canton players said, "Max, do you see that lightening over there?"

"Only half of it," said Max.

Max wasn't just trying to be funny. He was also saying that conditions didn't warrant a stoppage of play, yet. But then, with two outs in the top of the fourth and the score still 4–0, the skies opened up and let fall with a downpour of Old Testament proportions. Richmond players and coaches and office staff and interns, raced over to the fence past the Canton dugout in front of the beer gardens, and under the direction of Cate and Cindy Blunk grabbed the tarp, unrolled it, and spread it over the infield as effortlessly as if they were making a bed on a lazy Sunday morning.

It was a good thing that the extended Richmond grounds crew were so efficient because the rain continued to pound the field and, if anything, increased in intensity. Somebody asked how long we had to wait before the umpires could call the game, and the answer came back that a half hour wait minimum was a league rule. "Like all Frontier League rules, though, it's flexible," interjected David Knight. "I could come back in five minutes and tell you to drive home safely."

Ezra Firkins got ahold of Bob Masewicz in the Blues Brothers bus and asked him how the weather looked on radar. "It looks bad," said Bob.

"Yeah, but how bad is it?" pressed Ezra.

"I haven't seen anything this bad-looking since we were in San Antonio when they had that killer tornado."

It seemed impossible that the game could be resumed, and everyone began to assume that the umpires would call it shortly. An unidentified voice came over Troy Derengowski's walkie-talkie: "Knock, knock."

"Who's there?" said Troy.

"Bang."

"'Bang' what?"

"Bang the game."

The drain in the Roosters' dugout was partially clogged. Before anyone realized that, the water level began to rise so fast that the dugout had to be abandoned. Before long the water there was waist high.

Remarkably, few fans had left the ballpark, possibly because they would have gotten drenched trying to get to their cars but also because they were hoping to see the rest of the Blues Brothers' show, as well as the Roosters' anticipated victory. Fate relieved them of the former concern. The Blues Brothers had a rare off-day on Thursday and did not have another gig lined up until Friday, when they would rejoin the Crocodiles for a show in Canton. Like all the best acts, the Blues Brothers worked under guaranteed contracts—they got paid, rainout or no rainout—and they were under no obligation to stay over for another show—especially a show performed gratis—but that's exactly what Bob decided to do. Eventually, the downpour slowed to a hard rain which eventually slowed to a steady drizzle. At this point, Bob walked onto the field and announced that the Blues Brothers would be back tomorrow to perform a complete show. It was a gracious, classy thing to do. Of course, Greg felt that he needed to do something to reinforce the idea that the act was worth coming back for, so Jake Blues ran precariously around the bases and then made a whopper of a belly flop slide onto the tarp covering the home plate area, parting the water for ten yards like a steel-belted radial in a tire commercial.

As the drizzle slowed, it began to dawn on us that the game just might be resumed, as inconceivable as that had seemed a half hour earlier. Boredom was becoming a distinct possibility as we resigned ourselves to waiting out the rest of the delay.

I quickly learned to never underestimate the ability of young ballplayers to find a way to have fun in almost any circumstances. I wasn't expecting much when Troy announced over the P.A. that Phill Kojack and Bobby Chandler were going to do some imitations to entertain us, but there was no remote control to change the channel with.

As Chandler, the Roosters' pigeon-toed, high-waisted, hard-throwing closer with the made-for-Hollywood smile, walked towards home plate carrying a bat, Kojack, his cap turned sideways, headed towards the pitching mound. Kojack took one step up the hill, then tripped and fell flat on his face. It looked so unintentional it was impossible not to laugh, but Tincher told me he could have predicted it. "Kojack does that all the time," he said. "He tripped when he was about to be handed his high school diploma; he tripped at his college graduation; he trips in department stores and knocks the manikins all over the place. He's got a video of himself tripping during all the important occasions in his life. I've never seen it, but the other players say it's hilarious."

With Kojack standing upright on the mound peering towards the home plate area, we turned our attention towards Chandler, taking his batting stance. Holding the bat almost straight up, he took a fairly wide stance with both knees turned inwards a bit. "Sammy Sosa," announced Troy. Kojack wound up, lost his glove which flew backwards behind the mound, and threw an imaginary meatball towards home. Chandler took a mighty swing, dropped the bat carefully, took a couple of steps towards first, leaped into the air with his feet together, then spread his arms wide like an airplane while he made an abbreviated trip around imaginary bases. He leaped onto home plate triumphantly, then with his first two fingers tapped his lips a few times, tapped his heart a few more times, and finally made a "V" sign towards the grandstands.

Next up was Barry Bonds. Bending over to pick up an imaginary rosin bag, Kojack looked behind himself towards the first base grandstands and shook his rear end back and forth, eliciting squeals of delight from a group of teenaged girls who were watching his every move. Batting left-handed, Chandler kept his back foot planted in the batter's box but stepped out with his front foot. While still holding the bat, he adjusted his batting gloves; tugging several times first at the batting glove on his right hand, and then tugging several times at the glove on his left hand. Back in the box, he choked up on the bat and wiggled it impatiently, almost spastically. Kojack delivered, and then Chandler knocked it out of the park with a short, compact stroke. Pretending to circle the bases, Bobby aka "Barry" ran as if his feet were set in blocks of concrete; and after he crossed home plate, he sullenly pointed towards the grandstands as if he were putting a curse on his worst enemy.

"Rickey Henderson!" said Troy. Batting right-handed again, Chandler got into a crouch with his legs spread as far apart as they would go, yanked up both sleeves of his jersey, and lowered the bat over his shoulder level to the ground. After hitting a no-doubter, he contemptuously flipped the bat away from himself with both hands, indicating that nothing grander could ever be done with such an instrument again.

Batting last in this parade of pantomimed players was none other than the Bambino, Babe Ruth himself. He moved into place on little mincing steps. He tipped his cap to the crowd, tipped his cap, tipped his cap, tipped his cap. He took a wooden swing which nevertheless sent the old horsehide soaring, soaring into the night and out of sight, and then went into his affable home run trot, which was designed neither for showing off or for showing up somebody else. Those little mincing steps were taken quickly now, quickly, quickly, quickly, and as he rounded first, he tipped his cap again, tipped his cap, tipped his cap.

The whole thing was a wonderful performance, but the piece de resistance was the Babe Ruth bit, which was like watching an old grainy, silent, black & white newsreel from the 1920s come to life. I remembered Bob Masewicz and thought to myself that, although he was actually a Frontier League relief pitcher, for those moments we'd just witnessed, Bobby Chandler most definitely *was* Sammy Sosa, Barry Bonds, Rickey Henderson, and Babe Ruth.

The rain finally stopped completely, and the tarp was pulled off around 10:30. Bags and bags of Diamond Dry were emptied at home plate, on the mound, and around the bases, and a dozen rakers spread the stuff in an effort to make the field playable. Somebody unclogged the drain in the Roosters' dugout, and interns carried pickle buckets full of water to a drain behind the dugout to speed up the process. Everybody was in a hurry because radar showed that another storm cell was on its way.

With the delay approaching two hours, there was no chance that the Roosters' starter, Jeremy Robinson, was going to warm up again. Instead, John Cate went right to his closer, the talented imitator Bobby Chandler who took the mound as himself. When play resumed, Chandler got the final out of the fourth; and, after the Roosters added another run to make it 5–0, he also pitched a scoreless fifth, allowing nothing more than one base on balls. The rains came back in the bottom of the fifth with two out and two on. It wasn't the pounding rain of before, but it was hard enough to cause Max and Deron Brown to wave the players off the field.

I hustled down to field level and found Max standing in the doorway to his clubhouse, smoking a cigarette and looking bushed as he watched the Roosters' grounds crew, its former contingent reduced by half, make a half-hearted attempt to get the tarp on the field.

"Max, what's going on?" I said. "Two hours ago the Roosters busted ass getting the tarp on the field, and now they look like The Three Stooges trying to pitch a revival tent."

Max merely gazed at me wearily.

"If they don't hurry up and get that tarp spread out, there's no way this game is going to continue. The field just can't take any more water," I added. Home plate was already starting to puddle, and the grounds crew were still moving slower than Fred Sanford after a big meal.

"Unless ... Oh, I get it," I said. "Duh! It's already an official game, and they don't *want* to get the tarp on. ... I don't know what I was thinking. ... Why didn't you say something, Max?"

"I knew that you'd figure it out if I let you keep talking," he said.

"Well, even so, they aren't hustling at all. Shouldn't you or Deron make them at least try to get the field covered?"

"Nope. And I'll tell you why. Because if we were in Canton, they'd do the same exact thing over there."

Five minutes later Max made it official, and we didn't hear a peep from the Canton coaches or players as they scampered past us on their way to the visiting clubhouse, having dropped the first two games of the series.

Right before the game ended in the bottom of the fifth, Mike Zerbe had been involved in a memorable, if not, particularly significant play. Leading off the inning Zerbe hit a line drive over shortstop that got through the legs of center fielder Matt Griswold. Despite a pulled hamstring Mike was able to lumber safely into second and even to advance to third on a ground out to second. He pushed his luck though when Ryan Anholt hit a rocket to short. Eric Clement made a gutsy play staying with a tough in-between hop and fired home a bullet that reached catcher Shaun Argento just a split second before Zerbe plowed him over like a middle linebacker. Zerbe got to his feet instantaneously and continued running to the dugout, without waiting for Deron Brown's "Out" call, as if he'd scored the run. Zerbe and Argento saw each other later at Applebee's, the Roosters' post-game hangout. "That shit hurt," said Argento.

"Much respect," said Mike, as he raised his hands to bump fists with the Canton catcher.

We were beginning to think that Greg Walters had decided not to join us at The Wheel when he barged in, complaining about how much trouble he'd had getting a cab after the game. His complaint set up one of our regulars for the best line of the night.

Greg had kept us laughing almost non-stop for about an hour, when apropos of nothing at all, he blurted out, "I know, let's get a hooker!"

"And you think it's tough to find a cab in Richmond," said David Knight.

As part of their act, the Blues Brothers had intermittently broadcast sound bites from the movie over the P.A. system during the game and the long rain delay:

"They're not going to catch us. We're on a mission from God." (Elwood)

"This money is for the year's assessment on the St. Helen of the Blessed Shroud Orphanage in Calumet City, Illinois," (Elwood). "Five thousand bucks. ... It's all there, pal." (Jake)

They didn't use my favorite lines from the movie, but Max did. After we'd done our duty at The Wheel, Max backed the Buick into the street and let it idle in neutral for a moment. Staring straight ahead, he repeated the immortal words of Elwood Blues: "We're a hundred and six miles from Chicago; we have a full tank of gas and a half a pack of cigarettes. It's dark, and we're wearing sunglasses."

As I pointed forward, I uttered Jake's response: "Hit it."

The next day, for the series wrap-up with Canton, I drove over to Richmond without Max, but accompanied by my son Nolan and his other best buddy, a crew-cut kid and all-around good athlete named Michael Spears. I gave them a couple of bucks, told them to behave themselves, and turned them loose.

I ran into Mike Zerbe heading onto the field for BP and told him that I'd missed his home run the night before because I'd been kidnapped by the Blues Brothers. I said that I was happy for him that the Roosters got the game in so the home run counted. "I heard it was a tape measure job too," I added.

"It went pretty far," he said. "Hit the volleyball court across the street. That wasn't my longest though. Last year I hit one that landed in the middle of the Little League diamond, on the other side of the volleyball courts."

"Wow! How did you know it went that far?"

"A Little Leaguer saw it when it hit and brought it to the game the next night for me to sign."

"Did you give the kid a new ball and get the home run ball for your trophy case?"

"No," he said frowning. "I'd never do that. I wouldn't ask a kid to take a substitute ball. It wouldn't be the same. Besides, the memory is enough for me."

During batting practice I finally got a chance to talk with Duke Ward. Duke was a tall dude with a wild mustache and a bowling pin figure. Although he was balding on top, his blond hair was long and curly on the sides. Duke was the easiest member of the Roosters' management team to find. He maintained his station in the busy area between the home team dugout and the first base grandstands so steadfastly that the Roosters might as well have put up a sign designating the space as "Duke Ward's Office." Like John Cate and more than two dozen other minority stock holders, Duke owned a small slice of the team. He also had a number of other business interests—he owned a record store, a commercial janitorial service, and a property management company. Nevertheless, I wasn't at all surprised to learn how much time he spent on the Roosters on game days: "six or seven hours minimum with phone time."

I found Duke to be very knowledgeable and passionate about both the Roosters and the Frontier League as a whole, but what impressed me the most was his take on the city of Richmond, his adopted home, which he moved to "on purpose."

"I grew up in Houston, Texas," he said, "but I didn't like it there. I wanted to move away because I was sick of the South and sick of big cities. Richmond is the best of both worlds. In a lot of ways it's like a small town, yet it's only an hour's drive from three major metropolitan areas. People here complain about having to drive an hour to get to Indianapolis, but in Houston I had to drive an hour just to get from one side of town to another. The main thing, though, is that I feel safe in Richmond. I can walk around the neighborhood at three A.M. and don't have to carry a gun to protect myself.

"There are so many murders in Houston that it's no big deal there anymore. In Richmond, a murder is front-page news for three days. And I *want* it to be front-page news for three days!"

The Roosters won again, 5–4, to sweep the Crocodiles. It was their fourth straight victory, got them closer to .500 at 6–8, and enabled them to climb out of the East Division cellar over Canton. Aaron Sledd, with two doubles and a home run, and Mike Zerbe led the Rooster attack. Zerbe went hitless in two trips to the plate, but it was his seventh-inning sacrifice fly which produced the game-winning RBI.

Nolan and Michael had a big time, as I knew they would. Before the game, towards the end of BP, they walked up to me and Duke Ward with their tee shirts, like nets full of fish, pulled out in front of them and bulging with baseballs they'd found beyond the right field wall. Conscious of every Frontier League team's need to watch their pennies and a little worried at how the boys' scavenging might look, I began to explain to them that they might have to return the balls to the Roosters for batting practice use. Duke graciously waved away my trepidations and told the boys they were welcome to keep their hauls.

I've never been able to lavish a lot of money on my children, but

I've tried to compensate for that in other ways. Thanks to the Blues Brothers, I was able to give Nolan an automobile ride he'll never forget.

In the bus before the game Bob and Greg tried to make Nolan feel like one of the gang, which means they harassed the hell out of him.

"How old are you, Nolan?" asked Bob.

"Eleven," Nolan said. It was the last answer he was able to articulate.

"Yeah? ... Have you got a girlfriend? ... Have you got a boyfriend! ...What sports do you play? ... Where were you last night? Come on, quick! Come up with an answer!!!"

"Nolan, do you know what to do?" asked Greg. "Did your dad show you the dance steps you have to do? ... Hey, you know what you ought to do tonight, Nolan? Go up to a hot chick in the stands and yell 'You are so hot!' Then grab her and pull her down and make out with her. You're under 18; you can get away with it."

"Do it now, when you still can," advised Bob.

"Yeah, I wish I knew when I was your age what you can get away with when you're young," said Greg.

Ezra Firkins came over the walkie-talkie and said, "Eight outs remaining. Eight outs remaining." A few minutes later he was back, saying, "Nine outs remaining. Nine outs remaining."

"Max must have stayed out too late last night," said Greg. "He's giving 'em an extra out!"

Nolan and I were sitting in the backseat of the Bluesmobile just outside the right field gate. I was sitting on the driver's side behind Bob, while Nolan was behind Greg on the passenger side. We had been talking about baseball team mascots, and I ventured the opinion that even the lamest of them were at least enjoyed by the little kids.

Bob agreed saying, "Our contact in Omaha once told me, 'You could dress a guy up in a turd suit, and the kids would still come around him for autographs.'"

Greg instantly envisioned how such a scenario would play out: "'Mom, that guy gave me a piece of shit.' 'That's nice, Honey. Just don't bring it into the house.'"

The last couple of outs were taking forever to complete. Looking out of the car to his right, Greg noticed that we were being watched by a little girl and two young boys, standing on a foot bridge that crossed over the creek running behind the ballpark. Greg jumped out of the car, ran towards the kids, and shouted "WAZ UP!!!"

Although Greg got no reaction from the kids, Nolan and I laughed at his antics.

Greg bent over, picked up some pebbles, and pretended to throw the rocks at the kids. "Get outta here. Go on, get outta here," he said.

Nolan and I laughed at this too, but again the kids didn't budge and gazed at Greg impassively.

Talking to Ezra over the walkie-talkie, Bob said, "I'm going to say, 'For all you beer drinkers, please drink responsibly. That means to hold your beer cup with two hands.'"

Back in the car, Greg tried once more with the three interlopers, snorting at them like a pig. This finally brought a faint smile to the face of the little girl.

"Aren't you supposed to be doing something?" Greg said.

"No. Aren't you?" was the comeback from the suddenly emboldened little girl.

"No. We just sit here for hours ... in black polyester."

The third out of the bottom of the second was finally made, and, with "Peter Gunn" blaring over the P.A. system, we were rolling towards the right field gate.

"Don't worry, Nolan. Only three people have been killed while riding in the back seat of this car when it crashed," I said.

Greg turned around and said, "We've never crashed! ... on purpose."

We didn't crash, of course, but this ride was different than the one I'd enjoyed the night before. As we roared past the Canton bullpen in the left field foul ground, one of the Crocodile pitchers ran up close to the Bluesmobile with a king-sized plastic beer cup full of water and flung it towards Greg in the front seat. In an instant, Nolan was dripping from head to toe. "Dad, I got soaked!" he said laughing.

Greg turned around and said, "That's the third time that's happened. Whenever I see a player with a cup of water, I dive down on the seat towards Bob."

I was laughing too. In fact, we were practically worn out laughing from being around the Blues Brothers. "You took one for the team, son," I said.

After the game, in the nearly empty McBride Stadium parking lot, Nolan, Michael, and I sat for a moment with the van in neutral. Staring straight ahead, I said, "We're a hundred and six miles from Cincinnati; we've got a half a tank of gas and a van full of baseballs. It's dark and we're not wearing sunglasses."

Looking at me as if I'd lost my mind, Nolan and Michael said, "Huh?"

It was time, I realized, to head back to the video store.

6

Of Paints and Dragons I Sing

MAX NOW HAD ANOTHER, longer break from the Frontier League, which was going to last until July 5th, when he was supposed to start a series in Canton against Chillicothe. That meant that he would miss the next three series in Richmond, when the Roosters were scheduled to host the Evansville Otters, Dubois County Dragons, and Chillicothe Paints. As the league supervisor of umpires for Richmond, Max was sensitive to the wrong impression players can get when they see the same umpires on every visit to a particular opposing team's ballpark; and he was deliberately absenting himself from Richmond for a time in order to prevent such an impression from forming. Max was also trying to give his protégés as much Frontier League experience as possible; so that when he retired from umpiring and moved on to full-time assigning, his stable would be full and his horses ready to run.

That didn't mean that he was going to be on vacation. No way. He was going to be working harder than ever.

From June 16 through July 5, Max was going to be doing two big American Legion tournaments in Lima and Marietta, Ohio, as well as a number of Great Lakes League games. And it didn't hurt that working so many amateur games in such a short period of time meant some extra money in his pocket. When Max worked a Legion doubleheader (two sevens) and a Great Lakes Game, he pulled in $155 for the day. On a few occasions he even did double-header double duty (a pair of Legion games plus a pair of Great Lakes games) when his take for the day grew to $180.

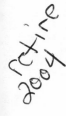

Of course, even without Max, the Frontier League season went on. In fact, two of the most important things in the history of the league happened during Max's absence, and neither involved an actual Frontier League game.

On Tuesday, June 20, the first alumnus in Frontier League history graduated to the major leagues, and it wasn't Morgan Burkhart.

Brian Tollberg, a righthanded pitcher who'd begun his professional career with the Chillicothe Paints, became the first player to put the stamp of legitimacy on the Frontier League when he made his major league debut for the San Diego Padres against the Arizona Diamondbacks. His appearance in the game validated the vision of the league's founders, the faith of the league's owners, the allegiance of the league's hard-core fans, and all the hard work that everyone associated with the league had put in for nearly a decade. Most of all, it rejuvenated the players still in the league and, like a game-winning home run by a slumping slugger, lifted their spirits, if only for a while, over the wall of skepticism and long odds they faced every day.

None of this had been on the mind of Tollberg when he first toed the rubber at Bank One Ballpark in Phoenix on July 20, as he wasn't even aware of the added significance of his debut. "I didn't realize I was the first Frontier Leaguer to make it until Bill Lee called to congratulate me. I think that's great," he told John Wend in a phone interview, after holding the D-Backs to one hit over seven innings and picking up the victory in the Padres' 3–1 win.

What seemed to be an extra justification for hope among current Frontier League players was the fact that Tollberg had not been a superstar for Chillicothe. It was encouraging to think that he'd had a merely good year for the Paints in 1994, compiling a 7–4 record with a 2.83 ERA. That good year had been enough to get Tollberg noticed and signed by the Milwaukee Brewers. Given a chance, Brian used pinpoint control and an effective change-up, the same weapons his success in the Frontier League had been based on, to move steadily through the Brewers' and Padres' farm systems. At the time of his callup, which came after 102 minor league starts, he had been 6–0 with a 2.83 ERA for the Padres' Triple-A club, the Las Vegas Stars. Tollberg's promotion to the big leagues proved the premise upon which the Frontier League had been founded: as good as they are, as thorough as they try to be, scouts overlook players with the ability to play in the major leagues. It does happen. And, in fact, it happens all the time.

Case in point: before Frontier League aficionados from London, Ontario, to O'Fallon, Missouri, could get used to the idea of having an ex–Frontier League player in the big leagues, debut lightening struck again for the second time in a week. To replace outfielder Trot Nixon

who went on the DL with a bad hamstring, the Boston Red Sox called
Morgan Burkhart up from Pawtucket, where the switch-hitting former
Richmond Rooster had been hitting .283 with 17 homers and 54 RBI.
To no one's surprise, Burkhart too immediately showed that he belonged
in the big leagues, singling in his first at bat against the Orioles' Mike
Mussina, one of the best pitchers in baseball. Burkhart was later walked
intentionally in the same game, although not with the bases loaded.

Even without the prospect of getting to watch Max umpire, by the
end of the month I had to get to a Frontier League game. I was hooked.
Wednesday, June 28, was an off day, but on Thursday Nolan and I
drove over to Chillicothe to watch the opener of a series between the
Paints and the Johnstown Johnnies.
I immediately headed for the press box. Two Paints players, Andy
Lee and infielder Chris Dickerson, were already there, in uniform, seek-
ing to get new music they'd selected as their introductory songs approved
by John Wend and Aaron Lemaster.
"Hey, Andy, how many starts have you had since the no-hitter?" I
asked.
"Three."
"How have you been doing?"
"I haven't given up an earned run since my first start of the season."
Wondering how close he'd come to duplicating Johnny Vander
Meer's double no-hitter feat, I said, "How long did you go before you
gave up a hit in the game after the no-hitter?"
"I gave up a hit to the first batter. I had him 0–2, but he stuck his
bat out and blooped one down the right field line."
"We looked at each other in the press box and went, 'There goes
the suspense,'" said John.
After Lee and Dickerson left, John told me that he and Aaron had
to carefully scrutinize the music the players wanted to use because many
of them favored inappropriate heavy metal that John likened unto
"satanic rock." Dickerson hadn't even wanted his own song but was in
a slump and superstitiously felt that adopting one might change his
luck. He'd picked out "Seek and Destroy" by Metallica, the Paints'
favorite band.
John and Aaron were still excited about Brian Tollberg's recent
major league debut, and John informed me that it had been even more
smashing than I'd realized. Tollberg had beaten the Reds in Cincinnati
in his second start and been named National League Player of the Week.
Not bad for a rookie who'd started his pro baseball career in Chillicothe,
Ohio.
There were also personnel changes for me to catch up on. Gone

were catcher Wes Brooks; pitchers Rip Fleming, Eric Bentley, and Matt
Buirley; outfielder Mick Celli; and first baseman Dave Masterson. Celli
and Masterson had been in the starting lineup on Opening Day but were
let go because of their insufficient contributions to the offense. "You
get about two weeks to prove you can hit," John told me. Fleming and
Bentley had both been released because they'd had arm problems, but
Buirley had been signed by the Cincinnati Reds and immediately dis-
patched to their Double-A farm team in Dayton, Ohio. The Reds had
discovered Buirley by accident when one of their scouts had come to
Chillicothe to watch the Paints' number two starter, Josh White, pitch.
The Reds were still interested in White, but John surmised that a gentlemen's agreement between the Reds and the Paints prohibited the
Reds from taking any more of the Paints' pitchers until later in the season. At least John was hoping that that was the case. "Our number one
starter, Byrd, is hurt—he has a bad elbow. If we lose our number two
starter, White, or our number three, Andy Lee, we'll be in big trouble.
Hell, we're in a pennant race." Even having lost their last two games,
the Paints were in first place in the East Division, one game ahead of
London and Johnstown.

The six new Paints were pitchers Rick Blanc and Jamie Detillion,
catcher Josh Lamberg, infielder Joey Choron, and outfielders Justin
Graham and Matt McCay. All were rookies except for Choron and Blanc.
Choron, who had played for Chillicothe in 1999, had an outstanding year
for the University of South Alabama as a junior. He entered his senior
year as a pre-season Division I third-team All-American, but a knee injury
cut short his season. Blanc too had been a Paint before, in 1998, but
the slightly built righthander had spent 1999 in the Northern League
with the Sioux Falls Canaries. Rick had started 2000 in the independent
Western League with the Yuma Bull Frogs. He'd stayed around long
enough to strike out former major league slugger Kevin Mitchell, playing for the Sonoma County Crushers, but he didn't like the Western
League. He'd called Roger Hanners and said, "Have you got a spot for
a pitcher?"

"Would the spot be for you?" Roger asked.

"Yeah, it's for me," he said.

"When can you be here?" came the reply.

Nolan came up to the press box for some hot dog money, and after
he left John asked me what his favorite sport was. I told John that
although at the moment Nolan preferred football, it was obvious to me
that his future as an athlete lay in basketball since I was certain Nolan
was destined to be 6' 7" or 6' 8". This reminded John of a story about
a kid he'd once coached in football named Little John Coker.

"Coker was called 'Little John' because his dad, who'd been an All-

American football player at Oregon State, was known as 'Big John Coker,'" said Wend. "Anyway, I was twenty-two years old when I was coaching this eighth grade football team. Little John Coker was on my team, and he didn't like to hit anybody, and he didn't want anybody hitting him.

"His daddy showed up at practice one day, and I thought, 'Uh, oh, he's gonna ask me why I'm not playing his kid more.'

"I felt this giant bear claw of a hand grab me by the shoulder, and I thought, 'Here it comes.'

"'Hello, Coach,' he said.

"'Hello, Mr. Coker.' I said.

"'My boy doesn't like this game, does he?'

"'No, sir, he doesn't.'

"'Well, don't throw him to the wolves,' he said.

"'Whew!' I went to myself.

"I was in the Army during Vietnam, and when I came out of the service in 1967, I went to a high school football game in Nelsonville in Athens County. There was this big tight end playing a helluva game, and so I asked somebody, 'Who's that kid?'

"'John Coker, Jr.'

"'That's Little John Coker! Well, I'll be a son-of-a-gun,' I said. Little John went on to play tight end at Oklahoma State, and he's now a dentist in Dayton."

After John finished his "You never know" story, I told him how impressed I was with the team's constant promotional efforts. It was Wendy's Baseball Card Night, and on the way into VA Memorial I had been given a set of the cards. It was a glossy, high-quality 27-card set, that included cards of Roger Hanners, his coaches Marty Dunn and Jamie Keefe, "Clubbie" Aaron Queen, and mascot Chief Krazy Horse. My comment about promotions reminded John of another story, this one about a popular Cincinnati radio comic named Gary Burbank.

"Burbank comes to Chillicothe once a year to promote his afternoon drive time radio show on WLW, which we can pick up here in Ross County," said John. "He always comes out to VA Memorial, and we treat him like a celebrity; let him throw out the first pitch of the game, stuff like that. One time I introduced him to this lady who said she was his biggest fan, and Burbank said, 'I have to apologize: I'm usually taller than this.'

"He came up to the booth to announce a few batters and said, 'How many do you want me to do?'

"I said, 'I don't care. Do however many you want to do.'

"So he says, 'What's the name of the team, again?'

"'The Ohio Valley Red Coats.'

"As you know, Burbank has five or six characters he plays, and the bits he does with them are hysterical. Probably his most famous character is the red neck guy he calls Earl Pitts. So he gets into his Earl Pitts voice and says, 'Now battin' for the Ohigher Valley Rednecks is Tyrone Williams.'

"And of course the batter was a black kid. He looked up at the press box along with everybody else.

"Then Burbank says, 'Tyrone? ... What kind of a name is *that* for a redneck!'

"The kid had to back out of the batter's box, he was laughing so hard."

John was off and running now, and I was happy to let him continue to spin out the stories. "The best celebrity guest we've ever had was Pete Rose," he said. "Pete was here in 1997 to speak at a luncheon during the season, and he came out to the ballpark after lunch to watch batting practice. As you know, you have to pass two big prisons to reach VA Memorial. Pete said, 'I saw those prisons and was a little worried there for a minute that you guys brought me into town to keep me here.'

"During BP Pete was leaning on the cage joking around with everybody. Scott Pinoni, our big home run hitter, was batting, and Scott was spraying the ball to all fields.

"Pete said, 'Hey, Big Boy, betcha can't hit one out.'

"Pinoni said, 'Excuse me.'

"Rose said, 'I bet you can't hit one over the fence.'

"Scott hit the next pitch over the trees behind the left field fence. Rose looked at me and said, 'That's not the first bet I've lost!'

"Part of the deal we made with Pete was that he was to sign two autographs for everybody at the luncheon. The luncheon was sold out, of course: 230 people plus the players. They brought the players into the room to see Pete first, before the luncheon started, because they wouldn't have time to stick around like everybody else. Now, we were in first place at the time by seven or eight games.

"The first five or six guys to come into the room were all white. And Pete shook their hands and listened to them tell him their names. The next three guys to come in were black: Mitch House, Jackie Jempson, and Danny Collins.

"Pete smiled and said, 'I knew there had to be some brothers on this team for you guys to be in first place.' And the black guys just loved that!"

"Aaron, have you picked out the Beer Batter, yet?" asked John.

"Yeah. Let's go with Vanrobays, Johnstown's catcher," said Aaron. "He's only struck out seven times in 50 at bats coming into tonight's game."

Ah ha, I thought, the fan-friendly Paints were generous with their offer to sell beer at half price for the rest of the inning if the Chillicothe pitcher struck out the Beer Batter during the designated at bat, but they weren't stupid about it.

When I told John that Max wasn't scheduled to work the series with Johnstown, his thoughts raced back to the previous homestand against the Cook County Cheetahs. "Those guys were out of control," he said. "I wish Max would have been here. Max would have thrown out about three of 'em the first night. You know, Ron LeFlore manages that ballclub." I did know that and I was looking forward to meeting LeFlore, the ex-con who had turned his life around and become a star in the major leagues with the Detroit Tigers and Montreal Expos after being given a tryout, while still a convict, by Billy Martin.

"He was a nice guy in the dugout before the game—he was joking around and everything—but during the games he was a jerk. And his players were even worse. They bitched the whole series," said John. "In the first game, after their third baseman, Sanchez, took a called third strike, he threw his bat and his helmet back to the screen. He pitched a fit at home plate, walked halfway back to the dugout, turned around, and hollered some more. That's an automatic ejection in any league, but the ump just took it.

"One of their outfielders, Brandon Pollard, I think it was, he did the same thing. Argued at home on a called third strike. And they were both good calls. They looked like cock shots from here.

"In the second game Sanchez tried to steal second with Cook County down by three runs with two outs in the ninth. He was out, and it wasn't even close. He got up and bitched about that, started cussing out the ump.

"Then in the third game Jason Baker hit a home run his first time up. He hit it right down the left field line and couldn't tell if it was going to stay fair. Nobody could. He waved at it like Carlton Fisk did in the World Series, saw it go out fair, and ran around the bases. Well, LeFlore didn't like that.

"His second time up he hit one even farther. It went high into the trees over the scoreboard. It was like a golf shot, and he stopped and watched it for a moment a few feet from home plate. He wasn't pimping it; he just couldn't believe he hit one that far. But there was no way he was pimping—he's the most religious kid on the team, the one who leads the prayer service on Sunday mornings in the clubhouse. And when they collect the fines from Kangaroo Court for a big party at the end of the season, Baker is the one who holds the money—he's the only one they all trust. And he plays the violin, for Pete's sake. ... You should have heard him play the "Star-Spangled Banner" before the game on Opening Day. It was beautiful.

PISS-POOR - FUCK'D UMPIRES!

"Anyway, when he got around to third base, LeFlore jumped all over him and was jabbing his finger at him. They tried to hit the next batter, Chris Poulsen. We know they tried to hit him because they threw behind him. Their second baseman Mike Davis started running his mouth too. Well, Byrd, who was coaching at first base, defended the Paints—Byrd's got a hot temper anyway—and he got into it with Davis. Byrd actually started onto the field after Davis, but fortunately the ump grabbed him before he could get very far. I'm telling you, I have never seen a display like that, and it's absolutely unbelievable that none of the Cook County players got tossed. The only good thing about the series is that we beat 'em two out of three. I wish we had swept 'em."

WELL THE UMPIRE FINALLY GOT HIS HEAD OUT OF HIS ASS.

The game turned out to be a doozy, as exciting a game as you could ask for on any level. I don't think his new song had anything to do with it, but Chris Dickerson did break out of his slump by hitting a solo home run over the left field wall in the second inning. You could tell instantly that it was gone by the way it took off and by the sound. In the top of the third Paints' starter Josh White made the beer drinkers in the ballpark happy by finding a way to strike out Vanrobays, the good contact hitter.

The Paints got another run in the third, but Johnstown tied it up with a pair of runs in the fourth. Chillicothe immediately retook the lead in the bottom of the inning with a clutch two-out single to left by Mike Horning, the Paints' baby-faced second baseman. In his third year with the team, Horning was extremely popular with his teammates. He was a heady player who made the most of his abilities, and he'd actually made the East Division All-Star team in 1999, but he didn't have much power or speed. "Roger wants to cut him every year," said John Wend, "Every spring he says, 'We've got to find a second baseman.' But he always winds up keeping Horning because he loves him so much."

White held Johnstown at bay as he worked into the eighth, but with Johnstown third baseman David Ferres on first and two out and the Paints still clinging to a 3–2 lead, Roger Hanners relieved him; and not with a pitcher out of the bullpen but with his designated hitter, Jason Baker. I was surprised at this move, but Aaron Lemaster explained that Baker, after beginning his pro career in the Dodgers farm system as an outfielder, had converted to a relief pitcher for two seasons before deciding that he wanted to switch back to hitting in order to play every day. In this light the move made some sense, especially taking into consideration the fact that, as Aaron said, "He throws 92 miles per hour." The rules covering the DH made the move additionally risky though. By sending Baker to the mound, the Paints would lose their DH; and if Baker was replaced by another pitcher, that pitcher would have to hit for himself.

Baker ran into trouble immediately. Johnnies first baseman Gabe Memmert singled to right, and then Mike Horning booted DH Trevor Mosely's grounder to load the bases. Left fielder Dan Morse stepped into the batter's box with the game on the line. Baker started Morse off with a beautiful curveball that buckled Morse's knees. Jim Schaly started to raise his right arm to signal a strike but didn't. Immediately Roger Hanners started walking towards the plate, and immediately Schaly pointed Hanners back to the dugout. Roger didn't stop, so Schaly ordered him back to the dugout again. When Hanners kept coming, Schaly pulled off his mask and gave the Paints' manager the old heave-ho. Roger made a few comments and then left rather quietly. One pitch later Schaly threw Stephen Byrd out of the game too.

Baker wound up walking Morse which forced in Ferres with the tying run. Acting manager Marty Dunn then brought in Woody Fullenkamp to face Vanrobays. With more than half-priced beer riding on the outcome, Woody walked the Johnstown catcher on five pitches, and the Johnnies led 4–3. Woody struck out shortstop Eliott Sarabia to end the inning, but the damage had been done. The Paints had given up the tying and go-ahead runs via an error and two walks, with two outs.

Johnstown starter Joel Filipek gave up ten hits and walked two in his eight innings of work, but he had the lead when he handed over the ballgame to John Lewter to start the bottom of the ninth.

Catcher Chris Poulsen, 0–3 on the night, was scheduled to lead off for the Paints, but Marty Dunn sent up rookie Josh Lamberg as a pinch hitter in Poulsen's place. A couple of weeks earlier the Paints had sent for Lamberg, sight unseen, when they found themselves in need of catching help and didn't know where else to turn. "Hey, Roger, remember that big kid from the University of Richmond who faxed us his resume?" Aaron Lemaster had said to the Paints' manager.

At 6' 4" and 230 pounds, Lamberg was the biggest player on either team, but he didn't look much like a ballplayer. His uniform hung on him sloppily as if he were wearing pajamas a size too large, and his awkward movements reminded one more of a rambunctious puppy than a seasoned pro. However, the Jewish Lamberg was full of moxie and not intimidated by the situation. He took a vicious cut at a Lewter fastball and missed. "He should be starting," said Aaron. "He's five for eleven since we picked him up. The pitchers like Poulsen receiving, but Lamberg can hit." The count went to 2–1, and then Lamberg took another mighty cut and missed. Whatever Lewter threw next was the wrong pitch because Lamberg jumped all over it. He completely crushed the ball and sent it in an instant high into the dark trees beyond the left field fence. "I told you he could hit!" shouted Lemaster above the happy applause of the crowd and the song "Celebrate" coming over the P. A. system.

The fans could smell a victory now, and the Paints almost ended the game right there. They loaded the bases after two were out on singles by Justin Graham and Mike Cervenak and a walk to Joe Colameco, but Chance Melvin grounded out to short to end the threat. The hit by Cervenak was somewhat questionable. It was a soft liner hit right back to the pitcher, which Lewter dropped and could not pick up in time to throw Cervenak out at first. "Should I give him a hit on that?" asked John Wend, who was acting as official scorer in place of Aaron.

"Does he need it?" I asked.

"Yeah. He's got no hits tonight. He's 0–3 with a walk."

The decision was more important than usual because Cervenak had a 21-game hitting streak on the line.

"Then, yeah. Give him a hit. For whatever reason, the pitcher was obviously fooled by the ball." And so, Cervenak's streak continued.

As the fans settled in for extra innings, John made an unscheduled announcement over the P. A.: "Attention: There's a little boy in the press box named Jake who says his daddy is lost."

After batting, Lamberg had to stay in the game and catch, and, as things turned out, Chris Poulsen was probably glad that he did.

The game remained tied at four heading into the twelfth inning. Johnstown's hard-nosed, veteran right fielder Kirk Taylor was on second with two outs when pinch hitter Matt Kuseski dropped a soft base hit in front of Paints' left fielder Justin Graham.

Graham charged in, scooped the ball, and fired a seed to Lamberg standing in front of the plate. Lamberg caught the perfect throw chest high in the air; and a second later Taylor, who'd been running all the way with the hit, slammed into the big catcher, knocking him to the ground. When the dust settled, the prone Lamberg pulled the ball from his mitt and, with Taylor still laying on his legs, showed it to Schaly, who made a dramatic "OUT!" call. The fired-up Lamberg bounced up, showed the ball to Taylor, and then spiked the ball over his shoulder for emphasis before turning and heading for the dugout. After the game Lamberg spoke like a veteran about the play, giving all the credit to his teammate: "I didn't have to do anything but hold onto the ball. Kuseski hit that little fly and I knew it was going to fall. Graham threw it right on the money. I couldn't have asked for a better throw." Asked about his gesture towards Taylor, he said, "He gave me a pretty good shot, so I figured, 'Here's one for you.'"

Ben Gerkin singled to open the bottom of the twelfth—it was his first hit of the season in 13 at bats—and then Chris Dickerson walked. That brought pitcher Ryan Sawyers to the plate, by necessity. Because they lost their designated hitter position in the eighth inning when

Jason Baker came in to pitch, the Paints' pitchers had been in the batting order ever since, and now there were no more pinch hitters to call off the bench. Sawyers, the Paints' sixth pitcher of the game, hadn't picked up a bat since his college days at West Virginia Wesleyan, but he was able to get down a sacrifice bunt that moved the runners up to second and third. With first base open, Johnstown manager Mike Moore walked Lamberg intentionally to set up the double play.

Baseball games between well-matched teams often work themselves out key play by key play and come down to a conclusion that has the same feel of inevitability as the ending to a chess match between weary but unyielding grand masters. And so, this marathon contest wound down to one more crucial, possibly final, confrontation. It pitted hard-throwing Jim Stuart, a new acquisition not listed on the Johnstown roster found in the program sold at VA Memorial, against Mike Horning, the second baseman who clung to the Paints like a stray cat that wouldn't take a hint and move on.

Every player in a Paints uniform besides the four on the field were standing at the fence in front of the home team dugout, cheering on Horning, who took Stuart's first pitch for a ball.

The crowd came to their feet and started clapping in unison. Stuart fired in another fastball that sailed high and away. Horning checked his swing: Ball two.

If Horning felt pressed to make up for his error that had helped Johnstown take the lead which caused the extra innings, he didn't let it affect his judgment at the plate. He took another pitch: Ball three.

Now all the pressure was definitely on Stuart. This game, just as life itself almost always does, had lasted long enough for its potential goat to get a chance to redeem himself. Stuart took a deep breath, rocked, and fired. Tenacious, sagacious, patient Mike Horning took ball four, dropped his loaded but unfired Louisville Slugger, and trotted happily down to first base with the game-winning RBI to his credit, as his teammates swarmed Ben Gerkin at home plate.

The next morning Max checked in over the telephone. After I told him about Schaly's ejection of Roger Hanners, he said, "Who else did he get?"

"Byrd," I said. "How'd you know there was somebody else?"

"Jim always gets 'em in pairs. He says that all the time: 'If I throw one out, it's gonna be two. I always eject 'em in pairs.'"

"Hey, Max, is it possible that you could get through this Frontier League season without throwing somebody out of the game?"

"No," he said simply.

Max answered so confidently that I assumed there were Frontier

6. Of Paints and Dragons I Sing   147

League ejections in his past. There were, but only two of them. These I had to hear about. Who in the world, I thought, would act up enough to deserve getting thumbed out of a baseball game by a one-eyed umpire who had the guts to do the job, especially when that umpire was Max?

"The first Frontier League player I threw out was a black kid who played center field for London," said Max. "I can't remember his name, but he could run like a scalded dog, and he was a good ballplayer. He got picked up by somebody in affiliated ball near the end of the season, and by then we were good friends. Anyway, I called a third strike he didn't like, and he started to draw a line with his bat to show me how far outside the pitch was. I told him, 'Don't draw a line,' but he went ahead anyway. 'You're gone!' I said.

"Andy McCauley, the London manager, didn't argue about it, but he asked me, 'Max, why did you run him so fast?'

"I said, 'Andy, he didn't just draw a line, he dug a trench you could plant corn in!'

"My second ejection happened last year in Richmond when I threw a guy out for accusing me of being a homer. That's essentially what he did. It started the night before when Deron Brown was the home plate umpire. Dubois County had this new catcher who'd only been with the Dragons about a week, and he showed Deron up all night by turning around and arguing pitches. I told Deron at The Wheel, 'I'm not trying to run your game, but you should have run that guy. He was an ass. If I can see it, everybody in the stands can see it. I guarantee you, now I'll have to run him tomorrow night.'

"Well, the next night the first time the Richmond batters came up, they were talking to me at home plate: 'Hey, Max. How's it going? How you doing? How's the season going for you?' Stuff like that. The players on both teams were doing it, but this new guy didn't know that. He thought I only umpired Richmond's games and that I was friends with only the Richmond players. He turned around on me in the second inning, so I told him, 'Hey, if you want to talk to me, you keep looking straight ahead at the flag pole in center field.' I didn't hear much out of him after that until the seventh inning when there was a pitch he wanted and didn't get. He turned around and said, 'Boy, you sure are pretty close to the guys on this team.'

"Deron Brown knew what was going on, and he told the Dragons' first baseman, a guy they called Iceman, 'Uh oh, Max is getting pissed.' Iceman said, 'No, no he isn't. I've never seen Max get mad on a baseball field.' Just as he said that ... BOOM!

"I said, 'Oh, yeah? Well, for your information, there's six or seven guys on your team I know better than anybody on Richmond's team, and you'll never get to know me as well as those six or seven guys do, especially tonight!' I stepped back, pointed at his back, and threw him out. 'Number 35 … You're gone!' He didn't even see me do it.

"After the game the guys on his team explained things to him at The Wheel."

I knew without even asking Jim Schaly why he had tossed Roger Hanners. Technically, you are not ever allowed to argue balls and strikes. You can do it, but you have to do it the right way, and you can only do so much of it. One thing you definitely can't do is leave the dugout and walk out to home plate in the middle of an at bat to argue balls and strikes. Not with an experienced, no-nonsense umpire like Jim Schaly.

The thing that amazed me was how fast Schaly reacted. Roger took only one step before Schaly warned him to get back into the dugout. How did Jim even know that Roger was coming out? Is his peripheral vision that good? Perhaps Jim was looking in that direction because the Paints were chirping over the call, or maybe it was because he knew he'd looked indecisive in starting to raise his arm and then changing his mind. In either case, he knew instantly he wasn't going to allow the Paints' manager to come out to home plate and argue with him, and he knew instantly as well what to do to stop him.

I didn't know what Roger Hanners had been thinking though, so I asked him before Friday night's game.

"I felt he blew the call," said Roger. "It was a crucial situation in the game. We wound up walking the batter and it hurt us. And I was upset about some earlier calls too. My players were upset with the calls, and I wanted to support them. I hadn't been thrown out yet this season; in fact, I hadn't even argued hard yet. But last night I felt it was time to say something."

Even though Johnstown had lost the game, their manager, Mike Moore, had managed to stick around for the duration. Moore was a moon-faced, broad-shouldered young guy who didn't look much older than his players. In fact, he wasn't that much older and had retired from the league as a player only a couple of years before. Johnstown had made the playoffs in 1999, losing in the first round to London two games to none, and everyone felt they were going to be a contender in 2000 too. The Johnnies liked playing for Mike Moore, and despite the extra-inning loss the night before, they were loose and confident going into Friday night's game.

Johnstown drew first blood with a single run off Andy Lee in the third and then padded the lead with three more runs in the fifth, aided by a rare, two-base error by center fielder Greg Strickland. The Paints were not about to quit though, especially at home where they played with extra confidence. They immediately wiped out the Johnnies' lead by hanging a 5 on the scoreboard, the big blow being a grand slam by first baseman Chance Melvin.

By this time I had met, and even become friendly with, all the Paints' front office employees, including General Manager Bryan Wickline, a two-time winner of the league's Executive of the Year Award. It was impossible not to notice the workaholic Wickline. He was in constant motion throughout every game, hustling through the aisles, communicating with subordinates via walkie-talkie, and fussing over operational and promotional details like a mother hen tending her brood of chicks. I realized how on top of everything Wickline was when I overheard him tell somebody on the other end of the walkie-talkie that there was a light out in the scoreboard—one light, out of the hundreds of lights in the scoreboard. Though I had been looking continually at the scoreboard I hadn't noticed the burnt out bulb. "Pepsi takes care of the scoreboard," said Wend, "and it'll be fixed by tomorrow's game."

It was also impossible not to notice Wickline's girlfriend, Karen Manson, a pretty blonde with short hair, who seemed to be at every Paints' home game. Vivacious and outgoing, she was the Paints' unofficial good will ambassadress, and she moved around, visiting with as many people as possible, nearly as much as Bryan did.

In contrast to Wickline, Paints owner Dr. Chris Hanners kept such a low profile that I had not even seen him yet, much less met him. There was no owner's luxury box at VA Memorial, so I knew he didn't make it a habit of hiding out there. Nevertheless, I thought it a little strange that I hadn't run into him, and I asked John Wend if Chris came to many games. John said that Chris was at nearly every game and could always be found over by the beer wagon, parked behind the Paints' dugout and to the right of the Paints' clubhouse. On the way over there it dawned on me that by hanging out near the beer wagon Chris made himself eminently available to one and all, and that if anyone had been hiding out, it had been me, in the oasis of the press box.

Wearing shorts, sneakers, and a white short-sleeved dress shirt, Hanners was standing with his arms folded in front of him, yet he somehow gave the impression that he was as open to some shmoozing as a man welcoming friends to a backyard bar-b-que. He was about six foot tall, appeared to be in excellent shape, and still had a head full of hair which he wore in a youthful, Don Johnson style, parted down the middle. I was not surprised to learn later that he had been an outstanding athlete at Canal Winchester High School, near Columbus, Ohio, where he had earned a total of 12 varsity letters in baseball, football, basketball, and track. He had a handsome, intelligent face that was nevertheless tinged with melancholy.

I started to introduce myself and explain why I wanted to talk to him, but Chris interrupted me, saying, "I know who you are and what you are doing. I know a lot about you. In fact, I know the names of your kids. Let's see, there's Mickey, Casey, Nolan Ryan, and ... there's one more with a baseball name... what is it ... shoot, I can't remember the other one."

Needless to say, I was flattered and impressed that Hanners had taken the trouble to do a little research about the guy who wanted to interview him, and his calling attention to the names of my kids was an effective ice-breaker for us both, for which I was grateful.

"The other one's name is Babe," I said. "Her first name is actually Brigid, but her middle name is Ruth after a favorite aunt or a great home run hitter—take your pick—so she gets called 'Babe' as much as Brigid. My oldest child didn't get a baseball name, but I've offered to help her change her name from Meg to 'Lefty' or 'Mookie' or something like that."

"Your wife must be a saint," Chris said.

"Close to it," I admitted.

Chris and I had an enjoyable, wide-ranging talk about the Frontier League, and what impressed me more than Chris' grasp of the diverse elements which go into the successful operation of an independent minor league was the mixture of pride and humility with which he spoke. He was rightfully proud of the tremendous strides the league had made but personally humble about his own contributions, which I knew to be enormous. The thing that had struck me from afar as being most impressive about the man was the fact that he'd been elected president of the league every year since the league's inception. For the other owners in the league to overlook such an obvious conflict of interest indicated that they had tremendous respect for and trust in Chris Hanners.

I began by asking him why he'd bought a franchise in the Frontier League. "Because I thought it was a good investment," he said. I was surprised a little, not that Chris said this, but that it was the first reason he gave for getting involved with the Frontier League. He repeated what I'd heard before about the franchise fee appreciating to over half a million dollars; surprised me again by informing me that the league was debt-free—"That's something that is very unique in independent baseball," he said—; and outlined the league's plans to expand to 16 teams with two eight-team divisions. Rockford, IL; Kankakee, IL; Waukegan, IL; Greensburg, PA; Washington, PA; Butler, PA; a western suburb of Cleveland; and former league member Kalamazoo, MI, were all serious candidates for expansion.

"Plus, I liked the idea of bringing professional baseball back to a small town like us," he added, restoring my faith that he was at heart a romantic like myself. "The National Association had such a grip on minor league baseball, that Chillicothe and the other little towns we started in would never have gotten a minor league franchise because of the Association's stringent standards for facilities. So we thought we'd do it ourselves and by-pass the affiliated minor leagues by starting our own league."

After complimenting him on the way the Paints had renovated VA Memorial and the way they maintained the ballpark, I asked Chris if the ballpark would meet current Association standards. "No, it wouldn't," he admitted. "The lights are not quite good enough, nor are the dressing rooms for the players or the umpires. There's a lot of things we want to do here to improve our facilities, but we have to be realistic. Chicago has a new double-decked stadium, but then they have half a million people to draw from. We have 23,000 in Chillicothe."

Chris' mention of the Cook County team which was located in Crestwood, Illinois, a suburb of Chicago, set up a question I'd been anxious to ask. "Why is the Frontier League moving into the suburbs of big cities like Chicago and St. Louis?"

"Because we are always trying to bring in people who are smarter than the guys we already have at the table. The owners we've brought in lately are better businessmen, and they have deeper pockets and more assets. Those guys enhance our entire operation, and we can learn a lot from them. And they want to be in big markets."

"Yeah, maybe so, but why should fans in Chicago and St. Louis go watch the Cheetahs or the River City Rascals play when they could just as easily go watch the Cubs or the White Sox or the Cardinals play?"

"Because it's not that easy to go to a major league game. In fact, it's usually a major hassle. You have to fight traffic, you have to pay for parking, you get ripped off when you buy a beer, ticket prices are going through the roof—and that's when you can get them.

"And it's a different type of experience at a Frontier League game. For example, a bunch of us went to Riverfront Stadium last week to see Brian Tollberg. The kids hated it. After two innings they were bored, but they had to sit still in their seat for the rest of the game. Here, they can get up and run around, and their parents don't have to worry about 'em. We even built that playground over there behind the metal bleachers on the third base line for them. We call it "The Fort," and we covered it with netting to protect the kids from hard hit foul balls. The adults get up and walk around too. The fans here love baseball and they watch the games, but they also socialize and do business at the same time. ... By the way, you see the metal bleachers we added over there on the other side of the visitors' dugout on the third base line? I call that section 'The Vatican' because that's where all my Catholic friends like to sit.

"We try to keep it safe, inexpensive, and close. If we do those three things, we'll be successful; and so will our teams in Chicago and St. Louis. The concept has already been proven. Last year was the first year in the league for both River City and Cook County, and they finished first and third in the league in attendance. River City averaged 4,000 per game.

"The other thing is that there are so many more people to draw from in the suburbs of big cities. Sixty per cent of the people who walk through our gate are not from Chillicothe. We draw from seven counties, but those seven counties still don't add up to twenty minutes from Chicago; that is, the number of people who live within twenty minutes of the Cheetahs' ballpark in Crestwood. That's such a big pool of people that we know the Frontier League and everything we offer is going to appeal to a certain percentage of them, and that will be enough to support the franchise."

Although Max was not going to do any Frontier League games in either Chicago or St. Louis, I was planning to visit both franchises because I wanted to get a complete picture of the Frontier League. I didn't want to prejudge either franchise, but I couldn't help feeling a certain resentment against them for the dwarfing sizes of their markets which had to give them a huge advantage over Chillicothe and Richmond, the two Mayberry-like Frontier League towns that I had emotionally adopted.

"Chris, isn't this push into the suburbs of big cities against the league's original mandate to bring professional baseball back to the little towns of the Midwest?" I asked.

"Well, maybe, but it's a question of survival. We started in the small towns, but the small towns can't do it. They don't have the funds to build the facility they'd need. They don't have the market it would take to retire the debt. Those rocky infield, chicken-wire backstop franchises in the small towns had to sell out to better financed franchises in bigger towns. So we've been through that already.

"I miss something about going to those small towns like Zanesville and Portsmouth and Lancaster and Newark, but it's not realistic in such places these days."

The Paints had scored twice more in the seventh, so that as the game drew to a close, Andy Lee carried a 7–4 lead into the ninth. I shut down the interview to let Chris enjoy the final inning of the game. As I headed back to the press box, Chris said, "I'd like to see Andy finish this game."

I don't believe in jinxs, buuuttt ...... Chris might as well have put Andy on the cover of *Sports Illustrated*. Ben Crowley opened the ninth by singling sharply to right, and then shortstop Eliott Sarabia, bunting for a base hit, got it when the ball rolled to a stop right on the line half-way between home and third base. That was it for Lee, who was replaced by the submarining rookie Eric Frodsham.

Mike Pilger hit a hot grounder into the hole at second. Horning did a good job just stopping the ball and should have been content with that. Instead, he made an off balance throw that got past Melvin at first. Crowley scored and Sarabia went to third. Second baseman Paul Esposito sacrificed Pilger to second, 1–3, for the first out of the inning. Shortstop David Ferres walked to load the bases, and then Frodsham hit Gabe Memmert in the shoulder to force in Sarabia with another run. The inning and the Paints' lead was unraveling fast, but with one out and a one-run lead, Chillicothe would still win the ballgame with a double play, which is why the sinkerballing Frodsham was still on the mound.

From Little League on, every baseball player is taught to think ahead when playing defense so that he'll know what to do before the ball is hit to him. It's good advice, but you still have to be able to think on your feet and do what the play requires if it unfolds differently than what you foresee in your mind.

Chance Melvin at first base had "game-ending double play" on his mind, but that predisposition led him into making a bad decision.

Trevor Mosley hit a high chopper down to first that Melvin fielded above his head. Since the ball was hit too slow to get a double play, Melvin should have gone home for the force on Pilger. That would have prevented the tying run from scoring. Instead, he went to second.

Melvin's throw forced Memmert at second, as Pilger crossed the plate; but usually heady Mike Cervenak compounded the mistake by trying to compete the double play. When his return throw to first bounced in the dirt and got past Melvin, David Ferres who had started the play on second came around third and scored the go-ahead run for the Johnnies. Frodsham finally got out of the inning when he induced Dan Morse to hit into a 6–4 forceout. Unbelievably, Johnstown had scored four ninth-inning runs on three hits, a walk, a hit batter, and two errors, not counting the two mental mistakes. In the bottom of the ninth the Paints exhibited none of their former never-say-die, comeback confidence. Instead, grim-faced and mechanically, they went down 1-2-3 against Johnnies reliever Steven Vickroy to complete the dismal, shocking loss.

As usual, I waited around for Aaron to print me out a box score and a play-by-play summary of the game. By the time they were ready, VA Memorial was empty, except for the groundskeeper, Jimmy Miner, who was already tending to the field; employees who were tying up loose ends; and the stragglers, who were simply reluctant to leave. I was happy to be among the latter as I had come to enjoy the quiet and stillness that loomed over the place as preternaturally as, I imagined, they must have descended upon smokey Civil War battlefields after last shots had rung out, the injured and dying had been removed, and the living had retired for the evening.

Chris Hanners was a straggler too. He sat sprawled out in a grand-stand seat surveying the diamond as if the game were still in the fifth inning. When he saw me, he said, "My dad won't be able to sleep tonight after a game like that. I saw my mom tonight for the first time in a long time, and she said he won't go to bed tonight. He'll play it over and over again in his head all night."

It was a tough loss, but at least the Paints, most of them anyway, went to bed in first place.

With the first month of the 2000 Frontier League season in the books, the standings looked like this:

East Division	W	L	Pct.	GB	West Division	W	L	Pct.	GB
Chillicothe	16	12	571		River City	16	12	571	
London	14	12	538	1.0	Cook County	15	13	536	1.0
Johnstown	14	12	538	1.0	Dubois County	13	13	500	2.0
Richmond	13	14	481	2.5	Springfield	13	15	464	3.0
Canton	10	17	370	5.5	Evansville	11	15	423	4.0

One of the great things about baseball is its long season. There's always another game tomorrow, it seems, which is a god-send when you throw away a win like the Paints did on the last day of June.

Overnight the first-place Paints regained their aplomb and went out and took the rubber game from Johnstown 5–1 behind the gutsy pitching of rookie Sean Boesch. In scattering eleven hits over seven innings while giving up the lone Johnstown run, the shaved-headed Boesch bested Johnstown's ace Matt Sheets, who in eight innings of work also gave up eleven hits. The play of the game came in the top of the fifth with Chillicothe leading 2–0, when Justin Graham threw a bullet in from left field to nail another Johnstown runner at home plate. Graham put so much into the throw that he fell flat on his face while making it. This time it was Ben Gerkin who got run over and who held onto the ball. "I guess Johnstown didn't see Thursday night's game!" I said, laughing, to everybody in the press box. "Either that or they didn't believe what they saw."

"No. I guess they didn't," said Aaron. "He's got a gun!"

When the Paints seemed to have the game in hand, I moseyed over behind the Paints' dugout to hang out with Chris Hanners for a while.

When I remembered that John Wend had told me that the bullpen wasn't going to do the Chicken Dance, I mentioned it to Chris and told him how disappointed I was not to see the routine.

"Byrd and Woody don't like to do the Chicken Dance when they're not going good," explained Chris. "Byrd's been hurt, and Woody's been getting lit up. He was the closer last year and at the beginning of this year, but last night Dad went to Frodsham late in the game in a save situation, and I saw Woody's head drop in disappointment."

The Joe DiMaggio story that I had modified for Woody's benefit at The Dock didn't seem so funny then; and it didn't get any funnier when Woody stayed down in the bullpen while Jason Baker pitched a scoreless eighth and Nate Gardner a scoreless ninth.

Late in the game John Wend announced that a ladies' wrist watch had been found in the bathroom and turned in. "Come up to the press box and describe your watch and you can claim it," he said.

I told Chris how impressed I was with the honesty behind such an act. "Last week we had a ladies' purse turned in that had $200 in it," he said. "That doesn't happen anywhere but in Chillicothe."

I agreed with the spirit of Chris' remark, even if I didn't quite accept it literally. As much as I had come to love Chillicothe, I knew that there were good people to be found everywhere. It was time for me to seek out some of the other good people around the rest of the Frontier League.

On Friday July 7, I left Cincinnati on a 12-day/5-city tour of the West Division of the Frontier League. My first stop was Huntingburg, Indiana, home of the Dubois County Dragons and, with a population of 6,000, *the* smallest city in professional baseball. I was more intrigued by the Dubois County franchise than any of the other franchises in the West simply because I couldn't believe that tiny Huntingburg, located in the southwestern corner of the state just off Interstate 64, was able to support a professional baseball team. The team was named to encourage support from the entire county, but even so that brought the population of the larger market up to less than 40,000. Making things worse was the fact that a longstanding coolness existed between Huntingburg and Jasper, the county's largest city with a population of 10,000, that lay only seven miles north of Huntingburg. The indifference of Jasperians to the Dragons was something that the Dubois County franchise could ill afford.

The most unfortunate thing of all, and something I found to be ironic as well, was the fact that the Dragons could also not count on any support from the baseball fans in the third largest city in the state, Evansville, which was only 48 miles southwest of Huntingburg. Not because Evansville had its own pro team in an affiliated league, but because the Evansville Otters were a member of the Frontier League themselves.

Although it didn't translate into extra fannies in the seats, the Dubois County franchise had one of the more interesting histories in the league in that it owed its existence to a baseball movie, *A League of Their Own,* director Penny Marshall's feel-good film about the All-American Girls Professional Baseball League that was created during World War II.

It all started when Mayor Connie Nass saw a chance to put Huntingburg on the map if she could convince Columbia Pictures to pass over candidates Danville, Illinois, and Madisonville, Kentucky, and make her city the site of the movie. Columbia did choose Huntingburg for its small town atmosphere, the cooperation it was promised by city hall, and the friendliness of its residents, many of whom wound up working as extras in the film; so in August of 1991 three big stars—Tom Hanks, Madonna, and Geena Davis—plus an outstanding supporting cast which included John Lovitz, Rosie O'Donnell, and Megan Cavanagh came to town to film the baseball scenes in the movie.

A key factor in Columbia's decision was the existence of Huntingburg's City Park field, in use since 1883, which Marshall agreed would be a perfect vintage home, with a little fixing up, for the movie version of the women's team the movie was about, the Rockford (IL) Peaches. Columbia told the city that the fixing up could be done in one of two ways. A temporary set using inexpensive materials could be erected and then dismantled when the shooting was finished; or the ballpark could undergo a real near-total reconstruction that would remain in place when the studio left town. Naturally, the city chose the latter option.

Built in 1894 the original City Park grandstand was rectangular in shape, not semi-circular, and 260 feet long. By 1985 the sections on both ends had deteriorated from neglect and were removed so that only the center section, seating about 500, remained. Columbia's construction crew moved this grandstand north ten feet and raised it six feet and added grandstand wings down both base lines so that the final capacity grew to 2,800. They also added in-ground dugouts; made substantial improvements to the playing surface, including the installation of a new sprinkler system; and replaced the chain-link fence around the outfield with a new plank fence made of cedar that was painted with period advertising. It was all done in eight short weeks, using the finest materials and with such attention to detail that all painting was done in a way to create a weathered look, while the use of circular saws was eschewed since wood was cut straight back in the 1940s.

The filming of *A League of Their Own* in Huntingburg did a lot for the city. It pumped millions of dollars into the local economies, boosted the civic pride of Huntingburg citizens, and did indeed put the city on the map, at least with the movie industry, which subsequently came to town for the making of two more motion pictures: an HBO production about Jackie Robinson breaking the color barrier called *Soul of the Game*, starring Blair Underwood, and a 1998 action film called *Hard Rain*, starring Christian Slater and Ed Asner. *A League of Their Own* also provided Huntingburg with a new ballpark, which was renamed League Stadium in honor of the movie. Columbia's "$800,000 gift to the city" was not only the largest prop ever built and left behind by the movie industry and a new tourist attraction for an area dependent on tourism; it was also a quality facility fit to become the home of a minor league baseball team.

Like a dictator filling a power vacuum, the Dubois County Dragons came into being in 1996 to play in Huntingburg's new League Stadium. The Dragons joined the Will County (IL) Cheetahs, the Anderson (IN) Lawmen, and the Lafayette (IN) Leopards to form the Heartland League.

The Heartland League was the thirteenth independent league to organize since the Northern League and the Frontier League had started the ball rolling in 1993, and its formation was a by-product of the instability and precariousness of the entire industry. Of the twelve independent leagues to precede the Heartland, one (the North Central League) had lasted two years; two (the Great Central and Mid-American Leagues) had finished their inaugural seasons, then disbanded; and two more (the Atlantic Coast and Golden State leagues) had not even been able to complete their first-year schedules. (A sixth league, the Mid-South, announced it had formed but folded before its initial season of 1995 even started.) Equally unstable and precarious were many of the independent team franchises which moved around in dizzying fashion. For example, Anderson and Lafayette came to the Heartland League from the defunct Mid-American League, while Will County came over from the North Central after it "went dark," as they say in the business.

The Heartland expanded to eight teams in 1997, picking up Altoona, Pennsylvania, and three teams from the Big South League: Columbia (TN), Clarksville (TN), and the Tennessee Thumpers (of Winchester, TN). This expansion was hardly a sign of strength though, as the league began 1998 reconfigured as a shaky six team circuit, made up of three original members (Dubois County, Will County, and Lafayette), Tennessee, the Tupelo (MS) Tornado, and the Huntington (WV) Rail Kings. Tupelo and Huntington folded soon after the season began, wreaking havoc on the league schedule, and even the strongest franchises in the league suffered dramatic declines in attendance. The Heartland was history when Will County and Dubois County joined the Frontier League for the 1999 season. Will County moved into a new stadium in Crestwood,

Illinois, became the Cook County Cheetahs, and joined the Frontier League as an expansion franchise; while Dubois County bought an existing Frontier League franchise, that of the Ohio Valley Red Coats, which is why the Dragons began the 1999 season with eight former Ohio Valley Red Coats' players on its roster. The transfer of the Ohio Valley franchise to Dubois County had left Chillicothe as the only one of the eight original Frontier League cities to retain its franchise.

Around noon I found League Stadium at the end of First Street, only a 1/2 mile from US 231 which runs right through the middle of town. With its weathered wood facade and the pillars and support beams visible under the roof, the place from the outside did look pleasantly archaic, but the illusion was spoiled somewhat by the setting which the ballpark shared with Huntingburg's large public swimming pool, in full and boisterous summertime use. Since the stadium was locked up, I drove back to 231 and took a leisurely look around Huntingburg. The heart of the town and the business district was Fourth Street, a long avenue of restored Victorian-era buildings housing numerous antique and specialty shops that stretched across both sides of 231. I found the Dragons' office on East Fourth Street next to The Overtime, Huntingburg's only sports bar. The Dragons were headquartered in a small former bank. I knew that because I parked behind the building and saw a large steel vault door with a combination dial on it leaning up against the back wall.

Inside I met Heath Brown, the Dragons' thirty-something-ish General Manager. Heath was the Dragons' only full time front office employee, and he continued to work with stacks of tickets in his office as we talked through a large opening in the wall separating the office from the lobby, cluttered with a couple of racks of Dragons apparel for sale and boxes of supplies and Dragons' squeeze bottles that would be given away in an upcoming promotion. Heath, who had experience with affiliated teams, gave me a brief history of the franchise and outlined what he was doing to help the Dragons make a go of it in Dubois County. According to Heath, the main reason the front office was so thin was the low unemployment rate in Huntingburg, the fourth lowest in the state. "Everybody here has a job unless they're pregnant or crazy, and some of the crazy people have jobs," he said. "We also have a hard time getting interns from college sports marketing programs to come here, and we can never keep them for long. Huntingburg is too small a town for them, and they get bored." Sensing my skepticism, he summed up the situation by saying: "Can we make it? Yes. Will it be easy? No. Will any of the owners get rich? Certainly not. But they can make a little money if we're successful."

As I started to leave, I made a comment about how far Huntingburg was from the major leagues for the Dragons' manager, who'd had a nice career as a third baseman for the Montreal Expos and Los Angeles Dodgers.

"Not the same guy," said Heath. "You're thinking about Tim 'Wallach.' Our guy is Tim 'Wallace.'"

"Jeez, I can't believe I got them confused," I said, both surprised and annoyed at myself for the mixup.

"You'd know it as soon as you saw him anyway."

"Why is that?" I said. "Is Wallace some kind of geek?"

"No. He's black."

11-4-2004

I still had plenty of time to get to the ballpark, so I paid a visit to the offices of *The Huntingburg Press*, across the street and down a few doors from the Dragons' office. Because *The Press* was a weekly, it didn't make sense for the paper to cover the Dragons on a regular basis. Nevertheless, publisher Bill Matthews was a baseball fan, and he did what he could to provide coverage of the team: mainly, publishing pre-season editions about the team every year, as well as special editions about noteworthy events, such as the Dragons' hosting of the 1999 Frontier League All-Star Game. Bill and I talked a good while in his private second floor office, and he spoke to me candidly about the difficulties facing the franchise. As Bill saw it, the basic problem was not the area's lack of interest in professional minor league baseball, but the franchise's previous mistakes. First, one of Heath Brown's predecessors, "not a people person at all," had alienated a lot of fans and potential advertisers. Second, the franchise, which had suffered substantial losses some years, owed money in the form of back debts to several people and businesses in the area. Bill expressed confidence that Heath Brown would, if given enough time, turn things around, but his revelations did little to assuage my fears about the viability of the franchise.

Fortunately, before I got depressed over the problems facing the Dubois County franchise, Bill concluded our interview with a light-hearted story about his involvement as an extra for *A League of Their Own.*

"I played ball at the University of Michigan but never umpired a day in my life," he said. "But I guess because I was tall, they hired me to play an umpire.

"There's a well known scene in the movie when Geena Davis is catching and Madonna is batting. Davis was supposed to run back towards the screen and slide at the last second to make this great catch on a foul pop. The ball was actually being dropped by a guy standing on a ladder, but Davis couldn't catch the ball. I think it took something like 43 takes before she caught one.

"Anyway, as the home plate umpire, I was supposed to run back towards the screen with her, flip off my mask, and call 'Out!' when she made the catch. 11\14\04 2308

"Now, it was a really hot day when we were filming this scene. They had a celebrity mess tent there where we could eat lunch, and they always had great food. That day I'd eaten some steak and some swordfish, and maybe too much of both. And here I was wearing this heavy wool clothing from the 1950s and a heavy chest protector and an iron mask, and it was hot as blazes. Well, after going through this scene a couple of dozen times, I started feeling bad. But I was still determined to make it ... this was going to be my scene in the movie.

"Penny Marshall, the director, noticed that I wasn't feeling well because she said, 'Hey, you're not going to faint on us, are you?'

"I told her I was okay, but after a few more takes, I knew I wasn't going to make it. My face was really red, and I felt terrible. Penny said, 'That's it. You're done.' She called one of my friends in to take my place, a guy who really was an umpire. He did the scene, and he's the umpire in the movie.

"Two days later I was umpiring the bases for a game the actors played, just to have some extra footage in the can, some filler stuff in case it might be needed. There was a play at second base, where one of the ladies slid in and she was out. I called her out, but immediately I saw the ball trickling away from the bag. I realized that the second baseman had dropped the ball, so I changed my call to safe. A few seconds later I turned around, and there was Tom Hanks, right in my face. I mean his face was two inches—if that—from my face, and he gave me hell for four or five minutes. He wasn't really mad—he was just acting, and I think he wanted to see how I would handle it. And I did okay. I didn't throw him out of the game, but I held my ground with him.

"The following spring my wife and I were in Chicago attending a White Sox game. Halfway through the game they ran a trailer for the movie which was about to be released, and the trailer had my argument with Tom Hanks in it. My wife got really excited. She was telling everyone around us, 'That's my husband! That's my husband!' And she said to me, 'Honey, I've never been more proud of you!'

"I was pretty excited too, but later on I got to thinking about it, and I thought maybe I should be compensated for appearing in the trailer. I talked to my lawyer in Huntingburg and showed him the contract I had with the movie company. As extras we got paid $50 a day, whether we worked three hours or thirteen. My lawyer showed me a clause in the fine print that said by signing the contract I relinquished all claim to further compensation from the use of my image in any form whatsoever at any time. He asked me if that was my signature at the bottom of the page, and I said yes, that it was. So that was that. I didn't make any more money, but I did get my ten seconds of movie fame."

When I walked inside League Stadium, six or seven Dragons' hitters were gathered inside the cage down the right field line, receiving group instruction from an athletically-built black man I assumed was Tim Wallace. It wasn't Wallace but Mike Samuels, the hitting coach. Tim was sitting in the dugout, watching the pitching coach, Mike Nichols, put the Dragons pitchers through some routine fielding drills. After Tim and I got the basic introductions out of the way, he told me I could call him by the nickname everybody else used: "Pops." When I told him about Max, he made a polite grunt, then asked, "Is he a good umpire?"

"Yes, he is. Everybody I've talked to has tremendous respect for him."

"He probably works at it twice as hard as anybody else."

"I think you're exactly right, Pops. I know that nobody cares more about doing a good job than Max."

"That's half the battle right there," he said. "More than half."

LIKE HOW'S THE FAMILY JEWELS?

When old friends in baseball run into each other, there's two questions they usually ask to get things going: "How's the family?" and "How are you guys going?" I couldn't ask Pops the first question, so I asked him the second—even though I already knew what the basic answer to the question was: not good. Earlier that day I'd bought a copy of *The Herald,* a fine tabloid-sized paper that was published in Jasper and which covered the entire county. Unlike *The Huntingburg Press, The Herald* did cover the Dragons on a regular basis; and judging by the July 7, 2000, edition, I judged the coverage to be excellent. Sports editor Jim Priest's thorough game story (along with an artful photograph of Johnnies catcher Jeff Davis breaking up a double play) had run on the front page of the sports section; below the headline story of the Carolina Panthers' Fred Lane being shot to death by his wife, and above a story about basketball coach Roy Williams' turning down the University of North Carolina to stay at Kansas. Priest's story had made it clear that the Dragons had not only just dropped a doubleheader to the visiting Johnstown Johnnies, but that they had also done so in a very uninspiring fashion.

THE ASSUMPE WENT TO UNC.

According to Priest: "The Dragons went from losing a close first game by blowing a number of chances to a lethargic two-hit performance to drop the second contest."

As I had suspected he would, Pops recounted the previous day's losses, complaining mostly about the team's lack of clutch hitting—in the doubleheader the Dragons had been 1–13 with runners in scoring position. But then, as he went on, his focus moved away from easily recognizable failures of physical execution to more critical intangible spiritual deficiencies. "These guys are happy to be here," he said. "They're happy to have a uniform, but they don't cherish the opportunity. You can see it in the way they play.

"I try to stress to them 'Don't be satisfied. Stay hungry. And don't be satisfied to stay here any longer than you have to.' Most of the guys we get here are players who didn't get drafted out of college, or they're players who did get drafted but then couldn't make it coming out of spring training and got cut. I tell them, 'Hey, this is where you prove 'em wrong, all the people who doubted you ... the scouts, the coaches, the personnel directors.' Every player here should play with a burning desire to get better, to prove the doubters wrong, and to move on. Every player. Every day.

"And I tell 'em 'Don't do it for the owners of the team. Don't do it for your girlfriend. Don't do it for the manager. Do it for yourself.'".

Pops had played the game himself, for 14 years, he told me, all in the minors. A second baseman-shortstop, he spent time in the farm systems of the Angels, Padres, and Cubs. The highest he ever got was Double A. He had a chance once to move up to Triple A, but it would have been as a utility man. He chose to stay down in Double A because he wanted to play everyday. In addition to his stints with affiliated minor league teams, Pops had also played pro ball in foreign countries—Mexico, Italy, Nicaragua—and, as his playing career wound down, in several independent leagues—the Northern, the Western, and the Northeast Leagues. It was in connection with the Duluth-Superior Dukes of the Northern League that he mentioned the name of Mal Finchman.

"Mal Finchman!?" I blurted. "How do you know him?"

"Mal was my manager, on several teams. He's been real instrumental in my career, and I love him to death."

I was stunned by this statement. Mal Finchman was as big a legend in the Frontier League as Morgan Burkhart. The only difference was that Mal's legend was a little tarnished, say like Jack the Ripper's. I had heard numerous stories about Mal, who was no longer associated with the league and was said to be scouting for the San Diego Padres; but never once did anyone say he liked the guy, much less express real affection for him. In fact, if Morgan Burkhart might be described in baseball terms as the universally respected and even beloved "Lou Gehrig of the Frontier League," then Mal Finchman was definitely the Frontier League's hated John McGraw. Or maybe its despised Leo Durocher. You get the point.

One Mal story I'd heard was about the time he got thrown out of a game—a common occurrence for him—then confiscated the team mascot's costume, put it on, and came back to hang around the dugout, from where he tried to continue managing the game.

Another time Mal became so angry he burned his own shirt in the dugout. Mal it seems had a superstition against the color black, dating back to a terrible season one of his teams had had while wearing black undersleeves. He'd promised himself that his teams would never wear black again, but the players on one of his Frontier League teams convinced him to try black again. After the team promptly got stomped, Mal whipped off his black shirt and set it on fire. Word spread around the league so quickly—sort of like wildfire, I guess you'd say—that when Mal's team went on their next road trip, they were greeted at the home team's ballpark by fire engines at the ready and banners proclaiming it to be "FIRE PREVENTION WEEK."

Finally, there was the infamous brawl between Finchman's Springfield Capitals team and the River City Rascals, managed by ex-major league slugger Jack Clark. The fight, the biggest in Frontier League history, resulted in more than twenty ejections and the arrests of both Clark and Mal. While Clark's arrest was a mere formality—the cops allowed Clark to turn himself in the next day—Mal was taken away from the ballpark in handcuffs. During the melee Mal lost his favorite pen. The cop, who'd ordered everybody off the field, told Mal he wasn't allowed to look for the pen. When Mal persisted, the cop arrested him on the spot.

This was quite a bit of mayhem to be caused by such a little guy, who was also no spring chicken; a circumstance that made Finchman all the more intriguing to me. Max had shown me a photo of Mal standing at home plate in Richmond for pre-game ceremonies honoring Morgan Burkhart prior to Morgan's last game in the Frontier League. Mal appeared to have the size and physique of a kid entering junior high school. Eventually I heard another Mal story related to his scrawniness. At a league-wide tryout Mal went up to a group of hopefuls and astonished everyone by telling the skinniest, most untalented kid in the camp that he was going to draft him. "Do you know why I'm going to draft you?" Finchman asked the bean pole.

"No," came the reply.

"Because you're the only one I know who looks worse in a baseball uniform than I do."

Had he ever played baseball, at any level? I had wondered later. And how had he come by his considerable knowledge of baseball and his keen ability to judge baseball talent? These traits he possessed, I knew, because Mal Finchman had won the Frontier League championship three times with three different teams (Erie, Johnstown, and Springfield); yet ... he had never been named Frontier League Manager of the Year. I couldn't wait to hear what Pops Wallace had to say further about the mighty, the legendary, the supposedly curmudgeonly Mal Finchman.

7

A Visit to the FL Big Time: Ron LeFlore and His Cook County Cheetahs

I WAS SITTING IN THE Dubois County Dragons' dugout, talking to a baseball lifer, a guy who'd never had a career other than professional baseball. Directly in front of us, the Dragons' pitchers, wearing shorts and T-shirts, were taking turns running a drill usually left behind in spring training. The purpose of the drill they were running is to get the pitchers to instinctively cover first base on balls hit to the right side of the infield, just in case the first baseman can't field the ball and beat the runner to the bag. After the pitcher throws a half speed pitch to the plate, a coach hits a grounder to the first baseman wide of first. The pitcher then cuts over to the baseline on an angle, runs parallel to the baseline, catches a toss from the first baseman, and steps on the bag. Without a doubt, the Dragons' pitchers had done this drill a million times before, but they were still participating in it enthusiastically, cheering on a teammate one time, and ragging on another teammate the next. Past the mound, which looked tantalizingly close, and past the infield and the long outfield lawn stood the fence that marked the boundary of this insulated world. And on those artificially weathered boards were painted the signs that had helped Hollywood create an even more illusory world:

"Read about the Rockford Peaches in the Morning Star."

"Don't Be Late Again. The Axis Won't Wait."

"Steinkamps Lumber Supports the Peaches."

"RCA Victor Hit Phonograph Records by Xavier Cugat, Benny Goodman, Tommy Dorsey."

"For Rockford Peaches Uniforms and the War Effort … It's Singer Sewing Machines."

"The first time I met Mal Finchman, I thought, 'What an asshole!'" Pops Wallace was saying. "But once you get past his personality, he's outstanding. He's a great baseball man and the best teacher of baseball I've ever been around. I'd do anything for that guy. I love 'im.

"Well, why is it that most everybody else seems to maintain the first impression that you had of him?" I asked.

"Because Mal doesn't fuck around. He is strictly business. Everything is by the book with him, spit and shine. He has a curfew, and he insists that everybody come to the ballpark to get in early work. Everybody hates him, but he's not a bad guy. They're just not able to see through his act like I did. They say, 'What a weird guy!' and they never get past that.

"But see, Mal is like that on purpose. It's a psychological thing. He weeds out the crybabies because he doesn't want them around.

"To give you an example, Mal was a jerk to me the first day I ever talked to the man. This was right after I'd been released by the Cubs. I had an offer to play for the Miami Miracle, which back then was an independent team in the Florida State League; but I lived in California, and I didn't want to go to Miami. I heard that the Boise Hawks were having tryouts so I called them. They were another independent team, in the Northwest League, and Mal was the manager.

"I got Mal on the phone, and right off he said, 'Why are you coming to the tryout?'

"'Why do you think?' I said.

"'What makes you think you can play for me?'

"I started telling him about my background in baseball, and he interrupted me. He said, 'I'm going to Florida. I can't talk now. Call me next week.' Click."

In the telling of this story Pops spoke in a deep scratchy voice out of the side of his mouth in fond imitation of his mentor, and the remembrance kept a smile on his face and a twinkle in his eye.

"So I'm thinking, 'What the hell was that all about?' I called Jim Essian, who's a friend of mine because I knew that he knew Mal. Essian said, 'He's checking up on you.'

"So I called him back, and he said, 'Don't think you're going to make my team just because you played Double A.'

"'Hey, I just want a chance,' I said. NB

"The tryout lasted three days, and for those three days I was the best ballplayer in the country. I could do no wrong. I was diving in the hole to catch the ball, making perfect relay throws, hitting lazers from both sides of the plate. After the second day guys were coming up to me saying, 'Man, you're in. You're a shoo-in to make the team.' So what did Mal think? He called me over and said, 'Don't do any more of that fancy shit. You're gonna ruin my team. They're all gonna think they've got to do that fancy shit to make the team. Just field the ball and make a normal throw to the shortstop.'

"He knew I could play though because when the tryout was over, he called me into his office and said, 'I've got a problem. I had the team all set, but now you've fucked things up. I want to offer you a contract, but I can't afford you.'

"I told him, 'Mal, I'll sign. I want to play, man. Just make me a decent offer.' And he did. I wound up hitting .317. I made the All-Star team and was voted onto Boise's All Decade Team. Like I said, I was able to see through his act, and I realized he's not a bad guy. I loved playing for him, and he later gave me a shot on his team at Reno in the California League and on his team at Duluth in the Northern League. … Everybody hates him, but they shouldn't because he gets the best out of all his players."

If Mal Finchman was such a great baseball man why hadn't he ever been hired to manage an affiliated team I asked.

"Because he didn't want to deal with their bullshit. In affiliated ball they tell you who to play, what to do. He wants to do things his way."

By this time the Johnstown Johnnies had come onto the field to start warming up. Pops called over Johnstown manager Mike Moore, who was standing near home plate.

"What do you think of Mal? Really, tell the truth," he said to Moore.

Moore looked at us to see if he could tell whether Pops had asked him a trick question. Satisfied that Pops had no hidden agenda, he answered, "He's got no personality."

"He's gonna call him," Pops said, nodding his head towards me.

"He'll hang up on you," said Moore. "He'll say … 'I'm on the other line with Abner Doubleday.'"

Pops and I laughed, and then Pops went back into Mal's voice: "'Who do you work for? … You're writing a book? So what. I don't have time to talk. I've got a call on the other line. … Max McLeary? He's an umpire. So what. I don't like him. … What's your name again? I've got to go. Call me back tomorrow.' Click!"

I hadn't had much news about the Frontier League in almost a week, so I was anxious to look over the game notes in the League Stadium press box prior to the tilt between the Johnnies and the Dragons. According to the notes, Chillicothe and Richmond had both won the night before. Chillicothe beat Canton 10–3 behind the pitching of Sean Boesch and the hitting of Justin Graham, who went 3–4 with a triple and four RBI; while Richmond spanked London 14–6. In the latter game my fellow Bluesmobile passenger, J.T. Engstrom, picked up the win and got plenty of support from his batterymate, Steve Mitrovich, a new addition to the Roosters' roster, who went 3–5 with a homer and six RBI. Chillicothe was still in first place in the East with a 21–13 record and a two game lead over Johnstown. Richmond was in fourth place, five and a half back at 15 and 18. In the West, River City was on top with the same record as the Paints. Dubois County's 15 and 17 slate put them in third place, five games off the Rascals' pace.

The notes also showed that Chillicothe was dominating the stats. As a team the Paints led the league in batting (.313) and pitching (3.49 ERA). Justin Graham's .423 was the league's best batting average, and the Paints had three other players in the Top Ten: Mike Cervenak (.363),, Joe Colameco (.362), and Jason Baker (.344). Shortstop Mike Cervenak, having an MVP-type season, was also leading the league in home runs (9) and RBI (36). As for individual pitching leaders, Paints Josh White (5–0) and Sean Boesch (4–1) were 1–2 in the league in ERA at 1.05 and 1.24.

The Dragons had two players among the league leaders. First baseman Fran Riordan was eighth in the league in batting at .349, and closer Chris Viel was leading the league in saves with seven. Both players, along with shortstop John Tavares and catcher Adam Patterson, had been named to represent the Dragons in the upcoming All-Star Game, scheduled for Wednesday July 12, at River City.

Brad Boyd, a 6' 8" rookie righthander from Australia, was scheduled to start for the Dragons. He had a strange record so far in 2000. In six starts his ERA was an unacceptable 6.11, he had given up 35 hits in 28 innings, and he had a bad strikeout-to-walk ratio of 14/22; yet his personal record was only 0–1, mainly because the Dragons were averaging 8.67 runs per game in his starts. Despite his overall bad stats, he had turned in three quality starts and could easily have been the winning pitcher in those games if he had been allowed to stay in the games a bit longer or if the Dragons had scored some of their runs earlier in the contests.

Friday night's game proved to be a typical Brad Boyd affair. Boyd was constantly in trouble—in 4.2 innings he surrendered five hits and six bases on balls—yet he gave up only two runs (both earned), left with the Dragons trailing 2–1, and wound up with another no-decision after Dubois County scored three runs in the eighth to tie the game 4–4.

During the pitching change when Pops brought Nate Rister in to relieve Boyd, I chatted with Keith Gearhart, Johnstown's personable young radio broadcaster I had gotten to be friends with, about the size of the crowd at League Stadium. I was always checking attendance figures, and, quite frankly, I was worried about the survival of the three teams that were not drawing well. The attendance at League Stadium of 859 was close to the Dragons' average of 909, but it was disappointing for a Friday night game. As poorly as Dubois County was drawing, Richmond (an average of 897), and Canton (503) were doing even worse. Johnstown was fifth in the league with an average of 1,566 per game, which was not bad, but I was still shocked when Keith told me that the Johnnies had drawn a crowd of 10,000 on July 4th. Seeing the astonishment on my face, Keith quickly explained the reason for the gaudy attendance figure: a concert and fireworks display were scheduled to take place after the game and the Johnnies let everyone in for free!

That salient fact had hardly sunken in before Keith told me there was even more to the story. It seems that the Johnstown–London game on July 3rd had been suspended in the second inning due to rain. That meant that the single game scheduled for July 4th was changed into a doubleheader. Originally, the schedule for July 4th called for the baseball game to start at 4:05; the two-hour concert, featuring a symphony orchestra and "The Sons of Tennessee" (two fiddlers and a guitarist who played on horses), to begin at 7:00; and the fireworks display to commence somewhere between 9:00 and 9:30.

Apparently unconcerned about the tightness of this schedule, the Johnnies' front office was a little lax in getting the wet and tarped field ready for play, and so the resumption of the suspended game was delayed for an hour until 2:05. Worse, the first game wound up going fourteen innings, London winning 7–6.

The Werewolves immediately took the lead in the second game on a solo first-inning home run by Jason Borghese, but Johnstown tied the score in the bottom of the first when Paul Esposito's grounder to short scored Mike Pilger who had tripled. Then, with third baseman Matt Kuseski batting, the mayor of Johnstown grabbed the P.A. microphone in the press box and announced: "Attention, ladies and gentlemen ... due to the length of the first game, we are going to have to cancel this game in order to get the orchestra on the field and the show on the road."

According to Keith, 10,000 fans, or a good number of them anyway, began booing as if the city had just banned beer at the ballpark, and the umpires and players all looked up towards the press box in stunned disbelief.

The home plate umpire called the mayor down to the field and then told him, "Look, I'm in full control of this game on the field. Nobody can suspend it but me. And I assure you that we're not going to suspend it for a concert and a fireworks show. I'm sorry that the first game went so long, but we *are* going to finish this game."

With that said, the umpire walked back to his position, pulled on his mask, and shouted, to the cheers of the crowd, "PLAY BALL!" The next day the local newspaper reported that for three hours on July 4th, the umpire was the mayor of Johnstown, and that his decision to overrule the real mayor was the best call he made all day.

After Dubois County tied the game 4–4 by scoring three times in the eighth, neither team scored in the ninth, so the game went into extra innings. From the seventh through the eleventh, Jason Tangi, Kris Draper, and Chris Viel kept Johnstown off the scoreboard, as the Dragons' offense squandered opportunity after opportunity. Watching this, I got the distinct impression that the longer the game went, the better chance Johnstown had of winning it. Sure enough, Johnstown finally broke through for three runs in the top of the twelfth. The Dragons came back to score twice on a single by outfielder Dan Horgan, but they lost by a run, 7–6, when they made the third out with the tying and winning runs on base.

The four and a half hour marathon, in which Pops used all six members of his bullpen, was made even longer by an incident that occurred in the bottom of the eleventh. The game was suddenly interrupted by home plate umpire Mike Rust who walked back to the screen and called Dragons GM Heath Brown over for a conference. In the press box we wondered what was the matter. We soon found out when Heath came up to the press box and told the P.A. announcer, Scott Sollman, that he'd been thrown out of the game. Sollman had played a computer-generated growling noise to punctuate the complaining that the fans had just done about Rust's strike call on a Dragons' batter. I had hardly even noticed the growling sound, but obviously the umpire had. And he neither liked it nor approved of it. "You're arguing balls and strikes," he said to Heath.

Sollman didn't say anything, but he didn't move either. "He's not going to restart the game until you leave," Heath told him. "We'll forfeit if you don't leave," he added for emphasis.

Rust got rid of Sollman and the canine commentary over the P.A. system, but the fans in the box seats behind home plate took up the cause and for the rest of the game they growled at Rust like junk yard dogs protecting their supper dishes.

The Dragons got another nice game story written about them in

Saturday's *Herald*, but I was surprised to read some of the quotes attributed to Tim Wallace: "It was a very poor effort on our part. They have
no desire to go out and win a ballgame." The first statement is the sort
of thing managers and coaches say all the time, but the second sounded
as if it crossed over the line of constructive criticism into blatant dis-
respect. Pops basically called his players a bunch of gutless pansies—he
"dissed" them in contemporary jock parlance—and there really is no
greater insult for an athlete. Pops' remark was the inflammatory, "we'll-
make-you-eat-those-words" kind of statement that coaches love to cut
out of the newspaper and post on the locker room bulletin board, as
long as it's made by the opposing coach. One of the unwritten rules of
baseball is that a manager doesn't rip his players in the press. He might
rip them, but not in front of the entire reading public. Perhaps Pops
was intentionally trying to anger or embarrass the Dragons into playing better; if so, it was a gutsy and risky strategy, as there is always the
distinct possibility that such a strategy will backfire and lead not to
improvement but to mutiny.

At League Stadium I ran into Robert Lee, the Dragons' radio broadcaster, another guy who looked young enough to be broadcasting for
college credit instead of a pay check. Despite his youth, Robert was hardly
awed to be working in professional baseball. He wasn't afraid to speak
his mind, and in fact he was critical of most aspects of the Dragons' operation. Fortunately, he had a very chipper personality which muted the
negativity of his criticisms and made them easier to listen to. Knowing
that I'd get the truth, as he saw it, I asked him if the dissension I was
starting to sense was real.

Robert told me that some of the players were indeed unhappy, with
what they considered to be Pops' overly-aggressive managing. According
to Robert's source, a pitcher he declined to name, the players felt that
the team was over-bunting … bunting too early, too often, and with two
strikes … and they were running so aggressively that they often ran
themselves out of innings. Similarly, on defense they would do things
like play the infield in with a runner on third and less than two outs in
the very first inning. Besides not being good baseball, these moves showed
the players that their manager had no confidence in them.

Robert's source also indicated that there was also some racial tension on the team, not necessarily among the players themselves, but
between the white players and their manager. "There's been some grumbling that there has been some racial discrimination in player selection,"
said Robert. "It does seem that every new player we get is black. Worse,
some of the new black guys are definitely not as good as the white players they replaced. Some of them have been terrible. Another one has
been hurt for three weeks and won't be back until August first. He's

being kept around because he's one of the manager's "boys." He's useless. All he can do is pinch run because he hurt his hand. Normally, in this league, if a player can't play, he's gone. Some of the white guys also feel that the black guys can get away with more because they're black."

Robert suggested, in an attempt to describe the situation as fairly as possible, that the player selection might have had as much to do with geography as with race: Pops and both his coaches lived in the Bay Area, as did seven players on the current roster, including four of the black kids on the team. He also pointed out that one black had been cut from the team (for unspecified behavior off the field, not his performance on it). I really had no way of assessing the accuracy of this characterization of the Dragons' manager, nor did I know how wide spread among the players the dissatisfaction with him was. Nevertheless, I'd heard enough to know that Pops had a sticky situation on his hands. I also knew that it was nothing that winning wouldn't cure.

I didn't confront Pops with what I'd heard to get an angry reaction from him so that I could sensationalize "the story" even further. I don't like that kind of "reporting." Besides, my own inclination was to give Pops every benefit of the doubt. I'd heard him be critical of his players, but he hadn't singled out just the white kids. I figured he knew more about baseball than any of his players or myself; so I would have been reluctant to criticize his strategy, even if I'd had considerably more than a single game to go on. I also felt it was his prerogative to pick the team as he saw fit. His job was on the line and more dependent on the team's won-loss record than his players' jobs, and so it only made sense to me to believe that he picked his players on the same basis as white managers: he tried to get the guys he thought could help him win.

Perhaps because the loss the night before was the first time all season the Dragons had lost three in a row, Pops and his hitting coach Mike Samuels were grousing about the team in the dugout as the Dragons took BP, even without any prompting from me.

"We can't score no motherfucking runs," Pops said to no one in particular. "That's why I have to get my pitchers outta there so fast. I can't wait. We gotta stop 'em right away because we don't score any runs. … None of those guys tried to do what you practiced with them yesterday in the cage, did they, Mike?"

"No, they didn't," said Samuels.

I asked Samuels what he had been teaching the Dragons' hitters. Mike gave me a long dissertation on hitting, but the gist of his instructional efforts was summed up in one lesson. "We're trying to get them to get the head of the bat out in front by using their hands, not their arms. The idea is to throw the bat at the ball," he said.

"But these guys don't listen," he continued, bringing the conversation back around to the players' attitudes. "That's why they're here."

"We can't give 'em anymore information," said Pops. "They've got all the information they need. Shit, they got more information than we've got. The trouble is they don't know how to put it to use. They can't take knowledge and put it into action. ... They're trying; we know that. But they've made up their minds already. ... And most of these guys are running out of time, if it's not already too late for 'em. ... There's an old saying that baseball scouts use: 'If he's 23, that's all he'll be.' In other words, when a player gets to be 23 years old, what you see is what you get. He ain't gonna get much better than he already is."

Pitching coach Brian Nichols came into the dugout, and I decided to ask him the same question I'd asked Canton pitching coach Doc Schaedler: "Why is there a prejudice against short pitchers?" While Doc had said that the preference for tall pitchers was mainly due to a belief in their being more durable than short pitchers, Nichols framed the issue in terms of comparative effectiveness. "It has to do with the angle at which a pitcher throws," he said. "Taller pitchers throw on more of a downward angle, while short guys throw on a flatter, more level plane, which makes their ball easier to hit. Also, taller guys have a longer reach, so the ball gets to the plate sooner." Although I knew the question was a complicated one, not subject to one simple explanation, Brian's answer made a lot of sense, and I told him that I thought so.

After watching batting practice for a while longer, I began to make my goodbyes. I was going to Mass at 5:00 before the game, and it was time for me to go. I shook hands with Pops and Mike Samuels, thanked them for their time and courtesy, and wished them well for the rest of the season. Pops asked me where I was headed to next. When I told him Cook County, he said, "Hey, do me a favor. We're going to Cook County right after the All-Star Game. Tell LeFlore I said we're coming to Cook County to kick his ass."

"You got it, Pops," I said.

As I gathered up my stuff to leave, a Dragons' hitter who had just finished spraying line drives all over the ballpark in BP, climbed down into the dugout to get his glove. It was John Schmitz, a rookie third baseman from San Mateo, California. A white rookie, who began the day with a .243 batting average.

"Hey, Smitty, if you don't start hitting like that in the game, we're going fishing ... without no fishing poles. ... You understand what I mean?" asked Mike gently.

Schmitz nodded, grabbed his glove, and hurried back onto the field.

I'd decided to go to Mass on Saturday afternoon, which would meet my Sunday Mass obligation, so I could get an early start Sunday morning on my trip to Chicago to visit the Cook County Cheetahs. When I was younger, it was easy to find good excuses for missing Mass on Sunday. Traveling was one of the most convenient. Being from out-of-town, I would tell myself that I didn't know where the nearest Catholic church was—and even though I was perhaps 500 miles from home, ten miles out of my way seemed like a monumental detour—I didn't know what time the Masses were, and, on top of all that, if Sunday were the return-home travel day, as it often was, I needed to sleep late to make sure I wouldn't get drowsy on the road. In fact, I was pretty sure I had an obligation to all the people who loved me and wanted to see me arrive home safely to stay in bed until I'd gotten all the rest I could stand.

That's the way I thought when I was younger. As I got older and wiser to my infinite ability to rationalize, I began to remember what my dad would say when we were on vacation and he would lug the whole family to Mass, no matter how far away it was from where we were staying: "If I don't make every honest effort to get to Mass on Sunday, I don't think I have any right to ask the Lord to watch over me and my family while we are traveling."

There weren't going to be any excuses for missing Mass while I was in Huntingburg, Indiana. St. Mary's on North Washington was the only Catholic church in town, but there were other Catholic churches all over Dubois County, 22 of them according to Friday's edition of *The Herald*; not to mention the Monastery Immaculate Conception in nearby Ferdinand. The Monastery, which sits like a medieval castle on a hill, is a spectacular edifice, and its beautiful dome can be seen from miles away. Every little community in the county, some hardly big enough to have their own post offices, seemed to have its own Catholic church. The fact that a good number of these churches in the tiniest communities had to share a pastor with the church in another tiny community may have pointed to the shortage of priests that is bedeviling the Church in many places, but it was also an indication that the people clung to these parishes with the same devotion and tenacity that was exhibited by the German-Catholic immigrants who had settled much of the area more than a century and a half earlier.

With a 3–1 record, a 3.35 ERA, and the longest innings-pitched-per-start average on the team (6.2 innings per start), rookie starting pitcher Jamal Gaines was pitching better than anybody else on the Dragons' pitching staff, with the exception of closer Chris Viel. The sumo-sized Jamal had a surprisingly smooth delivery, and he threw hard, his power coming as much from his big rear end and thick thighs as from his right arm. "The Big Dogg," who patterned himself after Atlanta Braves pitcher

Greg Maddux, was another California kid and black as coal to boot, but no one could say that he wasn't pulling his own considerable weight. Especially not after he shut down the first-place River City Rascals 2–1, while turning in only the third complete game recorded by a Dragons pitcher all year. The impressive outing solidified his position as the ace of the starting rotation, and, perhaps, as its stopper as well.

Towards the end of Jamal's Maddux-like outing, I left the press box to visit one more time with Dale Helmerich, a former mayor of Huntingburg and a big booster of the Dragons. Mr. Helmerich had chaired the committee responsible for staging the 1999 Frontier League All-Star Game at Huntingburg's League Stadium, and he'd told me proudly that the sellout had made the League a $6,000 profit, which was $4,000–$5,000 more than usual. Unlike many others I'd talked to, Mr. Helmerich was confident about the Dragons' future in Huntingburg. This seemingly unfounded optimism may have stemmed from Mr. Helmerich's fond memories of that All-Star Game success which put the fanny of a baseball fan in every seat in League Stadium, or it may have simply been wishful thinking from someone for whom community failure was unthinkable; in either case the upbeat former mayor would not countenance talk of impending doom for the Dubois County professional baseball franchise.

The Dragons had begun the season with a trainer, but by the time I got to Huntingburg, he was no longer around. Not having a trainer was a serious infraction of league rules, which not even the pollyannaish Mr. Helmerich could gloss over, as well as a practical problem for the team and a detriment to morale. Also missing, and more noticeably so from the fans' point of view, was the Dragons' mascot. Although I never got an explanation about why the Dragons were having to do without a trainer, I did find out, thanks to Mr. Helmerich, why the team was mascot-less.

Mr. Helmerich introduced me to a tall, gregarious red-headed man named Bill Bavirsha, who as "Sparky" the dragon, had once been the greatest mascot in Frontier League history to ever bite off the bald head of an old man or do the "YMCA" dance with a chorus line of gawky pre-teen aged girls. Bavirsha had created Sparky not as a mascot for the Dragons, but as a mascot for the sports teams of the University of Illinois at Chicago when he was a student there. UIC's teams had been ill-advisedly christened the "Flames," an amorphous nickname that was almost impossible to impersonate. Bavirsha's association of "Flames" with the fire-breathing capacity of dragons was a stroke of genius which allowed him to concretize the nickname in a character that people could relate to and which Bavirsha could make a costume for.

Sparky was a furry red giant of a dragon with bulging eyeballs, big teeth, and a thick sweeping tail that kids had to hop over whenever he turned to one side or another. He was friendly, funny, and inventive; a real crowd pleaser. He was perfect for the Dragons and undoubtedly boosted attendance, but Sparky was seen in Dubois County only during the summers of Bavirsha's college years when Bill worked in the Dragons' front office as Facilities Director by day and as an entertainer at night. Once Bill graduated and became UIC's "Director of Athletic Facilities," Sparky remained home in Chicago. The Dragons did not bother to find a replacement for Sparky, but perhaps they would have had they realized how much he meant to their fans, especially their youngest fans.

"In the middle of the summer, the temperature inside the costume gets up to about 110 degrees, and the suit gets pretty sweaty and smelly," said Bavirsha. "After most games I would let it air dry at the Stadium, but eventually it would need to be washed, so I'd take it to the laundromat. Of course, I didn't want any of the kids to see me doing this, so I tried to be as inconspicuous as possible.

"One day I went to the laundromat and carried the suit there in a large black plastic garbage bag. I put it in one of those big commercial washers with the window in the door, turned it on, and sat down to read a newspaper. A mom came in to do the family wash, and she had a little boy with her who was about four or five. He was running around playing while his mom was busy doing the laundry. He came running past where I was sitting, and when he saw my washer with the red costume spinning around inside it, he stopped dead in his tracks. He dropped the toy he was carrying, walked up close to the washer, started moving his head around and around in a circular motion, and shouted. 'Sparky! ... Sparky! ... Sparky!'

"I couldn't help but laugh, but I couldn't say anything, so I hid behind my newspaper. Fortunately, the little boy's mother was quick-witted. When he expressed his concern for Sparky, she calmed him down by telling him, 'He's just taking a bath.'"

In the bottom of the eighth inning with Dubois County ahead 2–1 and a Dragons' runner on first with no outs, left fielder Scott Marple bunted twice, unsuccessfully. On his second attempt, more of a slug bunt than a straight-up sacrifice bunt, the bat flew out of his hands and indicated to me that he didn't really have his heart in sacrificing. Pops left the bunt sign on with two strikes, and Marple struck out when his third attempt went foul.

Was this an example of the dubious strategy that Robert Lee's unnamed source claimed some of the Dragons complained about? If so, the malcontents were way off base. Keeping the bunt on with two strikes was a calculated risk but also a way for Pops to emphasize, without saying a word, the importance of getting the sacrifice bunt down. His point was proven by the outcome of the inning. Roy Muro's single to center field might have driven in the insurance run the Dragons were playing for had the runner on first been sacrificed to second. As things were, he was left stranded on base after a second strikeout and a pop fly ended the inning.

After the game a few Dragons lingered on the field by the far end of the dugout, signing autographs and talking to the host family parents who'd adopted them for the summer; but most of the players, intent on making a party out of what was left of Saturday night, bolted for the clubhouse, where pounding rap assaulted the hearing of anyone over 30 years old and repelled them the same way that high frequency gadgets plugged into the wall promise to keep away rodents and insects. The park emptied quickly, and with no where else to go but an empty hotel room, I hopped over the grandstand railing onto the diamond and walked into the Dragons' dugout. The dugout was already deserted except for Adam Patterson, the rookie All-Star catcher who'd gotten my attention in the first inning when he'd hustled down the first base line on a ground out to back up a throw from Fran Riordan to Jamal Gaines.

Patterson was sitting on the top ledge of the dugout bench, five two-by-fours wide, with his feet resting on the seat of the dugout bench, rather than the dugout floor. His white Dragons uniform with purple pinstripes and teal sleeves was soaked in perspiration, and he rested his chin on the knob of a Louisville Slugger which he held between his knees. At this point in his career Patterson was an offensive player playing a defensive position. His bat was a big asset for him, and his batting from the left side an extra plus as it made him more useful as a pinch hitter; but his future in professional baseball would not get much brighter until he improved his capabilities as a backstop.

We sat there together a few moments, silently soaking up the palpable feeling of victory that still suffused the dugout, then slowly began talking.

"Jamal threw a hell of a game tonight," I said.

"Yes, he did," said Patterson. "It's like a Nintendo game when a guy's pitching like that. The only time he gets hurt is when he misses his spot. Tonight he had a good game hitting his spots."

"It looked to me as if he had a good fastball out there."

"Jamal's fastball was pretty straight and flat tonight, but we set the batters up for it. ... Which is what you have to do. You can throw 110 miles an hour and get ripped if you don't know where it's going. There's a lot of guys in this league like that."

"Is the fastball his out pitch?"

"Not really."

"Well, what is his out pitch?"

"He doesn't really have an out pitch. It's a different out pitch for every batter. We basically let the batters get themselves out. We try to move the ball around, keep the hitters off balance, and never throw one right down the middle."

Jamal obviously was a long way from being as good a pitcher as Greg Maddux, but the approach that he and his catcher took to the art of pitching did sound a lot like the Maddux M.O.

I shifted the conversation from Gaines to Patterson himself, and in telling me about his own nascent professional career, Adam spoke often and appreciatively about his manager. It occurred to me that Patterson's regard for Pops was the foundation of a relationship that might grow into one similar to the relationship that existed between Pops and Mal Finchman.

Patterson had played his college baseball at Catawba, a small Division II school located in Salisbury, North Carolina, at the western edge of the state's central plains, about an hour north of Charlotte. Undrafted out of college, he had tried out for the New Jersey Jackals of the Northern League. New Jersey didn't sign him either, but they were interested in him as a future Jackal and told him he should get a year of seasoning in the Frontier League. Patterson took a 13-hour bus ride to get to the league-wide pre-season tryouts in Richmond and wound up being chosen as the number one pick of the Dubois County Dragons by their manager Tim Wallace. "After the tryouts Pops took me home with him and let me stay with him," said Patterson. "I didn't know anybody in town or have anybody to stay with yet, so I really appreciated that."

Patterson went on to explain how Pops had also been helping him adjust to professional baseball: "I'm a rookie and I'm not used to batting with wooden bats, so Pops keeps me in the middle of the batting order behind Fran Riordan, who's a veteran. He also tries to keep me away from lefthanded pitching which, as you know, is tougher for lefthanded batters like me to hit. He doesn't always sit me against lefhanders, but he tries to keep me in situations I'll be successful in. And it's working because I'm 8–12 against lefthanded pitching. In college I would have been upset if I wasn't starting, but Pops told me before the season started, 'Don't wig out if you're not playing. It's a long season. I'm going to give you days off even if you don't need them.' And I think that's working too because I've gained four pounds this summer."

Patterson told me that he too was going out to drink a few beers. He'd been in no big rush to get ready though because his drinking buddy was going to be his batterymate, Jamal Gaines, and Jamal wasn't going anywhere until he'd iced down his pitching shoulder. Still, there seemed to be meaning behind Adam's having stayed in the dugout, so I asked him why he was still there.

"Most guys, whether they're really happy they did something right or unhappy because they screwed up, rush right into the locker room," he said. "I don't like to do that. Now that I'm a professional ball player, this is my office, and my teammates are my family. At the end of the day, I like to leave my emotions at the office. I don't take them home to the family."

The stadium lights were turned off, and we were suddenly in darkness. As we both stood up to leave, he added, "You know, I also hang around in the dugout because I just hate to leave. I wouldn't care if they put a bed out here for me. I'd sleep in it. I really would. I love it that much."

Crestwood, Illinois (population 12,000), is one of the numerous suburban communities, villages, and towns that combine in a huge sprawl to form one of America's greatest cities; often referred to locally as "Chicagoland," as if the place were a continent and not a mere megalopolis. Located on Chicago's southside off I-294, Crestwood supports a minor league baseball team in the shadows of not one but two major league franchises, the Cubs and the White Sox. "Chicagoland" is so populous and such a hot bed of baseball fever that another minor league team, this one the Kane County Cougars who are affiliated with the Florida Marlins, prospers on the city's northside. Even so, the Frontier League in Chicago? It was a miracle and a travesty, a mad gamble and a brilliant coup all at once.

Like the Dubois County Dragons, the Cook County Cheetahs were refugees from the defunct Heartland League of independent professional baseball clubs. The team began life in 1996 as the Will County Cheetahs, and they started out playing home games in Romeoville, Illinois, at a small college whose baseball facility was woefully inadequate for professional baseball, even after the Cheetahs built wooden grandstands to accommodate 1,200. Such humble beginnings almost doomed the franchise; but in a scenario that has been played out all over America on both the major and minor league levels, a deal for a publicly financed new stadium became the salvation of the team. With Mayor Chester Stranczek, a former Philadelphia Phillies farm hand, leading the way, the city of Crestwood hired the same architectural firm that designed Camden Yards in Baltimore and the new Comiskey Park in nearby Chicago; and $9 million later the Cheetahs had a new state-of-the-art ballyard which gave the franchise the credibility it needed in the savvy suburban Chicago baseball market. The Cheetahs joined the Frontier League as an expansion franchise after the 1998 season, and

Hawkinson Ford Field, named after a local automotive dealership, opened in June of 1999, just in time for Cook County's first go-round in the league. I arrived at Hawkinson Ford Field on Sunday afternoon a couple of hours before the game's five o'clock start. My impression of the ballpark was that it was clean, spacious (3,200 capacity), and functional—as ordinary, in other words, as the typical new upscale shopping mall, designed to maximize spending and profit. Its upper deck which extended down one foul line (left field) only gave the park a half-finished, asymmetrical look and brought to mind public sculpture fashioned by artists intent on breaking rules and instigating controversy. The only other feature of note was the trailer parked on the plaza in the left field corner which housed the main ticket booth and the Cheetahs' administrative offices. For once, it wasn't the umpires and their needs which seemed to have been an afterthought or low priority.

After exploring Hawkinson Ford Field, I went over to the office trailer, where I met some of the staff and picked up some background information on the team. Going over the Cook County roster I noticed that the Cheetahs appeared to have an Outback pipeline, as six of their players were from Australia: pitcher Chris Oxspring, catcher Andy Uting, infielder Ben Foster, and the entire starting outfield: Grant McDonald, Brandon Pollard, and Darren White. GM Gerry Clarke explained how this had happened. In 1997 the Australian Baseball Federation team played a series of exhibition games across the United States. "They were phenomenal," said Clarke. Their head coach, Mike Young, was a Chicago native and a friend of one of the Cheetahs' assistant coaches. Since the baseball seasons in the two countries are on opposite ends of the calendar, Cook County and the Queensland, Australia, team agreed to swap players. The 2000 season was the third year of the arrangement.

Also hard to miss on the roster was Justin Pierro, an infielder whose weight was listed at 265. I was immediately intrigued by Pierro because I've always had a spot, as soft as a Milky Way on a hot day, in my heart for the calorically challenged baseball player. My all-time favorite player has always been the incomparable Willie Mays; who, by the way, astonished Army doctors during his induction physical by having the lowest body fat they had ever measured. Once Willie retired, I never really rooted for another player until Dale Murphy came along. After Murphy, there was nobody besides Cecil Fielder. I took to big Cecil, I think, because the weight fascists were so opposed to him. They acted insulted that such a huge guy had the nerve to believe that there was a place for him in major league baseball, and they ridiculed the impressive home run hitting he did in Japan. I rejoiced when Cecil came back to the states and feasted off American League pitching.

Pierro probably wasn't aware of it, but there has always been room for fat guys in our National Pastime. Back in the twenties when it wasn't a crime to poke fun at such things, Tigers' outfielder Bob Fothergill was actually called "Fatty." Fothergill wasn't thrilled with the nickname, but he didn't let it keep from swinging a mean stick as he averaged .325 for his major league career. There have been plenty of other guys who deserved the nickname as much as Fothergill; guys like Boog Powell, George Scott, David Wells, and even Babe Ruth, all of whom were good guys and good ballplayers. The fattest ballplayer of all was probably Jumbo Brown, a pitcher for the Yankees and Giants in the 1930s, about whose weight of 295 pounds Bill James said: "So far as I know, that is the grossest tonnage ever acknowledged by a major league player." The fat guy who had the most fun with his weight was relief pitcher Terry Forster. David Letterman called him a "big tub of goo," and instead of suing, Forster got himself invited to appear on Letterman's *Late Night Show*, where he upstaged the host with cracks like "A waist is a terrible thing to mind" and "My weight snacked up on me."

Sunday evening's game was going to be between the Cheetahs and the Evansville Otters. The last-place Otters had come to town after being swept in River City, but they'd won Saturday night's opener against Cook County 3–1. I'd seen Evansville in Canton and had not been that impressed with their ballclub, but Max had told me not to count them out of the pennant race; not as long as they were managed by Greg Tagert. Tall and skinny, Tagert wore glasses and always had a stop watch in his hand or stuffed into his back pocket. He did a lot of jogging and looked a whole lot more like a high school track coach than a professional baseball manager, but he was considered one of the best managers in the Frontier League.

When it was time for the exchange of lineup cards, three umpires, not two, walked out to home plate. I took this to be an indication of Cook County's appreciation for the importance of umpiring and made a mental note to tell Max about it. Later someone told me that I was giving the Cheetahs more credit than they deserved. The Cheetahs, it turned out, were spending the same $150 per game as other Frontier League teams; the umpires were merely splitting the money three ways instead of two.

Going into the game the Cheetahs stood out in one statistical category: stolen bases. No other team was even close to their total of 94 (runnerup River City had 52), but their success as base thieves hadn't made them a winning team or even a good club offensively. They were a mediocre sixth in runs scored and eighth in batting average. The Cheetahs' pitching looked even more dismal, statistically. They led the league by a wide margin in hits allowed, and the team ERA of 4.80 was next to worst.

Sunday's game didn't improve things any. Cheetahs' starter Gerald Yuscavage gave up only two earned runs in five and a third innings; but, aided by Cook County errors, the Otters scored four runs on only one hit in the sixth and won the game 9–5.

I hated to admit it to myself, but I was more entertained by the P.A. announcer, Kevin "Your Honor" O'Connor and his guest than by the game itself. O'Connor regularly punctuated the action on the field with carefully-timed sound bites from the *Andy Griffith Show* and Chris Farley and Jim Carey movies. His guest was a man named Dennis Duffels who imitated Harry Caray. Duffels wore ridiculously big, black eye-glass frames à la Caray, but he was too slight of build, was not enough of a Bud man, to resemble the Cubs' former broadcaster physically. On the other hand, he *sounded* exactly like Caray. At times Duffels would make unsolicited comments; with Cook County trailing late in the game, he lamented: "Why couldn't we have had eight guys on base when Darren White hit that home run?" At other times O'Connor would play straight man to Duffels' Caray:

O'Connor: "Harry, do you play golf?"

Duffels-Caray: "Yes, I do, Kevin. ... By the way, do you know that golf spelled backwards is flog!"

What made the whole thing seem surreal is that O'Connor sounded, naturally, just like actor Tom Hanks. At one point, O'Connor announced that the ladies who'd played in the All-American Girls Professional Baseball League would be coming to a future game at Hawkinson Ford Field for a reunion. He said, "By the way, that reminds me ..." and then he played a sound bite from the movie *A League of Their Own* of Tom Hanks saying, "There's no crying in baseball!" He could have skipped the recording and simply said the words himself because no one would have been able to tell the difference. O'Connor sounded like such a dead ringer for Hanks that it was like listening to Hanks visiting with Caray in the Cubs' broadcast booth at Wrigley Field.

After the game I called the Chicago home of a couple who were dear friends of mine and my wife, despite the fact that we seldom got to see each other. The last time I was in town I'd gotten to know and love their two young teenagers, one girl and one boy, and I was particularly anxious to see them again. Nicole answered the phone, and after we chatted briefly about why I was in town, I expressed my desire to see everybody.

"Do you need a place to stay?" she asked.

"No, I don't need a place to stay," I said, "but I would like to see you and Danny and the kids."

"Well, you're welcome to stay here, Mike, but I can't cook for you like I did last time," she said.

"That's okay. I don't expect that. In fact, why don't you let me take everybody out to dinner?"

There was a silence, which I later realized was Nicole wondering what to say and how to say it. In the end she decided to just come right out with it.

"Mike, Danny has moved out," she said.

I looked at the outfield grass to see if it were still green, and I checked the twilight sky to see if the stars were still in their places. Suddenly, the world didn't make sense anymore. I couldn't have been more stunned by what Nicole had just said had it been proven that Babe Ruth was really a woman. Danny and Nicole had been married for more than twenty years, and everyone who knew them knew that no couple could be more devoted to each other than they were.

I fumbled out expressions of disbelief and questions about "How?" and "Why?" and "When?" until I realized that there was no way I could just tell Nicole, over the phone, how sorry I was and go on with my own life, which now seemed like a non-stop holiday. I knew that I'd never been regarded as a very empathetic person, but it was time for me to try to be one.

"I'm coming over, Nicole," I insisted. "Just tell me how to get there from here."

The next day I was hanging around the Cheetahs' office trailer, still trying to come to grips with the dissolving marriage of my friends, when Ron LeFlore showed up. He had on Nikes with no socks, a gray T-shirt that said "Expos Baseball," a gold bracelet on his right wrist, two gold chains around his neck, and an expansion-era Montreal Expos baseball cap. Everything he was wearing looked new. He had graying hair, bulging eyes, and a pot belly, but he still moved with the grace of a man who'd once run fast enough to be a champion base stealer in the major leagues. In LeFlore, the Cheetahs offered their fans a manager who was not only an ex-big league star, but also an ex-con whose life had already been turned into a book (*Breakout: From Prison to the Big Leagues*) and a TV movie (*One in a Million: The Ron LeFlore Story*) two decades earlier. In naming the movie, Hollywood had shown uncharacteristic restraint, as LeFlore's incredible journey—he went from the state penitentiary to the starting lineup of the Detroit Tigers in about a year's time—was not a million-to-one but a billion-to-one shot; especially, given the fact that he had never played baseball on any level before he was sent to the State Prison of Southern Michigan in Jackson to serve a 5-to-15 year sentence for armed robbery. LeFlore hadn't even been a baseball fan before he went to prison. He considered football to be his sport, and his hero was Jim Brown. LeFlore started playing baseball only because he thought it would help him gain an early parole.

LeFlore had played nine years in the big leagues and compiled a more than respectable record. He'd led each league in stolen bases (swiping 68 for Detroit in 1978 and 97 for Montreal in 1980), made the American League All-Star team in 1978, and finished with a career .288 batting average. More importantly, he'd stayed out of trouble and kept his promise to himself that he would never return to prison. Once was more than enough for LeFlore, who'd learned his lesson well. "Really, prison was the best thing that could have happened to me," he'd told a Canton newspaper reporter earlier in the year. "If I hadn't gone to prison, who's to say I would be alive right now. All my buddies I grew up with, not one of them is still living."

LeFlore had come into the office to go over the itinerary for his players' trip to the All-Star Game in River City (pitcher Tim Pulizzano, catcher Jason Imrisek, second baseman Mike Davis, outfielder Brandon Pollard, and the big boy, Justin Pierro, were the Cheetahs who'd been selected to the West Division squad). I learned later that he argued for and won an increase in the players' per diem for the All-Star break from the $12.50 the team had budgeted to $20. "It's bullshit to give these guys $12.50. This is a special event, and they should get $20 at least," he'd said. This concern for his players was in keeping with what I'd heard the day before from Josh Wilkie, a rookie outfielder from Butler University who'd been in the Cheetahs' starting lineup until he crashed into the wall making a great catch at Thurman Munson Stadium in Canton. Wilkie had shattered his wrist which was now held together by a gruesome-looking device of five metal pins and a bar called an external fixator. I'd almost passed out listening to Wilkie describe how the doctor had set the broken bones in his wrist.

"Ron is a class guy who really takes care of his players," said Wilkie. "They can be kind of cheap here, but he got us things we needed in the clubhouse: tooth paste, shaving cream, shampoo, stuff like that. When we started out this year, we didn't have any shorts or baseball sleeves to work out in, but he got 'em for us two weeks into the season. He also got us some Mizuno pullovers that he paid for out of his own pocket. Ron may not be as good at teaching the fundamentals as the coach I had in college, but he's learning every day; and he's very aggressive, which personally I like a lot. He's also very fair and honest. He shows no favoritism, and he tells it like it is. He lets you know that if you don't hustle or don't perform, you'll be out of here. Which is the way it should be: we're not in Little League anymore. Ron is just a players' manager, and the relationship he has with the players is the best I've ever seen a coach have."

When LeFlore came out of the meeting, I introduced myself and explained that I was writing a book about the Frontier League and one of its umpires, Max McLeary, who did games in Chillicothe, Richmond, and Canton. We talked about the Cheetahs and the whole idea of independent professional baseball for a while, and then he asked me how he could help me with the book.

"Well, I've heard you're not very happy with the umpiring," I said. "Since my book is mainly about an umpire, I wanted to get your take on the subject."

"Well, I don't know this guy you're writing your book about," he said, "but I'll tell you this: the umpiring in this league is so bad I'm going to call a press conference to tell the media that the umps need to be reined in."

"Really?" I said, astonished that he would contemplate doing such a thing.

"Hell, yes," he said. "They cuss at the players and nothing happens to them, but whenever the players cuss they throw the players out of the game. That's not right."

"The umps really do that much swearing?"

"Damn straight. They'll say, 'Get the fuck out of the fucking ballpark. I'm telling you to get the fuck off the field.' And you can't do nothing about it. I've heard the umps have it in for me and the Cheetahs because I stand up for my ballclub to incompetent umps. … They can be pissed at me, but don't take it out on my players.

"This league has been around for eight years, and what's keeping it from getting more recognition is the poor quality of the umpiring. These umps don't know what they're doing. And I can't help it if I played ten years in the major leagues and know more about umpiring than they do."

In half a summer I'd learned a lot about umpiring from Max; enough that by this time I was suspicious of any non-umpire who claimed he knew more about umpiring than the umpires. When I told LeFlore this, he informed me that he wasn't boasting idly. He told me that he'd wanted to be a professional umpire himself and that he'd graduated from Joe Brinkman's umpiring school in 1989. I was surprised and impressed to learn this about LeFlore, who wanted to make sure I understood exactly where he stood in regard to the umpiring in the Frontier League.

"I don't have any respect for the umpires in this league because they don't have any respect for me," he said. "… Why is that? Why won't they give me any respect? Do they hold it against me because I came out of prison and spent ten years in the major leagues and was successful there? That's the way I feel. That they hold my success against me."

"Every team in the league gets the close calls at home. Not us. Every team has a home field advantage but not us. The fans are great everywhere I go, all around the league. But not the umpires. They don't give me any respect, and I don't have any respect for them. They can't even *earn* my respect. That's how bad they are.

"The other night in Springfield I got thrown out of a game, and all I did was ask the ump to make a call. 'Would you please make a call?' I said. I didn't cuss at him, but he threw me out. I can't accept a fine for simply asking the guy to make the call."

Justin Pierro and catcher Andy Uting walked past us on their way out of the trailer, and LeFlore asked them, "Did I cuss at the ump the other night in Springfield? ... before he threw me out?"

Both players agreed that their manager hadn't sworn at the umpire, prior to being ejected.

Ron told me he needed to get down on the field, so we left the trailer too. As we walked, he continued his harangue against the umpires. "Two weeks ago in Chillicothe the umpire hit me with a baseball. Did he get a fine for throwing a baseball at me?"

"The umpire threw a baseball at you?" This was an image I had a hard time picturing.

"Yeah, I had a baseball thrown at me in Chillicothe by the umpire," he said. "Chillicothe had a left-handed batter up who hit a roller down first. Pierro fielded it and stepped on the bag, and then the ump called it foul. I asked him why the ball was foul. He said because the ball hit the batter's foot in the batter's box. I told him, 'Check the ball then and see if there's a shoe polish mark on the ball.' He picked the ball up, looked at it a second, then threw it at me and hit me with it. So I threw it back at him."

"Wow, Ron, you've really had a rough time with the umpires this year," I said.

"Yes, I have," he said. "but I'm going to write Bill Lee a letter and tell him I'm gonna call a press conference to let the public know how things in this league are being run by the umpires. ... And the owner of the Chillicothe team."

When we got into the dugout, LeFlore grabbed a walkie-talkie and told somebody on the other end: "This music is putting us to sleep. We need something with a little rhythm, a little bump."

LeFlore excused himself, saying that he needed to get dressed for the game. I thanked him for his time and candor, then delivered the message I'd promised Tim Wallace I would give him. "Tell Pops to kiss my ass," was LeFlore's reply.

I'd found LeFlore to be likable, articulate, and cooperative, and he had given me quite an interview to say the least. I felt that he'd probably exaggerated the mistreatment he'd received at the hands of the umpires, even though I was sure that it had felt real enough to him. It seemed obvious to me that he was unfortunately making things harder for himself by becoming an enemy of the umpires; on the other hand, I recalled that some of the most successful managers in major league history hated and were hated by the umpires: John McGraw, Leo Durocher, Billy Martin, Earl Weaver. Maybe Ron LeFlore would follow in their footsteps and succeed despite his antipathy for the umpires in the Frontier League.

One of the Cheetahs' assistant coaches, Scott Spero, was sitting in the dugout, and I asked him if he agreed with LeFlore's assessment of the umpiring Cook County had been receiving. "I wouldn't say they're out to get us, out to screw us … they're missing shit. They're inconsistent," he said. "We'll accept in and out but not high and low too. Make it one or the other." Spero was referring to the tendency of some umpires to enlarge their strike zones in both directions.

On this note, Carlos May, the Cheetahs' hitting coach who was also a former major leaguer, chimed in. "I played in the big leagues," he said, "and guys would have a low strike zone or a high strike zone, but whatever it was, it would stay the same for the whole game. Here, we'll be rolling along, and all of a sudden things change. Ron will ask them, 'Where was that pitch?' and they won't even acknowledge the question! On the road we'll even throw 'em right down the cock, and we don't get the call. For an instructional league, for lack of a better term, it ain't helping the pitchers who are as confused as we are as to what is a strike. Everybody is looking for pitching, but the umpiring makes it harder to graduate guys out of the league."

I took these comments in and then asked if anybody could tell me how LeFlore had come to have a baseball thrown at him by an umpire, if it had actually happened at all. Doug Wellenreiter, a local high school baseball coach, who said that serving as the Cheetahs' pitching coach was a "once-in-a-lifetime opportunity" for him, began speaking: "Juan Mendoza was pitching for us against Chillicothe, and he didn't like the ball and strike calls, said the ump had a pretty narrow strike zone. 'You gotta do something,' he told Ron. So Ron said some things in support of Mendoza's pitching. Right after that the ump made an 'I'll show you' call. Mendoza threw one right down the cock, and he went 'BALL!' Our whole team got upset.

"The batter hit a ball down to first, Pierro caught it, stepped on first, and then the ump called it foul. Ron went out to question the call, and the ump said it was foul because it had hit the batter's foot in the batter's box. Ron said that if it hit 'em it would have a mark on it, so check the ball. They had to get the ball from the bat boy because the base ump had taken the ball from Pierro and tossed it to the bat boy. When the plate ump got the ball back, he stuck it in our catcher's face: 'See!'—it did have a black mark on it—and then he rolled it towards Ron who was walking back to the dugout down the path between home and the dugout. It bounced up and hit Ron in the back of the leg. Ron said, 'What the fuck! Did he throw that?' Everybody in our dugout said, 'Yeah, yeah! The ump threw it!'

"So Ron picked the ball up and threw it back at the ump, who was bending over the catcher, ready to resume the game. He didn't whiz it. He didn't drill him. It was a dart shot. It arched and went about 20 feet in the air, but it did hit the ump in the back. Ron got ejected from the game, which would have been his second ejection of the season; but Bill Lee, the Commissioner, said, 'We won't count that one because the ump basically started it by hitting Ron first.'"

Cheetahs players, wearing their red jerseys with black and gold trim, were going in and out of the dugout now, and I was able to corner Justin Pierro for a couple of minutes. Pierro had a broad friendly face and something of a double chin; he wore his cap pulled down tight onto his head and sort of squinted from underneath its bill. He told me that he'd played his college ball at Loras College, a Division III school in Dubuque, Iowa. He had signed with Evansville out of college in 1999, but they released him before the season started. The Cheetahs' Assistant GM, Larry Millar, called him and invited him to try out with Cook County. Millar told me later, "I was shocked when I first saw him. I knew he was big, but not that big! But then when I saw how far he could hit the ball I was delighted we'd been able to pick him up. He also surprised us by being so nimble at first base. He has great feet for a guy his size."

Although the Cheetahs occasionally used him at first base, Pierro was basically a designated hitter, so I asked him if he minded being cast in that role. "I do enjoy playing the field once in a while because then I'm too busy to worry about bad at bats. When you DH you have too much time to sit there and worry. But I like to hit, and DHing is what keeps me in the lineup."

"Has anybody ever referred to you as 'The White Cecil Fielder'? I think that would be a great nickname for you."

He laughed and said no, nobody had ever called him that. Besides, he already had a nickname: Bing. "Bing?"

"Yeah. When I first got here last year nobody knew my name, but they had to call me something because I was hitting the ball over all the place in batting practice. They started calling me 'Big New Guy' or BNG, for short, which eventually morphed into Bing."

Before I headed up to the press box, I asked if anybody had any funny stories I could put in my next baseball anecdote book. Neither Spero nor May nor Wellenreiter could come up with anything on the spur of the moment, but Ron had returned to the dugout and said he had one.

"This happened when I was playing for the Tigers in Detroit," he said. "Joe Brinkman was umpiring at third base that day, and right before they played the National Anthem, Alex Johnson started out of our dugout and said, 'Who shit on the field and called it the umpire?' Brinkman threw him out the game before he even got on the field."

The game turned out to be a Frontier League rarity, a pitcher's duel decided by one late-inning at bat in a crucial situation.

Going into the bottom of the eighth with the Otters ahead 2–1, Evansville starter Jeff Blitstein was working on a three-hitter, but Aussie center fielder Grant McDonald doubled to left field to start the inning and set in motion the decisive showdown of strategies and skills. The second spot in the batting order is seldom manned by a catcher, but Cheetahs backstop Jason Imprisek showed he was capable of hitting in the two hole by laying down a perfect sacrifice bunt that moved McDonald over to third. Managing by the book, Greg Tagert brought the Otters' infield in to the grass, and the gamble paid off when Darren White hit a ground ball right at shortstop Paul Bartolucci, who was able to hold McDonald at third as he threw across the diamond to retire White.

That brought the big boy, the Cheetahs' designated hitter, Justin Pierro to the plate with two out. After the game Wellenreiter told me: "It's kind of crazy to pitch to a home run hitter in that situation. You walk a guy like that and take your chances with the next guy. At least I know I wouldn't pitch to him in that situation. They'd been getting him out all night with the slider, but the sliders were all down in the dirt. Pitchers sometimes hang a pitch in that situation and get hurt, and that's what happened."

The count went to 3–2 on Pierro, who'd flied out, struck out, and grounded out previously. Blitstein's next pitch may have been a slider that didn't slide, as Wellenreiter assumed it was, but it looked like a fastball to Pierro, the fastball over the plate he'd been looking for all night. Justin jumped all over it and sent it soaring, a no-doubter, over the left field wall. As Pierro rounded third, with the go-ahead run that became the winning run after the Otters went down 1-2-3 in the ninth, LeFlore gave him a Bash Brothers high five (balled fists knocked together instead of the slapping of open palms) that had been popularized by the Oakland A's.

It was a great ending to my visit with the Cheetahs. Baseball fans adopt players as their favorites for all sorts of reasons. One thing that always helps solidify such a relationship, especially in its budding stages, is for the favorite player to come through with a big play in the clutch. My favorite Cook County Cheetah had done just that in made-to-order fashion. Now that I was twice the age of my new-found hero, I got to do something that I'd only dreamed about doing four decades earlier when I was a Little Leaguer rooting for the Jacksonville Suns, the Triple-A affiliate of the Cleveland Indians and later the St. Louis Cardinals. I got to go down on the field right after the last out of the game was made and ask the star of the game, my favorite player, how he felt about what he'd just done.

His face was still beaming as he headed back to the dugout from near home plate where he'd been talking with the Cheetahs' radio color commentator, Milt Pappas, a former Chicago Cubs pitcher who'd pitched a no-hitter for the Cubs and won more than 100 games in both major leagues.

I congratulated him and said, "Not bad for The White Cecil Fielder." He laughed and said thanks. Then I asked him how he felt.

"I feel great," he said. "We needed this win, bad, and it's nice to come through for the team. Things are going great for me: first, I made the All-Star team, and now, this home run that won the game. It's been a great week ... and it's only Monday!"

PS JBUS '89

CHEETAHS IN 2000
← MANAGER RON LEFLORE
HITTING COACH CARLOS MAY

RADIO COLOR: MILT PAPPAS

—NOT BAD—

8

An All-Star Show in St. Louis; Same Old Thing in Chillicothe

O'FALLON, MISSOURI, LESS THAN a half hour from Busch Stadium in downtown, St. Louis, represented the western boundary of the Frontier League in 2000. Although small (population 18,698), O'Fallon had been dubbed "the fastest growing city in America," and there was no impugning the league's wisdom in having decided to locate the River City expansion franchise there. In the second year of their existence the Rascals were leading the league in attendance at the All-Star break with an average of 3,655 per game, which was slightly ahead of the league-leading pace they had set the year before of 3,610.

The franchise had everything going for it: a new $4 million ballpark; excellent press coverage from both the *St. Louis Post-Dispatch* and the *Suburban Journal* of nearby St. Charles; the league's best logo—a rascally-looking beagle with one black eye and a baseball in its mouth; and a good team. In fact, after having finished last in the West Division the year before with a 39–45 record, River City went into the 2000 All-Star break with the best record in the league, a 24–14 slate that put them six full games ahead of second-place Cook County. The Rascals were such an unqualified success that the league had already committed itself to adding another franchise in the area, the Gateway Grizzlies who would begin play in 2001 in Collinsville, Illinois, a short distance from St. Louis on the other, eastern side of the Mississippi. The Rascals and Grizzlies were doubtlessly destined to become rivals on a par with the Paints and Roosters.

All-Star Game headquarters were at the Holiday Inn Select on I-70 in St. Peters, Missouri (less than ten miles east of O'Fallon), and when I got there, the Board of Directors' meeting was just adjourning and then partially reconvening in the hotel lounge. The most laughter seemed to be coming from a table where Alfredo Portela, Duke Ward, and John Wallenstein, the GM of the Springfield Capitals, were holding court. Also sitting at the table were two of Alfredo's young lieutenants, David Skoczen, the Canton Crocodiles' Director of Public Relations and Broadcasting and attractive Kristin Dolan, the Crocs' Ticket Manager. This trip was part of their continuing education, and they sat quietly in the background, nursing their drinks and hanging on Alfredo's every word.

The conversation eventually got around to promotional acts, and the consensus at the table deemed the three greatest acts in minor league baseball to be The Famous Chicken, The Blues Brothers, and Myron Noodleman, a comic in the Jerry Lewis vein. About The Chicken, aka Ted Giannoulas, Duke Ward said: "Ted is a great guy and an absolute professional. Nobody puts on a better show than Ted. But sometimes he gets carried away with himself. One time he was supposed to be the Grand Marshall of a parade in Richmond and ride in a convertible at the front of the parade. Well, he was late for the parade, and they started without him. He got pretty mad about it, acted like he'd been highly insulted, and couldn't believe they didn't wait for him. He said, 'If it had been Michael Jordan, they would have waited for him.' I said, 'Yeah, but you're not Michael Jordan. You're just a man in a chicken suit.'"

I listened to some more shop talk for a while, then decided to rest a little in my room before heading over to the Rascals' ballpark for a buffet dinner and social hour. As I was leaving the lounge, I was waved over to another table by Kevin Rouch, the Chillicothe radio play-by-play broadcaster and the league's official legal counsel as well. The sanguine Rouch was a notorious card, always ready with a joke or a pun, so I was not surprised that he had something humorous to convey to me. "Hey, I just wanted to make sure you knew about something that I said one time that might help you with your book," he said.

He asked me if I'd ever heard of Jamie Irving, the Harvard graduate who'd spent time in the Frontier League as an ambidextrous pitcher. I assured Kevin that I had heard of the kid.

"I don't know if you knew this, but Irving hurt his right arm in high school his junior year and taught himself to pitch with his left arm," said Rouch. "Later, in college his right arm got better, and so he started using both arms. Well, one time we were playing Johnstown, and Irving did his thing: he started an inning pitching righthanded after he'd been pitching lefthanded. When I realized what he was doing, I said, 'Jamie Irving is relieving himself on the mound with his right hand.' I said that on the air, and as soon as I did, the other guys in the booth realized what I'd said and started laughing. I went: 'Did I really say what I think I just said?'"

I hitched a ride over to T.R. Hughes Ballpark (located at 900 Ozzie Smith Drive in O'Fallon) on the Chillicothe team bus, a somewhat antique yet highly serviceable model, painted maroon and adorned with the Paints' logo. As a reward for their service, the entire Paints staff had been invited to make the trip. Four Paints' players were on the bus: pitcher Sean Boesch, shortstop Mike Cervenak, and outfielders Joe Colameco and Greg Strickland; and all three of the position players were going to start the game. Two other Paints, pitchers Josh White and Andy Lee, had been named to the All-Star team but were unable to play due to injury and hadn't made the trip. Also on the bus were the Roosters' All-Stars whom the Paints had picked up in Richmond: catcher Keith Fout, outfielder Aaron Sledd, and pitchers Bobby Chandler, J.T. Engstrom, Rich Jelovcic, and Phill Kojack. Unusual as it may seem, Chillicothe's good deed was typical of the relationship that existed between the two old-time Frontier League franchises. As Chris Hanners had told me: "I have the deepest respect for John Cate and Duke Ward as individuals and businessmen and baseball people, and we share ideas and resources with them and try to help them out whenever we can. ... But when the games start, we try to kick their ass, and they try to kick ours. We are each other's biggest rival."

Somehow the Rascals had built their new park for less than half of what the Cheetahs' new stadium had cost and gotten a facility that in no way took a back seat to Cook County's. The 4,080 person capacity of the place was mainly accomplished by a single concrete grandstand, stretching from the right field foul pole to behind third base, that felt like a natural, outdoor amphitheater by virtue of its being completely roofless. Even more appealing than this exhilarating openness were the asymmetrical distances down the foul lines (325 in left, 300 in right) and the "Big Dog Wall," a massive, towering combination of billboard, barrier, and scoreboard in right that gave the diamond an intimacy and focal point it otherwise would have lacked, while taking away any chance whatsoever of the cheap home run.

The buffet was set up on a large party deck in the right field corner. I made a couple of trips through the buffet line and spent most of that time socializing with the players, but eventually I made my way over to a table where John Wallenstein was sitting with a tall, clean-cut 34-year-old named John Kuhn, who happened to be the President and General Manager of the London Werewolves. I'd heard somebody who didn't care for Kuhn sneer that the only reason he held the position he did was because his father, James Kuhn, was the majority owner of the Werewolves. I'd also heard that Kuhn the younger (no relation to the former commissioner of major league baseball, Bowie Kuhn), had ambitions of becoming Frontier League Commissioner. I didn't let such commonly-made and often jealously-based criticisms prejudice me, and so I formed my own favorable impression of Kuhn as a capable and witty guy who was fun to be around. Kuhn was ambitious (so what? why did that make him a bad guy?), and he told a story simply to amuse me and John Wallenstein that nevertheless illustrated his ambition, tenacity, and experience.

"In 1990 when I was 24 years old, I worked as the assistant director of marketing for the Ft. Meyers Sun Sox of the ill-fated Senior Professional Baseball League," said Kuhn. "After the league folded, I got a job as a school teacher, but I still had the itch to work in baseball. My mom knew this, so she told me to call Mike Veeck, the president of the Ft. Myers Miracle, who were in the Florida State League, and ask him for a job. The Miracle were terrible. They were a co-op team with players that belonged to the Twins, Indians, and Rangers. They went something like 52–80, and their leading hitter batted .262.

"Anyway, I called Veeck and left a message for him because he wasn't in. The next day I received a return call from him. 'Is this John Kuhn?' Veeck said.

"'Yes, sir.' I said.

"'Do you know who this is?' he said.

"'Yes, sir.' I said.

"'Well, you called me. What is it I can do for you?'

"'I want a job with the Miracle,' I said. 'I know this town, and I can sell baseball to this town.'

"'You can, huh?'

"'Yes, sir.'

"'Before we go any further, let's get one thing straight right now,' he said. 'If you call me "sir" again, I'm going to crawl through this telephone line and kick your ass.'

"'I've seen pictures of you, sir, and, frankly, I don't think you can do that,' I said.

"'Get over here to my office and we'll see about that,' he said.

"'I'll be there in fifteen minutes,' I told him.

"When I got there, Veeck said, 'Okay. What is it you want to do?'

"'I want to work for you,' I said. 'I want to get back into baseball, and I know I can sell professional baseball to this town.'

"He goes, 'Yeah, right.' And then he asks me, 'Can you be here tomorrow at 6:00?'

"'Yeah, sure,' I said. The next day, I taught school and coached my high school baseball team, and then went to work for the Miracle. And Veeck started me out with a real plum assignment: selling programs. But that's how I got back into baseball. By the way, as a neat piece of trivia, when I got hired, the team already had a woman employee named Commiskey, so that gave us three famous names in baseball working for the team: Veeck, Kuhn, and Commiskey—even if the woman spelled her last name with two m's.

"I may have started out at the bottom, but Veeck had bigger plans for me, and it wasn't long before he asked me to be the Phantom of the Ballpark. This was a stunt that Veeck had used before to capitalize on the popularity of the Broadway play, *Phantom of the Opera*, when he was with Pompano Beach. I wrote up a story about the Phantom of the Ballpark based on what Veeck told me, and we put it in the program. The Phantom supposedly was a Pompano Beach second baseman named Bix Bixby who had died in a collision with the center fielder and later had his ashes strewn about the old Pompano ballpark.

"The costume I put on for the part was homemade but quite elaborate. I wore a black Lone Ranger mask to hide my face and over that I wore a catcher's mask, half of it painted white and half of it left black. I had a black 'Cheers of Ft. Lauderdale' sweatshirt that I turned inside out, and somewhere I found a black cape from an old Dracula Halloween costume. I'd also carry a black baseball bat with me and a finger flasher which I got from a magic store. A finger flasher hooks over one of your fingers like a ring and has a button on it. And when you push the button, it shoots a miniature fireball of sparks.

"Now, normally, at some point during the game between innings we'd start playing *Phantom of the Opera* music, and I'd come out of the office where I dressed and into the stands to do my thing. Whenever the kids got close to me, they'd practically molest me, trying to pull off the costume to see who the Phantom was. They kept getting bolder and bolder, so we decided to do something different. Veeck said, 'Can you bungee jump off the light tower?' There was no way I was going to do that. I'm afraid of heights. So we decided that I would make my entrance by coming over the outfield wall.

"*The Phantom of the Opera* music was my cue, and when it started playing I climbed up on top of the left field wall. The wall was about ten feet high, and once I got up there I got scared. I was holding the bat in one hand and trying to keep my balance with the other. There was a walkie-talkie in my pocket and on it I could hear them calling me: 'Phantom, come in! Phantom, come in!' They didn't see me at first because they thought I was supposed to come over the right field wall.

"In a little while the music stopped, and I knew I had to do something, that I couldn't stay perched up on the wall forever. I didn't want to do it, but I jumped. I'd never broken a bone in my life, but I knew this time I'd broken my ankle—I hadn't, it was a very bad sprain. Worse, when I hit the ground my thumb hit the button on the finger flasher, and the sparks flew out and caught my cape on fire! I mean, it started blazing! I rolled around on the outfield grass to put the fire out, and then, with my ankle killing me, I started limping across the field like Lon Chaney.

"This got the kids really excited, and they chased me all the way through the stands up to the door of the club offices. I rushed through the door and then slammed it shut behind me. I was leaning up against the door, out of breath, half burned alive, and in tremendous pain from my throbbing ankle. I looked up, and there was Veeck standing in front of me. He started clapping, slowly, and then he said, 'Outstanding! Do it again tomorrow.'"

I laughed and laughed at the story and thought that even if a paternal connection had helped Kuhn get his position with the Werewolves, he had also definitely paid some dues.

Bill Lee walked by, and I was reminded of what Ron LeFlore had told me he was going to do.

Although many people at first assume differently, the Frontier League's Bill Lee is not the same person as "The Spaceman," the flaky left-handed Red Sox and Expos pitcher who delighted sportswriters and infuriated the baseball establishment with his maverick behavior and counter-culture opinions back in the 1970s. It was the Spaceman who responded, "Thirty-two pounds per square inch at sea level" when someone asked him how much pressure he felt on the mound; and it was the Spaceman who was fined by Bowie Kuhn for saying, after first denying that he *smoked* marijuana, that he sprinkled marijuana on his pancakes. Even so, the coincidence makes it easy for even the most casual of baseball fans to remember the name of the Frontier League Commissioner (which was often used as if the first and last names were a single entity: BillLee), and it gave Max the idea for a one-of-a-kind Christmas present.

In the Fall of 1998 Max was umpiring in a national men's over-30 amateur baseball tournament in Arizona, and Bill Lee, the ex–major league pitcher, was playing in the tournament. One game Lee caught while Max worked the plate. Afterwards, Max asked Lee to autograph a baseball for his friend, the Commissioner of the Frontier League. The Spaceman was glad to do it. He took the Wilson A1010 Official Frontier League baseball from Max and on the sweet spot opposite the Commissioner's printed signature, he inscribed, "To Bill Lee, from Bill Lee. Earth, 1998." Driving from Cincinnati, Max hand-delivered the present to Bill Lee at his home in Zanesville, Ohio, the Friday before Christmas. On the same trip Max delivered a present to Jim Schaly in Marietta, Ohio. Again, the gift was nothing ordered out of a catalog or picked up in a department store off a bargain table but something highly personal that derived its value out of experience that Max had shared with the gift's recipient. At the Frontier League All-Star Game played in Richmond that summer, Max had gotten a crazy idea and talked Schaly and Chuck Robinson, the other base umpires, into going along with it. Max's wife, Patty, had made and sold some tie-dyed T-shirts to raise money for a summer camp for disadvantaged kids. A few of the unsold shirts had been left in the trunk of Max's car, and when he realized they were there before the game, Max knew it was time to brighten up their traditional umpire's blue attire. Everything looked normal until the ninth inning, when the three base umps removed their standard issue powder blue shirts and emerged from the Richmond dugout wearing their psychedelic tie-dyed Tees. "We know where the umpires were before the game," remarked the P.A. announcer. " … At the big garage sale in downtown Richmond!" Schaly's present was the tie-dyed shirt he'd worn during the All-Star game. Before framing the shirt, Max affixed a Frontier League patch to the sleeve and an apple pin, compliments of Patty, to the collar. The pin was Max's way of officially congratulating Schaly, the substitute grade school teacher, for finally getting his teaching degree, after 19 years of working towards it. "I figured you deserved a fitting memento of the achievement of getting your degree, since you've been working on it for half your life!" joked Max.

The first time I'd talked at length to the Frontier League's Bill Lee, a tall man in his late forties with glasses, a mustache, and a ready wit, I'd met him at his office in downtown Zanesville. Bill had established the league headquarters there in 1994 because he liked living in small Midwestern towns and because, at that time when the Greys were still in business, Zanesville was the geographic center of the league. When the league approached him, Bill was living in Seattle, where he worked for a top notch amateur hockey club, the Seattle Thunderbirds, that was equivalent, in its players, facility, operations, and fan support, to a minor league team. Both the sport and location were foreign to Lee, whose extensive baseball background had begun with his father in Illinois.

At Max's behest, the 1998 Frontier League All-Star Game base umps wore tie-dyed tee shirts. Left to right: Max, Rob Stevens, Jim Schaly, Chuck Robinson.

Roy Edwin Lee was a left-handed pitcher who appeared in three games for the 1945 New York Giants. The Giants finished fifth in the eight-team National League that year but boasted two Hall of Famers on the roster, right fielder and manager Mel Ott and catcher Ernie Lombardi. During the war Roy Lee was stationed at the Air Force base in Belleville, Illinois, and pitching for the team at the base he beat Satchel Paige and the Kansas City Monarchs 2–1 in an exhibition game. Bill Lee has a newspaper clipping about the game which quotes Satchel asking Roy: "White boy, how can you throw so hard?"

After Roy retired as a player, he settled in the St. Louis area and went into college coaching, first for St. Louis University and later for Southern Illinois University at Edwardsville. Roy's first son wasn't much interested in baseball, but his younger boy, Bill, took to the old man's game like sportswriters to free food. Bill wound up playing first base for his dad at SIU-Edwardsville, and in his senior year the team finished as runners-up in the Division II World Series. After going 8–16 in the Series and making the all-tournament team, Bill was told by scouts that he'd be drafted, but the call on draft day never came. At that point he decided to pursue a career in broadcasting, his major in college, and even had a hard-to-get internship with Jack Buck at KMOX lined up; but the

Braves invited him to a tryout in Atlanta. Lee hit well at the tryout, was signed to a contract, and reported to the Braves' rookie club in Bradenton, Florida, in the Gulf Coast League. After the Braves released him, he played a final year of professional baseball for Beeville, Texas, in the independent Lonestar League. "I hit .370 in my two-year minor league career," Lee told me; "… .190 the first year and .180 the second year."

Before he signed with Beeville, Lee spent spring training that year with the Boston Red Sox in Florida. He recalled what happened when he was grouped with the minor leaguers assigned to Boston's Winston-Salem farm team. "They put my name over one of the lockers in the minor league clubhouse, and when everybody saw it they assumed that Bill Lee, the major league pitcher, was being sent down. The first day of camp the clubhouse guy saw me sitting at my locker, and he said, 'Hey, you can't locker there. That's Bill Lee's locker.'

"'I am Bill Lee,' I said.

"'No, you're not.'

"'Yes, I am.'

"Then it finally dawned on him. 'Oh, my god! You mean there's two of you!' he said. He wasn't the only one confused. The kids saw my name in the program and wanted my autograph, so I signed my name for them all spring long and never told them that I wasn't Bill Lee, the Spaceman."

After Lee retired as a player, he went to work as a salesman for the friend who had invented Diamond Dry, the corn cob product that helps dry wet baseball fields. With the hope of still getting a shot at a broadcasting job in baseball, he attended the Winter Meetings in 1980, resume in hand. He wound up being hired as the Assistant General Manager and Public Relations Director of the Birmingham Barons, after the owner of the club told him, "I want you to come work for me. If you can sell that shit (Diamond Dry), you can sell baseball." After four seasons with the Barons, Lee moved on to become General Manager of the Chattanooga Lookouts, a post he held for five seasons. In Seattle he missed both baseball and the Midwest, and was receptive to the overtures of the Frontier League, made after Chris Hanners and fellow owners, Bob Wolfe (Zanesville Greys) and Steve Sturgill (Portsmouth Explorers), realized the league needed a full-time, impartial commissioner.

Bill Lee took the job as the first commissioner of the Frontier League in 1994 in time for the league's second campaign, and his biggest challenge was easy to define: it was simply to ensure the survival of the league. "I always say that there are four things that make a franchise successful," he'd told me. "The market, the facility, the ownership, and management. If you have three of the four you can survive. When I took the job, in most cases, we had a poor market, a poor facility, weak ownership, and bad management. We had nothing going for us! At the time Chillicothe was one of our better markets, one of our bigger markets too. Chillicothe is still a good market, but it's no where near one of our bigger markets anymore.

"I remember my first official night on the job, which was opening night of the 1994 season. It was June 17, the same night as the O.J. Simpson white Bronco chase. I was in Newark, Ohio, and things were so lax and poorly run I couldn't believe it. I was sitting with the Newark owner behind home plate when a foul ball came directly back to the screen. The guy was so inexperienced, as a fan, that he got scared and spilled his beer all over me. That's when I knew I was in trouble!"

Although Lee had been hired, like Kennesaw Mountain Landis, to basically save the league, it wasn't long before his authority was challenged. "We had a meeting in the Fall of '94 on a Saturday afternoon, and some of the owners wanted to bring a TV into the room to watch the Ohio State football game," he said. "Well, we had some important things to discuss, so I went on a tirade and read them the riot act. One of the owners said, 'I feel like I've been taken out to the woodshed.'

"I told him, 'Consider it that exactly.'

"Then he said, 'I don't have to take crap like that from you.'

"'Well, don't!' I said. 'Fire me if you want to. But you hired me to tell you how things need to be done, and until I'm fired that's what I'm going to do.'

"Since then things have worked out pretty well. Every so often somebody takes a run at me, but the bad apples always seem to weed themselves out. And I'm still here. I know one thing for sure: every decision I've ever made as Commissioner has been with the best interests of the league overall in mind, and nobody can say any differently."

By all accounts, Bill Lee had provided outstanding leadership for the Frontier League. He was particularly proud of having presided over the league's expansion into increasingly bigger markets and the tremendous growth in the value of a Frontier League franchise. With Bill Lee at the helm, the Frontier League had evolved from a shaky collection of under-financed small town operations that played in inadequate facilities and were run as glorified semi-pro teams to a credible professional sports collective that was anchored by a group of well-established teams, some of which actually turned a profit.

Despite his success and his standing as one of the seminal figures in league history, Bill Lee was not a pompous, stuffed shirt in the mode of Bowie Kuhn. He was instead a good old boy who took his job seriously but not himself. To entertain the crowd, he took batting practice before the 1997 Frontier League All-Star Game and came through nicely by muscling a home run over the fence. He loved to eat and found the best restaurant in every city in the league, information he shared with the public via a page in the media guide entitled the "Frontier League Commissioner's Dining Guide." Bill had a policy of never drinking beer at Frontier League games, but afterwards he could often be found at The Wheel and The Dock and the other watering holes around the league that the players and umpires frequented, where he would do his share of drinking, pool playing, and singing with great gusto. Happy Chandler was the original "Singing Commissioner" of baseball, but his renditions of "My Old Kentucky Home" were more sentimental than artful. "Bill Lee can really sing!" Max had once told me. "You should have heard him sing 'Devil with a Blue Dress On' and 'Johnny Be Good' in Chillicothe when they were having one of their 'Party with the Paints' nights. He brought down the house!" In short, Bill Lee had a blast being commissioner of the Frontier League.

I had never seen Bill Lee in a coat and tie, and when he walked past the table where I was sitting with John Wallenstein and John "Phantom of the Ballpark" Kuhn; he was dressed in his usual attire: shorts and sneakers and a sports shirt (black) embroidered with the Frontier League logo, a smiling baseball face wearing a Davy Crockett-style coon skin cap.

I kept an eye on him, and when it appeared as if he were leaving the party deck, I walked over and engaged him in conversation. We talked a few minutes about the Rascals' gorgeous ballpark, and then I told him about my trip to Cook County and asked him if he'd heard about Ron LeFlore's intention to call a press conference to complain about how the league was being run by the umpires. As the words left my mouth, I got a mental image of myself as Wiley Coyote, pushing down the handle which would ignite a keg of dynamite that would blow up in my own face.

Bill Lee turned abruptly, and while standing nose-to-nose with me like an enraged umpire responding to an out-of-line ballplayer, he informed me that he had heard from Mr. LeFlore and that, furthermore, he was happy to repeat for me what his response to Mr. LeFlore had been. It was short and sweet, and as thunderous and withering as anything the righteous Landis could have come up with in his hey day when he banned the eight Chicago Black Sox from baseball for life. "DON'T FUCK WITH ME!!!" he roared.

Later that evening I was looking forward to relaxing in my room while watching the major league All-Star Game being played in Atlanta's Turner Field. When I went down into the lobby to hit the pop machine, I ran into Chris Hanners who invited me to go along on a trip he was organizing to the casino off I-70 on the Missouri River.

"Thank you for asking, Chris, but starving artists and writers like me don't have money to lose at casinos."

"That's not a problem," he said. When I frowned at what sounded like his offer to pick up the tab for my gambling, he added. "It's really not."

The next day I heard that Chris had handed out $100 bills at the casino to everyone in the Paints' entourage. Maleine Davis, the Paints' Director of Finance, was standing nearby, and I said to her, "Wow! Chris sure is generous, isn't he, Maleine?"

"Yes," she said, "and sometimes he's too generous."

The Braves' Chipper Jones hit the game's only home run, making him the 13th player to hit an All-Star Game home run in his home stadium; but the American League won the game, 6–3, for their fourth consecutive victory. Shortstop Derek Jeter, who went 3–3 with a double and two RBI, was the game's MVP. Surprisingly, Jeter's three base knocks were the first All-Star Game hits of his career, and his All-Star Game MVP Award was the first ever won by a New York Yankee. The latter circumstance would have been cause for a congressional investigation had it not been for the fact that the Award had only been around since 1962; when it was actually awarded twice. Two Awards were made in 1962 because for four years, 1959–62, the major leagues staged not one but a pair of All-Star Games. The experiment ultimately failed because playing two games caused too much disruption to the regular season schedule. The last two players to win All-Star Game MVP Awards in the same season were the Dodgers' Maury Wills, who won for the game played in Washington, D.C. on July 10, 1962, and the Angels' Leon "Daddy Wags" Wagner, who won for that year's second game played July 30 in Wrigley Field.

As usual, the Frontier League was staging a single All-Star Game in 2000; and, as usual, mid–July in St. Louis was hot enough to melt Astroturf. I hated to leave the air conditioning of the hotel, but a late morning workout for the All-Stars in front of major league scouts was scheduled at T.R. Hughes Ballpark, and I wanted to be there for it.

By the time I got to the tryout, a round of batting practice was well underway. About a dozen scouts were on hand, scattered in the seats on the first base side of the grandstand. The major league affiliations of some of them were identifiable by the caps or embroidered sports shirts they wore, while the attire of others offered no clue as to the business they were engaged in. I studied them for a while; then, with the BP session winding down, I decided to sit down next to a scout named Nick Hostetler. He was wearing an Atlanta Braves shirt and didn't appear to be much older than some of the players he was scouting. The first thing I asked him was how much the recent promotions of Brian Tollberg and Morgan Burkhart had to do with his being at the Frontier League All-Star Game.

"Oh, a lot," he said. "Scouting this league is something we've put an emphasis on because of those guys."

When I asked if he'd attended any regular season Frontier League games, he said he'd been to four or five games in Canton. "They've got a big left-handed pitcher named Justin Wallace I've been keeping my eye on. I was hoping he'd be here," he said.

What was he looking for in the players working out before us? "Every scout looks for something different," he said. "I basically look for guys who can hit. If they can run and throw and field, that's fine, but they gotta be able to swing the bat. And that's what can be hard to judge. If some kid hits two home runs off a guy throwing 85, 86 mph, that's not necessarily impressive because he'll have to hit off better pitching than that in the league he'll have to play in if he signs with us. So for me, a hitter's gotta have strength and good bat speed.

"To be honest, being in the Frontier League, these guys here have to do everything well because they're older than guys just coming out of college. Their bodies have matured and they're done growing. They aren't going to improve that much now, so they have to possess above average skills."

Out of curiosity I asked Hostetler if he'd signed anybody I might have heard of. "Have you heard of A. J. Zapp?" he asked. No, I hadn't, and Nick hadn't signed him either, but he'd been the first one in the Braves' organization to be high on him. The Braves had taken the first baseman from Benton Central High School near Indianapolis in the first round of the 1996 draft (and paid him $675,000 to sign a contract), and Nick was pleased that Zapp, as a member of the Braves' High A club in Myrtle Beach, had recently made the Carolina League All-Star team.

After the batting cage was rolled away from home plate, the All-Stars began taking infield. It was obvious that most of them were throwing the ball as hard as they possibly could. They were in fact over-throwing and sailing many throws over the heads of the fielders they were throwing to. You could read their minds, that they'd rather make a bad throw that sailed over somebody's head, indicating arm strength, than bounce a throw in the dirt, which would indicate arm weakness. The catchers, especially, seemed to be trying too hard. They were asked to throw to second with their masks on after receiving a pitch from the mound. One catcher put so much into his throw that the force of it spun his mask to the side of his head. THE MAJORS DO THIS ALL THE TIME, WATCH PUDGE!

I asked Hostetler if the scouts took into consideration the fact that the players might not be showing their best because they were trying too hard. "Yeah, we know they're pressing," he said, "but the great ones don't do that.

"If they can't perform at their best under this amount of pressure, what are they gonna do when they're in Turner Field in front of 40,000 screaming fans? Besides, you can still see their tools."

He had a point to be sure, but I still couldn't help but think that the emphasis on physical tools is exactly what caused the scouts to miss Burkhart and Tollberg. You have to get to know a player well, you have to watch him day in and day out, to begin to see the intangible things that might separate him from other players, even those who have more tools. After all, some things can't be measured, only recognized: things like savvy, character, dedication, heart.

A home run derby contest was held before the game, with the three leading home run hitters from each division slated to participate. All three West Division representatives, the Capitals' Bobby McDonald, the Cheetahs' Justin Pierro, and the Rascals' Brian Fuess, went into the competition with five regular season homers to his credit. On paper the East lineup looked more imposing, as the Paints' Mike Cervenak had 11 homers under his belt; the Werewolves' Rick Nadeau, nine; and the Johnnies' Kirk Taylor, five. The Roosters' Aaron Sledd, who'd also hit five homers so far, was odd man out for the East.

With more than half of what would be a sellout crowd already on hand, the contest started. The two divisions took turns batting, and each player was allowed to take ten swings. Taylor led off and hit two over the outfield wall. McDonald managed only one homer, and then Nadeau hit two. The crowd stirred in anticipation when the Big Boy stepped up to the plate. He didn't disappoint. His first two homers were ordinary line drives, which did seem disappointing; but the second two, parabolic blasts worthy of the power plant from whence they came, flew over the outfield bleachers and completely out of the park. Pierro finished with five homers. Mike Cervenak came close to equaling Pierro with four. Brian Fuess, the host team's representative and a crowd favorite, was left-handed, which put him at a distinct disadvantage. He did manage to loft two shots over the Big Dog Wall in right field, but it wasn't enough to keep up with Pierro and Cervenak who advanced to the final round.

Mike Cervenak didn't look like a home run hitter, but he could definitely hit and hit with power, even out of his somewhat odd stance, sort of a half crouch, as if he were beginning to sit down. When I'd remarked to Chris Hanners about how good a shortstop I thought Cervenak was, Chris told me that Cervenak was playing out of position. At the University of Michigan Mike had played third base, his natural position. Chris couldn't believe that Cervenak had not been drafted out of college, and he knew that the kid wouldn't remain Paints property for long. He simply had too much ability for others not to see it. In fact, at least one other Frontier League team had been hot on Cervenak's trail. Cook County assistant coach Scott Spero had told me: "I keep up with kids in college on my computer. I track 'em and look to see if they are making progress from one year to the next. I was following Cervenak at Michigan, and I wanted to go see him play. I told the Cheetahs that I'd go scout him just for gas money. I didn't ask for anything else, no pay, no hotel room, not even meal money. They wouldn't give it to me, and my wife wouldn't let me go without it. Then we go to Chillicothe, and who do I see playing shortstop for them? Mike Cervenak. I said, 'Son of a bitch!'"

Probably because they were trying too hard, Pierro and Cervenak hit one more homer each in their next ten swings. That led to a sudden-death round. Cervenak reached the seats in left field on his first swing, and when Pierro's hump-backed liner into left-center hit the ground, it was over. The players in the East dugout, especially the Paints' contingent, applauded enthusiastically when Cervenak was awarded a plaque for winning the contest.

The East out-hit the West when it counted too, winning the Frontier League's All-Star Game 10–5. It was the East's second victory in the seven-year history of the contest. The West opened the scoring with single runs in the second and third innings, but the Paints' Greg Strickland tied the game with a two-run double in the fifth. The East took the lead in the following inning on a two-run homer by Canton's Travis Copley and won going away by scoring three in the seventh, one in the eighth, and two in the ninth. London outfielder Rick Nadeau was voted the game's MVP for going 3–5, including a two-run homer in the top of the ninth. Immediately after the game and before the start of the fireworks display which concluded the evening's festivities, Bill Lee presented Nadeau with his Award which, he explained, was named after Alex Gammas, "a very talented young man who played for the Zanesville Greys and was killed in a tragic auto accident two days before he was to go to the 1995 Frontier League All-Star Game." The tribute to Gammas caused to flash through my mind the words of the most well-known stanza from A. E. Housman's "To an Athlete Dying Young," the spare and achingly beautiful poem about the transience of fame (and, by implication, of life itself):

Smart lad, to slip betimes away
From fields where glory does not stay

And early though the laurel grows
It withers quicker than the rose.

Perhaps the fate of Alex Gammas gave Nadeau pause to ponder his achievement in the face of his own mortality. But probably not. I found him to be, as he was entitled to be, absorbed in the moment, which he told me in the dugout was "definitely the highlight of my career." Besides, he was already preparing himself to deal with a more imminent death, the end of his career as a professional baseball player. "The Frontier League has been a great learning experience," he said. "The league has definitely got talented players who got passed up for one reason or another by affiliated baseball. My feeling is that if you have a great season in this league, you should get seriously looked at. But I'm 24 years old. If nothing happens for me this year, it'll be time for a reality check. I've got a management job in a manufacturing plant waiting for me if this is the end of the line for me in baseball."

On the way out of the ballpark I passed the six Roosters All-Stars who were assembled on the plaza behind the East team's third base dugout. They were having their picture taken by a couple of diehard fans who'd made the trip over from Richmond. All the players were in a great mood, but especially Phill Kojack; who, by kneeling in his shoes, turning his cap sideways, and contorting his face, was doing his impression of a midget-sized Crazy Guggenheim for the pictures. It was the capper to his All-Star Game performance, which included, besides his two innings of effective pitching, his trademark trip and fall. The latter, which needlessly caused four thousand people to feel embarrassed for the poor boy, had come as he'd walked off the mound in the bottom of the fourth. "Hey, Phill," I hollered. "Nice trip."

"Thanks!" he said.

"I heard you're planning to get married. Don't tell me you're going to trip during the wedding."

"No, I'm not," he said. "My fiancée won't let me. … But don't worry: I'm going to trip at the reception!"

Thursday, the day after the All-Star Game, was an off day for the Frontier League. When I'd left Cincinnati, my plan was to stay over in St. Louis to catch the Rascals' next game on Friday against Richmond and then to move on to Evansville for a pair of games between the Otters and the Springfield Capitals before winding up the trip with a visit to Springfield, Illinois, for two games between the Capitals and Cook County. That schedule would have left me with only two more Frontier League cities to visit: Johnstown, Pennsylvania, and London, Ontario; however, when I woke up Thursday morning, I knew I'd never finish my itinerary as planned. On my many previous travels, I'd always missed my family but never as badly as I found myself missing them then. The marital catastrophe that had befallen my friends was still preying on my mind and made the continued absence from my family that I was contemplating seem unbearable. While wolfing down a Grand Slam breakfast at Denny's, I decided I was going home. Right after I drove over to Hazelwood West High and interviewed the school's assistant principal, the man who'd thrown out the honorary first pitch of the Frontier League All-Star Game.

Frank Burkhart seemed to be a sober, no-nonsense, very focused man, exactly the way most everyone had described his son Morgan. Mr. Burkhart's office at Hazelwood West was as bare as an army barracks except for one thing: the big bulletin board hanging on the wall that was covered with photos and newspaper clippings about Morgan and his two younger brothers. I'd heard nothing about younger Burkhart brothers, but apparently they were pretty good ballplayers too. All three boys had gone to Crowder Junior College, ten miles south of Joplin; Lance, a catcher, had gone on to Southwest Missouri State and been drafted out of college in the fifteenth round by the Montreal Expos. Damon, a second baseman, would be entering his senior year at Missouri Baptist in St. Louis in the fall.

As the interview proceeded, I got a sense that Mr. Burkhart had definitely had a strong influence on his son Morgan, as I'd suspected; but it appeared that Mr. Burkhart had guided with a gentle touch and had led more by example than exhortation. One thing Mr. Burkhart showed his sons was perseverance. He'd been at Hazelwood West a long time and had been the first head coach of the school's baseball team (1974–81). Morgan was the bat boy for his dad's teams, but Mr. Burkhart quit coaching before Morgan had a chance to play for him. "I thought it would be hard on my sons if they played for me," he said. "There would always be some parents who'd say, 'He gets to play because his dad's the coach.'

Nevertheless, Mr. Burkhart, like almost all fathers, from the most athletically inept to ex–major leaguers, was Morgan's first baseball coach; and he played an instrumental role in developing a key part of Morgan's game. "When he was four or five years old I pitched whiffle balls to him in the backyard," he said, "and he couldn't decide which way he wanted to bat. When he was six I started him out switch hitting, and we'd alternate: right, left, right, left. He hit the ball farther right-handed, so one day he said, 'Dad, I really need to hit right-handed all the time.' I told him, 'No, you're going to kept switch-hitting.'

"Even though the scouts like him better from the right side, I like him better as a left-handed hitter. I still think he has a better swing from the left side. And it's got to be a big plus for him as a professional, that he can hit from both sides of the plate. I know that Boston's manager Jimy Williams was impressed when Morgan turned around and got a big hit left-handed after he'd batted right-handed in the first three games he played."

Had Mr. Burkhart pushed Morgan into baseball, even a little bit? "No. I didn't have to," he said. "All Morgan ever wanted to do was play baseball. He was always dedicated to the game. He played other sports, but by grade school baseball was his favorite. He played four years of football in high school—he was a quarterback—and he started about half the time his senior year. He played basketball too but gave it up his senior year to work in the weight room for baseball.

"The thing about Morgan is that he really worked at it. He had a tremendous desire to get better and to excel, and Morgan did keep getting better every year. I stressed that to him: 'If you want to keep playing baseball, you better be getting better. If you take 150 cuts a day and really work at it, you'll be ahead of the guy who takes 150 cuts a day but doesn't really work at it. And you'll be way ahead of the guy who takes only 50 cuts a day or none at all. You have to make yourself better.' And Morgan did that. When he came out of high school, he was a good player … he was first team all-conference … but he wasn't all-state. And, as I'm sure you know, he was never drafted. He went to Crowder Junior College, and it was the perfect place for him. The coach there, a guy named Gary Roark, works your fanny off, and that's exactly what Morgan wanted. It's the kind of program where if you stay, you're going to get better. And Morgan did. When his brother Lance was trying to decide where to start college, Morgan told him, 'Hey, Lance, this is where you want to go.' And then Lance said the same thing to Damon: 'This is where you want to go.'"

Why did it take the scouts so long to decide to give Morgan a chance? "I think it was because he doesn't fit the profile," said Mr. Burkhart. "They want first basemen to be 6' 2" or so, and Morgan's only 5' 10" or 5' 11". With the numbers he put up in the Frontier League, no other explanation makes sense. Morgan certainly had a hard time understanding why he wasn't signed out of the Frontier League before he was.

"In my opinion, the Red Sox still weren't completely sold on him when they signed him. I think their feeling was 'Here's a guy who can fill a spot in our system.' I don't think they expected him to advance the way he did, but he kept opening their eyes a little wider. I watched him at every level he played at, and he always stood out as one of the best hitters, at every level. I felt that if he ever got a chance, he could play in the major leagues. You need a break … you need to be in the right spot at the right time, and that's what finally happened for Morgan. Somebody went on the DL, he got his chance, and he proved he could play."

After we talked a bit more, mostly about the first days of Morgan's young major league career, I was ready to conclude the interview. Even though it was summer break for the students of Hazelwood West, their assistant principal had work to do, and I had a long drive home to make. I had just one more question: What would Morgan have done if the Red Sox had not signed him? "Well, I know he wasn't about to quit," said Mr. Burkhart. "We never had a conversation where he said, 'Dad, I'm thinking about quitting. We've had conversations about him not hitting, and I've given him advice; but I've never had to talk him out of quitting because he's never been down on the game. If the Red Sox hadn't signed him, he would have gone to play in the Atlantic League or the Northern League, independent leagues that don't have age-maximums, because he was going to keep playing baseball, one way or the other; and he'll keep playing ball as long as he can. I know this because he's my son, and I know how he thinks. ... And as long as Morgan has a uniform to put on, as long as he is playing the game, he'll be happy."

On Friday, July 14, the Paints were opening the second half of the season at home with a series against the London Werewolves, and Max was scheduled to umpire all three games. I was anxious to see him—I'd missed him too—but I was worried about rushing off again before I'd spent even one whole day at home. I hadn't gotten back to Cincinnati until late Thursday night, and if I left with Max on Friday afternoon to go to Chillicothe, I wouldn't see Kathy again until Saturday: she was going to have to get up early and go to work Friday while I slept in. She probably wouldn't have said anything, but I knew how she would have felt: that I couldn't really have missed her as much as I said I did if it were that easy for me to leave again so soon. There was also the fact that we had a tentative get-away for the weekend planned. The get-away was for a Friday/Saturday-night stay at a rustic log cabin in Paintsville, Kentucky, that Kathy had purchased in a charity auction. Under normal circumstances, I would have been eager to get away with my wife, but I felt an obligation to Max and the book; and I was, as before, worried that if I were not on hand when Max was umpiring, I might miss something important.

Max and I talked on the phone Friday morning, and when I told him about my dilemma, he urged me to take the weekend off and spend it with Kathy. Besides, he said, the weather forecast called for steady rain all weekend, and he had a feeling there wasn't going to be much baseball played in Chillicothe.

Friday was rainy all day. Paralyzed by indecision, I neither left for Chillicothe nor committed myself to the trip to the log cabin in time to do either. Max called in the morning to say that they'd been rained out Friday night. He'd collected his $35 rainout fee before the first pitch was thrown, turned around, and driven home.

The Paints now had a doubleheader scheduled for Saturday, but the rain kept falling in Cincinnati, so around lunchtime I told Kathy I wanted to make the drive to Paintsville. As we headed down I-75, I comforted myself with the thought that there was a good chance the doubleheader might be rained out too. A couple of hours later, as we drove on the Combs Mountain Parkway through the Daniel Boone National Forest in eastern Kentucky, I felt even better about the situation. For more than half an hour we sloshed through a pounding rain that was the fiercest downpour I ever remember driving through. Had there been much traffic on the road, I would have pulled over and waited the storm out. As it was, we plugged along slowly with me becoming more cheerful and more relaxed the longer the drenching continued.

After passing it on a winding country road and doubling back, we found the driveway we were looking for. The driveway led into a densely-wooded holler that had been cleared enough to accommodate the cabin, set on a knoll on the right, and, about a hundred yards away on the left, a modern home, built against a hillside. The canopy of trees which hung over the entire clearing made for a pretty, peaceful, and spectacularly private setting; and the whole thing belonged to our hosts, Ralph and Sharon Scott.

Three other couples, including the Scotts' daughter Natalie and her husband Ric Boyer, were staying in the cabin for the weekend. When we arrived in the late afternoon, the three couples had already departed for an evening out at a dinner theatre. With no one at the cabin, we drove over to the big house to see if anyone was home there. We suspected not, as there was not a light on in the house to offset the impending darkness being brought on prematurely by the overcast sky and the shrouded setting.

We pulled up to the side of the Scotts' house which was positioned perpendicularly to the cabin. A walk to our right led around to a spacious deck on the front of the house, which faced a creek that ran along the bottom of the sloping lot. We followed a path around the lefthand corner of the house which led to a less formal but obviously more frequently utilized entrance under a car port at the rear of the house. And there we encountered our hosts who were sitting under the car port in the fading light, patiently waiting for the return of the power which had been knocked out by the storm.

We introduced ourselves, got comfortable around each other, and then spent the next several hours conversing quietly while enjoying the ceaseless patter of rain drops. I actually got my mind entirely off baseball for a while; but eventually I found myself talking about Max and the book when questions about our occupations were raised. To my surprise, Ralph had heard of the Frontier League. His son was married to the sister of Johnnie LeMaster, he said. In a flash I remembered having read on the backs of his baseball cards that the skinny light-hitting shortstop, who'd anchored the infield of my beloved San Francisco Giants during a perennially disappointing period in their history, listed Paintsville, Kentucky, as his home. Ralph remembered that LeMaster had managed the Frontier League team in Pikeville, about 35 miles south of Paintsville.

Known as the Kentucky Rifles, the Pikeville contingent was an original member of the Frontier League and lasted two full seasons, before the franchise folded and was replaced by Richmond. It was a miracle the franchise lasted as long as it did. The team played its home games in a municipal ballpark built to accommodate amateur baseball, and the sound of gunfire made by feuding families sometimes echoed in the hills beyond and accompanied the more familiar sounds of the ol' ballgame. From the start the club could not draw flies. Roger Hanners' memories of Pikeville on this score were quite vivid. "It was horrible there," he told me once. "They'd have one or two people in the stands; I'm not exaggerating. One time the umpire made a bad call, a terrible call, and we complained about it. He cleared the bench and made us sit in the bleachers. We were the only ones there. How they thought they'd make it I'll never know."

Realizing that Pikeville (population: 6,300) would not be able to support the team by itself, owner Billy Shelton hoped to draw from throughout Pike County, which numbered 80,000 residents. The unforeseen problem was that the mountainous roads of the county made it nearly impossible for many fans to get off work and reach the ballpark by the starting time of 7 P.M. An early–September issue of *Baseball America* in 1993 reported the grizzly attendance numbers: an average of 145 fans per game, good for last in the league. Pikeville's isolation—the town is located near the eastern-most tip of the state and the border with Virginia—didn't help any either, as few fans from out of the immediate area ever made the trek to Pikeville. Even Bill Lee himself, whose first year as commissioner of the league coincided with the Rifles' second and last year of existence, never once showed up in Pikeville.

Jim Schaly did Pikeville though, and the experience left an indelible impression on him. "There was only one motel in town, the Daniel Boone Motor Lodge, and we stayed there," he told me once. "And you went to bed hungry in Pikeville if the game went past 9:30, unless you wanted to go to Wal-Mart for a bag of chips. Chief Whitehead was the GM of the Rifles, and we never had enough baseballs. One time I said to him, 'Hey Chief, let me take you out to dinner after the game.'

"He said, 'Sure. Where we going?'

"I said, 'Wal-Mart. You want Fritos or Doritos.'

"On the way out of town after the last game I umpired there, I shouted at my partner, 'Stop the car!' We'd just passed the sign that said 'Welcome to Pikeville.' I got out of the car, went over to the sign, and pissed on it. Back in the car I said, 'Okay. We can go now. I'll never have to come back to Pikeville again.'"

The Pikeville franchise did have one moment of glory: capturing the East Division first half championship of the inaugural 1993 season with a 17–9 record. But that brief triumph was not nearly enough to sustain the franchise or even keep the manager on board. Rifles' skipper Roy Cutright and his coaches abruptly quit on August 10, leaving no one in charge of the team when the players arrived at the ballpark later that day. The manager and his coaches supposedly resigned because of "personal and philosophical differences," but more likely because they hadn't been paid. According to Schaly, "The players sprinted to their cars every payday. The first nine or ten checks would clear the bank; the rest didn't." LeMaster was Cutright's replacement and stayed on only until the end of the season. Which was just as well. LeMaster probably wouldn't have wanted to have anything to do with the Rifles' signing of 23-year-old outfielder Kendra Hanes the next year. A former fastpitch softball player at Oklahoma State University who was cut by the all-female Colorado Silver Bullets baseball team on the final day of their spring training before hooking on with the Rifles, Hanes was signed as a hoped-for gate booster. Although she didn't help the Rifles at the gate or on the field—*Baseball America* reported in its August 8–21, 1994 issue that she was 0–4 with three strikeouts and a ground out to the pitcher—Hanes did give the Frontier League an affirmative-action jump on the rival Northern League, which did not feature a woman player until 1997, when pitcher Ila Borders took the mound for the St. Paul Saints.

The spotlight never shined on the Kentucky Rifles again after the 1994 season, but the lights in Pikeville did come back on around 10 o'clock, and so the four of us went inside the Scott house to watch a little TV. When it was time for bed, the Scotts invited us to sleep in the big house instead of the cabin, and we gladly accepted. Late the next morning the cabin dwellers came over, and Sharon made a huge Southern breakfast for everybody, that included eggs cooked to perfection several different ways, long thick strips of bacon, hash browns, fried

apples, and, my favorite, grits with butter. The latter, a traditional Southern delicacy, is often unappreciated by Northerners; and this thought
reminded me of a story which I related at the breakfast table. When Phil
Rizzuto was inducted into the Baseball Hall of Fame in 1994, he gave
the funniest acceptance speech I've ever heard in Cooperstown. My
favorite part of the speech occurred when Rizzuto recalled making, as
a first-year minor league ballplayer in the New York Yankees' farm system, his first trip into the South. Rizzuto said that while nearing his destination of the small town of Bassett, Virginia, he ordered supper on
the train and found some strange white stuff on his plate. At this point
in the speech, Rizzuto couldn't even remember the name of the food
and turned around to ask for help from Bill White, the National League
president and Rizzuto's former broadcast partner with the Yankees, who
was sitting behind him on the dais.

"Grits! Yeah, grits," said Rizzuto. "That's the stuff. Anyway, so I see
this stuff on my plate, and hey, I'm a kid from Brooklyn! I don't know
this stuff. So I put a handful in my pocket."

Besides being physically beautiful, my wife Kathy is an adventurous
soul. Throughout our life together, she's introduced me to so many new
experiences and taken me to so many new places that I like to say,
"Honey, I'll follow you anywhere." I was certainly glad I'd followed her
to Paintsville. As short as it was, and despite the traveling it involved,
the get-away had re-charged my batteries. As we drove home through
more dreary weather on Sunday afternoon, I felt refreshed and serene
and ready to get back to work following Max on Monday. I was also
thankful that the weather had cooperated so beautifully. I figured the
odds were pretty good that because of all the rain I hadn't missed a thing
in Chillicothe.

I couldn't have been more mistaken.

When it happened, Stephen Byrd, the Paints' hot-headed starting
pitcher, said, "Not again!"

Mr. No-hitter, Andy Lee said, "There goes the good eye!"

And Chris Hanners said to nobody in particular, "Oh, my God! I
don't believe it." ... And then: "Where's Shannon?!!!"

Can you imagine what it feels like to hold the winning ticket in a
"Must-Be-Present-to-Win" drawing for a million dollars that you didn't
show up for?

The Saturday doubleheader, two seven-inning games, drew 2,700
fans to VA Memorial and started at 6:35. When the first game started,
with Max on the bases and Matt Neader behind the plate, the sky was

clear except for one huge black cloud in the west. Max thought the cloud was "the prettiest thing anybody would ever want to see because there was blue all around it." Max watched the cloud move towards the ballpark for three innings until it stopped right over the field and stayed there as if it were a dome. As he told me later, on Monday, "That was the baseball gods, telling me: 'Max, bang this thing and go home or you're gonna get hurt.'" With the cloud directly overhead, the teams played in a drizzle for two innings. Then in the fifth inning, Max heard the roar of a downpour coming through the trees in the beer garden down the left field line. He called time and ordered the grounds crew to get the tarps onto the field. Head groundskeeper Jimmy Miner and his minions got the mound and home plate covered fairly quickly, but by the time they started to unroll the big tarp, the rain was coming down so hard one couldn't see from first to third base; and the field was in danger of becoming unplayable.

Under the cover of the grandstands Bryan Wickline pleaded with the crew chief: "Max, we've already had two rainouts this year. We can't afford a third. We need to get this one in."

"We'll play if you can get the field into shape," said Max.

After a 45 minute drenching, the rain let up, but no one made a move to remove the tarps because radar showed that a second storm cell would hit the area in about 20 minutes. Alert fans knew that something was up when they saw Byrd and Woody Fullenkamp talking to Max, standing on the corner of the first base grandstand at the mouth of the wide aisle that led under the stands towards the umpires' dressing room. "You've always said you wanted to do the Chicken Dance with us before you retired," said Byrd. "Well, tonight's the night."

"I'll do it on one condition," said Max. "You have to have players on both teams involved."

"No problem," said Woody. "I'll go ask some of the London guys."

A buzz ran through the stands when the fans saw two benches placed end to end in the grass halfway between home plate and the grandstands and the players from both teams come out of the dugouts and kneel down in a semi-circle in front of the backstop wall. A new level of excitement was reached when London coach Ryan Pettit and two of his pitchers, Scott Conner and Ian Harvey, walked over to the benches, and the fans realized that the Werewolves were going to do the Chicken Dance with Woody, Byrd, and Ryan Sawyers. And then, when Max ran over halfway through the song and sat down between the Paints and Werewolves and did all the beaking, flapping, shimmying, clapping, and doe-see-doeing with players from each team, the place went absolutely crazy. The wet grass made the dancing treacherous, and there were some slips and near falls, but the crowd loved every minute of it and gave the performers what Byrd later said was "the best ovation we ever got."

When it was over and Max was back outside the umpires' dressing room, a man named Willard Seekatz came up and introduced himself. "Sir, I'd like to thank you for what you just did," he said. "I've been officiating high school and college basketball games for 35 years, and I understand how much it means when somebody comes up to you and says, 'Good job.' My wife has been to games and heard me totally abused because the fans don't realize that we're like everybody else. You just did more for our profession in five minutes than somebody else could do in 20 years of perfect officiating because you just humanized officials and umpires."

By the time London won the first game 3–2, it was almost midnight. Although many of the players on both teams would have been content to call it a night, only a couple of hundred fans had left the ballpark. Before making a decision, Max checked with Bryan Wickline and found out that the Paints' front office definitely wanted to get the second game of the doubleheader in, even starting at such a late hour. As Wickline explained to Max, the tickets for Saturday covered the second game, not the first; and if the second game were banged, rain checks would have to be issued. Ever accommodating, Max told Wickline that they'd play if the Paints would work some more on the field during the break between games.

It was about a quarter to two when London DH Chris Gavriel stepped in to hit against the Paints' Josh White in the top of the fifth inning. The Werewolves were trailing 6–3 but had runners on first and third with one out. Gavriel took the first pitch for a called strike, then swung at a high fastball and fouled it straight back. In an instant the ball went over catcher Chris Poluson's glove, blasted through the bars of Max's mask, and slammed into Max's face. Max stumbled backwards two steps, pulled off his mask which still held the baseball like a vise, took one halting step to his left, went down on one knee, and cupped his left hand to his face. His hand immediately filled with blood. As the trainers from both teams rushed to Max's aid, he lost consciousness and collapsed. Max told me later: "It was appropriate the Paints were playing London. My face was so bloody it looked like a werewolf had bitten and clawed me!"

When the Paints' Rodger Fleming and the Werewolves' Paul McCrimmon got to Max they immediately noticed two cuts on the bridge of his nose, which were bleeding profusely, and saw that he was also bleeding out of one nostril. They knew that he had suffered a broken nose and some kind of head trauma, probably a concussion. After they wiped the blood from Max's face and stanched the blood flow as best they could, Fleming revived him by passing smelling salts under his nose. Max was in a lot of pain, with the worst of it coming from the pressure London's trainer, Paul McCrimmon, was applying to stop the bleeding from the cuts on the bridge of his nose. They felt a little better about Max's condition when they saw that he could still joke around. When McCrimmon asked Max how he felt, Max borrowed a line from his favorite band, Pink Floyd. "There's someone inside my head, but it ain't me," he said, while gazing up at the dark side of the full moon.

A graduate of the University of Toledo and the former trainer of the Toledo Storm, an East Coast Hockey League affiliate of the Detroit Red Wings, the Paints' Rodger Fleming was one of the best trainers in the Frontier League. As the trainer for the home team, he took charge of assessing the seriousness of Max's injury. He wanted to get Max off the field so that he could conduct a proper neurological examination; so after Max recovered a little of his equilibrium, he helped him to his feet and guided him towards the gate at the end of the Paints' dugout.

Inside the umpires' dressing room Fleming decided that Max had sustained a grade one concussion. Max had all the textbook symptoms—dizziness, headache, ringing in the ears—except for nausea. After ten minutes, everything subsided except for the headache. Max's partner, Matt Neader, and Chris Hanners came into the room, and Neader asked how Max was feeling. "Gimme a cigarette and a beer, and I'll be okay," he said.

Neader laughed, then Chris repeated the question. "I'll be okay. Just give me a few minutes," said Max. "If Matt will put his gear on and work the plate, I can finish it on the bases."

"Max, are you sure? You don't have to do this," said Chris.

Max was sure. He just needed a little time to get himself together. As for Rodger, he felt that Max was capable of making the decision for himself.

Neader changed into his plate gear and went back out onto the field, as Max slowly changed out of his plate gear and into a fresh shirt.

When London manager Andy McCauley saw Neader walk onto the field, he asked McCrimmon what was going on. "Max definitely has a concussion, but he's thinking about finishing the game," he said.

"You've got to be kidding me!" said McCauley.

McCauley accosted Neader and said, "Look, we all know Max is a tough umpire, but this is ridiculous! My trainer says the guy has a concussion, so I'm not worried about finishing this game. Max's health is what I'm worried about, and finishing this game is not worth jeopardizing it."

"It's not my call," said Neader. "It's Max's decision. He's the crew chief. Max says he's fine, and the trainer says he's fine."

Recognizing guts and dedication when they saw it, the crowd stood and applauded heartily when the broken-nosed, Chicken-Dancing umpire walked slowly back onto the field. When Max got to home plate, he said, "Andy, have you got a problem with this?"

what ?
crowd ?
A blood fock'n crowd !

McCauley looked at Max and thought his friend was a mess. Max had gauze packed inside his right nostril, and a huge homemade bandage obliterated his nose. The blood from the two cuts on his nose had already soaked the gauze and was now beginning to redden the white trainers' tape that held the gauze over the cuts.

"Max, there was no doubt in my mind that you were not going to come out of that locker room and finish this game," said McCauley. "I'll tell you one thing: If I had 25 ballplayers like you, I'd take 'em into any trench and win the war. But, look, we don't have to do this. We can suspend this game and finish it tomorrow. And if we get rained out tomorrow, we can make up both games in the next series. We're coming back to Chillicothe next week."

"I know that," said Max, "but two things. One, tomorrow is get-away day for you guys. If we can finish this game right now, instead of tomorrow, that'll be three more innings you don't have to play before we can start tomorrow's game. You'll be three innings closer to London, and your guys will be able to sleep in a little more and catch up on their sleep. That's number one. And number two: I don't want anybody, Andy, either you or Roger Hanners or any of the players on either team saying that this game was called because Max McLeary wanted to go home early."

"Max, I know and Roger knows and all the players on both teams who know you know that that would never be the case. Nobody who knows you would ever say that or even think it. But, Max, you're in no condition to finish this game."

Having said his piece, Max didn't argue further and merely frowned in response to McCauley's entreaty.

By this time Max, McCauley, and Neader had been joined at home plate by Roger and Chris Hanners and the two trainers. McCauley appealed to Roger Hanners. "There's no way he should be out here trying to umpire a baseball game. He should be on the way to a hospital."

"Let's call it then. That's fine with me. It's past my bedtime anyway," said Roger, who turned and started walking back to the dugout.

After a moment's awkward silence, Chris looked at Max and said, "Well? How do you feel, Max?"

"Not that good. I feel a little light-headed, like I really don't belong out here."

"That's not what you said in the locker room a few minutes ago. In the locker room you said you felt fine."

"In the locker room I did feel fine."

A moment later Max attempted to put back on his stoic face. "Just give me a cigarette and a beer, and I'll be okay," he said, but this time it was too late. No one was buying the act now, nor did anybody want to listen to Max's sincere and profuse apologies for causing the game to be suspended because he'd broken his nose and gotten a concussion.

With the game finally suspended, the Paints turned their attention towards taking care of Max. Chris and Bryan Wickline insisted that Max not drive home but get a room at the Chillicothe Inn on Bridge Street at the team's expense. They also sent Rodger Fleming along to watch over Max. The two of them stayed up until five in the morning talking and drinking the six-pack of beer that Max somehow managed to get his hands on. The next morning Rodger, who had to work the Paints' baseball camp for Little Leaguers, was gone by 9:00. Max slept until 10:30, went to The Dock for lunch, and then, as Andy McCauley later put it, "showed up with bells on, ready to umpire" at VA Memorial Stadium by 1:00.

When Max got to the umpires' dressing room, he ran into Jimmy Miner, who told him: "Sometimes I feel like I can't get this field ready, especially when we get a lot of rain. But then I thought last night, 'If Max can go out and be ready to umpire after what he just went through, then, by God, I can get this field ready to play on.' I wanted you to know that."

"Thank you, Miner," Max said. "I appreciate you saying that, and I appreciate the job you do on that field every night because, you know, we're all in this together."

9

The Wheel,
Max Sets Off Fireworks,
and The Chicken

11/7/04
AFTER 2:00

MAX AND I FINALLY GOT BACK together on Monday, July 17, and we rode over to Richmond in Max's dark blue Buick Regal. Max had bought the Regal with 60,000 miles on it, and now that its odometer had climbed over 299,000, it had proven itself to be an automobile as indestructible as the man himself. Max looked a little tired; otherwise, the only visible effects of his recent ordeal were the wide bandage over his nose and some puffiness under his eyes. As usual, we stopped at the Village Pantry for cigarettes and a newspaper. Max wouldn't look at the paper, but I did and read that the Roosters had been swept over the weekend in their series against River City right after the All-Star Game. The Rascals had pinned the losses on three of Richmond's stalwart starting pitchers, Engstrom, Jelovcic, and Kojack, and had outscored the Roosters in the three games 25–5. The sweep was nothing new for Richmond, which was proving to be a very streaky ballclub. Six of their fourteen series so far had resulted in sweeps; unfortunately, the Roosters had lost four of them, including two to the Chillicothe Paints. The latter two sweeps had been brutal, as the Paints had outscored the Roosters 39–11 in the six games. The Roosters wanted and needed a little payback against the Paints. Coming into the series the Paints were in first by half a game over Johnstown, while the Roosters were seven back in fourth and in danger of falling out of the race.

When we came within view of our usual parking spot under the giant sycamore tree in the McBride Stadium parking lot, we saw that a trash dumpster had been left there. Max's sense of aesthetics was highly offended by this incongruity, yet he swung the car around the tree as if to find a different spot. "Max, you always park under the tree, don't you?" I reminded him.

"You're right. Let's don't break tradition," he said, as he completed the circle and inserted the car as far into our usual spot under the tree as the interloping dumpster would allow him to. Since it was the start of a series, Max had a lot of gear to take into the ballpark. As he was pulling his stuff out of the trunk, I noticed a small plaque off to one side. It was Max's Frontier League Umpire of the Year award for 1999. "I never noticed this before," I said.

"Bill Lee just gave it to me … a couple of weeks ago," said Max. I knew Max was thankful for the appreciation the award represented, but the actual plaque didn't mean that much to him, and it stayed in the trunk the rest of the season.

I too needed to prepare for the day. Opening a new notebook, I wrote my name, address, and phone number on the inside cover and added that there was a "Reward If Found." "Max, what's the date?" I said.

"You're asking *me?*" he said in a tone of voice that implied I ought to know that a man in his condition should not be expected to be cognizant of trivial details, such as the day of the week or the date. In the next breath he let me know that he was feeling the pressure again. "Man, I gotta get through this game tonight," he said, slamming the lid of the trunk. Halfway across the parking lot he expressed his anxiety once more, "This'll be a riot. I gotta get that first banger right."

Other than Max's accident, the big news around the ballpark centered on the Paints, not the home team Roosters. The Paints had learned Sunday morning that they were losing their team leader and the biggest bat in their lineup, shortstop Mike Cervenak. A New York Yankees' scout had seen Mike win the home run derby contest at the All-Star Game, been further impressed with his play during the game, and had offered Cervenak a contract.

Cervenak made his last hurrah with the Paints a good one. Chillicothe won Saturday night's suspended game against London first and then took Sunday's regularly scheduled contest, with Cervenak contributing two hits, including his league-leading 12th home run. The Yankees had Cervenak slated for their Single A Greensboro, North Carolina, team in the South Atlantic League, but before he joined the Bats in Greensboro, Cervenak was ordered to fly to Tampa, Florida, and work out with New York's Gulf Coast League team for a few days. Prior to leaving Chillicothe Monday morning, he explained to Doug Kimsey how bittersweet the signing was. "I hate to leave this team," he said. "They're a great bunch of guys. I'm close to them and to my host family, who are like second parents. Everyone in this organization and this town has been wonderful to me. Plus, I came back this year to help the Paints win the league, and I wanted a championship ring. It's a tough thing to have to do, to leave Chillicothe, especially now, when we've got such a good team, but it's the reason we come here: to get a shot at playing for a big league team."

As if losing Cervenak, who was leading the league in hits, extra-base hits, RBIs, and slugging percentage (in addition to home runs) at the time of his departure, wasn't bad enough; the Paints were also going to lose the Canadian Clipper, Joe Colameco, who had also been signed by the Yankees. In addition to being a terrific right fielder, the speedy Colameco could also hit. After Sunday's games, Joe was batting .367, good for fourth in the league; he was second in doubles; and he led the league in triples and on-base percentage. The Yankees were eventually going to send Colameco to Tampa for evaluation, but they were not able to obtain a visa for him right away, and so for the time being he was staying with the Paints and nursing a sprained ankle which he had recently injured. Outside the visiting team's clubhouse he told me how he'd learned the big news. "Yesterday I was eating a sub in the locker room before we got dressed for the games. Cervenak walked in, and I said, 'Congratulations, Mike!' And he said, 'Thanks, Joe. You're coming with me, you know.' I didn't know, and I didn't believe him until I heard it from Chris Hanners. And then I was so excited I couldn't finish lunch."

The upshot of all this was that although the Paints were in first place, they came into town looking over their shoulders. Holdovers from the year before remembered what happened when the star of the 1999 team, Gator McBride, was signed by the Boston Red Sox halfway through the season. The Paints' offensive production decreased by nearly three runs a game, and the team played sub .500 baseball for the rest of the year. The Paints still made the playoffs and even advanced to the championship round, but everyone felt that Chillicothe lost the championship to London not in September but in July.

In the press box I learned that there had been some changes in Richmond too. Official scorer David Knight and Gary Kitchel, the Frontier League's Ernie Harwell, were still on the job, but Troy Derengowski had resigned his P. A. announcing duties and been replaced by Scott Beaman, husband of General Manager Deanna Beaman. Troy had quit for the best of reasons: to be able to watch the games of a tee-ball player with the name Derengowski on the back of his shirt.

While losing Troy was a disappointment for the denizens of the press box, of more import for the fortunes of the Roosters was the addition of first baseman Macky Waguespack, who'd started the season with the Canton Crocodiles, and the loss of second baseman Key Voshell, who'd just signed with the St. Louis Cardinals. Waguespack, a good old boy with a thick Cajun drawl from Paulina, Louisiana, had been immediately popular with his new teammates. He had a tendency to strike out too much, but he also showed glimpses of becoming a serious home run threat. Voshell had clearly been Richmond's best player, but his departure was not that troubling, at least according to the *Paladium-Item's* Don Tincher. "In a strange way, not having Key here might help this team," he said. "They needed a place for Freddy Flores to play, and putting Ryan Anholt on second opened up a spot for Flores at third. Anholt has been getting on base a lot as a leadoff hitter, and Flores is one of those guys who always seems to be involved in the outcome. He's either going to win it for you or lose it for you."

We discussed the Paints' personnel losses, and Don told a story about a recent game in Richmond that illustrated how little the Roosters would miss Colameco. "Chillicothe was here on July fourth, and they were up 2–0, when the Roosters were batting with a man on first. Dan Wydner hit one over the right field wall at the Oberle Rigging sign. The ball went out of the ballpark, but Colameco jumped up and brought it back into the park. His bare hand hit the sign, and he dipped his gloved hand over the fence—it was actually below the fence on the other side—caught the ball, and brought it back over. Then he threw the runner out at first. He was standing at second base going, 'What happened? That was a home run, wasn't it?' My lead for the story in the paper the next day was 'The game was tied and then it wasn't.'"

The game started slowly as a pitcher's duel between the Paints' Sean Boesch and the Roosters' Steve Carver. Neither team scored for four innings, but the Roosters eventually tallied five runs off Boesch; two of which were unearned because of errors by Joey Choron, who had the unenviable job of trying to replace Mike Cervenak. Carver, a crafty little lefthander, kept the Paints off balance for seven innings and allowed only a single run in his final inning of work on a homer by DH Josh Lamberg. The final score was 8–1 after the Roosters tagged Eric Frodsham for three more runs in the eighth, while Bobby Chandler shut out the Paints over the last two innings.

Don Tincher told me that Mike Zerbe's parents were at the game, so I left the press box to join them in the first base grandstands.

Bill and Jan Zerbe were sitting with the Smithkamps, the couple that was hosting Mike for the summer. As expected, I found the Zerbes to be very sociable and upbeat people. They had come to see Mike play, all the way from Tampa, Florida, where Jan taught marine biology at Gaither High School and Bill ran his own insurance business after having retired from a 21-year career in banking. Naturally, they were friends with the Smithkamps, who sent them pictures of Mike playing for the Roosters. "As a parent, it's nice to know that Mike has a support system like the Smithkamps away from home." said Mrs. Zerbe. To my surprise, the Zerbes told me that they had another son who was playing professional baseball. Chad Zerbe, I learned, was a lefthanded pitcher, currently assigned to the San Francisco Giants' Triple A farm club in Fresno, California, one step away from the major leagues. "We're very proud of our boys," said Bill, "but the best part of it is that we've made a lot of friends through baseball and have had more fun than the kids." When I told the Zerbes why I'd formed such a good first impression of their son, they beamed with pride but didn't seem surprised at all by the account of Mike's courtesy, thoughtfulness, and maturity. Jan said, "Mike has always been a people person. He's a big supporter of his two brothers, one older and one younger; and when he was in school, the girls just adored him, but Mike was more interested in protecting them than dating them."

The game was in the bottom of the fifth, and Zerbe was batting. "Come on Z!" shouted Jan Zerbe. "Step towards the pitcher!"

"He calls home after every game and ends the conversation with 'I love you.' I don't hear a lot of men saying that, but that's the kind of person Mike is," she continued.

According to Mrs. Zerbe, who had e-mailed Mike that she was bringing some stoogies with her from Tampa, Mike was always a hard worker and the type of athlete who wasn't happy unless his uniform was the dirtiest. He gave up football in the tenth grade to concentrate on baseball and worked so hard at the game that it wasn't long before his mom began to think "Maybe things will happen for this young man."

Baseball did help pay for Zerbe's college education, and when he wasn't drafted, his parents encouraged him to continue his career, even if it was only in the Frontier League. "I told him that he should follow the dream, that he should ride the wave and see what happens," said Jan. Bill Zerbe, who'd been content to let his wife do most of the talking, added: "His philosophy is that 'One day I'll probably have to get a job, but right now I'm going to enjoy this and love every minute of it. ... They're going to pay me to play baseball? I'd do it for free!'"

"I would assume that coaching is a good possibility for Plan B," said Jan. "Mike loves the game that much. He loves the smells of baseball, putting on the uniform, the practices, talking to kids, ... everything."

Steve Mitrovich had led off the inning with a single to center, and with the game still scoreless, John Cate put the bunt sign on. Zerbe got it down, and although the pitcher was able to field the ball, he had no play except at first. "What was that?" asked Jan.

"A sacrifice," said Mr. Zerbe.

"Way to move the runner, Mike!" shouted Mrs. Zerbe. The Smithkamps praised the play in agreement with Mrs. Zerbe and pointed out that the Roosters had been having trouble executing the sacrifice bunt.

The Zerbes had no illusions about how much of a long shot it was for their son Mike to get to the major leagues, but they believed in helping their sons take their best shot; and they appreciated the wisdom for both their sons behind the advice Giants coach Sweet Lou Johnson had given Chad: "Never take the uniform off. Make them take it off you."

With his sacrifice bunt in the fifth inning Zerbe had figured in the first run the Roosters scored, and he also had a hand in the scoring two innings later. I was rooting even harder than ever for him when he batted in the seventh, 0–1 in the game, because I was also rooting for his parents. Mike worked the count full against Boesch, a tough customer; and then, in that moment of relaxed tension right before the pitcher goes into his windup, when the pitcher is looking in for his sign and the batter is trying to clear his mind and focus on an imaginary box off the pitcher's shoulder from which the ball will issue, a string of fire crackers went off in the grandstands. Schaly called time and had everyone wait out the interruption. Moments later Boesch delivered the 3–2 pitch, and Zerbe hit a broken bat liner that barely got over Joey Choron's head at short. "Yeah! Yeah! Yeah! Thataway, Mike!" shouted a standing Jan Zerbe. "That felt good," she added as she sat down. Ryan Peavey pinch ran for Zerbe and later scored on a single by Dan Wydner.

As the inning drew to a close and I got ready to return to the press box for the rest of the game, I asked Jan how she and Bill first met Max. "He came right up to us and just started talking to us about baseball," she said. "It's nice to see that he has a sincere interest in the ballplayers. And Mike just adores him. Max said Mike works hard every game, and that's what every parent wants to hear, whether in baseball or not."

"Broken-nose McLeary," as some of Max's umpiring buddies were calling him, virtually had the night off until the bottom of the eighth inning, which started when Freddy Flores hit a smash off first baseman Chance Melvin's glove that bounded into right field. Two pitches later, with a great jump off Eric Frodsham's submarine delivery, Flores took off for second and slid in well ahead of catcher Chris Poulsen's throw. Max delayed his call for a second or two, and then rang up Flores, who was still on the ground touching the bag with his left foot. There were only 716 fans on hand, but they let out a howl of protests and catcalls. As Max jogged back towards the first base line, Roosters third base coach Woody Sorrell sprinted across the diamond to accost him. And in the press box Gary Kitchel's partner for the day leveled a measured criticism of the call. "I like Max, but that was as bad a call as I've seen in some time. ... Unless Flores came off the bag, which we couldn't see up here," said Tom Parkevich, Earlham College's head baseball coach.

Sorrell never got the chance to argue the call. When he got to Max, Max said, "I'll talk to Cate" and abruptly turned away. John Cate did come out of the dugout, walking, but he didn't stay on the field long and there were no more fireworks. Max repeated for Cate the conversation he'd had with the prone Flores.

Looking upwards at Max, Flores had said, "My foot is on the bag!"

"It is now," Max had replied.

And to Cate Max said, "John, he tried to hook slide. His foot came off the bag for a second, and the shortstop slapped a tag on him."

The always intense, sometimes fiery Cate accepted Max's explanation with grace and wonderful sportsmanship; something the Roosters' 5–1 lead may have played some small part in.

At the Wheel Max and I were joined by Schaly, Kitchel, Zerbe, and Tom Arnett. Max was content to unwind quietly and make sure that the waitress kept the infield sprinkled, while Jim Schaly and his big personality dominated the conversation. As was his custom, Schaly had pulled his chair up to the table backwards. He was straddling it and hanging over its backrest, which practically functioned as a tether to keep him seated when he became excited, lifted off the chair, and leaned forward over the table towards his enthralled audience. "Mike, what's your favorite drink?" he said to Zerbe.

"You mean to drink or to make for a customer when I'm bartending?" asked Zerbe, after he took the cigar out of his mouth.

"To make for a customer."

"Oh, that's easy. A Red-headed Slut."

Schaly smiled, nodded his head, and said, "One time I was on the plate, and Zerbe swung at a pitch in the dirt. I said, 'What are you swinging at, you red-headed slut?' He laughed."

Max had a Zerbe moment to relate too: "One time Zerbe stepped out of the box and said, 'Max, that wasn't a strike.'

"'I called it a strike,' I said.

"'Yeah, but was it a strike?' Mike said.

"'It was that time.'

"'Well, it sure didn't look like a strike,' he said.

"'It must have been on my bad side then,' I said."

Morgan Burkhart's promotion to the major leagues was still a hot topic in Richmond—the *Paladium-Item* had started a "Burkhart Watch" as a sidebar on the front page of the sports section—and Schaly, like almost everybody who'd known Burkhart, had a comment to make that illustrated Burkhart's dedication to maximizing his talent and his constant dissatisfaction with anything less than perfection. "He would go 4–5 with four home runs and be pissed off about the one out he made," said Schaly.

"That's why he's in the major leagues," said Kitchel. "I talked to him on the phone when he was still in Pawtucket, and he said, 'Kitch, I'm not hitting worth a shit. I'm getting good pitches to hit. I'm just not hitting them.' I thought, well, at least, he isn't being overpowered; he knows he can hit the pitching. Three days later he was called up."

"Morgan's a helluva ballplayer, but he's not a classy dresser," said Schaly.

"That's for sure," said Kitchel. "He never cared how he looked. He'd straggle onto the bus wearing sandals, jeans, and an old T-shirt. He just never thought much about what he was wearing because he was always thinking about baseball. I heard that when he first went up to the Red Sox, Jimy Williams was fining him $1 a day for going around with such a ratty traveling bag. He finally went out and bought a new one."

"Morgan may not have paid much attention to his wardrobe," said Max, "but he cared what the baseballs looked like. One time I threw a new ball out to the pitcher. The pitch came in, and Morgan turned around and said to me, 'Max, what'd you rub that ball up with, black shoe polish? Throw it out. It's too dark. I can't see it.'"

"I said, "Hey, Morgan, like my dad Wilson used to say: 'Monkey can't dance ... don't blame floor.' But I did throw the ball out."

Word of the Paints–Cheetahs game that Ron LeFlore had been tossed out of by Matt Neader had gotten around via the league grapevine, and the mention of black shoe polish reminded Kitchel to ask Schaly about it.

"Matt made the right call," said Schaly. "but he was wrong to roll the ball over towards Ron. I told him later, 'Matt, you're lucky I wasn't LeFlore. I'da hit you in the head with the ball. You just don't do that. You made LeFlore look bad; you made the Frontier League look bad; and you made me look bad because I'm the one who hired you into the league.'

"What he should have done was held the ball up and said, 'See, Ron! The ball's got a black mark on it. It hit the batter's foot, just like I said: Foul ball!' LeFlore would have said, 'Fuck you,' and then you throw him out. But you don't roll the ball at him. Neader did that to piss 'im off.""

Cook County had recently given LeFlore his pink slip. No one knew for sure why LeFlore had been fired, but the assumption was that the Cheetahs' disappointing record was reason enough. After all, Canton's Dan Massarelli had been let go before LeFlore for not getting the Crocodiles untracked, and the managers of other poorly performing clubs were probably going to get axed also before the season was over. On the other hand, Schaly felt that LeFlore's rocky relationship with the umpires in the league had had a lot to do with his demise. "I'm not saying you need to kiss ass, but if the umps hate you, you're screwed," he said. "And Ron did not have a good relationship with the umpires, to say the least.

"Last year Chuck Robinson and I were umpiring in Canton right after Ron took over Cook County. Before the game Ron came up to Chuck and said, 'Hey, Bro! It's good to see you here.'

"Chuck said, 'Why's that?'

"'Because we can't catch a break from all the white umpires in this league, I know that.'

"And Chuck said, 'I played professional baseball like you. I didn't get as high as you did, but I played professionally, and I spent enough time in pro ball to know that you have enough to worry about besides being screwed by racist umpires. And if you think you're gonna win this game tonight because a black man is umpiring the game, you're dead wrong.'" 11\8\2004

Zerbe's parents came into the bar and were royally welcomed by both Max and Schaly. "You were in the bucket!" said Jan Zerbe to Schaly. This reference to working the plate, which I'd never heard before, prompted Schaly to summarize the game; which, from his point of view, boiled down to one thing: the outstanding control exhibited by the Roosters' Steve Carver. "He pitched a great game," said Schaly. "He reminded me of Tommy John when I had him in Triple A. John's fastest pitch was 75 mph, and his change was 60 mph. Yet he only gave up one hit, and he yelled at the catcher for calling the pitch when he gave that up. Carver was pitching so well I hated to see John Cate go to his bullpen. I told John, 'I'll umpire the plate every fifth day for you when that kid is pitching, and I'll make him an All-Star!'"

As the Zerbes didn't know Schaly as well as they knew Max, Jan began to make polite, conversational inquiries about him. Schaly was only too happy to fill the Zerbes in. Most of what he told them I knew already, but I hadn't known that Jim was one of three brothers and that one of those brothers was a college baseball coach (at St. Leo's in St. Leo, Florida), like Schaly's dad. Another interesting tidbit that came out was the fact that Schaly's dad owned an authentic game-worn Roberto Clemente jersey, a sleeveless flannel, no less. The jersey had come from Kent Tekulve, who'd played for Don Schaly at Marietta College before enjoying a fairly long stint as the Pittsburgh Pirates' best short reliever. According to Schaly, after Clemente's tragic death in 1972 "everybody robbed his locker." Tekulve made off with the flannel jersey; added a pair of Vernon Law's baseball pants and one of his own caps; and gave the pieced-together Pirates' uniform to his old college coach. Don Schaly probably never even wondered about the monetary value of the Clemente shirt, but I knew it to be considerable, perhaps even astronomical, in the hyper-inflated sports memorabilia market of our time.

At some point the conversation got around to football, and Schaly and Jan Zerbe discovered that they shared a passion for the Pittsburgh Steelers. This united them against Mike, an equally passionate Cleveland Browns fan, who refused to acknowledge their claim that the Steelers were the grandest franchise in professional football history.

Max and I were both getting tired; and so, with the Steelers–Browns debate still in progress, we said our goodbyes and called it a night. I offered to drive home, but Max declined. He'd be fine, he said, if I'd just pop open and hand him in a timely manner the two Coors Lights he needed to get home. The first one was for the trip from Richmond to Liberty; the second one, for the trip from Liberty home. We talked less than usual and listened more to music, which was supplied by the CD player in the trunk of the car, loaded with 12 of Max's favorites: Shania Twain, Annie Lennox, Match Box 20, Rod Stewart, Tina Turner, Fleetwood Mac (live), The Tractors, Bob Seger, The Commitments, Dance Party '97, John Cougar Mellencamp (live), and Frankie & Louie's Greatest Hits (that's Budweiser's talking ferret and lizard, not Frankie Avalon and Louie Armstrong). I particularly enjoyed a kick-ass remake of "Mustang Sally" by the Commitments and was surprised when Max told me that the CD it was on was the soundtrack for a movie by the same name as the band: about, of all things, a dysfunctional Irish group that nevertheless did the greatest hits of Motown as soulfully as their original artists. "You and Kathy have gotta stay in one night and rent the movie," said Max. "You'll love it."

After we got to Max's place, I opened the door of my mini-van and stood there in the wet grass a few moments, with Max still in the driveway, his back to the house, while we coordinated our plans for the next day. As usual, Max thanked me profusely for spending so much time on our project. Waving aside his thanks, I thanked him and told him the pleasure was all mine. Knowing that tomorrow would be a big day for him, I urged him to sleep late and get plenty of rest. "Yeah, right," he snickered. "I've got to be at the shop by 8:00. But I appreciate your concern." Just before I ducked my head and slid into the front seat, he added, "You know, when people ask you what was the toughest part of the book, you'll say, 'Keeping Max alive.'"

Early Tuesday morning Max received a package at the shop. It was from friends of his who ran a sporting goods store for umpires. They'd heard about his injury Saturday night in Chillicothe and immediately sent him a new Wilson metal protective mask to replace the plastic "Death Mask" that had let him down twice.

"You are going to use the new mask tonight, aren't you?" I said, as we got ready to leave for Richmond.

"Hell, yes," he said. "I may be crazy, but I'm not stupid."

Once we arrived at McBride Stadium, I headed for the box seats by the Roosters dugout to watch a little BP. On the way over I saw a wispy young woman sitting in the third row intently watching the Roosters work out. She had freckles and long auburn hair and wore a small gold cross around her neck. I suspected that she was a ballplayer's girlfriend since there were rarely any fans in the ballpark at that time of day besides relatives and girlfriends of the players.

The early bird turned out to be Phill "The Tripper" Kojack's fiancé, a Tarheel from Newburn, North Carolina, named Corina Hansen. She and Phill had become good friends while they were students at Liberty University in Lynchburg, Virginia, but their relationship did not progress to the dating stage for over a year because Phill was afraid of losing her as a friend in the event that a courtship didn't work out. The turning point in their relationship occurred one weekend when Phill stayed on campus to go on a blind date and Corina traveled to Knoxville, Tennessee, to visit her best friend, Faith, who decided they should go for a little hike up Mt. LeConte.

I have always been a sucker for good stories about how true romances get started, and Corina's had the added enticement of involving an adventure I could completely relate to. Climbing to the top of Mt. LeConte near Gatlinburg in the Great Smoky Mountains was one of the many unforgettable adventures of our married life my wife had talked me into going on. Although we didn't appreciate its benefit when we started, a constant drizzle kept us cool as we sweated for hours walking the rocky, slippery trail that wound upwards around the mountain. I remember being certain throughout the final two-hour leg of the hike that the top of the mountain had to be just around the next bend. In all, the ascent took us six seemingly-endless hours of almost continual climbing. As part of the package we'd paid for, we were entitled to an overnight stay in one of the tiny, pioneer-like cabins on top of the mountain, and we were so exhausted that we went to sleep almost immediately after supper. After wolfing down breakfast the next morning, we made our descent down the mountain. The trip down took only two and a half hours, but with every painful step our aching muscles reminded us of how badly out of shape we were. Before we'd started our trek up the mountain, I'd sneered at the self-congratulatory "I Survived Mt. LeConte" T-shirts we'd seen in the gift shop where we'd picked up our bag lunches. After we reached the bottom of the mountain though, I understood why people bought the shirts.

Corina's experience with Mt. LeConte was even more unforgettable than mine; as she, Faith, and two male friends of Faith's decided to conquer the mountain in one day. "It took us five hours to get up the mountain," she said in a decidedly Southern twang, "which wasn't bad. The problem was that we got a late start, so that by the time we started down the mountain it was completely dark. Worse, it was raining and there was no moon out. We held onto each other and made a little train with Faith in the lead. She would give us directions, like 'Step down … step up … rock to your right.' She had a little flashlight at first, but it went out after about an hour. It was really scary because we couldn't see a thing, and at one point Faith almost stepped off the trail and went over the side of the mountain. When that happened, I told Faith, 'Tell Phill, if I don't make it down, that he's the only person I ever thought I'd marry.' After we finally got down, we ran into a park ranger. When we told him what we'd just done, he said, 'That was really stupid.' 'Yeah, we know,' we said.

"The next day I talked to Phill on the phone, and I asked him how his date was. He said it was terrible, and I thought, "Yes!" That was when I admitted to myself for the first time that I was in love with him. When I told him about coming down the mountain in the dark, I said that I told Faith, 'Tell Phill goodbye if I don't make it.'

"A week or so later we were talking on the phone again, and I told him the same story except that this time I said I told Faith, 'Tell Phill I wish we had dated.' Phill said, 'That's not what you said the first time you told me the story.'

"'Do you want to know what I really said?' I asked him.

"He said he did, so I told him. And all I remember hearing from the other end of the phone line was dead silence, which really scared me. I thought, 'Uh, oh. I've really blown it now.' But I hadn't. He said he was glad I felt that way, and we started dating. And all our friends said, 'It's about time!'

Next to Kojack's dad, Corina became Phill's biggest fan. Whenever possible she slipped away from her job at the college library to watch Liberty's home baseball games. "I remember sitting in the stands and hearing the other girls ooh and ah over him. Some girl would say something like, 'Phill's so cute. Why don't they put him in?' And I'd think. 'No library card for you, sister!'"

I'd been completely charmed by Corina's story and the sweet way she had of telling it; and I hated to go from the sublime to the ridiculous, but I had to ask her what she thought about Phill's peculiar talent.

Amusingly, Corina had found out from Kojack's mother that Mr. Kojack had always been a tripper too—he tripped on his first date with Mrs. Kojack, and his specialty was tripping on curbs—and so she accepted Phill's little idiosyncrasy as something that simply ran in the family. Not only that, Phill had never known about the family legacy, until Corina told him that he was a trip off the old block.

Corina was also able to tell me about Kojack's most infamous trip to date. It had come when he returned to Liberty University to visit old roommates after he had already graduated. On the morning of his departure, Kojack told his friends goodbye and left the campus, but he changed his mind and decided he wanted to stay another day and night. By the time he returned, the entire student body was attending a chapel service held on the floor of the 9,000-seat Vines Center, the home of the Liberty Flames basketball team. So that he wouldn't remain locked out of his friends' dorm room all day while they attended classes, Kojack felt that he had to get their attention in order to let them know he was still on campus. He walked around to the empty seating section at the end of the building behind the stage; climbed to a walkway that ran well above the gym floor; and then, when he was certain that most everybody in the audience couldn't help but notice him, he tripped, eliciting gasps and muffled cries of alarm. To reassure his audience that he was okay and to make sure his friends knew it was him, he climbed all the way up to the exit and again fell flat on his face when he reached the top step. The 6,000 students at the chapel service couldn't help but laugh this time; but the school's founder, the Reverend Jerry Falwell, didn't think it was funny at all, and Kojack was banned from the campus for three months.

In contrast to the lovely time I had talking to Corina, the game, which matched Andy Lee against Jeremy Robinson, turned out to be an ugly spectacle.

Andy gave up only one run in seven innings but watched the Chillicothe bullpen blow the game by allowing three runs in the bottom of the eighth. Although Robinson gave up only two hits and one run in five innings, he wasn't around when the Roosters took the lead; so Chad Sosebee, who surrendered two runs while working the sixth through the eighth innings, picked up the win and Bobby Chandler, the save, for tossing a one-hit ninth.

Max was in trouble from the start. The Paints' center fielder Greg Strickland struck out looking at a pitch that appeared to be outside to lead off the game. Former coach Jamie Keefe, pressed back into service by the Paints' desperate need of a steady shortstop, hit second and also struck out looking at a pitch that appeared to be up. When Keefe ran out to his position at the end of the inning, he turned to Schaly and said, "Jim, does Max have no heart? I haven't swung the bat in two years."

"You didn't swing it then either," joked Schaly. In the third after Keefe doubled to right-center, Schaly said, "Jamie, do you want the ball (as a trophy)?" "Fuck you, Jim," said Keefe with a smile on his face. An inning later, a frustrated Roger Hanners barked, "We've got one damn hit, and an old man's got it! Let's go!"

In the bottom half of the first, Max called Freddy Flores out on strikes, prompting Gary Kitchel to make a veiled crack about Max's umpiring: "There's a called third strike on Flores. ... Jim Schaly, who's on the bases tonight, has had his ups and downs, but he's a very good umpire, and he's very consistent with balls and strikes."

By the time Max rang up Dan Wydner in the bottom of the second and Mike Horning to lead off the top of the third, players on both teams were questioning his strike calls. By the fifth inning, the dissatisfaction with Max's judgment was becoming blatant. As the Roosters' Ryan Anholt walked slowly back towards the dugout after having been called out on strikes, he looked back over his shoulder and said something to Max. And in the press box, Kitchel said, "Again, we see a pitcher's strike zone."

As poorly as things were going for Max, I was still stunned by what happened when Greg Strickland came to bat in the top of the seventh, with two outs, a man on second, and the game tied 1–1. The first pitch to Strickland was a called strike. The left-handed batting Strickland swung at the next pitch and ripped it down the first base line. First baseman Kevin Cassidy had no chance to field Strickland's rocket which veered towards the corner after it passed the infield for an obvious RBI-producing extra-base hit.

As soon as Strickland connected with the baseball, he turned his head around and looked at Max ... and continued to look at Max for several strides up the first base line. It all happened in a flash but was such a strange thing to see that it seemed to occur in slow motion. What, I wondered, was Strickland doing? As soon as the thought occurred that he might be checking to see if Max called the ball fair or foul I dismissed it. Everyone in the ballpark, including Richmond's mascot, Rowdy the Rooster, knew the ball was fair. No, something else was going on here, and it continued all the way around the bases with Strickland.

Longtime Paints third base coach, Marty Dunn, gave Strickland the "Stand Up" sign, but the speedy center fielder ignored it and slid into third, hard. He sprang to his feet, and clearly yelling now, stomped towards Max, who had run out towards third from behind home plate. Without hesitating, Max thumbed Strickland out of the game. This only increased Strickland's fury. He let loose an obscenity-laced tirade as he marched into the Paints' dugout to grab his bat and glove. Visibly furious, he stomped across the field towards the gate by the Richmond dugout. Schaly intercepted him near home plate, and, placing his hands on his shoulders, tried to calm him down. But Strickland was not to be pacified. Without slowing down or changing course, he bumped Schaly out of his way and steamed ahead off the field.

It only took me a few minutes to get from the press box to the Paints' clubhouse. Greg was already changing into his civilian clothes. Aaron Queen was straightening up, trying to look busy, but he was probably there just to keep an eye on Greg, since it's a well known fact that angry athletes sometimes do stupid things, like injure themselves while kicking and slugging inanimate objects.

Strickland and I had never spoken, and I knew he didn't know my name, but I felt certain that he recognized me as the writer who'd been hanging around Max McLeary all season. My impression of him was that he was a quiet, polite young man, in addition to being a helluva ballplayer. He also seemed to be a very sober person. Whether that was his natural disposition or an unfortunate result of his being the only black kid on the team, as well as the only black person besides Marty Dunn in the entire organization, I had no way of knowing. I did know that his outburst seemed completely out of character.

Without beating around the bush, I asked him what in the hell had happened to get him so fired up.

"He called a strike on me on a bad pitch and said, 'You guys have been whining all night. There's something for you guys to whine about.'"

"I told him, 'Hey, it's nothing but an AB for me, Big Guy.' But I thought, 'Why is he messing with me? This is the seventh inning, and I haven't said shit to him.'"

"From the press box it looked like you said something to Max after you hit the ball," I said.

"Yeah. I said, 'Like I said.' Meaning it wasn't nothing but one more AB for me."

"Did you say anything when you slid into third? Did you swear at Max?"

"No. I didn't say nothing. I just looked at him."

I didn't want to rile Greg up any further, so I didn't challenge his statements, but I had a hard time believing the conversation had gone exactly as he'd reported it. Before I could find a way to delicately question whether he might have made another remark or two of a slightly different color, he vented his feelings in a short monologue.

"I'll pay the fine," he said. "And I'm sorry for the F-bombs. I embarrassed myself, my family, my team. I shouldn't have lost my temper like that. It's just a ball game. I can't believe I let an umpire get to me.

"But I didn't start it. He started it. I told him that if he was going to give me shit for no reason, I wasn't just going to take it. I'm going to give it back to him.

"I'll apologize if he wants me to. I'm a man. I'm 24 years old. I've been a professional baseball player for four years, and I've never been thrown out of a game before tonight.

"But the guy was brutal! He was missing pitches all night, and he's got rabbit ears on top of that. I never said nothing to him all night. I was in my fourth AB of the night. I should be able to talk to my teammates. We were grumbling in the dugout, but I never said nothing to that umpire."

I returned to my perch in the press box in time to see the Chillicothe bullpen give the game to the Roosters. Strickland's triple had driven in the Paints' go-ahead run, and Chris Dickerson's sac fly to center in the eighth had driven in Justin Graham who'd led off the inning with a double to up the Paints' lead to 3–1. But that was it for the Paints. Before Roger Hanners could get him out of the game, rookie Drew Roberts, who'd recently come to the team from Kent State University, loaded the bases on a walk, a hit, and a hit batter. Woody Fullenkamp came on, but was unable to prevent all three runners from scoring. Josh Lamberg singled to open the top of the ninth and was moved into scoring position by pinch hitter Joe Colameco's grounder to second, but he died there after Mike Horning and Chance Melvin grounded to short. When Jason Guynn's game-ending peg flew across the infield and landed in Aaron Sledd's first baseman's mitt, an outburst of glee emanated from the fans, who were still feeling revved up by Strickland's ejection.

Max practically sprinted off the field, and the players on both teams studiously avoided talking to the players on the other team as they left the diamond.

When I walked in on Max and Schaly, Max was sitting slumped over in the chair in front of his locker. He had a lit cigarette in his hand but looked too tired and demoralized to care about smoking it. So far he had removed nothing but his chest protector and Carolina blue jersey.

"Three ejections in five years in the Frontier League ... That's an average night for Jim," he said.

"I always throw 'em out in pairs," said Schaly quietly. "If I get one, you know there'll be another."

"This mask will take some getting used to. It feels different, but I like it," said Max. There were a few moments of awkward silence; then Max said, "Couple of 'em high?"

"Yeah. The third one on Jamie especially," said Jim.

"I was real worried before the game," confessed Max. "I wanted to make sure I didn't flinch. My knees did buckle a few times."

David Knight came into the room and asked Max what Strickland's ejection had been all about.

"He came up to the plate mumbling," said Max. "I couldn't make out what he was saying because they were playing the music so loud during the warm-up pitches."

"But the first pitch was going to be a strike no matter what?"

"Yeah, pretty much. I thought, 'We'll see what he's made of.' So he hits the next pitch, and he turns around and yells at me. He's yelling all the way down to first base, and when he gets to third he's still yelling! Mitrovich says to me, 'Max, you gotta run him for that.' I said, 'Wait until he stops running.' See, if I'da thrown him out right away, the play would have been dead, and that run for Chillicothe wouldn't have counted. So, he gets to third, Jim calls him 'Safe,' and I call him 'Out' ... as in 'You're outta the game.'"

"What exactly did you say to him, Max?" I asked.

"'Hey, Strick! You're gone!'"

When I'd walked into the room, I'd never seen Max look as down as he looked at that moment. But in recounting the incident to Knight, Max had started coming out of his funk; and his little joke at the end even brought a chuckle out of him. I knew then that he'd be okay, especially once we got to the Wheel, where some cold Coors Lights would help ease the pain.

There was a good crowd at the Wheel for a Tuesday night, and most of the patrons were people who'd been at the Roosters' game. Naturally, everybody wanted to talk about the spat between Max and Greg Strickland, who received no sympathy whatsoever in the pro–Roosters bar. Everybody took a shot at him, including Tom Arnett, who said, "He was in the Braves' organization, you know. We figured he roomed with John Rocker and that Rocker traumatized him." Even when the conversation veered away from the Paints' center fielder, somebody usually found a way to bring it back to him. For instance, a big trade had been announced right after the game. The Roosters were sending center fielder Dan Wydner, utility infielder Ryan Anholt, and relief pitcher Jamie Blaesing to the London Werewolves in return for center fielder Jason Borghese, third baseman Todd DeGraffenreid, and pitcher Scott Conner. When the trade was mentioned, somebody shouted: "Who are we getting ... Greg Strickland?"

As usual, Jim Schaly had something to say, and I was glad to hear his remarks because they went a long way towards explaining how the situation had reaching the boiling point. "Max called a pitch on Strickland he didn't like," said Schaly, "and the next inning he came up to me and said, 'I used to respect you, but I don't anymore; not since you started showing up with these shitty partners.'

"'What did you say?' I said to him. He repeated the whole thing he told me the first time. So I said to him, 'Well, I never respected you, and I'll tell you something else: Roger has a team full of injured guys and he's missing some good players who've signed with affiliated teams, so I'm not gonna run you. But I am going to tell my partner, whom I do respect, exactly what you think about him.' When Strickland came up in the seventh, Max called that first pitch to him a strike and said, 'I hear you don't like me.'"

Later on I got yet another perspective, the one from the beer garden as relayed by Tom Arnett. "You know, Mike, we're not totally abusive assholes in the beer garden. No sir. What we are is hecklers with morals. We have rules we follow, like we don't cuss at the players or threaten them or talk about their mothers, wives, or girlfriends. Most of the players laugh at us and give us shit right back, but if we get under their skin, we really let 'em have it. Now, Max didn't exactly have his best game of the season tonight. One time the boys thought he missed a pitch, and they started to get on him, but I told 'em, 'Lay off Max. He's got post-concussion syndrome.' As for Strickland, in the first inning he took what he thought was ball four and started to first, but Max called him out. As he came back to the Chillicothe dugout, which is on the third base side next to us in the beer garden, I shouted at him, 'Hey, Greg, you were going to the wrong dugout!'

"'Fuck you,' he said. Oh, okay, if that's how you want to be, I thought.

"In the fifth inning he got stranded on second, and nobody brought his glove out to him. I yelled, 'Hey, Greg, it looks like your own teammates don't like you.' He didn't say anything to that because I think somebody with Chillicothe had told him to tone it down. After that we started calling him "Mickey Rivers," just to hassle him. Right after he slid into third, he called time and started walking down to home plate. Max walked about five steps towards third, and then Strickland shouted, 'You're a fuckin' jerk!' And that's when he got the thumb from Max."

I'd gotten versions of the incident from four different people, and each, I was sure, despite some contradictions, contained elements of the truth; which, if sifted and re-combined in some convoluted way I was unable to do, would yield a perfect account of exactly what had happened. As the night went on and I watched Max recovering his confidence and cheerfulness among the people he knew respected and loved him, I contented myself with pondering the irony in his having shown a lot of guts in climbing back on the horse that had thrown him and gotten nothing much more for his trouble than another ejection and bruised landing. Life certainly wasn't fair, and nobody knew that better than Max McLeary.

My consolation, our consolation, was, as always, fellowship, humor, and the blessing of another day and another game tomorrow. As we walked out of the bar and towards the parking lot across the street right before closing time, Max said, "Boys, I'm sure glad to get that one under my belt. ... I do like that mask, Jim."

"Wait until you get hit in the face. You'll love it!" said Schaly.

The next day Max got a break from the Frontier League, which probably wasn't a bad thing. He didn't take a day off though. He and Schaly rode up to Columbus to do a Great Lakes League game. I went back to Richmond on my own to finish up the series between the Paints and the Roosters. Everybody in Richmond was thinking "Sweep," but the Paints quashed that notion with a five-run second inning, highlighted by Greg Strickland's two-run single, and won the game 8–4.

The Roosters were their own worst enemy, as they committed five errors and left 11 runners on base. Ryan Sawyers picked up the win and ran his record to 4–0 but needed help from Stephen Byrd and Jason Harrison. The fact that the feisty Byrd came out of the bullpen meant that he was still fighting through some arm trouble, and the performance he turned in was quite mixed. All five outs he recorded were by strikeout, but he also gave up three hits, four walks, and two runs. He didn't like Rod Rollins' strike zone at all. More than once he walked a few steps towards the plate and glared at Rollins after getting the ball back from catcher Ben Gerkin; and when he was relieved by Harrison, all his body language showed his disgust. Walking off the mound he brushed rudely against Gerkin, and he looked with subdued rage over his shoulder at Rollins as he crossed the foul line and again as he was greeted on the top step of the dugout by his teammates.

For me the highlight of the game came in the fourth inning when Mike Zerbe hit his fifth home run of the season over the left field fence. The night before, Don Tincher had shown me two lists he was keeping updated as the unofficial records-keeper of the Richmond Roosters:

Frontier League All-Time Home Run List
Morgan Burkhart 86
Scott Pinoni 58
Mitch House 50
Mike Zerbe 40
Keith Habig 34

Roosters Career Home Run List
Morgan Burkhart 86
Keith Habig 34
Jason Kinchen 27
Mike Zerbe 18
Aaron Sledd 15

"I wrote in the paper that Zerbe's most recent home run was his 40th. He hasn't done anything since then. I told him I shouldn't have written it," Don had said to me.

"What did Zerbe say to that?" I'd said.

"'Don't worry about it' ... the typical Zerbe reply."

I was pleased to see Zerbe's name on both lists, and I felt that his ranking fourth on the league all-time home run list was an accomplishment he could be especially proud of when his playing days were over; an end, it was beginning to look like might arrive at the conclusion of the current season. I was also happy for Mike that he'd hit his 41st career homer in front of his parents, who were going back to Tampa after the game. The solo blast only cut the Paints' lead to 5–1, but in my book it was definitely a big hit in the clutch.

During the game I ran into John Wend, and I asked him what Roger Hanners' reaction to the fracas the night before had been. "I don't know what he said after the game last night, but I can tell you what he said before today's game," John said. "He read 'em the riot act today, boy, and he should have done it a long time ago. He said, 'The umpire last night let us know early in the game he was going to give a little on the inside corner and a little on the outside corner. And he was consistent all night, and he called it the same for both teams and for both pitchers.

"'You can't go up there your third or fourth at bat of the night, and he's been calling the same way the whole game, and start bitching about it. He let everybody know from the beginning of the game what his strike zone was going to be.

"'And I'm getting tired of guys bitching, throwing helmets in the dugout, and dropping F-bombs all over the ballpark. There are kids in the ballpark, and there's no reason for that stuff. I'm tired of hearing the F-word every time you strike out or have a strike called on you you don't agree with. I don't want to hear the F-word anymore. If anybody says "Fuck" anymore, it'll be me. And if I hear anybody else use that word, he'll be sitting next to me in the dugout.'"

As far as everyone on the field was concerned, the previous night's hubbub was over and done with, but that mindset didn't apply to the hecklers, for whom Greg Strickland was still an irresistible target. In the sixth, after the drinkers in the Beer Garden had had plenty of time to down the legal limit, Strickland came to bat for the fourth time. Tired jokes about his swing causing a nice breeze were made; several mocking refrains of "Strickkkk ... landddd" could be heard all over the park; and somebody yelled, "Hey, Strickland, it's the sixth inning. You're usually gone by now."

Greg wound up drawing a base on balls—ball four was clearly high—drawing the comment: "Max would have rung him up!" On the mound for Richmond was Matt Schweitzer, a rookie from Olivet Nazarene College that the Roosters had just picked up. A lefthander with a good move to first, Schweitzer was in the second of a three-inning hitless stint for the evening. His deceptive leg kick faked Strickland back towards the bag on his first pitch to Jamie Keefe, and there were hoots of derision on that. A couple of pitches later, Greg went but was thrown out at second by Keith Fout. That caused glee all around and even brought the hilltoppers out of their lawn chairs along the NW 13th Street wall enclosing the ballpark. "Hey, Greg, we were just kidding! You *aren't* Mickey Rivers!" one of them shouted. The hecklers had one last shot at him in the eighth, and Tom Arnett came up with the funniest crack of the night after Strickland flied out in foul territory down the left field line. "Hey, Greg, you're still in the running for Miss Congeniality tonight. Don't blow it!" he said.

Chillicothe broadcaster Kevin Rouch's guest on his post-game radio show in the McBride Stadium press box was Marty Dunn, the Paints' third base coach. Except for a handful of games at the beginning of Chillicothe's first season, Roger Hanners had been the only manager in club history; and, in fact, on June 15th he had managed his 500th game for the Paints. Hanners' right hand man during that entire long stretch of games had been Dunn, who had also been the head coach of the Chillicothe High School varsity baseball team for 12 years. I didn't want to beat a dead horse, a Paint or otherwise, but Marty had been pretty close to the action on Tuesday night, and I thought his perspective was worth getting.

To my surprise, Marty revealed that at first he had been as mystified by what had happened the night before as I had been watching from the press box. Marty said he didn't see Greg look backwards after he'd hit the ball, nor did he hear Greg say anything when he slid into third. He asked Max what happened and said that Max admitted to having baited Strickland: "I hear you don't like me. If you don't like me now, wait until you see this."

"I've been in the league for eight years, and I've known Max for several years," he continued. "My personal opinion is that Max was struggling a little. Both teams were jawing at him, and to his discredit Greg used some bad language in the dugout. Max recognized this and did what he felt he needed to do. But you can't tell me that a kid can go around the bases, running out a triple, and be jawing with the umpire the whole time.

"After the game I talked with Greg, and I asked him to think about two things. One, I said, 'We all know that you are a good person, but the language you used gave everybody a bad impression of you. Once you create a bad impression like that, it can be very hard to change.' And two, I told him, 'I know the fans in the corner were riding you, but you can't let other people, the fans or the umpire, distract you or put you in a situation that gets you out of the game. Baseball is a tough game that requires total concentration, and if you are worried about the fans riding you or an umpire screwing you, you're in trouble. This is a lesson that will apply later in life too. There'll be people who want to take your job, and you can't let them mess with your mind and cause you to lose focus on your task.' Greg was a lot calmer today, and he stayed within himself.

"I think what it boiled down to was that it was just one of those nights. Things got to Greg a little bit, and he was an easy target. It was an atypical night for Max too because Max is usually on top of things. I have a lot of respect for him, but everybody has a bad night once in a while: pitchers, hitters, umpires, third base coaches. We're all human; we all make mistakes."

On Thursday the 20th, Richmond started a series at home with London, but I skipped the game, won by Richmond 7–5, because Max and Schaly were still going to be in Columbus at Ohio State doing a game in the Great Lakes summer collegiate league. Max and Schaly were scheduled to work the final two games of the London series, but I was only going to catch the middle game on Friday night because I was leaving immediately after the game for Cooperstown, New York, to attend the Inductions at the Baseball Hall of Fame.

It would have made more sense to skip the game and make the long drive to Cooperstown during the day instead of at night, but on Friday night the Famous San Diego Chicken was going to be in town, and there was no way I was going to miss his performance.

I'd seen the Chicken perform once before, a long time ago, in Atlanta-Fulton County Stadium, and the only thing I remembered about his show was that it was hilarious and well-attended. At the time, crowds as low as 5,000 were nothing unusual for the lowly Braves, but 35,000 showed up to see the Chicken on a night when the Braves came in dragging a six-game losing streak behind them.

I caught up with the Chicken, aka Ted Giannoulas, in the Richmond clubhouse after the game. Giannoulas had brown eyes, an aquiline nose, and a head full of cropped dark hair. And, although he seemed taller out of costume than in it, he was short. Statistical information on mascots is hard to come by, but I did have the Chicken's 1982 Donruss baseball card to go by; which for the record lists his height as 5' 6". The Chicken was the first mascot to ever appear in a baseball card set produced by a major manufacturer. Purists protested as if Donruss had committed some kind of bubble gum card sacrilege, but I thought the card was an honor that the Chicken richly deserved. Sports teams had had mascots before Giannoulas came along; but they had all symbolized the nickname of the home team, and none of them had ever been even remotely as funny as the Chicken. The Chicken is independent of the teams whose games he works at—he symbolizes nothing but his own personality and its effects: egomania, sarcasm, treachery, and mayhem—and he is an outstanding entertainer, not just a cheerleader in a ridiculous costume. So in that sense, Giannoulas has always been, and he remains, a true original.

The table and chair that the Roosters had provided for Giannoulas in the middle of the room didn't offer any privacy, but at least Richmond beat Zanesville, where years ago at a Zanesville Greys game he'd had to dress in the ticket booth. After he showered, Giannoulas put on green shorts, a gray sport shirt, white socks, K Swiss sneakers, and a Rio Grande Valley WhiteWings baseball cap. I was curious about the cap, as I knew that the WhiteWings were members of another independent professional baseball league, the Texas–Louisiana. Ted told me that he wore the ball caps of minor league teams only because he didn't own a single major league team cap, out of spite. "The magic has been lost for me at the major league level," he said. "There is fabulous, ghastly wealth up there, and you'd think that the players were having a lot of fun, laughing all the way to the bank. But it's not that way. I see a lot of acrimony, uptightness, and a disgusting, non-fan friendly attitude up there. It didn't used to be that way. Back in the '70s and early '80s the attitudes in the major leagues used to be more the way they are around the Frontier League, but after the labor disputes and the big money, everything changed; or rather, the players changed. They've allowed the numbers in their bank accounts to change their personalities. It's sad. And I was getting the most attitude from the highest paid players." Because of the prevailing attitudes "up there," Giannoulas had quit soliciting gigs with major league clubs. He still played big league stadiums but only when they called him first. He said he averaged 130 dates a year and that so far in 2000 his only date in the big leagues had been in Kansas City. For the Chicken, the minor leagues were where it's at. And he especially loved the spirit he found in independent professional baseball. "The farther down the chain you go, the more spirit exists there," he said. "So yes, I definitely have an affinity for the Frontier League and the other independent leagues. Bless their hearts. The players here are still chasing their dreams." He also told me that the first question in his mind when he got to Richmond Friday morning was, "Does Morgan Burkhart have the same attitude now that he's made it to the big leagues?"

Not that favoring the minors was hurting Giannoulas, who didn't exactly work for chickenfeed. For each performance he commanded a fee that was equal to an average person's salary for two months or more, and he'd been working as the Chicken for two and a half decades. Unless he'd been extremely careless with his money, Ted was already a wealthy man.

And despite the story Duke Ward had told me earlier in the season, Giannoulas' wealth and fame had apparently not gone to his head. Before Friday night's game Gary Kitchel told me, "There's a reason Ted's been so successful, and the reason is that he's a very gracious person. The first year we had him here, when I was working for the Roosters in the front office, he went out in the beer garden in the eighth inning to sign autographs for free. The autograph line stretched all the way down the left field line and way around the home run fence. He stayed for about an hour and a half and signed every autograph. Then he came into the office—actually we were working in a trailer then—and talked baseball for another hour. He sent me a Christmas card every year I worked for the club. And Schaly says that one year Ted sent him a $200 gift certificate from Penney's for being so cooperative during his act."

According to Giannoulas, he got his start quite by accident. As a student at San Diego State University, Ted was working at the campus radio station in 1974 when a commercial radio station in town came looking for a college kid to help them with a promotion. They needed somebody to dress up in a chicken suit and give away candy and Easter eggs at the local zoo. "They said, 'It's $2 an hour,' he said.

"'I can't afford that,' I told 'em.

"'No. We pay you,' they said.

"'It's a deal!' I said.

"So that's how I got started as the KBG Chicken. They hired me on the spot with no audition and no training. The costume they had for me was bad. It was made out of papier-mâché and was so ugly it scared the kids."

A few days after his appearance at the San Diego Zoo, Giannoulas made his baseball debut when the radio station lent him to the San Diego Padres so that he could help pass out free records on Opening Day. Giannoulas displayed a natural talent as a visual comic, and the radio station soon began sending him to entertain at San Diego Chargers football games and at football and basketball games played by the Aztecs of San Diego State. Before long the Chicken was in demand all over town; and though he performed at a wide variety of events, he quickly became known as the San Diego Chicken because of his frequent appearances at Padres games. Honing his act the entire time, Ted kept working locally and for hourly wages for about five years; but eventually big-time events, such as the NBA Finals, came calling, and he realized it was time to stretch his wings. It took law suits for him to gain his freedom from the radio station and the Padres, who claimed exclusive rights to the character, but the courts ruled in his favor and he flew the coop. As part of the verdict in the suit against the radio station, the court ruled that Giannoulas had to re-design the costume; a job that was taken on successfully by Ted's mom. "Yep, Mom is still on the payroll," he told me. "I need her because I go through two costumes a year. But labor costs are going through the roof. Mom just asked me for a raise to $6 an hour!"

Attendance for the game was 1,284 which was about 400 more than what the Roosters had been averaging. A solid 8-inning/5-hit performance by Werewolves starter Cory Carr, three Richmond errors, and a pair of London long balls added up to a 6–2 win for the visitors. Hard-luck Roosters starter Phill Kojack, the victim of three unearned runs, took the loss, his seventh in nine decisions. Kojack didn't pitch all that poorly, but he did surrender home runs to All-Star Game MVP Rick Nadeau (his 12th) and to former Rooster Ryan Anholt. Anholt's two-run homer to right came in the fifth, and when the inning was over Phill ran off the diamond as usual. In the dugout though, out of view of most of the fans, he slammed his glove on the bench four times in frustration ... bam! bam! bam! bam! ... then plopped down in disgust. Kojack's little outburst was the most memorable thing about the game, which was otherwise completely overshadowed by the antics of a man in a chicken suit.

Right before the game started, the Chicken walked up to Max at home plate and got him on the old fake handshake trick. When Max reached out to grasp the Chicken's extended hand, the Chicken haughtily pulled his hand back, leaving the snubbed Max looking, if not actually feeling, sheepish. Stepping around Max, he came to a jump stop, extended both arms towards the London dugout, and put the tremoring hands-and-fingers voodoo hex on the Werewolves. He then lifted one leg into the air, as if he were urinating in their direction.

In the bottom of the first, he walked into the first base coach's box, hugged Richmond coach Brad Finken, and then shooed him away back into the dugout. Although the signs always come from the coach or manager in the third base coach's box, the Chicken went to town, flashing every sign known to baseball, as well as a few known only to himself, for the next thirty seconds or so. In between batters, Richmond's own mascot, Rowdy the Rooster, came out to meet the Chicken. Rowdy began to offer a handshake, but the Chicken eschewed it in favor of the canine method of introduction, meaning that he bent over and sniffed Rowdy's posterior.

In the bottom of the second while still "coaching" first, the Chicken tried to distract the Werewolves pitcher Cory Carr by showing him a poster of a gorgeous, buxom, bikini-clad young woman entitled "BABE." When that didn't work, he tried a second poster, of a Hollywood star, the pig that was the main character in the movie *Babe*. With one out Todd DeGraffenreid grounded out to short. The Chicken was so certain DeGraffenreid had beaten out the routine grounder that when base ump Jim Schaly calmly signaled "Out," the Chicken fell over in a dead faint ... more like a harvested bonsai than redwood tree.

As the Werewolves threw the ball around the infield, the Chicken walked towards home plate and unrolled a large eye chart for Max to look at. Dutifully and unnecessarily, Max put a hand over one of his eyes and attempted to read the chart. He must not have done very well because the Chicken threw the chart up in the air in disgust and pulled out an over-sized pair of glasses which he offered to Max to help him alleviate his obvious vision deficiencies.

With right fielder Ryan Peavey at bat, the Chicken directed his efforts once again towards trying to rattle the pitcher. He combined "ca ca ... ca ca" crow calls with mini-shouts of "Hey, pitcher!" but the strain of verbalization took a terrible toll on him, as his upper beak became bent and stuck inside his lower beak. With some panicky gyrations the Chicken was able to pop his upper beak back into place. Peavey doubled down the left field line, and as he pulled into second standing up, the Chicken accepted the applause for Ryan's hit by taking a big bow. Catcher Keith Fout was up next. When he took a called strike, the Chicken pulled out an aerosol spray can, held his nose, and sprayed air freshener all around to diffuse the stink of Max's umpiring. Fout took another called strike,

Max, the Famous Chicken, and the author.

and the Chicken turned his back to the crowd. When he spun around
a few seconds later, he was the stereotypical blind man, wearing dark
glasses and walking haltingly with a cane. A couple of pitches later, as
if it were part of the act, Fout looked at a called strike three. The Chicken
immediately held a skunk out in front of himself and held his nose
again to indicate what he thought of the call.

I SAW WHEN
THIS CAME
HE CAME
TO DAYTON
2000

While Phill Kojack warmed up before the start of the third inning,
the Chicken came onto the field leading four pre-schoolers dressed like
baby chicks. When the Chicken and his brood of flapping chicks got
near home plate, Kojack and Fout, paused and waited for them to pass.
As the five of them marched behind the standing Fout, each of them
in turn patted Fout on the butt. After huddling in front of the London
dugout, the Chicken and his chicks extended their arms and fingers and
hexed the Werewolves. They reached home plate on their way off the
field just as Max walked up to brush it off. As the Chicken passed Max,
he lifted his leg to pee on the plate, and each of the four chicks followed suit. The chicks each took a big bow and then left the field.

Werewolves center fielder Dan Wydner singled to open the top of
the third, causing the Chicken to say, "Get a DP, Roosters, get a DP!" A
couple of pitches after Kojack whiffed Dyterious Edwards, who was then
shooed back to the dugout by the Chicken; Wydner attempted to steal

second but was thrown out by Fout. The Chicken pulled out yet another prop, a sign which said, "You are so busted!"

In the middle of the third the Chicken became bolder than ever. Taking up a position midway between the third base line and the London dugout, he put the trembling finger hex on the Werewolves again. He was immediately pelted by five baseball gloves which came flying out of the dugout. The Chicken looked stunned … and indignant … and then he went right back to hexing the Werewolves. He was pelted again with four or five more gloves. Again the Chicken looked stunned and indignant, but after carefully surveying the litter of gloves on the field and peering into the dugout, he realized that the Werewolves were out of ammunition, and so he resumed his hexing with gusto and supposed immunity. That's when seven or eight Werewolves sprang out of the dugout, rushed the Chicken, tackled him, piled on top of him, and pummeled him. When the Werewolves unpiled and returned to their dugout, the comatose Chicken lay spread-eagle on the field. Two men in hospital uniforms rushed to the Chicken's aid, laid him in a stretcher, and carried him off the field. Unfortunately, when they swerved right to get around Max at the back of the home plate clay circle, the Chicken rolled off the stretcher and hit the ground with a thud. Completely oblivious to their carelessness in transporting injured poultry, the emergency squad guys continued off the field with their empty stretcher; leaving it up to Max to revive the Chicken with smelling salts.

The Chicken was not about to let the enemy, the visiting team, get the best of him; and his revenge came in the top of the fourth when the theme song from the movie "Rocky" came blasting over the P. A. Wearing boxing gloves and white & black trunks the Chicken came out bobbin' and weaving' and practice punching. He made his way over into foul territory in front of the London dugout, where five Werewolves stood waiting; three on the left, two on the right. The Chicken knocked each of them unconscious, one by one, with single punches. When they were all supine, the Werewolves third base coach stood nearby glaring menacingly at the Chicken. Undaunted and bouncing from one webbed-foot to the other, the Chicken made a "come and get it" wave to the coach. As the coach approached belligerently, the Chicken telegraphed the coming big knockout punch by windmilling his arm around and around and around; but when the coach was in range he didn't punch at all. Instead, he kicked the coach in the nuts; and then, when the coach was bent over in pain, he delivered an overhand pile driver that knocked him to the ground.

The Chicken showed that he was quite the Renaissance bird by moving gracefully from the martial to the terpsichorean arts. In the middle of the fifth he danced to a big band swing number with a series of progressively older partners, ranging from a tiny little girl in a two-piece lime jump suit to an old granny who leaned stiffly over a walker. As the Chicken whirled around the field with the little girl, the grade schooler, the teenager, the co-ed, and the middle-aged mother; the granny moved awkwardly towards the front of the line and we wondered how in the world the Chicken would be able to dance with her. When the middle-aged mother finished dancing, the Chicken beckoned to the granny to come out for her dance. She struggled with her walker through the gate by the Roosters' dugout, inched forward a few more steps with her head down, and then, looking up and apprehending the vision of the Chicken in all his glory, she became so inspired that she tossed away her walker, ran out to the Chicken, and danced with the vigor of a Radio City Music Hall Rockette as the crowd went crazy!

In the fifth the Chicken graciously took a picture of Max and Jim Schaly, standing next to each other and smiling expectantly; but then he ripped the film out of the camera, threw it on the ground, and stomped on it. In the seventh he came out in a top hat and cane and did a smooth soft shoe dance to "Minnie the Moocher." And later in the same inning, when the London pitching coach went out to the mound to have a word with Cory Carr, he held up a sign which said, "Dumb & Dumber." The most hilarious bit of the evening though may have come in the sixth when the Chicken got into it with Barney, the purple pacifist dinosaur with the green tail. The skit started with the Chicken dancing expertly to some Rap music. Barney the dinosaur came out and did some very lame, sluggish dancing. The Chicken stopped him mid-dance and, making an obvious challenge, went back to his own frenetic dancing. When he stopped, he gestured to Barney to "top that." Barney started the same lame dancing as before, which enraged the Chicken so much that he began smacking Barney around. The Chicken danced again and then issued another challenge. Barney moved his feet feebly as before, but then … he smacked the Chicken around and transferred into a totally different gear. He totally out-danced the Chicken by performing a complicated, well choreographed dance number that included multiple splits. There was nothing the humbled Chicken could do but pay homage to his better, which he did by bowing repeatedly to Barney from his knees. Showing the good sportsmanship we expected from him, Barney pulled the Chicken up from his knees and gave him a big hug. As Barney walked towards third base, the Chicken responded in character to the dinosaur's gesture of good will. The Chicken ran after Barney, tackled him, and, lying on top of him, pounded the turf like a WWF referee: "One! Two! Three! You're Pinned!!!" Ever forgiving, Barney hugged the Chicken again. But it was clear that the Chicken was not to be trusted. As the two new friends walked off the field together, arm in arm, the Chicken flipped Barney over his hip.

By the eighth inning, the Chicken's official show was over, and he retired to the plaza behind the grandstand where he sat at a table signing autographs for all comers. A half an hour after the final pitch, he was still there, joking with the last of the autograph seeking fans. A little boy who'd been trading barbs with him was the last to leave. As he walked away from the table towards the exit with two smiling parents, he called over his shoulder, "Goodbye, Mr. Wiener."

In his high-pitched bird voice, the Chicken replied, "Goodbye, Mr. Baggy-pants. And remember: eat fish for dinner, not chicken!"

10

After Cooperstown, Clouds Over Richmond and Chillicothe

THE FIRST BASEBALL HALL OF FAME inductions I ever attended were in 1986 for Willie McCovey, Bobby Doerr, and Ernie Lombardi. I'd never missed Induction Weekend since then, and over the years I'd been privileged to witness and cover as a member of the working media the inductions of some of the greatest names in baseball history, such as Catfish Hunter, Billy Williams, Willie Stargell, Johnny Bench, Carl Yastrzemski, Jim Palmer, Joe Morgan, Rod Carew, Fergie Jenkins, Gaylord Perry, Tom Seaver, Rollie Fingers, Reggie Jackson, Steve Carlton, Mike Schmidt, Jim Bunning, Earl Weaver, Phil Niekro, Tommy LaSorda, Don Sutton, Larry Doby, George Brett, Nolan Ryan, Robin Yount, and Orlando Cepeda. Upon reaching a certain age, each of my kids had been allowed to make the trip, so that the summer pilgrimage to Cooperstown had become a rite of passage and, at least for the boys, a family tradition. (A single trip seemed to suffice for the girls.) When I left Richmond late Friday night, I was accompanied by Nolan, my other son Mickey, and one of Mickey's neighborhood buddies, Keith Sands. At the end of the summer Mickey would be entering his sophomore year of high school; and despite his name, it looked as if he were going to wind up excelling at basketball, not baseball. The Mick was still a baseball fan—his favorite active player was Frank "The Big Hurt" Thomas—but I got the feeling that some of the luster of Cooperstown was wearing off for him and that he got as much of a kick out of helping friends, such as Keith, make their first visit there, as he got in revisiting the place himself.

With the exception of a catnap at a rest stop, I drove all night to get us to Cooperstown a couple of hours before lunchtime on Saturday. I was tired but able, as usual, to function on adrenaline.

We spent most of the day shopping but also toured the Hall of Fame Museum. I'm always interested in the special exhibits that change from year to year. New for 2000 were exhibits on Mark McGwire's home run record, Barry Halper's astounding collection of baseball memorabilia, and cartoonist Charles Schulz's "Peanuts" comic strip. The McGwire exhibit, called "The Great American Home Run Chase," included fascinating information and trivia about home runs throughout baseball history but focused primarily on McGwire's pursuit of Roger Maris' single-season home run mark of 61 set in 1961. Accorded special recognition were the fans who caught significant McGwire home run balls during the 1999 season and turned them over to the big slugger, instead of auctioning them off for huge paydays. Mike Davidson, a catering manager whose wife gave birth a month after his moment in the spotlight, caught #61 and was quoted as having said: "This means more to McGwire and to baseball than a million dollars does to me. Why be greedy?" Tim Forneris, a 22-year old Cardinals groundskeeper who caught #62, was quoted as having said: "It would brand you to sell it. It's sad to hoard things. Life is all about experiences, which I have here tonight." The exhibit summed up these gestures of generosity by saying: "These acts of pure selflessness affirmed our faith in both the game and the fans who watch it."

The second exhibit, set up in a room that reproduced part of the basement of super-collector Halper's New Jersey home, featured choice, truly historic objects, such as the WW II OSS (Office of Strategic Services) ID card which had belonged to Moe Berg, the second string major league catcher who became a U.S. spy; Babe Ruth's polo coat, his 1938 Brooklyn Dodgers cap, and a silver bat that was given to him by the San Antonio Knights of Columbus after he'd hit 59 homers in 1921; and several Shoeless Joe Jackson items, including his 1920 American League contract which was notable for two reasons. First, it was a three-year contract, for $8,000 per year, that Jackson had extracted from the penurious Charles Comiskey in an era when multi-year contracts were rare; and second, the contract had a Joe Jackson signature on it. The illiterate Jackson usually depended on his wife Katie to read and write for him, but for the occasions when she was not present to assist him, Joe copied off a card in his wallet on which Katie had written his name. The crude but legible signature on the contract was almost certainly one that Jackson himself had labored to produce.

The tribute to "Peanuts" and its creator was my favorite of the three new exhibits, as I was thrilled to see Mr. Schulz's contribution to what we might call the "culture of baseball" officially recognized in Cooperstown. The exhibit, set up in an annex to the Hall of Fame Library, provided some biographical information about Schulz—e.g., his father bought four different Sunday papers for the comics—and some insights into his thinking. Schulz realized, for example, that humor comes from life's mishaps and frustrations, not its successes. "Happiness is not funny," he said. Fortunately for us, he also realized that baseball, because there is a lot of failure in it, was the perfect setting and barometer for his main character, the bumbling but persevering Charlie Brown. The entire corpus of Schulz's baseball-related "Peanuts" strips is devoted to an exploration of the theme of perseverance in the face of personal inadequacy and adversity; and the strips included in the exhibit were well-chosen to illustrate this.

"Good grief," says Charlie Brown in one of those strips, "one hundred eighty-four to nothing. I don't understand it … How can we lose when we're so *sincere!*"

And in another strip Linus offers the following words of consolation to Charlie Brown: "Look at it this way, Charlie Brown … we learn more from losing than we do from winning."—"THAT MAKES ME THE SMARTEST PERSON IN THE WORLD!!" replies Charlie Brown.

For a perfect summation of the universal appeal of Charlie Brown, the exhibit quoted Joe Garagiola, the Hall of Fame broadcaster who made a career out of exaggerating his own ineptness on the diamond: "Charlie Brown is the hero of all Americans because he's the underdog, but you'll never convince him of that. He'll be out there on the mound everyday, even in the rain. There's a little bit of him in all of us."

The acceptance speeches in Cooperstown seldom disappoint, but the ones delivered on Sunday, July 23, 2000, were, as a group, the best I'd ever heard. Sparky Anderson, who led teams in both major leagues to World Championships, made his mark in baseball not only as a great manager but as a great person. The respect and genuine concern he had for everyone he ever met came through in every word of his folksy speech. And while we believed in the honesty of his humility, we didn't accept his self-deprecating assessment of his accomplishments: "I hope every manager gets it straight: the players *earn* this; managers come here on their backs. I've always believed that. I was smart enough to know that, and I thank them. … Did I have a secret? Not really. I got good players, stayed out of their way, let them win, and hung around for 27 years."

In the press conference after the Inductions, Sparky went on for five minutes in praise of his former player, Tony Perez, and the entire Perez family for the way they love one another. After making the point that people should be judged by their character and not by irrelevancies such as their race or skin color, Anderson said, "I don't care that Tony Perez can't speak English!" At this, Perez widened his eyes and looked out at the reporters with a look on his face as if to ask, "What's he talking about?" Sparky then delivered the punch line he'd set up. "If you'd given Tony 20 more years, a teacher, and a dictionary, I promise you he could have given a speech here today in English," he said. Actually, Tony did just fine, and we understood him perfectly, despite his thick Spanish accent, when he said things like: "I'm not the Hall of Famer in the family; my wife, Pitulka, she is the real one"; and "I carry three flags in my heart: one for the United States, where the best baseball in the world is played; one for Puerto Rico, the country that adopted me; and one for Cuba, where I was born."

As for Carlton Fisk, he went last and took by far the longest. In fact, his rambling, emotional 40-minute speech may have been the longest ever delivered by an Inductee—the suggested and usually adhered-to length is 15 minutes. Fisk's long speech may not have contained any purple passages—the closest Fisk came to eloquence was his statement that "I feel I carry a torch for this game"—but it was obviously a sincere and very personal effort to describe the fullness of his lengthy baseball experience, from the simplest pleasures in the daily ballpark routine to the most transcendent moments of glory achieved during competition. At times, Fisk acknowledged the inadequacy of words, as when he said that "Only a catcher can understand what it takes to be a catcher." At other times, he was more successful at conveying the meaning a special event held for him. For example, he recalled that when he hit his 300th home run, his son Casey, serving as the White Sox bat boy, was there to greet him at home plate. "He hugged me and kissed me," said Fisk. "That's all I needed." Afterwards, Fisk undoubtedly caught a lot of grief from his fellow Hall of Famers for the length of his speech; but the fans, used to the deliberate pace of every game that Pudge ever caught, listened patiently to every last word of his once-in-a-lifetime-and-for-all-time address.

The final big event of Induction Weekend is the Hall of Fame Game which is played at Doubleday Field on Monday, traditionally between one team from the National League and one from the American. The Hall of Fame Game for 2000 pitted the Cleveland Indians against the Arizona Diamondbacks. Regardless of which teams play and despite the fact that second stringers do most of the playing, the game is always a complete sell out.

In the past I never paid much attention to the pre-game home run derby, participated in by three members of each team; but Russell Branyan of the Indians and Alex Cabrerra of the D-Backs made me pay attention. The home run hitting display they put on was awesome and seemed almost super-human. The two players certainly looked the part; the part, that is, of a comic book super hero. With rippling muscles on top of muscles, Cabrerra was obviously into serious body building, as physiques like his simply do not occur in nature. Hardly "muscle bound," Cabrerra had a swing as smooth and quick as any wiry, lithe shortstop; and the mammoth drives he hit were still rising as they clipped branches from the tops of the pine trees beyond the left field wall of cozy Doubleday Field. Although not as muscular as Cabrerra, the broad-shouldered six-foot-three left-handed batting Branyan was, if anything, even more powerful with a bat in his hands than his American League counterpart. It's not a long way to Doubleday's right field seats, sure, but I'd never seen anybody reach them, as Branyan did, with what were obviously half-effort warm-up swings! When Branyan began cutting loose, I wasn't sure *the town* was going to be able to hold him; never mind the ballpark. Both Branyan and Cabrerra advanced to the finals, and Cabrerra wound up winning the derby by hitting seven homers in his final ten swings. I knew it before, but the size of these two behemoths, and their remarkable ability to knock a baseball out of sight, impressed on me further the enormous distance between the Frontier League and the major leagues. The distance seemed even greater when I stopped to contemplate the fact that, as good as they were, neither Branyan nor Cabrerra had yet been able to establish himself as a starter on the major league level.

A few minutes before the field was cleared of the media, I turned away from the diamond and saw Carlton Fisk, standing with his back to the grandstands, imperially surveying the scene before him. Fisk looked sharp in his olive green slacks, green and white checked sports coat, and snazzy tie; and he wore well the extra pounds that age had inexorably added to his frame. I went right up to him and began to speak; but as I did, a short man in a dark suit took a preemptive step forward, as if he were protecting the big man next to him who was twice his size. Fisk's body guard turned out to be none other than Dale Petroskey, the President of the Hall of Fame. "He's not doing any interviews," he said. After a quick glance at Petroskey, I told Fisk, who didn't deign to look in my direction as I spoke to him, that I was writing a book about a minor league umpire and that I wanted to ask him, as the man who'd caught more games than anyone else in major league history, if he could remember an umpire ever getting seriously hurt. "Did you check with our research staff about this?" interjected Petroskey. Before I could answer Petroskey's question, Fisk answered mine. "You're gonna get some bumps and bruises," he said, as he donned a pair of sunglasses and tilted back his head regally, "... but a broken arm is about the worst that ever happened to an umpire when I was playing." Emboldened by the answer, I asked a follow-up question. "The umpire I'm following got hit in the face with a pitch. Have you ever heard of that?" I said.

Without hesitation he said, "It had to be his equipment. It couldn't have been his positioning or the catcher's positioning."

"Your umpire was wearing a mask, and he still got hit in the face?" asked Petroskey.

"Yeah. The ball went right through the bars of the mask," I explained. "It was a lightweight model made out of some kind of resinous plastic. ... It was a million-to-one freak accident ... except that it happened to him twice."

Again, Carlton's comment came instantly. "I never said umpires were the smartest people in the world," he said. "...And they always blamed stupidity on catchers!" he added in afterthought.

Although four Reds had been inducted, Tony Perez was the star of the show for Reds fans, and so I made him the focus of the story I wrote for *Reds Report*. It was a fun story to write because Perez had been so obviously overjoyed the entire Induction weekend but also because there was a contrastingly negative background to his election experience. Tony had only been elected in his ninth, and next-to-last, year of eligibility, and before his election finally happened he had started to become angry and embittered about the injustice of his being annually overlooked.

While I included this unhappy element of Tony's Hall of Fame experience in my *Reds Report* story, I didn't dwell on it or frame it as ironically as I might have. After all, once Tony got in, all was forgiven; and, in fact, he himself handled the matter graciously in his speech. While thanking Sparky Anderson, his former manager, he said, "They made me wait so long so we could go in together."

Still, I couldn't shake the memories of Tony's lamentations and expressions of frustration that we read every January in the *Cincinnati Enquirer* for all those years when he came up short in the balloting; and as I wrote my sunny article for *Reds Report*, a darker-edged poem formed in my mind. I sent it to my editor, Steve Helwagen, in Columbus, along with the story, but I wasn't really surprised when he chose not to run it. Even so, it's another side to the story, that in its way is as truthful as the straight reporting I did for *Reds Report*.

Putting Tony Perez in His Place

Even red-necked Reds fans
pegged him as their boy
bragging about it as if
it somehow were to their credit.
They got off on all those rbi
by Doggie, Mr. Clutch, the Big Dawg.
They thought he above all
had the right attitude,
felt their own atrocious grammar
superior to his broken English,
reveled in the bush league tale
of his ordering the same old ham
& eggs by pointing at the menu.

At the first sign of less-than-spectacular
they panicked and cut him out
like an appendix or clubhouse cancer.
He packed up and went quietly
to Montreal where his broken English
was even less use to him, taking his
swagger, his trust, and his confusion with him.

When it should have been time to sit down
and talk with him like the good hands people
they brought him back to pad the gate,
but he didn't understand nostalgia,
thought he was still being paid to swing the bat.
Even worse in their eyes, he didn't know it
when it was time to go, so they orchestrated
his retirement unilaterally with a carefully placed
leak, leaving the chagrined sportswriters scrambling
for explanations and going-away presents.
Thousands of ignorant fans came late to his day,
an afterthought dropped on the table like a bad tip.

They made it up to him by naming him manager,
but they didn't really mean that either, their confidence
in him lasting one glorious quarter of a season.
One honor remained and they gave it to him but not
before their grudging finally brought out his anger,
which caused them to finally hear him when he said,
in perfectly good English, "I want to get into the Hall. I belong."

Tuesday was our travel day from Cooperstown back to Ohio. I took Wednesday off and picked Max up again on Thursday, the 27th, for the middle game of a series in Richmond between the Roosters and the Canton Crocodiles. From Max I learned that by skipping the opener, won 7–3 by Richmond, I'd missed Phill Kojack's third win of the season against seven losses. Before we talked about the games though, Max imparted some bad news; namely, that Roger Hanners had had a heart attack on Sunday when I was in Cooperstown. In fact, Roger had had two heart attacks, the second, milder one coming when he was on his way to the hospital in an ambulance. Max wasn't able to tell me much about Roger's condition, but he knew that Roger was at home and not in the hospital, which I obviously took as a very positive sign.

Losing causes turnover, and the revamped Crocodiles not only had a new manager, Jeff Isom, but they also had a lot of new players. Only eight of the 24 players currently on the team had been on the Opening Day roster. There were four new faces in the starting lineup, and three of them were rookie infielders: second baseman Billy Colome (out of the College of Charleston), shortstop J. D. Coy (St. Mary's University), and third baseman Curtis Sapp (University of Louisville). All three were noticeably short, particularly Colome and Coy who were listed, generously, I suspected, at 5' 9".

Frank Grubb, one of Max's protégés, had the plate and did a beautiful job in his first Frontier League game in Richmond. As did the pitchers on both teams. Control artist Steve Carver, who'd made life so easy for Schaly his last time out, gave up only six hits over six innings, but unfortunately one of the hits was a two-run homer by the stocky Sapp, his first of the season. Sapp's blast, which came in the second inning, sailed so far out of McBride Stadium that Gary Kitchel imagined for his listeners that the ball would disrupt a kid's game going on across the street. "Look out youth leaguers!" he said.

Chad Sosebee finished the game with three innings of hitless relief, but the two runs produced by Sapp's home run stood up; as Matt Baber, Lance Robinson, and Drew Thomas held the Roosters to a single run on six hits.

Once again, when Rooster runs were at a premium, Mike Zerbe came in for criticism at the hands of Gary Kitchel. The Roosters plated their only run in the fifth on a leadoff triple by Jason Borghese and a single by Aaron Sledd. After first baseman Macky Waguespack and catcher Steve Mitrovich flied out, Todd DeGraffenreid moved Sledd to second with a single to left. That brought Zerbe to the plate with a chance to knock in the tying run. Right before Zerbe struck out swinging, Kitchel said, "Now would be a good time for a Peacock Road shot."

After Gary recapped the inning and turned it back to the station for commercials, he turned towards me and *Palladium-Item* sportswriter, Vernon Redd, and said, "Zerbe is the worst two-out/runners-in-scoring-position hitter I think I've ever seen. The worst!"

"Careful, or I'll put that in my story," said Vernon with a grin.

"Go right ahead. It's K-I-T-C-H-E-L."

"From up here, it's hard to tell, but it looks to me like Mike doesn't change his swing to try to punch those curve balls to right field. Maybe if he did that, they'd quit throwing him so many curveballs," I said.

"He never does," said Kitchel. "Brad Finken has worked really hard with him, but Zerbe won't choke up or make any adjustments. ... He's the worst two-out hitter I've ever seen. He's also the *nicest* bad two-out hitter."

Because the Roosters didn't keep stats on hitting with runners in scoring position, Kitchel's opinion was based completely on observation. Nevertheless, he was at every Roosters game and I wasn't, so it would have been presumptuous for me to challenge his analysis. I did however point out, without getting Gary to change his mind in the slightest, that Zerbe had gotten a hit with a runner in scoring position in the second inning. The hit into right center did not score Todd DeGraffenreid from second base but only, in my opinion, because either DeGraffenreid or third base coach Woody Sorrell had decided to play it safe with one out. Or perhaps DeGraffenreid had simply gotten a bad jump. In either case, Zerbe had come through in the clutch without getting any credit for it.

The next day Patty rode over to Richmond with Max and me. We took our usual short cut through the back streets of Brookville, and just as we pulled up to the last stop sign before we turned right onto Route 104, it happened. Max turned around and asked for the camera from Patty, sitting in the back seat. He then aimed the camera at the Regal's odometer and took the picture proving that the car had reached 300,000 miles.

When we walked into McBride Stadium, Big John was already at his post outside the Roosters' clubhouse. He noticed that Max was dragging a little bit and asked him, "Are you tired?"

Max, who'd been traveling and umpiring and recovering from injuries almost every day since the end of February, was tired, but he didn't admit it. Instead, he asked Big John the same rhetorical question he'd asked Dan Massarelli earlier in the season. "You know where the definition of sympathy is in the dictionary, don't you?" he said. "Right between *shit* and *syphilis*. That's from Wilson, my dad. He had more one-liners like that than I would ever be able to come up with."

"PLATE"

It was Max's turn to be in the bucket, and when he was putting on his plate gear, Max mentioned that he couldn't wait to get the new shoes that he'd ordered. "Are you finally going to get a pair of steel-toed shoes like every other sane umpire?" asked Frank Grubb.

"No, I'm not," said Max. "When I left Johnstown Steel I vowed I would never wear another pair of steel-toed shoes again in my life, and I haven't."   *I THOUGHT HE WORE FUCKEN BASE SHOES WITH STRIPES!*

Friday night's game couldn't have been more different than Thursday's, as the Roosters scored a week's worth of runs and won the game 24–6. For all intents and purposes, the game was over after Richmond scored seven in the second and 12 in the third. The game was such a laugher that Canton manager Jeff Isom sent infielder Marcos Sanchez in to pitch the bottom of the seventh and the eighth. A native of the Dominican Republic, Sanchez was talented enough to have already played in three different major league organizations: the Yankees, Reds, and Padres. He had the most open batting stance I'd ever seen—he stood facing the pitcher so squarely until the pitch was on its way that he might have been chopping wood rather than batting—and his Pedro Bourbon-ish pitching was just as stylish as his hitting. He had long arms, threw the ball hard, and paused dramatically after every pitch in the follow through position. Perhaps the Roosters were tired of running around the bases by the time he took the mound; but for whatever reason, they did not score on Sanchez, who allowed no hits, walked two, and struck out three.

After the game there were fireworks, which accounted for the bigger-than-usual, unlucky-for-Canton crowd of 1,313. As Max walked off the field at the end of the game, Billy Colome, who'd been stranded at third by Roosters' reliever Alejandro Bracho, ran up to him. "Max, Max …" he said, "I just wanted to tell you thanks. Even though we were getting drilled, you didn't try to screw us on the strike zone just to get out of here faster."   *NICE COMMENT TO MAX BY CROC'S Colome PG 255*

Jeff Isom caught up with Max by the time he reached the umpire's dressing room. With the fireworks already going off beyond the center field fence, Isom said, "Max, I'm embarrassed. I know Billy already talked to you, but I just wanted you to know that I appreciate it too, the game you called under those circumstances."   *NICE COMMENT CROC'S ISOM*

Max appreciated the comments from Colome and Isom—everybody likes to feel appreciated—but I knew that hard work and complete dedication to the job were an ingrained part of Max's character, by nature and by upbringing.

Patty McLeary was a hard worker too—when she wasn't teaching school she was working for Max, installing new carpet or dashboards in the classic autos of well-to-do collectors—and she was the kind of person who did a job that needed doing without having to be asked to do it. Patty, in fact, had missed most of the game she'd come to Richmond to watch Max umpire because she spent that time working on Frank Grubb's car. I hadn't known it was possible, but a foul ball had veered over the roof of the Roosters' offices into the parking lot and gone through the back window of Frank's 1996 Toyota Corolla. From the second through the seventh innings Patty had painstakingly picked every shard and splinter of glass out of the carpet and upholstery of the car; and then, because there was rain in the forecast, she'd driven over to Wal-Mart and bought duct tape and sheets of plastic in order to fashion a temporary replacement window for the car.

At least Patty returned to her seat in time to see Dave Hornbach play the Argosy Casino Dash for Cash Game at the end of the eighth inning. Dave and the McLearys were old friends, and Max had left passes to the game for Dave and his son Jake at the ticket window. Dave, who taught printing at Colerain High School just north of Cincinnati, had been in Patty's sixth grade class at St. Lawrence years before and had met Max at the same time, as Max had taught art to Patty's students. "Back then Max had an afro out to here," Dave told me. "A white man with an afro!" Max later umpired some of Dave's baseball games when he played for Western Hills High School in Cincinnati.

The object of the game was simple: to run as many times as possible in thirty seconds between two buckets and transfer as much money from the large bucket filled with coins to the smaller empty bucket. It was surprising how slow the contestants on most nights moved and how little money they wound up with. The night before however had been different.

"What's your name and what do you do?" asked Megan, the young lady who MCed the Roosters' between-innings contests.

"I'm John, the tar man," said the plain spoken contestant, who sold tires for a living.

"Are you ready to win some money?" asked Megan.

"Ever thang I can get," deadpanned John.

True to his word, John repeatedly buried his large hands up to his elbows into the bucket full of coins and with his hands and arms pressed tightly together hustled one big scoop of coins after another over to his take-home bucket. When his time ran out, the interns and the cheerleaders known as Rooster Chicks picked up all the coins he'd dropped and added them to his take. John then received a nice hand from the crowd for having come away with what was easily the biggest haul of the year.

John's unofficial record lasted just one night. Dave used the same method of extraction and transportation that John had, except that Dave was also able to move faster than John had. Patty and Jake were both excited when they saw the two big plastic bags full of coins that Dave was taking home, and they spent the rest of the game taking guesses as to how much money it all added up to.

It was karaoke night at The Wheel, and the place was packed ... and loud. In fact, the place was so loud, it was impossible to carry on a conversation without practically shouting. Max, Patty, and I squeezed ourselves in at a table of Roosters boosters that included Kitchel, Tom Arnett, third base coach Woody Sorrell, and Bob Van Pelt, one of the original main investors in the franchise and a former NFL player who'd once played for the Philadelphia Eagles. Personally warm and low key, Van Pelt had played important roles in Roosters' history. He'd had the privilege of being Morgan Burkhart's host, and he'd once taken out a second mortgage on his home to keep the franchise going.

Because The Wheel was so noisy and so rowdy, we didn't stay as long as we normally would have, but I still had a couple of interesting conversations. Kitchel's guest partner for the game had been Bob Coddington, one of the host parents in the house where pitcher Rich Jelovcic was living. Coddington had decided to have a little fun at Gary's expense by asking him on the air if Gary had really set the Richmond High School record for strikeouts in a game with 18. "Yes, I did," said the embarrassed Kitchel, "but I think the record's been eclipsed by now. ... By the way, Bob, you read my notes very well!"

When I told Gary in the bar that I was impressed with what I'd learned about him from Coddington, he told me that the most memorable thing about the game for him now was not all the strikeouts, which he'd accumulated over 12 innings, but that his 2–1 victory had come over Anderson (IN) High's Gary Erskine, the son of famous Brooklyn Dodgers' pitcher Carl Erskine. Gary Erskine never followed his dad into the major leagues, but he did, Gary told me, get a full ride to the University of Texas as a hitter.

Max could tell that Kitchel was feeling a little down, and Gary admitted that he was having girlfriend problems. "You can't live with 'em, and you can't live without 'em," he said wistfully.

"'You can't put a price on that sniff,'" commiserated Max, using an unusual expression that we figured meant about the same thing as the cliché Gary had used. "That's another Wilson," he said to me.

While Max and Patty lent sympathetic ears to Kitchel, I chatted a while with Woody Sorrell, John Cate's right hand man who had been the head baseball coach at Dayton University for seven years before coming to Richmond. Like Jan Clark, Woody wore a crew cut that, while unfashionable in our age of self-indulgent self-expression, augmented nicely his disciplined, no-nonsense approach to life and his occupation. I hadn't talked much to Woody, but from the first time I met him early in the season I'd sensed that he was a very loquacious person who loved talking about baseball more than anything else in the world.

Woody told me that he loved working for the Roosters and that everyone in town had been great to him. The fans weren't always supportive, but Woody knew how to handle the ones who got out of line. "You say you weren't here for the first game of the series with Canton on Wednesday night," he told me, "but the fans on top of the hill behind the third base dugout started getting on me about a run that didn't score earlier in the game. It wasn't my fault that the run didn't score, but it was late in the game and the run was looming large. One of the guys on top of the hill, who'd probably had too much to drink, screamed at me, 'That run shoulda scored, and this game would be tied. That's why you got fired in Dayton … for holding up runners that you ought to send home!' So I called Tom Arnett over to the railing and told him, 'Tell that guy I said the reason I got fired in Dayton was because I went up into the stands and killed an asshole who was giving me shit.'"

After talking with Woody for a while, I began to think that, regardless of what the topic of conversation was, as long as it was baseball-related, he would be able to add something meaningful to it. Sure enough, after I told him what Carlton Fisk had said to me in Cooperstown about umpires, he had his own Fisk story to relate that shed some light on how Carlton had managed to last so long at the most demanding position on the field. "I was in Detroit for a game against the White Sox and the Tigers in 1990, I think it was," he said. "It was the year Bobby Thigpen set the record for saves in a season, whenever that was. Anyway, when the White Sox took infield before the game Ron Karkovice did all the catching. He made all the throws to the bases, and he had a cannon. His throws down to second were like bullets, and they were right on the money. When the White Sox took the field in the bottom of the first, Karkovice came out and caught every one of the warm-up pitches. Now I knew Fisk was in the game because he had hit in the top of the inning. Fisk finally came out of the dugout, and he stood outside the circle, with all his equipment on, until Karkovice was done warming up the pitcher. Fisk then stepped into the circle, stretched, arched his back, and squatted down real slow. The first pitch he caught all day was the first pitch of the game that the White Sox pitcher threw.

"And it was the same way all night. Karkovice came out and caught every warm-up pitch and made every throw down to second. And Fisk never made a throw all night during the game, except back to the pitcher. The White Sox won in a blowout—the game was 8–1, something like that—so the Tigers really didn't have much chance to test Fisk's arm. And he probably could have still thrown. He just wasn't going to do anything he didn't have to do. He wasn't going to expend any energy he didn't have to expend or make any throws he didn't have to make or do any squatting he didn't have to do. At first, I thought it was weird, but then I realized that Fisk had earned the privilege. And I later learned that he did the same thing all season."

Despite the Roosters' big win over Canton, the mood at the table over the future of Richmond's franchise in the Frontier League was pessimistic. The feeling was that the Roosters had some great fans and some loyal supporters in the business community; just not enough of either. From my point of view, the intangible value of the team to the life of the city was incalculable, but the hard fact of the matter was that the Roosters had to be able to pay their bills just like any other business; and if attendance didn't start picking up, it was going to be difficult if not impossible to do that.

Nobody liked to talk about it, but the possibility of Richmond losing its Frontier League franchise had been in the back of many people's minds all year. When the topic was raised at out table, Gary Kitchel didn't hesitate to say what such an occurrence would mean to him. "I love the Roosters," he said. "It would kill me if they left town. ... And I'll tell you something: Richmond will never get another professional baseball team if the Roosters do leave."

I knew that he had a history with the Roosters, but I hadn't known, until he started reminiscing about it, that Gary had been with the team from the very beginning. In listening to Gary's recounting of the early days of the franchise, I also learned a few things about how an enterprise like an independent professional baseball team really gets off the ground.

According to Gary, when Bill Lee came to town in the summer of 1994 prospecting for possible Frontier League franchise sites, he was delighted to discover McBride Stadium. Bill knew right away that with some minor improvements McBride would make a great home for a Frontier League team. And he was fortunate that the best baseball man in town, the man who would spearhead the effort to secure a Frontier League franchise for Richmond, was nearby. John Cate, the well-known and highly successful head baseball coach of Richmond High School, was on the field, getting it ready for a big American Legion tournament. Bill Lee introduced himself and said, "I've been told that you are the person I should talk to about bringing minor league baseball to Richmond."

Cate stopped what he was doing, looked at Bill Lee, and laughed derisively: "Yeah, right!"

Being the good salesman that he is, Bill Lee convinced Cate in no time at all that the idea of minor league professional baseball in Richmond was not laughable but do-able with the right people behind it. Cate went to work assembling an ownership group; and Kitchel, who eventually was named the team's first general manager, got involved with the franchise from the beginning because at the time he'd been working for Cate, helping John out with the mowing business that supplemented his teacher's salary.

Gary became animated remembering the excitement of those early days when the founding fathers of the team had to make decisions about everything. He remembered Cate agonizing over what colors to use for the team's uniforms. "Red was no good because it's too common and it's also the high school's color," said Kitchel. "We didn't want blue either because it's too common too. John really wanted something different, and he spent hours poring through uniform catalogs. Finally, I said, 'John, how about orange and green? No professional team has those colors, and they go good together.' So that's how we chose the colors."

As shrewd sports marketers know, uniform color selection is not an insignificant matter. The right, or wrong, choice and mix of colors can mean huge differences in sales of team souvenirs and apparel. And uniform colors and design can affect players too. As Roosters' fan Ray James had told me, "John Cate loves to dress his teams well. They've got black, green and orange tops, in addition to their white and gray pin stripe sets; so that altogether they have about 18 different combinations of shirts and pants. The first two years we were in the league, everybody wanted to come here to play … just for the uniforms!"

"Scott Porter, one of the four or five original investors who were really responsible for putting the whole thing together, was the guy who came up with the nickname 'Roosters,'" Gary continued. "John thought Porter was joking at first, but then he started thinking about it. I told him, 'No, John, Scott's not kidding, and I think "Roosters" would be a great nickname. We're talking about a feisty bird, a cock, not a hen. We can make a great logo for it, a mean-looking rooster. And, again, we want something unique, right? Well, nobody's got that name, plus "Roosters" sounds good with "Richmond." They alliterate.' So that was how we picked the team's nickname.

"We held a newspaper 'Name the Team Contest,' but it was a sham. We stuffed the ballot box!"

Kitchel needed a ride home, and so we headed South on State Route 227, instead of U.S. 27, out of Richmond. After we dropped Gary off at his house in tiny Boston, we headed West on 122 to pick up 27, only three miles away. Minutes later Max, Patty, and I all saw, at the same belated instant, the stop sign, which seemed to come out of nowhere in the pitch black darkness of the intersection. Max slammed on his brakes, but it was too late. We went past the sign, skidded into the intersection, and came to a stop in the southbound lane of U.S. 27.

It wasn't that Max had had a lot to drink because we left The Wheel fairly early. And it probably didn't have much to do with the fact that Max was a visually impaired driver. It had more to do with the fact that we'd been on a strange road in total darkness, paying more attention to our conversation than our safety. Nevertheless, we were all pretty shaken up. Route 27, which truckers use, can be a very busy road; and if a semi or even an automobile had been flying down 27 when we skidded out into the middle of the road, we all could have been killed. As Max finished crossing 27 and turned the car around, Patty gave me a look as if to say, "Now do you know why I can't sleep until Max gets home every night?"

In the same breath she asked Max if he were okay and if he wanted me to drive the rest of the way home. Max, of course, said he was fine. There was no need for me to drive, and he chalked up our brush with disaster to the darkness and his unfamiliarity with the road. I agreed that his mistake was one that could have happened to anybody. Still, I couldn't help but watch the road carefully the rest of the way home, as I thought about how lucky we were not to have wound up like those high school kids who'd lost their lives on U.S. 52 the year before, only miles from Max's home.

For the last three days of the month, Max was going to be in Chillicothe for a series between the Paints and Crocodiles. I decided to skip the opener on Saturday, the 29th, so that I could accompany my wife Kathy on a day trip to Tennessee to look at a piece of land we'd bought in the spring. This time I wasn't as worried as before about missing something because I figured, "What else could possibly happen to the guy?"

Saturday morning Kathy and I made the three and a half hour drive down to Lone Mountain Shores, a new development on Norris Lake near the little town of New Tazewell. We originally went down on a whim and wound up buying the sixth lot we looked at. We'd gotten a late start, and it was almost dark when our salesman, an ex–University of Tennessee basketball player, David Longhi, remembered one more lot he ought to show us: lot #63 which no other customers had seen yet because the developer had just rough cut in a steeply inclined driveway. Kathy was instantly swept away by the "million dollar view" the lot commanded of the lake and the mountain on the other side, and I knew in the next instant that Mr. Longhi had just made a sale. Although the lot cost twice as much as I was mentally prepared to spend (in the unlikely event that we bought any lot at all) and although we were, as I liked to say later, definitely the poorest people to own land in the development, I didn't have the heart to say no. In our married lives Kathy had had to compromise or settle for second or third-best too many times, and this was going to be one time when she didn't.

We really enjoyed visiting our lot, and the view was just as spectacular as we'd remembered it. But there wasn't a whole lot to do, and so after a couple of hours on lot #63, we went for a drive through the development. A half an hour into the drive, while we were trying to negotiate a particularly steep hill on the mountain, our '93 Ford Explorer gave out. I didn't know what was wrong, but we immediately suspected the transmission, which Kathy had had replaced less than a year before. I eased the car down the hill backwards until we'd reached a level place in the road, and then we sat there glumly for a moment, trying to figure out what we were going to do.

"Do you folks need help?"

That was the sound of two angels, who looked like human beings, coming to our aid. Their names were Bob and Katherine Merrihew, and they were not only one of the handful of couples to have already built in the development, but they were also one of the very few couples who lived there year round. The Merrihews had built a beautiful log home and made it bigger than they needed for the express purpose of providing temporary lodging for people in need, particularly the Vietnam veterans whom Bob counseled through his "Point Man International Ministries."

The Merrihews had our car towed back to their place and insisted that we stay in the "spare apartment" that made up the basement of their home. Nobody could look at the car until Monday morning, so the Merrihews invited us to spend both Saturday and Sunday nights with them. We made the best of it and wound up having a grand time socializing and becoming fast friends with our generous hosts. Bob and Katherine gave us the grand tour of the whole mountain, took us out on the lake in their pontoon, and shared with us their experience in building a log home and their knowledge of local contractors ... just in case we ever won the lottery and found ourselves in a position to build.

On Monday morning we had the car towed to the only garage the Merrihews knew of, a little hole-in-the-wall place called Troy's on the outskirts of town. While the mechanic on duty crawled under the car and had a look, we said goodbye to the Merrihews and urged them to go on home since the repair, even if Troy's could handle it, might take the rest of the day. I was having unsettling visions of having to have the car towed all the way back to Cincinnati. Turning back to the car, I noticed the hood up and the mechanic bending over the engine. I walked over and asked him if he knew what was wrong and if he could fix it. "It weren't nothing but a loose hose, and I done tightened her up already," he said. "Let me finish filling her up with transmission fluid, and you folks can be on your way." Kathy and I practically jumped for joy. After more goodbyes and promises to the Merrihews to get together again real soon, I asked how much I owed Troy's. "How 'bout ten dollars?" he said. I gave him a twenty and said, "Lunch is on me."

As we began the drive home, I turned to Kathy and said, "Can you believe this place? We're stranded and get taken in by two people who act like our guardian angels, and then when we're at the mercy of the repair shop, the mechanic charges us ten bucks total, which is what we would have been charged per quart of fluid in a big city, *if*... they didn't decide to tell us to come back in three days because the whole transmission was shot. We ought to call *Sixty Minutes* to come investigate!"

"No, don't do that," said Kathy. "We don't want the world to discover this place. We need to keep this place a secret."

Kathy took the events of the weekend as a sign that we were meant to buy the lot we bought. I was more inclined to say that we were just lucky to have benefited from the kindness of strangers, but the weekend did make me feel, like Kathy, a whole lot better about having invested in our own little piece of heaven on earth.

I finally got back together with Max on Monday afternoon. A hard rain had pounded Southwestern Ohio all weekend but spared Chillicothe, and the Paints and Crocodiles had gotten in the first two games of the series on Saturday and Sunday.

On our way north I noticed that the sunflowers lining both sides of I-71 had taken a bad weather beating. Their glorious summer faces had been tilted back and arched proudly towards the sun before, but now they drooped depressingly as if they had suffered some ignominious and debilitating defeat.

When we turned off 71 and headed east on state highway 35, Max told me that we were going to swing by a Champs sporting goods store in the Chillicothe Mall, if we could find the place in the extra twenty minutes he had allotted for the purpose. He was going to pick up the new pair of umpire shoes he had ordered over the phone. When the salesclerk had asked if Max knew the way to the Mall, he said, "No, not really. I've been to Chillicothe more than a hundred times, but I only know where three things are: the ballpark, The Dock at Water, and the Adena Regional Medical Center."

Nothing out of the ordinary had happened in Chillicothe over the weekend I had missed—and I was thankful that Max was still alive and in one piece—except that the Paints had won the first two games of the series, both in come-from-behind fashion. Winning two games in a row, especially against Canton, would have been no big deal for the Paints in the first half of the season, but things were different now. Even with a three-game winning streak, the Paints were four and six in their last ten, and if Sunday night's victory had not been won, the loss would have been their eighth in 11 days.

As soon as I climbed into the press box to have John Wend and Aaron Lemaster fill me in on the recent fortunes of the Paints, I could detect the siege mentality that permeated the ballclub. The Paints had already suffered several major blows, particularly the loss of Mike Cervenak and Joe Colameco, but they were becoming the Job of the Frontier League, their faith and resolve being tested to the limits of human endurance. In the players' parlance it was as if they had somehow pissed off the baseball gods.

No one knows who invented the colorful term "baseball gods"—the term cannot be found in *Dickson's Baseball Dictionary*, the most astounding such book ever compiled—but it is used frequently by players to refer to some indefinable force which seems to operate in the world of baseball, primarily as a sort of payback system for bad behavior. Get out of line or get too big for your knickers, and the baseball gods are certain to take you down a peg (that's assuming other players don't do it first). Even though it is nonsensical, the concept makes a certain sense to the players, most of whom are highly superstitious anyway and glad to have a pat explanation for why bad things happen to basically good ball players.

The Paints themselves would have had a hard time saying what they had done to deserve retribution at the hands of the baseball gods, unless the gods were simply angry at them for having achieved excellence. As the ancient Greeks and Romans knew full well, lower case gods are famous for their jealousy and capriciousness. Others around the league would have immediately said that the baseball gods were punishing the Paints for their arrogance.

While I wasn't worried about the baseball gods, I was concerned about Roger Hanners. I wanted to inquire about his health and about how his absence was affecting the team. I knew that Marty Dunn was a capable baseball man, but a team doesn't lose a man like Roger to a heart attack in mid-season without it costing the team dearly in many ways. As he went over the announcements he would have to make throughout the night over the P.A. system, John Wend told me about the Paints' stricken leader: "He's doing okay, about as well as can be expected, but he's awfully tired. You can barely hear him when you talk to him over the telephone. At this point I think they're more worried about his kidneys than his heart, although he won't say anything about it and neither will Chris. He's been having trouble with his kidneys all season, before the heart attack. He's keeping up with the team though and has to have a play-by-play report of every game."

I asked if there was any chance of his putting on a Paints uniform again in the 2000 season.

"He's probably finished this year," said John. "I know he'll come back next year if he can. I asked him once how long he was planning to manage, and he told me that as long as he can ride the buses and walk from the dugout to home plate to argue with the umpires he was going to do it."

Whenever a company or an organization or a team loses a person who has been integral to the success of that company, organization, or team for a long time, the survivors invariably pay a tacit tribute to that person at some point by telling favorite stories about him. And so it was with the Paints, who had spent one night at The Dock at Water telling Roger Hanners stories. John Wend repeated one of those stories for me in the press box as the Crocodiles continued taking their lethargic infield in the stifling late afternoon heat.

"Two years ago we had the best team we've ever had here, in my opinion," said Wend. "We had Mitch House, Scott Pinoni, and Gator McBride, all on the same team. As you know, they are three of the best hitters to ever play in the Frontier League, and they are the three guys whose retired numbers you see hanging on the outfield wall. There was a big buildup about the team before the season even started, and the papers were saying they were going to run away with the league.

"Well, they started out two and six. They weren't winning because they weren't scoring any runs. They were in Canton and lost another game when all they put up was one or two runs, and Roger really let them have it after the game. It was f-ing this and g-d that for about 15 minutes. It's rare for Roger to use that kind of language. He doesn't talk like that very often, but he'd lost patience with 'em.

"When he was about finished with his tirade he said, 'Who's pitching tomorrow?'

"Bob Spears raised his hand and said, 'I am, Coach.'

"Roger said, 'Can you strike out 15 or 16 and pitch a shutout?'

"Spears said, 'I'll try, but I can't guarantee it.'

"'Then there's no f-ing way we're gonna win the g-d game,' Roger said, 'because the most we can score is one f-ing run a game!!!'

"Pinoni, McBride, and House had been sitting there with their heads down, feeling sorry for themselves, but then when Roger said that they raised their heads and looked at each other, wide-eyed, as if to say to each other, 'Holy shit, ... we'd better get our asses in gear!' The next night they hit four home runs among the three of 'em, scored about ten or eleven runs, and won the game easily. They went on a tear after that, and with five games to go they had the first half championship all sewed up!"

Losing Cervenak, Colameco, and pitcher Matt Buirley was bad enough, but at least there was a positive side to their loss. After all, one of the main reasons the Frontier League exists is to help overlooked players get into affiliated ball. What was much more frustrating were the injuries. The way things were going the MVP of the 2000 Paints' season was going to be trainer Rodger Fleming. Rodger could not have been any busier or had his skills any more tested if the Paints had been playing hockey or football without any protective equipment, instead of baseball. Marty Dunn said of him, "I love him and I hate him. I love him when he helps get the injured guys ready to play again, but I hate him when I see him come out of the dugout and walk past me onto that field. I say, 'Oh, no. Here comes trouble.'"

The worst news of all was about Josh White, the righthanded pitcher the Cincinnati Reds had been following when they discovered reliever Matt Buirley.

White's arm had always hurt after he pitched. Some pitchers are just like that, and Josh had come to expect after-game pain. However, White had crossed a new threshold after his last start on July 15 in Max's second Mask Game. The pain was still there the next day, excruciating pain in his right elbow which, alarmingly, was also causing numbness in his fingers. Doctors re-examined him and told him he needed an operation if he wanted to continue pitching. Rather than undergo surgery, White decided to retire.

His retirement meant that the Paints were losing quite possibly the best starting pitcher in the league. Josh certainly had the best pitching stats in the league: a 5–0 record, a league best 1.38 ERA, and an outstanding 39 hits to 65 IP ratio.

The Paints' center fielder and the league's best leadoff man, Greg Strickland, was also continuing to battle injuries, as well as, on occasion, the umpires. Greg had re-aggravated his sore hamstring but had stayed in the lineup without telling anybody about his injury. One night with Stephen Byrd on the mound Greg didn't get to two balls hit into center field. To the ultra-competitive Byrd it looked as if Strickland didn't give a full effort. Byrd accosted Strickland accusingly in the dugout between innings, and Marty Dunn had to step between the two of them to prevent the argument from escalating into something more serious. Barely mollified with the revelation that Strickland had been playing hurt, Byrd growled, "If you're injured you need to tell somebody. And if you can't play, get out of the lineup!" Disappointed that his effort to play hurt was not appreciated, Strickland snapped, "Take me out then!"

Strickland sat out a few games but returned to the lineup on Sunday, July 30, for the middle game of the series against Canton. He played left field instead of center and was instrumental in Chillicothe's come-from-behind extra-inning victory. He made two circus catches in left, banged out two hits to raise his average to .340, and scored three of the Paints' eight runs, including the game winner.

He also suffered a new injury which knocked him right back out of the lineup.

After drawing a walk against Canton pitcher Drew Thomas with two outs in the bottom of the tenth inning, Strickland stole second base, then bounced up and moved to third when catcher Shaun Argento's throw went into center field for an error. Moments later shortstop J.D. Coy booted Justin Graham's grounder, and Strickland raced home with the winning run and ... a throbbing left thumb, which he had jammed sliding into second base. The next day the thumb was so swollen Strickland could not slide his fielder's mitt onto his hand. Incredulous at this latest in the string of injuries he had suffered in the 2000 season, Strickland said, "The DL ought to be called 'The Greg Strickland List,'" and that's exactly what the other Paints began to call the disabled list.

Justin Baker, the "Bible Belter," was scheduled to start in left for Strickland, who had already relinquished center in favor of Graham, but even here the Paints were not at full throttle. Baker had missed 16 games because of a deep contusion in his right quadriceps muscle. A hematoma or a pocket of blood had formed beneath the fascia, and Baker's thigh had been surgically opened to release the blood. Nineteen staples now held the wound closed, and Rodger's heavy wrapping of the leg beneath Baker's uniform pants was visible from the press box.

Despite the staples in his leg, Baker played like a wild man. As usual, he attacked the ball at the plate, ran the bases hard, and slid hard. He even slid head first when he deemed it necessary, causing Fleming to wince and momentarily shut his eyes, in the hope that when he opened them and looked at the ex–Dodgers farm hand again he would not see a red stain spreading across the thigh of his white baseball pants.

Another tough customer was outfielder Matt McCay, who had become the regular right fielder. The night before, after McCay had swung and missed at an outside pitch, he glared at the pitcher for a few moments. The pitcher stared right back and then, even with the count 0–2, hit McCay on the left elbow with the next pitch. The purpose pitch raised a big knot on his elbow, but McCay refused to leave the game.

PASE SHOES ON THE PLATE!
Max on the plate in Chillicothe; the "Bible Belter," Jason Baker, at bat.

And there was no way he was not going to play Monday night. When John Wend called his name during the introduction of the Paints' starting lineup, McCay sprinted onto the field at VA Memorial ready for battle, his true grit as conspicuous as the bandage that wrapped his elbow.

On Sunday, Richmond had somehow beaten first-place Johnstown in a doubleheader. That left the up-and-down Roosters three games below .500 and seven games back of the Johnnies. Even with Richmond's sweep of the twin bill and their own modest three-game winning streak, the Paints at 29–26 were in third place in the East Division, one game behind London and three behind Johnstown. They were also a few percentage points ahead of Evansville, the West Division's second-place team, in the race for the fourth spot in the playoffs. A third of the Frontier League season remained to be played, but it was obvious that Chillicothe needed to win, especially against the league doormats.

The Paints were thinking sweep, but for the third night in a row they got behind early. After starting the game by striking out Canton center fielder John Vollstedt, Rick Blanc got into trouble by giving up a single to Shaun Argento and a base on balls to Matt Gelotti, who'd had four hits the night before. That brought lefthanded DH Travis Copley to the plate. Copley, the Crocodiles' best hitter and a bona fide All-

Star, jacked one high over the right field wall to give Canton a 3–0 lead and present the Paints with another uphill challenge.

In the bottom of the first with two on and two out, righthander Ron Deubel plunked Matt McCay, on the left elbow. The crowd gasped at seeing McCay get hit in exactly the same place as the night before, but McCay hustled down to first and, with his right hand, waved Rodger Fleming back into the dugout before the Paints' trainer got near him. Third baseman Chance Melvin then grounded out to end the threat.

Chillicothe got a run back in the bottom of the second on a home run by first baseman Joey Choron, another player who had been a bench warmer at the beginning of the season. Although he'd had a rough series in Richmond, Choron had begun to hit and to make the most of his chance to play regularly. Short and chubby, Choron didn't have a good body, but he occasionally packed a wallop in his swing, as his long ball which sailed over the Budweiser sign atop the scoreboard illustrated.

The Paints got another run in the fourth, mostly through the efforts of McCay, who singled, stole second, continued to third on a bad throw by Argento, and scored on Melvin's single up the middle; however, they followed this up with some royally sloppy play in the fifth. First, Blanc, who had apparently settled down by blanking Canton for the previous three innings, walked the bases loaded. After the third free pass, Marty Dunn got long reliever Eric Frodsham up in the bullpen.

With Blanc still on the mound, Copley hit a soft liner into shallow right field on a 3–2 pitch. Two runs scored easily. Joey Choron cut off McCay's throw from right and caught Copley between first and second. Choron tentatively ran Copley closer to second; then, with the runner on third beginning to edge down the line, he wheeled and fired the ball over the head of Chance Melvin, allowing another run to score easily. Copley moved to third on a ground out and then scored on another soft liner into center field to make the score 7–2. With the damage done, Frodsham put on his jacket and stood impassively on the bullpen mound, watching Blanc retire two of the next three Canton hitters to end the inning without further scoring.

In the bottom of the inning, Marty Dunn stood bent over, hands on knees, in the third base coaching box, shaking his head disgustedly. Whether he was upset with his players or with himself, for having left Blanc in too long, it was hard to tell, but in either case Dunn didn't have much time to dwell on the previous half inning, for the Paints staged a four-run rally themselves.

Jamie Keefe opened the Chillicothe fifth by singling to center. Chris Dickerson flied out to left, but then Justin Graham hit a bomb into dead center which Canton's John Vollstedt misplayed into a triple. Vollstedt started in on the ball for a few steps, drifted to his left, then tried to retreat on the ball, but it was late. Seconds later Jason Baker hit another bomb into center that went even farther than Graham's. Vollstedt didn't misplay this one, but he still couldn't get to it, and Baker coasted into second with a standup double.

Matt McCay surprised everyone in the ballpark by bunting on the next pitch. Pitcher Ron Deubel fielded the ball on the third base side of the pitcher's mound but threw to first too late to nab the speedy McCay. First baseman Joe Whitmer then threw the ball past third trying to catch Baker running from second on the bunt for an error which allowed Baker to come home with the Paints' third run of the inning. McCay then stole second, went to third on a passed ball, and scored on Chance Melvin's single. In an impressive display of aggressive baseball the Paints had scored four runs on five hits and one Canton error, and they were back in the game.

After Eric Frodsham, the lanky submariner, took over for Blanc and kept Canton off the scoreboard in the top of the sixth, Chillicothe tied the game at 7–7 on Mike Horning's double and Graham's single.

As Frodsham warmed up to begin the seventh, I found Chris Hanners in his usual spot, behind the Paints' dugout in the area between the brick grandstands and the first base line metal bleachers. Because it's impossible to hold an uninterrupted conversation with Chris there, we took seats about ten rows up in the grandstands. After we talked a little about Chris's dad, the conversation turned to the indomitable spirit that the Paints were exhibiting on a nightly basis.

"This is a nasty bunch of kids," Chris said. "There's no quit in them. And that's a tribute to my dad. Quitting is a bus ticket home. We may not have the best team on the field anymore, but we'd be murder in a fight."

As we watched Travis Copley bat Chris spoke wistfully about him. "He's a great kid, a big, good-looking kid. He could be a model," he said. "We had him in the spring, and we knew he could play. But it came down to him and somebody like Chance Melvin. We thought they were even at the time, so we cut him. He was one of the last cuts we made. And it's come back to haunt us. Now it seems like he hurts the Paints every time we play Canton." With five RBI on the first inning homer and a two-run single, Copley had hurt Chillicothe plenty already, but he struck out looking this time.

I asked about Frodsham, confiding that I'd heard the Paints had been on the verge of releasing him several times. While neither confirming nor denying that Frodsham's spot on the roster had been so tenuous, Chris said, "He's flaky ... sometimes he acts like he's not all there ... but he's improved, he's really improved." Frodsham's stats weren't bad at all, and in fact he entered the game tied for the league lead in appearances with 24; yet, he was still a rookie and he often pitched like one. Further, he had no saves and was most often used in set-up or mop-up situations.

With the game tied Eric was now in a position to qualify for the win if he could hold Canton down long enough for the Paints to complete their comeback, but he couldn't do it. After allowing a single, a walk, and a sacrifice bunt, Frodsham was replaced by Nate Gardner.

Gardner finished the inning without allowing a hit or a base on balls, but he wasn't able to prevent both of Frodsham's runners from scoring. Altogether, Canton plated three tallies, two of them unearned runs which came home on Joey Choron's second throwing error of the game.

Unbelievably, the Paints stormed right back, batting around and scoring five big runs to take the lead, which was their first lead of the night, 12–10. Choron got back one of the runs he let in with an RBI triple, but the big blow for Chillicothe was a three-run homer by DH Chris Dickerson. All the Paints had to do now was "Hold 'em," and the come-from-behind-to-win-every-game sweep was in the bag. Marty Dunn turned to Woody Fullenkamp to lead the Paints to the promised land, but Woody was no longer pitching like the Moses of the Chillicothe bullpen.

In the top of the eighth Fullenkamp surrendered a booming two-run homer to third baseman Marcos Sanchez that re-tied the game, at 12–12. Then in the ninth he gave up another two-run homer, this time to Matt Gelotti. Out of comebacks, the Paints went down 1–2–3 in their final at bat, against Canton closer Drew Thomas. The 14–12 loss was a stunning, demoralizing turn-around, the kind of defeat which has ominous overtones for a once confident team suddenly struggling to hold their heads above water. If the Paints failed to make the playoffs, this surely would be one of the games the players would look back on most regretfully. 11/19/04

I took my time getting to the umpires "closet" to allow Max and Jim Schaly to unwind a bit in peace. When I got there they had only stripped down to their T-shirts which were thoroughly drenched in perspiration. They sat sprawled in exhaustion, and while they were drinking the Pepsis Butch Atteberry had left for them, they were apparently too tired or still too keyed up to have an appetite for the wrapped up chicken sandwiches that lay in a paper carton on the dressing table.

They had the same stunned looks on their faces that the Paints and their fans had on theirs. To them it was a matter that the game had taken so long to play, not that Chillicothe had lost, but they too were sensitive, in their own way, to Woody Fullenkamp's plight caused by his mysterious demise. "How do you go from being the best closer in the league one year to not being able to get any f-ing body out the next year?" said Max. It was a question nobody had a answer to, least of all Woody Fullenkamp, whose record dropped to 1–4 with the loss.

Anguishing over the loss, I lamented how Copley had killed the Paints, driving in five runs on his two hits. "Yeah, but he also struck out four times," said Schaly.

I quickly checked the box score Aaron Lemaster had printed for me. "No, he whiffed three times," I said.

"That's right, I remember," said Schaly. "All three were called strikes. The first one he thought was inside. The second one was right down the middle; he didn't say a word on that one. And the third one he thought was outside. When he came up for the last time, he asked me, 'Would you have rung me up if I hadn't been the beer batter?' I told him, 'Yes.' All three pitches he struck out on were legitimate strikes, but I do get the beer batter at least once every game. I make sure the fans get half price beer at least one inning every night."

The talk about beer reminded Schaly of something he wanted to ask me. "Did you see what I did last Saturday night in Richmond?" he said. I said I hadn't because I'd been in Cooperstown. "I was on the bases and in between innings I walked over to the fence in front of the beer garden," he said. "I went up to Tom and said, 'Where's *my* beer?' He looked at me kind of shocked and said, 'I dunno.' So I grabbed his off the picnic table and drank it. It was funnier than hell. Well, really it was only about half a beer. You can't do something like that in a close game. You need at least a four-run lead. … Actually, now that I think about it, it was a two-run lead. But nobody cared. Everybody thought it was hilarious."

"If you're going to shower, get your ass in there," snapped Max, ending Schaly's rumination on beer drinking and umpiring. "We've got to have one at The Dock tonight, and I want to get going."

When Schaly, naked except for a bath towel around his waist, stepped through the door separating the umpires' closet from the Paints' clubhouse on his way to the showers, Max said to me, "Don't ask Jim any more about that thing in Richmond. I'll tell you why later. You'll have to trust me on this. Just don't bring it up again tonight. Okay?"

"Sure, Max. No problem," I said.

Since it was a Monday night, Water Street was quiet and deserted. We still were not able to park in front of The Dock, but we did find a spot for Max's Buick almost directly across the street. As we approached The Dock's front door, Chris Hanners, on his way into the saloon, was ending a conversation with Mike Horning, on his way out.

"Mike takes losing as hard as anybody," said Chris. "He can't have a good time after a loss like that, so he's going home to bed."

The music inside The Dock was as good and as loud as ever, but a funereal mood reigned over the sparse crowd nevertheless. I found a few Paints in their usual spot, in the far corner, where they were sedately eating pizza and throwing darts. I watched them for a few moments, then turned to head back towards the front of the bar to rejoin Max and Schaly. That's when I saw Woody, sitting by himself at the controls of the sound system, headphones over his ears, losing himself in the music, trying to think about anything but the thing he loved most: pitching.

11

Sex, Tempers, and a Resignation

WE LEFT THE DOCK EARLY because Max realized all of a sudden that he didn't have his Frontier League ring on his finger. We raced back to VA Memorial Stadium, completely deserted except for Aaron Queen who was doing laundry, and Max found the ring exactly where he'd left it, in the top drawer of the little table in the umpires' dressing room.

On the way home Max explained why he hadn't wanted me to talk to Schaly. Although Schaly didn't know it, everybody did not think his beer-drinking stunt was funny. In fact, when the Roosters' front office got wind of it, they thought it was a serious enough breach of conduct to contact Bill Lee about, and some people even thought Schaly should be fired. When Bill Lee called Max to ask him about the incident, Max instinctively did what he had to do to protect the job of his best friend and partner: he lied. Thinking quickly, Max concocted a story that the whole thing had been nothing but a stunt and that the cup Schaly drank from had contained not beer, but water.

Max's fib had calmed the waters, but the situation was still very tricky. Bill Lee was too smart to really buy the story but also cagey enough to let it stand if it assuaged Richmond and headed off a major headache. So the Frontier League comish was not the problem. The danger, as Max saw it, was with Schaly himself. "I know how Jim is," he said, "and if he finds out that Richmond complained and that I had to cover up for him, he'll get pissed off, run his mouth, and cause a huge scene. The truth will come out, and then there'll be no saving his ass or mine!"

Was Jim really that much of a hot head and did the self-destructive streak in the guy really run that deep? I asked. Yes he was and yes it did, Max told me. And, no, Max could not count on Jim, if he found out what happened, to just let the whole thing die quietly, even if Max tried to carefully explain to him that doing so would be necessary for their mutual survival.

As unfortunate as it was that Schaly could be his own worst enemy, the situation was complicated by the fact that some bad blood existed between him and Richmond. Schaly had been with the Frontier League from the very start, and now that Roger Hanners was no longer in uniform, Jim was the only person on the field still left from the league's inaugural year. In 1998 Schaly had been made the Supervisor of Umpires for the entire league. One regrettable day that season he was about to walk out the door of his house in Marietta, Ohio, to start a ten-day trip around the West Division of the league, when his wife dropped the ultimate bombshell on him. She was leaving him for a younger man, a college football player at nearby Marietta College. And, oh yes, she was already pregnant with the other guy's baby.

Naturally, Schaly was devastated, and to make a long story short, he wound up taking his hurt and anger out on the people around him in the Frontier League. He had a particularly bad run-in with John Cate that resulted in his being effectively banned from Richmond. He lost his supervisory position and almost got run out of the league altogether. The only thing that saved him was the fact that he was a hell of an umpire, head and shoulders above the other arbiters in the league.

Max, who wanted to be able to work with Jim in the Frontier League ballpark closest to his home, later played peacemaker between Cate and Schaly and eventually secured Bill Lee's permission for Schaly to return to Richmond. Cate and Schaly managed to co-exist, but the past was never completely forgotten by either man. Keeping the peace in Richmond was clearly in Schaly's own best interest; but having been shafted by both love and baseball, Jim had chips on both his shoulders. And, as Max realized, they were a constant threat to trump even the most sensible considerations of self interest.

Tuesday, August the first, was a league-wide off day, but we were back in the saddle on Wednesday. On our way to Chillicothe I asked Max how Dave Hornbach had made out in Richmond playing the Dash for Cash Game. "After he counted it all up, he had $154!" said Max. "I have to umpire two nights to make that much. ... And I got him into the park for free on a pass, and Patty's the one who bought the program that had the lucky number on it." After I finished laughing at the irony of it all, I tried to comfort him by saying, "Well, maybe the book will embarrass the league into raising the umpires' pay."

"Heck, all I want is for the umpires, not the Rooster Chicks, to be the ones to pick up the coins the contestants drop," he said.

Although Max and I had been together for two months, there was still a good part of his life I didn't know much about. I didn't want to pry or bring up memories of old wounds, but there were things that needed clarification, especially the status of one Marty McLeary in Max's life. I knew that Max, like any good father, loved his son, but there was no way, as far as I could tell, that Max had a close relationship with Marty. Max was very proud of Marty, a strapping 26-year-old righthander pitching for the Boston Red Sox's Double-A farm team in Trenton, New Jersey, but there was apparently very little communication between the father and the son. Unlike the Zerbe's who got a phone call after every Richmond Roosters' game, Max never heard from Marty. Max rarely mentioned Marty, and he followed Marty's progress in professional baseball by reading *Baseball America,* just as any hard core Red Sox fan looking towards the future of the team might do. Marty had been raised by his mom in Mansfield, Ohio. In college he pitched for Mt. Vernon Nazarene where he went 36–2, with his only losses coming during his junior and senior years in the NAIA World Series. Max got to exactly three of his son's college games to watch him pitch, and he did so without ever letting Marty know that he had been there.

Max told me that he'd met Marty's mom, Barbara Camp, at Grace College in Winona Lake, Indiana, but we went back a little farther to 1966 and started with Max's freshman year in college which he spent at Penn State University. Max made the varsity baseball team at Penn State as a walk-on second baseman and actually saw considerable playing time in the spring of 1967. Penn State didn't have a very good program at the time though; so when he was recruited by Grace College—the minister of Max's church in Johnstown tipped off the coach at Grace—he left Happy Valley for greener pastures. The fundamentalist college was pretty strict, and, according to Max, "we couldn't smoke, drink, dance, swear, play cards, or go to the movies." The bans against smoking and drinking didn't bother Max any because "I didn't smoke or drink until I started coaching baseball when I was 27. Baseball coaching will cause anybody to start smoking and drinking."

Content with his studies, his steady girl Barbara, and sports—he also played goalie on the soccer team—Max stayed out of trouble until the end of his junior year in 1969, when he made the mistake of buying a six pack of beer for another student, the chaplain, who was the nephew of the dean of students. "I didn't drink the beer myself. And I didn't even give it to him," said Max. "I just told him where it was: in the bushes where I'd left it." A week before final exams the chaplain repented and confessed to his uncle. Max took finals on Thursday and Friday, helped the baseball team clinch the conference championship by sweeping a season-ending doubleheader on Saturday, and was thrown out of school on Monday morning right before he was to take his last exam. The dean and the president of the college told him he was being expelled for "violating the code of conduct you signed." Although he was kicked out of the dorms too, he stayed at the home of the athletic director all week so he could be there when Barbara, who was a year ahead of him, graduated on Sunday.

Max spent the summer umpiring college-age amateur baseball in Johnstown and then moved to Ashland, Ohio, in the fall to be with Barbara, who'd returned to her home town after graduation. After Max and Barbara got married that December, Max became the head soccer coach at Ashland University, as well as an assistant for basketball coach Bill Musselman, who later coached in the NBA. In addition, he enrolled at Ashland and got the college degree there he should have gotten from Grace. Their first son, Matt, was born in 1972, shortly before Max and Barbara moved to Dayton, Ohio, for job opportunities at Wright State University. Barbara took a job as assistant to the registrar, while Max became the trainer, the Sports Information Director, and the school's first soccer coach on the varsity intercollegiate level. In the summers Max also started umpiring professionally, in the New York–Penn League, after graduating from The Umpiring Academy, which later became The Harry Wendlestedt School of Umpiring. Unfortunately, Max's constant traveling put such a strain on his relationship with Barbara that by the time Marty came along in October of 1974, the marriage was on the rocks. "I just wasn't grown up enough," said Max. "I was on the road too much, and I had something going on in every town. I really messed up. It wasn't Barbara's fault. She's a very religious person, and she's been a great mom to the boys." Max described their parting as an "amicable separation," and I was sure that the term was accurate, as far as it went. What it left out was the tragedy brought about by the dissolution of the marriage; the tragedy of the boys having been separated from their father and of their father having been separated from his boys.

The Dubois County Dragons were in town to play the Paints, but I wasn't going to be able to renew my acquaintanceship with Tim Wallace, as I had hoped to do. While reading the "Transactions" section in the *Cincinnati Enquirer* that morning I'd noticed that Pops had been fired and replaced with first baseman Fran Riordan, who was going to be a player-manager for the rest of the season. Pops' two coaches had also been let go and replaced by two other players, shortstop John Taveras and outfielder Scott Marple, who were to assist Riordan.

I was pleased to see that Robert Lee, hanging around the visitors' locker room was still a Dragon and the same irrepressible, wise-cracking scamp I'd met in Huntingburg. "It's all up hill from here," he said with a wry smile, after he'd told me that GM Heath Brown had also been fired. When I asked him how Pops had taken the news, he said, "I think he knew it was coming. He told the players he would probably be canned. He said, 'Everybody else is getting fired. Why shouldn't I?'"

Why was Pops fired? "Mostly because he didn't want to promote the team or do any appearances," Robert said. "He didn't want to do anything but manage, and in Huntingburg we don't have that luxury."

While Robert and I were talking, a big Chillicothe cop in his early thirties, came over and began asking for Fran Riordan.

A few moments later the Dragons' new manager came out of the clubhouse to see what the cop wanted. "Are you Fran Riordan from Buffalo, New York?" the cop asked, as he took a small notebook out of his shirt pocket.

Yes, he was. I could see that Riordan, a tall, solidly-built, good-looking young man, understood immediately that the reference to his home town meant that the matter the cop was inquiring about related to him personally and not to him as the manager of the Dragons.

"Is 'Fran' short for anything?"

"It's short for 'Francis.'"

"Is there anything unusual about the spelling?"

"No, no. It's 'F-R-A-N.' ... What's this all about, officer?"

"Well, Mr. Riordan, I got a teletype from NCIC on you from the Buffalo police in connection to a bar fight. Somebody got seriously hurt, and there's a warrant out for your arrest."

"Are you kidding?"

"I'm afraid not."

"I can't believe this. ... You can't be serious."

"I wouldn't lie about something like this."

"I don't believe this."

"Why don't we go to the station downtown and get this straightened out, and maybe we can get you back before the game's over."

"Yeah. Okay, sure."

"Handcuffs aren't going to be necessary, are they?"

"Oh, no. No, sir."

"Good. Now, Mr. Riordan, if you'd just come this way," said the cop, as he took Riordan by the arm and led him around the corner of the grandstand, where, looking up, Fran saw a familiar, friendly face.

"GOTCHA!" said Max.

"Fran and I go back a long way," Max had told me at the beginning of our trip to Chillicothe. "I had him for a Triple-A-BA (American Amateur Athletic Baseball Association) tournament in Johnstown when he was playing for Buffalo; I had him from his freshman through his senior years when he was playing for Allegheny College; and I had him a couple of summers when he played in the Great Lakes League." And, it went without saying, Max had umpired some of the Frontier League games Riordan had played in. When Riordan had played for Richmond, Max saw him fairly frequently; but now that Fran was with Dubois County in the West Division, it was almost as if they were in different leagues. Max was truly happy about Riordan's promotion, and he'd been excited at the prospect of renewing their old friendship, within certain prescribed boundaries, of course. "He's not going to get any breaks, but it'll be just like Old Home Week tonight," he'd said.

Roger Hanners once told me, "I get so damned mad at Max, but he's such a great person I can only stay mad at him about five minutes." If the relieved Fran Riordan got mad at Max, his anger didn't even last as long as Hanners'. "You SOB," he said while trying to hold back a smile.

"Did we getcha? Huh? Did we?" Max said.

"Shit. My heart dropped to my stomach. I thought, 'Oh, no! My parents and my girlfriend are here tonight: this is going to be really embarrassing.'"

"I just wanted to make your first night on the job a memorable one. Welcome to management!"

"Thanks a lot. But, actually, this'll be my second game. We lost my debut, 11–2, to Evansville."

"Well, that was just my way of saying, 'Congratulations!'"

"Yeah, like I said, 'Thanks a lot, you SOB.'"

After Max and Riordan exchanged some pleasantries, I asked Fran how things were going so far. "I'm the first to say I'm not a manager," he said, "but something needed to be done. There was a lot of negativity before. Now the air has been cleared, and everybody is really loose. We know we're not going to make the playoffs this year. We just want to play good baseball the rest of the way."

Riordan was not just being careful of overconfidence when he said that the Dragons were already out of the playoffs, which were reserved for the two Division-winning teams plus the two teams with the next best records, regardless of which division they were in. Barring a miracle, the Dragons were out of contention, as the standings showed with two thirds of the season completed:

East Division	W	L	Pct.	GB	West Division	W	L	Pct.	GB
Johnstown	32	21	604		River City	34	21	618	
London	31	24	564	2.0	Evansville	28	26	519	5.5
Chillicothe	29	27	518	4.5	Springfield	27	29	482	7.5
Richmond	26	29	473	7.0	Cook County	25	32	439	10.0
Canton	21	36	368	13.0	Dubois County	21	29	420	10.5

Since the end of the first month of the season Johnstown and River City had established themselves as the teams to beat in each division. The Paints were not dead by a long shot, but everybody in Chillicothe had mentally revised the team's goal from winning the East Division to qualifying for the playoffs by sewing up the fourth and final playoff spot. And it was beginning to look as if the main competition for that fourth spot was going to come from the Evansville Otters, who had improved their record by ten games in July in climbing out of the West Division's basement and into second place.

The Paints hadn't been able to sweep the last-place Crocodiles, but they didn't make the same mistake against the last-place Dragons. Chillicothe put together good pitching and great hitting to win the three games 8–3, 12–6, and 8–3. Sean Boesch gave the Paints' worn-out bullpen a break by going all the way in the opener. Before the game John Wend told him, "Give us seven tonight, big boy." "Eight," promised Boesch, who then delivered nine. Andy Lee went eight strong innings in the second game and struck out eight to run his season strikeout total to 90, only two behind league leader Randy Eversgerd of River City. And in the final, sore-armed Stephen Byrd pitched well enough in 5.2 innings to pick up the win and run his record to 4–0. Woody Fullenkamp was still not right—he gave up four hits and two runs in the final inning of Andy Lee's game—but the bullpen answered the call in the finale, as the trio of Eric Frodsham, Jason Harrison, and Nate Gardner held the Dragons scoreless over the last 3.1 innings.

The Chillicothe offense got into gear early and roared continuously. In the first game two-run home runs by Jason Baker in the first and Justin Graham in the third set the tone for the entire series. In the press box John Wend called Justin's shot. "If he (Jamal Gaines) hangs the curveball to Graham, he'll take him deep," John said moments before Graham hit one over the right field fence with Chris Dickerson aboard via a base on balls. In the middle game the Paints pounded out 17 hits. Every player in the starting lineup got at least one hit. Dickerson, Baker, Matt McCay, Joey Choron, and Chris Poulsen all had two hits, while Chance Melvin picked up three hits for the second night in a row. In the Friday night finale, the Chillicothe attack was led by Greg Strickland,

Poulsen, and Phil Warren, a recently-acquired rookie who had played college ball at S. E. Missouri State. After having missed three games with the hand injury he suffered against Canton, Strickland went 3–5 with a double and a triple; Poulsen went 4–4; and Warren hit a monster of a home run to left center.

The series wasn't much fun for the Dragons, but Chillicothe fans had a blast, and the fun for them wasn't limited to the Paints' domination on the field. The opener came on another "Winning Wednesday" when the Nourse Family of Dealerships gave away a 1990 T-Bird and a '91 Taurus.

It's hard to argue with the Paints' description of "Winning Wednesdays" as the "best promotion in the Frontier League," but Friday night's promotion was no slouch either.

For the "Diamond Dig," sponsored by Kenrick's Fine Jewelry and Gifts, all ladies 18 years old and up, got a chance after the game to look for a ½-carat diamond ring that had been buried in the skin part of the infield. John Wend told me that Kenrick's owner, George Clayton, enjoys being known as "the only man who can get 100 women on their knees all at one time." John also told me that the Diamond Dig promotion is the one that GM Bryan Wickline and his staff are the most anxious about each year. "One year Bryan had to break up a brawl," John said. "The gals couldn't find the ring, so we started giving them clues. They all bunched up, and three of 'em found it at about the same time. That was a mess, let me tell you."

And then there were a couple of Chicken Dances during which the participants showed off some new moves during the waltz part of the song. One night the ever-inventive Woody Fullenkamp impersonated a rotating, intermittent lawn sprinkler; on another night he slipped into a basketball mode with some defensive slide movements and shooting motions. Eric Frodsham and big Josh Lamberg also got into the act. The gangly Frodsham did an amusing rap dance, while Lamberg did a dance that incorporated a series of foot slaps with the opposite hand. Lamberg had not been able to dislodge Chris Poulsen as the starting catcher, but he was a longball threat off the bench, and he helped keep the clubhouse loose. "They're not going to cut *me*. They might trade me, but they won't release me," he told Max. "They can't. Not when I'm the only Jew in the league."

Our appreciation for these finger-lickin' good performances put John Wend in mind of Chicken Dances Future and Past. John first told me that Richmond had issued the Paints a Chicken Dance Challenge to be held during the season's final series, which would be played in Chillicothe. The man behind the Challenge was Roosters reliever Bobby Chandler, who used to pitch for the Paints and was one of the originators of the routine. "Bobby will have some wild stuff planned, I guarantee you that," John said. "He's creative as hell." John was also reminded of the night when the Chicken Dance was used to pay tribute to a great Paints' player. "When Gator McBride left the Paints for affiliated ball, it was in the middle of the season, and he didn't dress for the game. The pitchers used the Chicken Dance that night for a salute to him during the ceremony when they retired his number. They all stood on benches in the bullpen, stuck their arms out, and moved them up and down like a gator chomping. Then at the end of the song they took their hats off and bowed to him."

The series also produced some memorable moments for me. I went on the radio with Robert Lee for an inning to talk about the book, and off the air he said, "If your book was about us, the title would have to be 'Shit Happens in Dubois County.'"

One night the winner of the Announcer for an Inning contest turned out to be a five-year-old named Shane B. Bush. He was wearing a T-shirt that his mom had marked up to say "Chance Melvin's #1 Fan." The first thing he said to Wend was, "I got two luse tuse." Shane wasn't the least bit nervous, and though he wasn't able to pronounce the names of the batters exactly the way John prompted him to, his pronunciations were recognizable and his bravery endearing to the crowd. John got such a kick out of Shane's pinch hitting that he let him do the entire inning instead of the first three batters as usual. When somebody came over the walkie-talkie to say that the previous night's Announcer for an Inning was complaining that he only got three batters, John said, "Well, Shane's better!"

Matt McCay, the new right fielder who was in the lineup because of Colameco's departure, was not only playing well. He also made every one of his at bats a miniature theatrical production. McCay had chosen as his introductory music the theme song from "The Dukes of Hazzard" TV show. I'd never watched the show, but I discovered that I really liked its catchy theme song, manfully sung by Waylon Jennings. Its quintessentially country sound, rhythm, and narrative made it refreshingly different from the rap and heavy metal preferred by most players in the league. McCay's leisurely amble from the on-deck circle towards the batter's box would give Aaron Lemaster the chance to play the entire opening verse of the song.

The piece de resistance was the little hop that McCay would take just as Waylon Jennings referred to the subjects of the song for the first time, thus connecting McCay in the minds of Paints fans with those "good old boys."

On Thursday night I ran into McCay outside the Dock, and he told me that he was relishing his opportunity to finally play. "I didn't have a great tryout in the spring—I'm not one of those guys who runs a 6.3 sixty-yard dash or drops bombs in BP—but Roger decided to keep me," he said. "It surprised me as much as anybody else. I came in as a utility player, somebody who could catch, play first, play the outfield. That was my role. ... The guys would say, 'Let's get an eight-run lead, so McCay can bat.'"

I'd seen in the program that McCay had played at the University of North Carolina, so I asked him if he'd played for Mike Fox. Matt said that he'd not only played for Coach Fox at UNC, but that he'd also played for him as a freshman and sophomore at little North Carolina Wesleyan College in Rocky Mount and been taken to UNC by Fox when the latter first took the job in Chapel Hill. I had played at Wesleyan years before Fox turned the Battling Bishops into a Division III powerhouse. I knew that the baseball program at N.C. Wesleyan had been turning out players good enough to go into pro ball since the start of the Fox era, but I'd never met one until I met Matt McCay. I also knew that this fraternal connection between McCay and myself was a lot more exciting to me than it was to him, but he humored me kindly. The next day I carried my old N.C. Wesleyan baseball jersey to VA Memorial Stadium. Standing by the Paints dugout, I slipped the jersey on over my sports shirt and called out to McCay manning first base during BP. It was a very fan-ish, even adolescent thing for a writer, twice as old as the players he was writing about, to do, but I couldn't help myself. McCay, bless his heart, gave me a big grin and a friendly thumbs-up sign.

As for Max, he had a fairly uneventful series on the field. The closest he came to any controversy was on a play in the first game that happened to involve McCay. In the bottom of the third with two outs, Matt chopped a hard grounder up the middle over the pitcher's mound. Jamal Gaines got a glove on the ball, slowed it down, and knocked it towards second. Second baseman Dennis Pelfrey fielded the ball near the bag and, spinning towards first as he threw, made a weak throw to first. Max called McCay out, but he looked safe to me, to some of the fans, and to John Wend, who said, "Come on, Max!"

At The Dock after the game I asked Max how the game had gone for him. "I had a couple of bangers," he said. "A few of the fans were bleeding paint on me, but that's to be expected." When I asked about the McCay play specifically and admitted that he'd looked safe to me, Max gave me another lesson in umpiring. "The rule is you don't reward a bad play ... you do reward a good play," he said. "For example, a one-hopper is hit to third. The third baseman drops it, it's a banger at first: he's SAFE! On the other hand, the shortstop goes in the hole and makes a long off-balance throw. The first baseman digs it out, it's a banger: he's OUT! Just like last week when Justin Graham was on second, and he took off for third on a ground ball to the pitcher. He was out by two miles. The third baseman put the tag down, but he didn't really tag the runner. He missed him, but Graham was out … for stupidity! And Marty didn't argue. Some of the fans did, but they don't understand. I wouldn't have called him out if the third baseman had ole'd 'im, but he made it close enough."

Max also thought he had a good idea for the book we were working on together. "I've got a new subtitle for the book," he said excitedly. "Here's what it should be: 'A Season in the Frontier League … as Seen *Through the Eye* of Umpire Max McLeary'! People will think it's a typo until they read the book!"

Even as the Paints beat up on Dubois County, the injury bug continued to plague the team. There were five new or recurring injuries in the third game alone. In the bottom of the third Joey Choron pulled up lame while going from first to third and was replaced at first base by Phil Warren at the start of the next inning. While running out a single in the bottom of the fourth, Jason Baker re-injured his bad quadriceps and was pinch run for by Josh Lamberg. As Byrd, who allowed ten hits and five walks, struggled to last the five innings he needed to be eligible for the win, John Wend pointed out that he was working without his full arsenal of pitches. "His two seam fastball which goes down is his best pitch," said John, "but he's afraid to throw it because it puts pressure on his elbow." And in the seventh, Rodger Fleming had to come out of the dugout to check on Chris Poulsen. Eric Frodsham grazed Dragons right fielder Adam Olow with a pitch that hit Poulsen's forearm on the ricochet. Poulsen was okay this time and stayed in the game after Fleming administered some anti-inflammatory cold spray to his arm; unlike the time earlier in the season when Poulsen missed three games after getting hit, while running to first, with a throw that opened a six-stitch cut in his forehead.

The scariest and potentially most serious injury occurred in the top of the first inning. With one on and one out, Scott Marple lined a smash down to Chance Melvin at third. The ball bounced up sharply, caught Melvin in the head, and knocked him to the ground. Melvin lay sprawled on his stomach, unmoving, in the grass. Shortstop Jamie Keefe got to him first, knelt beside him, and then waved to the Paints' dugout for help. Melvin came close to passing out, but Rodger Fleming helped him into a sitting position and kept him conscious until the Union Township Emergency Squad arrived fourteen minutes later. Fortunately, a minor concussion and a cut on his ear were the extent of Melvin's injuries. As Melvin was taken away in the ambulance, I couldn't help thinking, "Thank goodness; for once, it's not Max getting a ride to the hospital with the flashing lights and sirens going!"

FUCK THIS! I THOUGHT
THIS "GD" FUCK'N BOOK WAS
ON MAT + THE FL.?

✳ I got another weekend off because Max and Schaly worked the play-offs of the Great Lakes League. We'd meet again for the Tuesday–Thursday series in Richmond, Roosters against the River City Rascals.

After leaving Chillicothe, the Dubois County Dragons had gone home and finally gotten off the schneid under Fran Riordan in taking a doubleheader (which included a make-up game) from the Roosters on Saturday, despite home runs in each game by Macky Waguespack. On Sunday the Roosters had pounded out a 16–2 victory, but the Monday wrap-up had been cancelled, under questionable circumstances. As Gary Kitchel told me later: "It had rained overnight, and at 3:00 Monday afternoon the field was wet, but nobody was doing anything to work on it. We went back to the hotel and got a call that the game was being called. We left Dubois County at 5:00 with the sun shining and clear skies. Since we're finished with them, the game won't be made up. The cancellation doesn't hurt them, but it hurts the Roosters. John Cate was pissed. He said, 'It's a black mark against their franchise and a black mark against the league.'"

Schaly had spent Monday night at Max's, so on Tuesday the eighth, we all rode to Richmond together, Max, Jim, Patty and I, in Jim's 1989 light blue Dodge Caravan. The van, which clearly functioned as Schaly's office-away-from-home, was so well-stocked with the things Jim had come to know he would need that I felt compelled to jot down in my notebook its contents as follows: two big equipment bags, one for Jim's plate gear and one for his civilian and miscellaneous umpiring clothing; a clothes rod from which hung his non-folding umpire clothes: two light blue umpire shirts, three navy blue shirts, one red shirt, a pullover jacket, a dress blazer (for cold weather), and two pair of gray slacks; one lawn chair (for chairless dressing rooms); two brief cases; a tray of caps; a cooler containing two Miller Lites and two bottled waters; a case of Valvoline 10W/30 motor oil; a road atlas; a stack of newspapers; an umbrella; a large bag of peanuts; a rolodex; a box of Red Man chewing tobacco pouches; an empty Valvoline box (for trash); a plastic coffee mug; and a nasty pop bottle which he used as a spittoon. Like Max, Jim believed in getting his money's worth out of a car, but he had no illusions about how much longer his van was going to last, and he was starting to look around for a replacement. The case of motor oil was not, after all, an over-precaution. "If you follow me close enough, you can scrape oil off your windshield and put it in your car because it just flows out of mine," he said.

When Jim noticed me taking inventory, he pointed out a burn hole in the upholstery and said there were two more such holes in the couch back in his apartment. All compliments of Max, whom Jim had once caught sleeping with a lit cigarette. "I know you don't care if you burn

NOBODY
WANTS
to
McBride

down your house and kill yourself," Jim said to Max, "… I know that. But do you care if you kill Patty and the two dogs? All I can conclude is that you don't. Why is that, Max? Are you such a slave to nicotine?"

Max didn't really have a comeback to the hectoring, but Schaly continued in a vein meant to indicate he'd only been kidding. "Have you ever been smoking on the throne and dropped some hot ashes on the Big Guy?" he said. We all laughed, including Patty, and I said, "The 'Big Guy?' Where'd you get that one?"

"Oh, there's tons of 'em," he said. "Purple-helmeted yogurt slinger … one-eyed worm … bald-headed champ. There's a movie called *The Program* … if you want a list, watch that movie."

For most of the drive Patty and I, in the backseat, were content to listen to the conversation in the front seat, which was dominated by Schaly. Particularly interesting was Jim's account of a recent series between Richmond and Cook County which illustrated, as far as Jim was concerned, the lack of support given the umpires by the league office when players got out of hand. The story revolved around Rodney Rollins and Toby Sanchez, Cook County's foul-mouthed, hot-headed third baseman.

"Rodney was on the plate for the game last Thursday, August the third, in Richmond," said Jim. "He rings up Sanchez … strike three! … and Sanchez argues at the plate. He goes back to the dugout, throws down his helmet and his bat, and yells out at the top of his lungs, 'YOU'RE FUCKIN' TERRIBLE!' And Rodney did not throw him out.

"Now, Sanchez had already been ejected twice this season, so he was facing a $100 fine and a three-day suspension without pay if he got tossed a third time.

"I talked to Rodney about the game, and I told him, 'You should have thrown him out; you've got to run the game the way it's supposed to be run. Why didn't you throw him out?'

"Rodney said, 'I didn't want to go over to the dugout.'

"I said, 'You don't have to. *Look* over there and say, "Hey, Sanchez, you're gone!"'"

Max turned around and added an aside to Jim's tale: "Rodney's never thrown anybody out of a Frontier League game. That's his pride."

"Anyway, the next night Deron Brown has the plate; Rodney's on the bases. Deron rings Sanchez up in the sixth inning … same thing. He argues at the plate, slams down his bat and his helmet, and before he gets into the dugout he yells as loud as he can, 'YOU FUCKIN' SUCK!' Deron throws him out. Sanchez runs back to the plate screaming and cussing like a wild man. He's completely out of control, and the manager, a coach, and another player have to grab him and hold him back. Rodney runs in to help Deron and gets between Deron and Sanchez.

His mistake was getting too close to Sanchez. Rodney says, 'You need to leave the field.'

"Sanchez says, 'Fuck you!'

"Rodney says, 'You need to leave the field, NOW!'

"Sanchez breaks half way loose, reaches over, and punches Rod in the chest. The force of it knocks Rodney back three or four feet. What I'm upset about is that Bill Lee is apparently not going to punish Sanchez for the assault. The $100 fine and the three-day suspension was for the ejection; he's gotten nothing extra for the punch.

"Bill told me, 'Don't question my decisions concerning player discipline. I've told you before, and I told you before this season started, they're none of your business.'

"I said, 'Bill, when the incident is serious enough, when it involves a player touching or assaulting an umpire, then as a matter of justice and fairness, the umpires should have some say.'

"Bill says, 'A $25 fine hurts the players in our league a lot more than a $2,500 fine hurts a player in the major leagues.'

"And I say, 'Yeah, maybe so, but look at what other players in the majors got. Rose, all he did was push Dave Pallone, and he got thirty days. All Roberto Alomar did was spit and he got suspended six days, and the umpires protested that until they found out that that was the maximum the rules allowed.'

"Bill said, 'Well, I told Rodney he's free to file assault charges with the police if he wants to.'

"Obviously, Bill and I never did see eye-to-eye on how Sanchez should have been handled, and later on he told me he thought the umpires instigated a lot of their own trouble with foul language. The players and managers want that to be a one-way street, but it's not. For instance, a player says, 'Fuck you.' If I say, 'No, Fuck *you!*' then he gets all bent out of shape and says I started the whole thing by cussing him. That's bullshit.

"You think I'm kidding? The other day Richmond's pitcher didn't like a call, so he throws up his hands and says, 'Where the fuck was that pitch?'

"The umpire says, 'Outside. Now get back on the fucking mound.'

"John Cate comes out of the dugout and says, 'You can't talk to my players like that.'

"The ump says, 'Did you hear what he said to me?'

"Cate says, 'I don't care what he said. You don't talk to my players like that.'"

Schaly and Max went on for a while in a similar vein, commiserating with each other over the fact that the league didn't appreciate its umpires enough, didn't protect them enough, and didn't pay them enough. Nursing these grievances put Schaly in mind of someone I would not have imagined as an ally of the umpires, Mal Finchman. "Nobody liked Mal because they couldn't beat him," said Jim, "but in the early days when the umpiring in the Frontier League was borderline atrocious, he was our biggest supporter. He said if a player ever touched an umpire he should be gone.

"The Frontier League is lucky it still has umpires. We thought about walking out one time; we talked about it. If I didn't need the money to pay my rent, I'd be gone."

I didn't challenge Schaly's claim of being indifferent about umpiring in the Frontier League. I considered his statement more bravado than anything else. Like Max, he was tied to the league by more than his wallet. Long ago each man had connected himself to the league emotionally, psychologically, fraternally, and professionally; and this connection was not something either man would sever lightly.

River City took two out of three from the Roosters, Richmond salvaging the finale 13–3. While the losses hurt—the Roosters dropped even further behind Johnstown and London—their main effect was to bring the disappointing season and the team's problems to a head.

As we neared Richmond, Schaly told us how much he was looking forward to working the plate with Steve Carver going for the Roosters, but his envisioned easy-chair day never panned out.

Ironically, Mr. Pinpoint Control got himself into trouble by walking the leadoff batter of the game, River City's Travis Dawson. One out later third baseman Brian Fuess took a letter-high Carver fastball downtown to give the Rascals a 2–0 lead. The homer was Fuess' 11th of the year, which tied him for third in the league, while the two RBI boosted his league-leading total to 62. After the Roosters knotted the score in the second on doubles by DeGraffenreid and Borghese and a single by Flores, Fuess came to bat again in the third with one out. Fuess ran the count to 2–2, and then Carver plunked him in the back with a curveball. Before jogging down to first, Fuess eyed Carver reproachfully. Carver stared back at Fuess defiantly. Schaly pulled off his mask, stepped a few paces forward, and told Fuess to head down to first. As this happened, Rascals outfielder Benny Craig, who wasn't in the lineup, climbed up to the top step of the River City dugout and shouted towards Schaly: "Don't talk to our guy. He was the one who got hit!" Glancing towards the Rascals' dugout, Schaly pointed towards himself, shook his head, and mouthed, "You don't want any of this."

"Ooooh! We're scared!" said Benny.

Rascals manager Neil Fiala came out to talk to Schaly and wanted to know why Jim hadn't issued a warning to Carver for hitting Fuess.

"Because it wasn't intentional," said Schaly.

"How do you know that?" said Fiala.

"Because the pitch was a curveball."

"I thought it was a fastball."

"I guarantee you it was not a fastball," said Jim. "It was a curveball."

"I know it was a fastball," insisted Fiala.

"I bet you a beer it was a curveball. I'll ask the kid who got hit," said Schaly, as he looked towards Fuess down at first, which prompted Craig to make another comment.

"Neil, if I hear one more word from that guy, he's gone," said Schaly, as he pointed towards the Rascals' dugout.

"Are you pointing at me?" said Craig. "Don't point at me. That's rude."

Bang! Schaly threw Craig, who wasn't even in the game, out of the game. "That's it, Neil. He's outta here," Schaly told Fiala. Neither the fans nor Craig himself realized he'd been run until Fiala went over to the dugout and told Benny that he'd have to leave.

On his way to the clubhouse Craig stopped at home plate and asked Schaly, "Why'd you throw me out?"

"Because you're an idiot," said Schaly.

Benny was leaving, but he wasn't quite finished for the day. "Oh, yeah? Well, you don't even know how to throw somebody out of a game. I'll show you how to throw somebody out," he said to Schaly who'd already turned his back to Craig and stood facing center field as he jotted something down in his notebook. After rearing back with his left arm pointed upward and the right one pointed towards the ground, Craig sprang forward, spun around slightly, and thrust his right index finger into the sky with all his might, as if he were trying to poke Goliath in the eye. This mocking gesture of his own ejection drew laughter and a nice round of applause from the crowd.

In the Rascals' clubhouse Craig explained to teammate Joey Pipes, a pitcher, "I got thrown out by some guy with a big ego. I didn't even swear at him, didn't say even one cuss word. ... He's got a good strike zone, but he's an asshole."

After the game I asked Schaly why he threw Benny out. "I threw him out for being a dick," he said. "He pissed me off. He turned his hat sideways and said, 'Ooooh, I'm so scared.' I told Neil I was going to run him if he said one more thing. He said, 'Don't point at me.' Gone! He wanted to be Mr. Funnyman for his teammates, but he spent the last seven innings in the clubhouse."

When the inning was over, Jim got together for a minute with Max and River City's pitching coach, Randy Martz. "I'm taking a poll," said Schaly. "What was the pitch that hit Fuess?"

Benny Craig of the River City Rascals throws Umpire Jim Schaly (back to the camera) out of the game, while Max tries to intercede and Rascals manager Neil Fiala looks on.

"A curveball," said Martz.

"Thank you," said Schaly. "Max?"

"Curveball."

"Then it's unanimous. Randy, please tell your manager the pitch was a curveball. He thinks it was a fastball."

"Fastball???" said Martz.

As amusing as the Benny Craig incident was, it turned out to be merely an interlude between scenes of the Carver–Fuess drama. With one out in the fifth, Fuess came to bat for the third time with the game still tied 2–2. Carver's first pitch went behind Fuess, who turned around and looked at Schaly. "Oh, boy, here we go," I thought. Schaly called time, walked halfway to the mound, and issued official warnings to both dugouts. By doing this Schaly was putting both managers on notice that if any further brushbacks or bean balls were thrown, the offending pitcher and his manager would be automatically ejected from the game.

Carver's next pitch was inside for another ball, and his third a big breaking slider away from Fuess that Schaly called a strike. Carver came back with the same exact pitch, which was a mistake because it was exactly what Fuess was looking for. Fuess hit the ball so hard and so far that right fielder Freddy Flores didn't even move. Fuess didn't engage in any overt showboating, but he did take his sweet time making his second home run trot of the night, which probably accelerated the unraveling of Carver's equanimity.

Carver got catcher Bill Black on a fly to left, but he hit DH Darin Kinsolving, for the second time in the game, and then gave up another home run. This time Freddy gave chase—he leaped against the fence and fell down—but he was unable to keep the drive of first baseman Aaron Jaworowski in the ballpark. After left fielder Bret Haake singled to right, John Cate finally sent Woody Sorrell out to relieve Carver. Rookie lefthander Matt Schweitzer came on and, before getting the third out of the inning, gave up a double to T. J. Runnels which produced another run and a 6–2 lead for the Rascals. River City later scored off two more Richmond relievers, so that the final score was 10–3.

The highlight of the game was Aaron Sledd's booming home run, his tenth, to the biggest part of the ballpark in straightaway center field in the sixth inning. The most romantic part of the game came the next inning when Patty was named "Lady Fan of the Game" and received a bouquet of flowers. After Scott Beaman announced that base umpire Max McLeary and his wife Patty were celebrating their 19th wedding anniversary, Max turned towards the box seats and tipped his cap to Patty. Nobody minded that the drawing for "Lady Fan of the Game" had been obviously rigged by Max and the Roosters' front office.

In the dressing room Schaly reminded Max that he hadn't walked over to the Rascals' dugout in order to throw out Craig, and he felt that his having had Fiala deliver the bad news to Benny enabled him to avoid having to throw somebody else out. "I should have thrown Carver out for that weak-ass brushback, the pitch that went behind Fuess before he hit the second home run," Jim said. "It was definitely intentional. I don't like throwing at hitters, but I feel like it's part of the game. I don't think Carver tried to hit him though. The kid has such great control he would have hit him if he'd wanted to. And hell, he throws so slow it wouldn't have hurt Fuess if it did hit him."

On the way to The Wheel Max said to Schaly, "Hey, after you ran Craig and I was trying to get him to leave, I said, 'Come on, Benny and the Jets, let's go.'"

"You shouldn't try to kid around like that when guys are pissed off," said Jim.

"He wasn't pissed off."

"You still don't do it. ... You might get 'Rod Rollins-ed.'"

Patty giggled at the comment and said, "It was a good thing he didn't lay a finger on Larry, or the Lady Fan of the Game would have hit him ... with my plastic soft drink bottle."

We all laughed, and then Max and Schaly made more jokes about
the Lady Fan of the Game attacking a Rascals' player ... with her
umbrella, her bouquet of flowers, her pocketbook, and whatever else
she could find. Max said, "She would have hit him at least 19 times!"
We laughed again, and then I began singing, in my best imitation of
John Belushi and Dan Aykroyd, the only country song, besides "Raw-
hide," their Blues Brothers characters know and perform at Bob's Country Bunker—"Stand by Your Man."

At The Wheel we were joined by official scorer David Knight and
Bob Van Pelt. After a lot of discussion about how the game had unfolded,
Schaly said, "I told Max when we were getting undressed after the game
that there will be a brawl before this series is over."

"No there won't. There's not enough spunk on the team," said Bob.

"I agree," said Knight. "There's no leaders on the team."

"And River City has too much to lose," chimed in Max.

Somebody walked by wearing a black T-shirt that said "Fuck Everybody." "Hey, I like that T-shirt," said Schaly. "It reminds me of the saying I live by: 'Fuck 'em all but six.' The 'six' refers to the number of
people that it will take to carry your coffin. Every night, when I walk
onto the baseball field, I look up into the stands and say to myself, 'Nope.
None of my six are here. ... Fuck 'em all!'"

On any given night the conversation at The Wheel or The Dock
was liable to turn raunchy at some point, even when we had a woman
in the company. When it did, the guys always apologized ahead of time
and offered to tell their jokes later, yet invariably the woman, not wanting to be seen as the one to throw cold water on the party, would insist
that the joke-telling go ahead as if she weren't present. Although she
blushed often and feigned disgust, Patty was always a good sport and
usually laughed as hard as anyone else at off-color humor.

Schaly, in particular, was hilarious and totally uninhibited in discussing sexual matters, including his own sex life, which he portrayed as
being pathetically non-existent. He claimed that he hadn't had sex since
his wife left him, and he would periodically state how long to the day
his dry spell had lasted. "The last time I got laid was on Valentine's Day,
in a Holiday Inn," he said once. "That's the best sex there is ... hotel
sex!" If there was a cute girl in the bar, Schaly would express a desire
for her and say, "I'd make her see gawd!" And if there weren't any good-
looking women around to lust after, he'd stick out his hand, palm up,
and say, "I've got another date tonight with Miss Ohio." Although I was
sure that he exaggerated for our amusement, he acted as if he really
were as desperate as he talked, and he constantly hit on cute bar maids.
He claimed to have a fetish for small women, like one of the bar maids

at The Wheel, and he thought nothing of wondering aloud about her panty size. He even had no qualms about asking Patty what she thought the girl's panty size might be!

On Tuesday night Schaly started us down the road to bawdiness by saying, "Max, when was the last time you saw the serial number on a condom?"

"I never have," said Max

"That's because you don't have to unroll 'em far enough," said Schaly.

After we finished laughing at the way Max swallowed Schaly's set-up hook, line, and sinker, Van Pelt had a joke he wanted to tell that he said was apropos since it was Max's anniversary. "There's two guys who find out they have the same anniversary: a rich guy and a poor guy," he said. "The rich guy says, 'I bought my wife two anniversary presents: a Mercedes and a diamond ring.' The poor guy says, 'Why did you do that?' The rich guy says, 'Well, I figured that if she doesn't like the diamond ring, she'll be able to drive to the jewelry store and exchange it for something she does want.'

"'Oh, I see,' said the poor guy.'

"'What did you get your wife for your anniversary?' asked the rich guy.

"'A pair of fuzzy slippers and a dildo,'" said the poor guy.

"'Why'd you do that?' asked the rich guy.

"'Well, her feet get cold at night, so I figured the slippers will help keep them warm. And if she doesn't like the slippers, she can use the dildo to go fuck herself!'"

There was no turning back now, and after Max had the waitress sprinkle the infield, Schaly launched into a story about one of his personal sexual escapades. "First of all, you've got to understand that this happened in the middle of my drought," he said. "I'd been over a year without sex. So at that point I only needed two things: thin and no penis. Anything else was acceptable. Me and Max and a couple of other umpires were sitting around drinking at a bar in Cincinnati, and one of the umpires' girlfriends found out about my dire situation. She said, 'You wanna get laid? No problem.' So she started bringing girls over for me to check out, one at a time. 'Jim, how's this one?' Then she'd bring over another one: 'What about this one?' About the fourth one to come in was awesome. She was forty years old, she was a size three, and she was wearing a black mini-skirt.

"We start talking and getting drunker than shit, so before long we decided to leave and go get a hotel room. 'Alright!' I'm thinking, 'the drought is over!' We stumbled out of the bar and into the parking lot. When she leaned up against my van, we started kissing, and I started messing with her clothes. I unhooked her bra and pulled her mini-skirt up to her shoulders, and she had on nothing underneath the mini-skirt but a thong. We were so hot and bothered by that time, not to mention drunk, that we decided to do it right in the van. I slid the side door of the van open, and she laid down on the floor of the van with her feet resting on the ground. We were just about to get started, when a car pulled up five feet away from us, and the driver, a chick about twenty years old, said, 'Mom ... is that you?'

"'Oh, my god! That's my daughter!' she said, as she pulled down her dress and tried to fix her bra.

"'Tell her to go home!' I said.

"'I can't do that!' she said.

"'Tell her to come back in five minutes then!' I said.

"'I can't do that either!' she said.

"Needless to say, the drought continued."

"But that's not the end of the story, is it, Jim?" said Max. "A week later Jim was umpiring in Canton at a Crocodiles' game, and he was partnering with Chuck Robinson. Before the game Chuck had a little talk with the P.A. announcer up in the press box. After the guy introduced the starting lineup for the Crocodiles, he introduced the umpires. And when he got to Jim, he said, 'And umpiring at home plate is Jim Schaly ... MOM, IS THAT YOU?'

"I'd had a game in Chillicothe the same night, and when I was driving home, I got a call from Jim on my cell phone. 'That damn Robinson, I ought to kick his ass!' he said. 'And yours too! because I know you put him up to it!'"

All this talk about sex reminded Max of one of his favorite stories, and as soon as he started to tell it, Patty groaned in feigned dismay and excused herself to go to the ladies' room.

"Now this whole thing started near the end of last year at a game between the Roosters and the London Werewolves in Richmond. Here's the scenario: The game was being umpired by two guys from Chillicothe, a father-son combination, who weren't very good umpires. In fact, they were terrible. We'd been trying to get them out of the league for a while, and I didn't like assigning them Frontier League games, but Bill Lee was reluctant to get rid of the father because he'd been in the league since the beginning.

"These guys were so bad that both teams were getting on them from the start of the game. One of them threw Andy McCauley out of the game, and they pissed off John Cate so much that he wanted to get thrown out too. But they didn't want to throw John out after throwing Andy out because that would make them look bad. John tried everything he could think of to get thrown out of the game—he really verbally abused them both—but nothing worked, until he stood on the top step of the dugout and shouted, 'You guys are horrible! The only reason you're still umpiring in this league is that you're sucking Max McLeary's dick!' That finally got him tossed out.

"The next series was Richmond's last one of the year, and I was scheduled to work it. I got an idea to have Patty go out for the ground rules and say something, and I wanted her to do it before the last game. When I told her what I wanted her to say, she wouldn't do it. 'I can't say that, Larry!' she said. So I ripped out a page from her lesson plan book and wrote down what I'd wanted her to say, so all she had to do was hand the note to John Cate. I thought it was funny that I wrote the note on a page from a lesson plan book because Cate is a longtime school teacher, just like Patty is.

"Anyway, when it was time for the ground rules, Patty started walking out to home plate. It was the only time in league history that a woman went out for the ground rules. When Cate saw Patty instead of me, he thought, 'Oh, boy. What the hell is Max up to now?'

"Patty said, 'Hi, John.' John said, 'Hi, Patty.' And then Patty handed John the note which said: 'There's only one person in this league who's sucking Max McLeary's dick ... and I guarantee you it's not another umpire!' John laughed like hell, and he saved the note—I think he hung it up in his office—but he wasn't able to get me back because I'd waited until the last home game of the season."

The next day the *Paladium-Item* which I bought at the Village Pantry, and which Max wouldn't read, was worth 35¢ many times over. Its coverage of the Roosters' game the day before included a photo of Benny Craig showing Schaly how to eject somebody from a ballgame! Taken by the opportunistic Jason E. Suggs, the picture included all the principals. From left to right it showed Craig in his ejection windup; Max approaching Craig in order to usher him gently off the field; Rascals' manager Neil Fiala watching impassively with his hands in his back pockets; and Schaly, his back turned to both Craig and the camera, recording the ejection in his notebook. It was a great photo, one that captured a baseball moment as intriguing as it was unique and one that would have left the paper's readers scratching their heads in confusion had the caption not explained what the heck was going on in the picture.

Vernon Redd's game story was even more interesting than the photo of Craig's hijinks in that he conveyed the candid sentiments of a very unhappy John Cate. The last six paragraphs of Redd's story were given over to Cate's complaints about the lack of hustle by some of his players and his promise to wash his hands of the offenders in the future:

"What's frustrating is just really the lack of effort out of some players," Cate said.

"When you can't run a groundball out and you can't do some things hard, you shouldn't play.

"We have some players that are more conscious about what goes on after ballgames than we do during the ballgame itself. That's the part that just really hurts."

With less than a month left in the season, it seems that some of the Roosters might be burning their bridges.

"More than anything, you're not only playing for this year, you're playing for an invitation to come back next year," Cate said. "What a lot of players are doing is taking away their invitation because we won't go through this again.

"I just hope they're enjoying themselves while they do it because a lot of them won't be back."

I wasn't surprised that Cate would say such things to his players, but I was surprised and even shocked that he would blast his players in the newspaper. John's diatribe was much worse, for example, than Tim Wallace's mild criticisms in the Huntingburg press; and I felt that such strong words, made public, would surely have some serious consequences, one way or the other.

The consequences weren't long in coming. On Wednesday night, after another demoralizing Richmond loss during which the Rascals scored eight runs in the first two innings, Cate resigned. The resignation shocked me even more than John's newspaper comments had. Other people, including Max, weren't at all surprised. "He's burnt out. He's losing money, and the team is losing," Max said simply.

When I thought about it, I realized there had been some warning signs of John Cate's meltdown. In particular, there was an incident during the second game of a July fourth doubleheader that everyone regarded as just another funny story at the time but which in retrospect seemed to be a subconscious admission by John himself that he was being consumed by his burning dedication to the team and the organization.

The Roosters were playing the Paints in Richmond, and Deron Brown had the plate while Brian Jackson was on the bases. In the bottom of the fifth inning, with no outs and Steve Mitrovich on first, Kevin Cassidy hit a ground ball to Chris Dickerson at third base. Dickerson's throw pulled second baseman Mike Horning towards first base, but Jackson ruled that the Paints made the forceout on Mitrovich anyway. When Cate went out to argue that Horning had missed the bag, Jackson warned him, "Don't go to the base": meaning that Jackson was not going to permit Cate to show him up by demonstrating how far away from the bag he thought Horning was when he caught Dickerson's throw. Naturally, Cate made a bee line for the base, which prompted Jackson to eject him. Incensed now at the ejection *and* the call, Cate picked up the base and, wheeling around like a discus thrower, attempted to toss it across the infield. The base landed on end and tumbled over and over until it came to rest, much to Cate's surprise, only about five feet away from Jackson, who jumped out of the way.

"He tried to hit me!" said Jackson to his partner Deron Brown.

"I don't think so," said Brown. "It just slipped."

Jackson, who wasn't at all sure he bought Brown's conclusion, tried to reassert his authority over the Roosters' manager. "You call the groundskeeper and get him to come out here and put the base back where it belongs," he demanded of Cate.

"For your information," screamed Cate as he marched off the field, "I *am* the groundskeeper! ... I'm the president of this ballclub, the director of personnel and scouting, the manager, and the groundskeeper, and I'm not putting anything back! ... Fuck you!"

Woody Sorrell took over for Cate and actually ran the team Wednesday night. Since Cate didn't officially resign until after the game, the 9–6 loss went on his managerial record. Cate finished with a 28–35 slate for 2000, making his lifetime record with the Roosters 165–151.

After Wednesday's game Don Tincher and I visited Woody in the Richmond manager's office. I started by offering my congratulations. "You know, I don't look at it as a 'Congratulations!' type situation," Woody said. "This is just my turn to step up to try to help John. If he told me that my job was to shag balls behind the left field fence, I'd say okay." His explanation for Cate's resignation supported the conclusion I was coming to: that Cate had quit not because he didn't care about the Roosters but because he cared too much.

"Frankly, we all knew something was going to have to give. With John always worrying about front office matters, organizational details, budgetary problems, players moves, and on and on, there was just too much pressure on him. The other day somebody in the front office brought a check into the dugout for John to sign, right in the middle of the game. John has always taken too much on himself, and the stress of it finally caught up with him. John was so upset he couldn't even address the team today."

"John has his kids, then it's the Roosters. They are his baby," added Tincher.

"The losing really got to John too. I respect guys who take losing hard, but you can't take losing personally. You won't last in this job if you do, and getting beat is very personal to John," continued Woody.

What about the Roosters' financial situation and the poor crowds the team had been drawing? Did they have something to do with Cate's resignation?

"I think so," said Woody. "John would never say so in public, but I think he feels like the community has let him down."

Woody and I talked late into the night, and I discovered that there was a lot more to him than baseball. He told me he'd majored in history with a concentration in Southeast Asia and that he had read classic books about the Vietnam War, such as *The Best and the Brightest* and *The Making of a Quagmire.* He said he was currently taking a course on Hemingway and asked me to make him a list of the best baseball books, in case he would ever get the time to read them.

As usual, I was impressed with his knowledge of baseball. During his years as a college coach Woody had spent a lot of time talking to major league scouts, and he had become conversant in the language of the profession and very familiar with the scouting philosophies of different organizations, such as the New York Yankees. "A New York Yankees scout has to remember," he said, "'I'm scouting for the Yankees ... somebody who can play for the Yankees is not somebody who can play for anybody.' For instance, the Yankees won't draft a righthanded-hitting first baseman unless he's the best on the board. If he's a second round player, they won't draft him. You also never see the Yankees draft little outfielders. They have no interest in guys like Tom Goodwin or Willie Wilson. They know they never win by stealing a lot of bases in Yankee Stadium. They want big outfielders with power who have enough speed to cover center field. They also want switch-hitting catchers, left-handed hitters at the corners, and power pitchers. They draft with very specific needs in mind, and that's one of the reasons the Yankees are the best run organization in all of sports."

Being able to judge talent is a talent itself, one that is crucial for successful coaching and managing, and Woody seemed to have developed a keen eye for baseball ability. Earlier in the season a major league scout had asked Woody to write up reports on the six best players in the Frontier League after the Roosters had been around the league once. Woody had sent in reports on Chillicothe's Mike Cervenak and Matt Buirley, River City's Randy Eversgerd and Mike Robertson, London's Ian Harvey, and Richmond's Chad Sosebee; all six players had been signed by major league organizations.

Woody was no less perceptive, I thought, in assessing the talent level of the teams in the league and the probable outcome of the pennant race with the Frontier League season winding down. "Chillicothe and River City were the two most talented teams in the league at the start of the season," he said, "but they got hammered by affiliated ball. The talent around the league is very even now. Johnstown, London, and River City are just about locks to make the playoffs, so everybody else is fighting for the fourth playoff spot. We told our guys at the All-Star break that one team would pull away for that fourth spot, and it looks like it's going to be Evansville. Something happened to pull them together, because they're playing so much better now than they were before. Johnstown is going to win the whole thing, and the reason they'll have rings on their fingers is that they have made as few moves as possible. They've had the most continuity, the most cohesion, the most unity. There are 24 happy guys on that club, and everybody knows his role right down to their utility infielder. He knows he's not starting, but he knows that if somebody gets injured or if a pinch hitter is needed in a certain spot, he'll be the guy ... he knows there's not 14 guys on the team ahead of him or guys not even on the team that management is waiting to bring in. Johnstown is a group of happy guys, and you have to give their manager, Mike Moore, a lot of credit."

While I was at it, I asked for Woody's opinion of my two favorite umpires. "We all love Max," he said. "Even if I thought Max was having a bad night, I'd never do anything to show him up or let the crowd know I thought he was having an off night. As for Schaly, he has such great judgment, and he's such a frigging great umpire, but he has this attitude that 'I'm God.' Tonight he asked me, 'Was that pitch I rang Waguespack up on low?'

"'Yeah it was low,' I said.

"'Was it *real* low?'

"'Yeah.'

"'Oh, shit. I like that kid. I didn't want to hose him.'

"I was shocked when he said that because it's the first time I've ever heard Schaly admit he was wrong."

If the Roosters were going to climb over Chillicothe and Evansville to secure the fourth playoff spot, they had six full series left in which to get the job done. They concluded the series with River City and began the Woody Sorrell Era with the 13–3 win on Thursday night. The key to the victory was a bevy of extra-base hits: doubles by Jason Borghese and Todd DeGraffenreid; triples by Jason Guynn and Aaron Sledd; and home runs by Kevin Cassidy, Brian Brown, who'd been traded by the Rascals to the Roosters after Key Voshell was signed by the St. Louis Cardinals, and Aaron Sledd, who hit a pair of dingers. As Woody said after the game, "There's no substitute for extra-base hits with runners on base. None whatsoever. You get a run and a runner back in scoring position. Eight of your 11 hits are for extra-bases ... you can't lose!"

Sledd's second homer, which came in the fifth was really tagged and sailed way over the trees beyond the right field fence. "Wow! That was a moon shot, wasn't it," I said to Don Tincher in the press box.

"Yeah, but Morgan Burkhart used to hit one like that every other game," said Don.

After having walked three times the night before, Mike Zerbe went 0–3, partly because the hamstring, which he'd injured back in June, was still bothering him. After grounding out to third in the second inning, he came up limping. "Wheels really hurting?" asked Max.

"I'm on rims," said Mike.

Rich Jelovcic also had a lot to do with the victory. He had a one-hitter going into the eighth inning and was relieved only because he was hit in the hand by Darin Kinsolving's single back to the mound to lead off the inning. "I'm glad that Jelo's turn came up today," said Woody, "because he was able to redeem himself against the only team that's hit him hard all year. River City beat him to death at their place. It was so bad it might as well have been me out there pitching. What was the difference tonight? I don't know.

"I do know that he deserves another chance in affiliated ball. The Yankees didn't give him much of a chance. They thought his fastball didn't have enough movement, and they didn't like his mechanics. But Rich has good control; the number of walks he's given up is unbelievably low for a guy with his speed. And he's the kind of pitcher that gets better as the game goes along. You have to get to him early. If he gets in a groove and gets his confidence going, watch out!"

The play of the game came in the top of the sixth, involved Max, and resulted in the second ejection of the series. Even though the Rascals were trailing by six runs, center fielder Travis Dawson attempted to steal second. Roosters catcher Steve Mitrovich was as startled as anybody else to see Dawson running, and he hesitated for a second before uncorking his throw. Dawson thought he had the base stolen easily, but Max called him out. At the end of the inning, as Dawson jogged out to his position, he said to Rascals' shortstop, Kevin Lucas, "He said he tagged me on the helmet as I slid by. He can't see that with one eye."

Max, who was standing in the grass behind second, said, "Oh, yeah? Well, I hope you can see this with two eyes: You're outta the game!"

"I wasn't talking to you," protested Dawson.

"If I can hear it, you might as well have been," said Max.

"Well, I still say you can't see good enough with one eye."

When River City's pitching coach, Randy Martz, heard about Dawson's comments, he said, "That's fucking bullshit. Wait until I get him in the clubhouse."

"That's a pretty hot button to push right there," said Woody.

According to Schaly, "That's the same thing as calling a black guy 'nigger,' the same exact thing."

"It goes with the territory," said Max.

WELL SAID JIM!

12

Hitting the Jackpot in Evansville: Heartbreak in Springfield

ON AUGUST 11TH, MAX, Schaly, and I moved from Richmond back to Chillicothe for a weekend series between the Paints and the first-place Johnstown Johnnies. I knew it was just an illusion, but with about two weeks' worth of games left in the 2000 Frontier League season, time seemed to be speeding up. One thing I was sure of. When the season was over, it would seem as if the summer had flashed past my life like one of Jelovcic's or Kojack's fastballs. Knowing this, I made a conscious effort to savor every moment left in the dwindling season.

Max and Schaly weren't at all rueful about the season coming to a close. After all, it wasn't their first nor would it be their last summer in the league. Besides, they were way too busy and tired to worry about it. All week they'd been working doubleheaders in a big National Amateur Baseball Federation tournament in Dayton, in addition to a Frontier League game at night; which meant that they were umpiring 27 innings per day. "You should see our motel room," said Schaly before Friday night's game. "There's umpire clothes hanging everywhere. The maids won't come into the room to make the beds. They just throw in some fresh towels. Last night I went to Wal-Mart at two in the morning to buy laundry detergent so I could wash our clothes in the bath tub."

304

"I couldn't get all the soap out of my clothes," said Max, "so I was afraid that if I got caught in the rain, I'd start bubbling all over."

Schaly asked me rhetorically how many ways I'd seen a baseball game interrupted. "I've had games interrupted by rain, lightening, thunder, snow, hail, wind, animals, … and now I've got a new one: flooding," he said. This enumeration was prologue to a story, of course, and the story was about a NABF game Schaly and Max had umpired earlier in the day at the University of Dayton.

With seven outs to go in the game, one of the starting pitchers got yanked. In a fit of pique he kicked a little cooler next to the water fountain in the dugout. The cooler banged into and burst the water line running up to the fountain, so that a big geyser of water arched 30–40 feet into the air and onto the field. The shut off valve on the supply line to the fountain was broken, and for 45 minutes nobody could locate the main water source, which turned out to be in a dormitory on a hill above the diamond. By the time the water was shut off, the left side of the infield was completely flooded. "The kid's dad coaches at Florida Atlantic University, and I'm friends with him," said Schaly. "I called him up and said, 'The next time you send your kid up to Ohio, make sure he behaves himself and doesn't make a mockery of our great National Pastime.'"

I paid a visit to the Paints' clubhouse and got there at the tail end of their pre-game meeting. Marty Dunn's pep talk had apparently focused on the team's admirable resilience in the face of all the departures and injuries. "Nobody but the people in this room know how hard this season has been for us, and I'm really proud of the way so many of you guys have gone out there and played hurt, and I'm proud of the love you guys have shown each other all year long," he said. As customary, Marty ended the meeting with a prayer to "Our heavenly Father," which concluded: "… and we ask that you watch over us and keep us free from injury and give us the courage to never quit but to always do our best, and we ask these things in the name of our Lord, your son, Jesus Christ." Everyone in the room said, "Amen," except for Lamberg, who added his own affirmation: "Mazel tov!"

Up in the press box John Wend brought me up to date. The Paints were coming off a disastrous road trip during which they'd lost five straight: two in Evansville and three in Canton. The inability to win on the road was nothing new, as Chillicothe's home (23–9) and road (9–23) records were mirror images of each other. The Paints' bad luck with injuries had also continued. Coach Jamie Keefe, who'd been activated to replace Mike Cervenak at shortstop, was the latest victim. In Evansville

Jamie had broken his thumb while backhanding a ground ball. Chris Dickerson took over for Keefe at short, and Jamie resumed his third base coaching duties with a cast on his left hand.

As the Paints' starter, the slender Rick Blanc, threw the last of his warm-up pitches, I told Wend that I thought Chillicothe had a bunch of good guys on their team. "We really do," said John. "There's not one prick on the team. And Blanc ... he's a great kid. He's not even close to being a prick. He's always smiling ... heck, I've never even seen him have a bad day! He's really a reliever, not a starter, but he knows we don't have any choice, and he doesn't complain."

Blanc certainly didn't have a bad day on the mound, as he pitched a four-hitter over eight innings and bested Johnstown's ace, Matt Sheets, 2–1. There were major league scouts in the stands to watch Sheets, but he didn't want to sign until he had helped Johnstown will the Frontier League championship.

In the first inning with one out Greg Strickland took ball four but remained at the plate for an inordinate length of time, as if he were waiting for Max to tell him it was okay for him to trot down to first. After the game I asked Max if it had been a case of Greg being overly cautious because of their earlier run-in. "No," Max said, "he just forgot the count." In the fifth with a 3–0 count, Greg started to leave home plate, but Max called the fourth pitch to him a strike. The 3–1 pitch was definitely outside, and Greg didn't hesitate. He flipped his bat away and hustled down to first. A couple of pitches later Strickland stole second easily. At this point, with the game still 0–0, Phil Warren hit a groundball into the hole at short. When Eliott Sarabia uncorked his long throw to first, Strickland broke for third, and Max ran out from behind home plate to make the call as the first baseman's throw came back across the diamond. Although Strickland made it close, Max called him out. "I know it's not a good play," said John Wend, "but Strickland was trying to make something happen. He's gotten away with it a couple of times this year."

Conspicuous by his absence was Chief Crazy Horse. When I noticed this and asked John about it, he said that the Paints' mascot was at the county fair. A few minutes later a matronly woman stood at the press box window to also inquire after Chief Crazy Horse's whereabouts. John gave her a different answer, one which caused her face to turn red. "He had a prior commitment," he said. "He's out to stud."

The Paints got on the scoreboard first when the Johnnies' center fielder misplayed fly balls by Chris Dickerson and Justin Graham into back-to-back doubles in the sixth inning. Chillicothe got an insurance run in the eighth on a single by Graham and a triple by Matt McCay down the right field line. The insurance was needed because of a wacky ninth inning pitched by Nathan Gardner.

With one out and runners on the corners, catcher Charles Vanrobays hit a come-backer to the mound. Instead of going to second for the game-ending doubleplay, Gardner started running Matt Kuseski back to third. He made a low, errant throw which caught third baseman Chance Melvin off guard. Melvin retrieved the ball while Kuseski scored and then threw past Gardner covering third, so that by the time the Paints regained control of the situation, Johnstown had the tying run on third and the potential winning run on second. Fortunately for Gardner, who came into the game with a 2–8 record, he pitched out of his self-made jam. He ended the game with a pair of strikeouts, sandwiched around an intentional walk. After the game Gardner told Wend, "I have no f-ing idea what I was thinking." The next day he told me, "I saw the runner pretty far off third, and I just forgot the situation. It was a mental error." The irrepressible Blanc adopted an "all's well that ends well" perspective on the outcome. As he told the *Chillicothe Gazette's* Paul Warner: "That ninth inning was definitely nerve racking. I think I lost a couple years off of my life from watching it. But Nathan got the job done and we got the win. That's the bottom line."

We were already on our second round of beers when Paints players began coming into The Dock. Sean Boesch, the big rookie starting pitcher who kept his head shaved, walked right up to Max and put his arm around Max's shoulder. Boesch had heard about Max's recent ejection in Richmond and the reason for it. "I didn't even know until two weeks ago that you only have one eye. You and Schaly are the two best umpires in the league," he said, as he kissed Max on top of the head.

"What are you doing? Trying to get your next win!" said Max as we all laughed.

Boesch did in fact get his next win the following night, allowing just one run in seven innings, to run his record to 6–5, and he didn't need any help from Max. He got all the help he needed from his teammates and the Johnnies, who played like anything but a first-place team.

Johnstown started another good pitcher, Takuro Seki, who came into the game with an 8–4 record and 91 strikeouts, good for third in the league; but Takuro did not take his A game to the mound. He started his night by hitting Mike Horning and then turned Greg Strickland's grounder to first baseman Gabe Memmert into a hit when he failed to cover the bag. Three infield errors later, the Paints had a 4–0 lead. The four runs were achieved with only a single bona fide hit, a double by Justin Graham, and only two of the runs were earned. Seki gave up three more runs in the second, on a homer by Jason Baker; and after his own fielding error led to another unearned run in the fourth, his night was finished. The final score was 10–3, Paints.

It looked for a moment as if the brawl that Schaly had predicted for Richmond and River City would take place in Chillicothe. With one out in the fifth George Hlodan skipped a pitch off the top of Chance Melvin's batting helmet. One out later he beaned Mike Horning too. Exclamations of anger and impatience in accusatory tones emanated from both the stands and the Paints' dugout, but Aaron quelled the unrest a little by playing Elmer Fudd's voice over the P.A. "There's something squew-wey 'round here!" said Fudd. Calm was further induced by what seemed like a bit of poetic justice: Greg Strickland's two-run double over center fielder Mike Pilger's head, a shot that bounced off the center field wall. "Greg made him pay for those bean balls!" shouted a happy John Wend over the din of the celebrating crowd.

An inning later though we were again only a spark away from a con-flagration of tempers and testosterone. Johnstown pitchers committed their fourth HBP of the game when Hlodan plunked Jason Baker in the back. Baker, who'd hit the three-run homer in the second, was visibly upset and hung around the plate, as if he were using every ounce of his self-control not to charge the mound. Everybody in the Paints' dugout had stood up and was ready to follow Baker into battle, but Jason slowly cooled off and trotted down to first without abusing Hlodan or challeng-ing him or even looking in his direction. Hlodan had no idea how for-tunate he was that it was Baker whose poise had been tested.

It wasn't generally noticed by the fans, but another mini-drama unfolded during the game and centered around a scorer's decision. In the top of the sixth inning Mike Horning went into the 4–3 hole to stop a grounder hit by right fielder Kirk Taylor. Horning's off-balance throw beat Taylor to first but pulled Phil Warren off the bag, and Taylor was ruled safe by Max. Aaron said he was leaning towards ruling the play an error, and John agreed with him. Moments after Dick Whitney put the "E" on the scoreboard, I noticed that Jamie Keefe, sitting in a fold-ing chair outside the Paints' dugout next to Marty Dunn, was objecting strenuously to the ruling. With a disgusted look on his face, Jamie was staring in our direction and had his arms spread wide in a gesture meant to say, "Are you kidding me?"

Bryan Wickline, visiting the press box, said, "He's losing it."

When I asked why Jamie was so bothered by the decision, Bryan said, "That's his boy. ... He's that way with Horning and Chance."

When I glanced back down towards Keefe, I saw him clearly mouth a directive towards the press box: "Change it!"

And that's what Aaron did. The error came off the scoreboard, and Taylor was credited with a hit. "I don't mind the questioning," said John, "but I do mind the attitude."

After the game a still somewhat agitated Keefe suddenly appeared in the righthand entrance to the press box. "You give an error when a guy doesn't make a routine play," he said. "Not when a guy runs his ass off just to get to a ball and then makes a bad throw that's meaningless in a 10–1 game. That's not an error. … It's about the definition of what is and is not an error, and that's all I've got to say." Aaron and John didn't say a word either during or after Keefe's visit.

I skipped Sunday's getaway game (for both teams) and so was spared the disappointment of watching the Paints fail to complete the sweep against Johnstown.

Although Max was not going to be there, Richmond was at home from the 15th through the 17th for three with the Springfield Capitals, and I drove over by my lonesome for the middle game of the Roosters' next-to-last home series of the year.

Having won their final two games in Canton and the opener against Springfield, the Roosters came into the game Wednesday night sporting a modest three-game winning streak. Since I'd last been with the team, Ryan Peavey had gotten hot and worked himself into the starting lineup. He'd gone 3–4 the night before and was batting .500 (11–22) over Richmond's last ten games. Newcomer Chris Lotterhos had also taken over at second base for Brian Brown. Lotterhos, who'd played at Mississippi State University for Pat McMahon, an old high school classmate and teammate of mine, lived in the same neighborhood in Germantown, Tennessee, as his buddy Aaron Sledd, and was quite a character. At Mississippi State Lotterhos had to take a ceramics class, and he made the best of it by making a spittoon for his course project. Right before he left Starkville, he buried his baseball glove at second base on Dudy Noble Field, along with a bull riding glove that he'd kept in his back pocket in honor of his hero, rodeo star Lane Frost. "I think it was cool that he died doing what he loved to do," Chris said of the man whose life the movie *Eight Seconds* was based on. Lotterhos also told me that he was an inventor. One of his inventions concerned hunting, another baseball, but he couldn't tell me anything more than that. "My lawyer says that I can't tell anybody what the inventions are until we get patents on them," he said.

Retiree Ray James was exactly the kind of fan that Richmond needed. He rooted for the Roosters to win, of course, but he attended every home game, not in the expectation that they would win, but simply because he loved baseball and the players. He had been attending the Reds' Dream Week fantasy camp for years and had become so friendly with some of Cincinnati's old players that Roy McMillan had given him a very special memento: McMillan's gold ring that commemorated the 1956

Reds having tied the National League record for home runs in a season, with 221. Earlier in the afternoon Ray had handed Mike Zerbe a store bought Larry Walker model bat and said, "Use this. It's got three hits in it tonight."

"Okay, I'll give it a shot," said Zerbe. "Ray, you're either going to be a prophet or a crazy old man."

"I can't lose," said James. "I win either way."

Jan Clark went on the radio with Gary Kitchel, and as Phill Kojack struck out the side in the top of the first, they discussed who might come back for the 2001 season. "What about John Cate?" asked Clark.

"No, I think he's retired," said Gary.

In the bottom of the first Chris Lotterhos hit a foul ball down the right field line that totally sawed off his bat at the handle, causing Jan to wonder if the handle would be included in the Roosters' upcoming broken bat give-away promotion. "You used to beg the players for broken bats at Reds' games when you were a kid, didn't you?" asked Kitchel teasingly.

"Yes, I did, Gary," answered Jan.

"And did you ever get one?"

"Yes, I did. I got one from Pete Whisenant. Actually, he was a coach. I looked into the dugout and saw that Whisenant had a bat in his hands. When the Reds made a bad play, he slammed it down and broke it, and that's the bat I got."

As Phill Kojack racked up strikeout after strikeout, his teammates pounded out 14 hits, which were good for eight runs. Mike Zerbe came close to making Ray James a prophet. He did get two hits, doubles in the second and the sixth, and he hit the ball hard a third time in flying out deep to center field in the fourth. Lotterhos and DeGraffenreid hit triples, Peavey homered, and Aaron Sledd knocked in his 100th run as a Rooster in the first inning; making him only the fourth player in Roosters' history to reach the century mark. The most memorable hit of the game though came in the sixth off the bat of Keith Fout. Although Keith had made the All-Star team, he had been losing his grip on the starting catching job ever since Steve Mitrovich joined the team. Mitro was a big, muscular guy who hit for power and for average, and his presence made Fout face the fact that he didn't have much of a future as a professional baseball player when he wasn't even the best catcher on his own team. He decided that it was time for him to hang up his spikes, but he wanted to go out in style. Fout, who came into the game with one homer on the season, decided he would quit immediately after he hit his next home run. That homer came in the sixth inning off reliever Matt Beck with Mike Zerbe on second base. After Fout rounded the bases, he slapped Zerbe's hand at home plate and kept right on running, off the field, through the gate by the dugout, and into the Richmond locker room and retirement. Mitrovich was forced to finish the game for his former caddy.

After Fout's swan song home run which put the Roosters ahead 7–2, I walked out to the beer garden beyond the third base dugout to talk to Tom Arnett, who'd become even more of a celebrity there for having coached first base for the Roosters the night before.

It was Woody Sorrell's idea to suit up civilians and have them coach first base. The coaching ranks had been thinned out—that was true—by Cate's retirement and the departure of Brad Finken, who returned to Olivet (Michigan) College where he worked as an assistant football and baseball coach. But Woody really saw his call for help as a great public relations move. His philosophy was "They're all good fans if they're at the ballpark," and he continually urged his players to always thank the fans for coming to the Roosters' games.

Although getting to dress in a Roosters uniform and actually participate in the game was supposed to be its own reward, that hadn't stopped Tom Arnett from trying to milk the opportunity for something extra when Woody called him on Monday, a league-wide off day.

"Tom, would you be interested in coaching first base for us tomorrow night?" asked Woody.

"Yes, I would," said Tom. "And I'm available for the right price."

"What's that mean?"

"You need to cover my lost time from work and pay me at least the minimum wage."

"I can't pay you, Tom."

"Okay. I want a jersey then."

"I can't do that either."

"A hat? You gotta at least give me a hat."

"Okay. I think I can swing a free cap," said Woody. "But you have to promise me you'll be on time (4:00) and not show up drunk or drink beer during the game."

"Don't worry, Woody. I give you my word: I'll be professional," said Tom.

Tom's professional coaching debut had turned out to be interesting, to say the least. In Tuesday's opener Freddy Flores led off the bottom of the first for Richmond with a single. When he came back to first after rounding the bag, Tom said, "Freddy, please don't do anything to embarrass me."

"I love you way too much to do that to you, man," said Freddy, who was promptly picked off by Capitals' pitcher Tony Harden.

Flores reached base again in the sixth on an error by the shortstop. When reliever Mike Riveles heaved a wild pitch, Freddy took off for second, decided he could make third too, and was thrown out by catcher Aaron Voldness. Out number two on the bases. Freddy didn't even make it all the way to third, as his slide came up about a foot short of the bag.

Freddy completed his unusual hat trick the very next inning. He singled to left for his third hit of the game but rounded first too aggressively, got too far away from the base and his rookie first base coach, and was thrown out by the left fielder before he could get back to the bag! Although Freddy and Tom both felt like crawling back into the dugout, their recklessness didn't doom the Roosters, who won the game handily, 12–6.

I wasn't surprised that Tom's partner in crime, or at least his partner in "criminal base-running," had turned out to be Flores. I'd learned that if you kept your eyes on him, you'd see Freddy often doing things out of the ordinary. Before Wednesday's game I had seen Freddy, the women's fastpitch softball coach, playing catch on the right field foul line, using a windmill motion and an underhanded release as if he were a fastpitch softball pitcher warming up. And then, after he struck out in the sixth inning for the second time in the game, he played with his bat all the way back to the dugout like a drum majorette his baton. He windmilled the bat around and around and around, as if he were going to throw it as far as he could, but he held onto it, dropped it over his right shoulder, and pulled it between his legs. He passed it around his waist, again and again, flipped the bat into the air, caught it by the barrel, tossed it to the ground handle first, and then caught it niftily, by the handle again, on the rebound. Freddy's bat fandango was a very cool demonstration of a ballplayer keeping his cool. "It's my stress reliever," Freddy told me later. "I wanted to throw the bat and my helmet so bad ... by the time I got to the dugout I had blown off enough steam."

In the top of the seventh with one out Capitals second baseman Billy Bone hit a two-run homer to make the score 7–4. As Kojack shut down the Springfield rally by striking out the next two hitters, his 12th and 13th victims of the evening, I asked Tom if he'd learned anything from his coaching experience the night before. "Next time I'll be more active," he said. "The only disappointing thing about it ... and I'm grateful on the one hand ... is that nobody pulled a practical joke on me."

That wasn't entirely true in that the Roosters did in a sense pull one on Tom, as I learned when he continued. "Around the fourth inning," he said, "one of the guys in the bullpen said, 'I'll give you $10 if you can get Schaly's shoes dirty.'

"'Fuck the $10. I'll do that for nothing. That's a challenge,' I said. When Schaly came over towards first base, I got him talking about high school sports. With one foot I dug up some dirt, and with the other one I spread the dirt on one of Schaly's shoes. Then I did his other shoe. I would have gone for a mountain if I could have done it. When Schaly noticed what I was doing, he said, 'You asshole! Don't ever do this again' and he started wiping his shoes off on the backs of his pants. The guys in the bullpen were busting up laughing. I told Schaly I was sorry, but then I tried it again in the eighth inning. The second time I couldn't get much of a mound built up. If I'd had spikes—I had on turf shoes—I could have really done a number on him. This time Schaly tried to wipe his shoes off on my pants, and it looked like he was trying to trip me."

The Roosters got a run back in the bottom of the seventh to make it 8–4, so I figured that the only suspense left in the game revolved around Phill Kojack: would he be able to go all the way? and how many strikeouts would he finish with?

I figured wrong. The Capitals never gave up, and although Kojack struck out 16 of them to tie the Roosters' record (set in 1997 by Jeff Montfort), they loaded the bases on him in the ninth and with two outs brought the tying run, in the person of Greg Schelhaas, to the plate. Kojack had fanned Schelhaas four times already, so even though he was Springfield's best hitter, Capitals' manager Don Herron was not inclined to try the Schelhaas–Kojack matchup a fifth time. He pinch hit Jesse Smith for Schelhaas, causing Woody Sorrell to counter by calling to the bullpen for closer Bobby Chandler. As Kojack walked off the diamond, he got an appreciative hand from the crowd of 1,001 and congratulations from everybody in the Roosters' dugout. The drama didn't last long. Chandler fired a strike to Smith and then, on the next pitch, popped him up to second for the ballgame. The save was Chandler's 11th, good for second in the league; the win, Kojack's fifth against nine losses.

After the game I hung around the Richmond clubhouse for a while before heading home. Without Max, the trip to The Wheel was neither obligatory nor would it have been as much fun as usual. I noticed that Woody was trying to make John Cate's office feel just a little bit like his own. Sitting on John's old desk was one of Woody's most prized possessions: a spittoon attached to a home plate. "It's pretty nasty, isn't it?" he said. "I get Big John to hose it out for me when we go on road trips. ... I really need to quit chewing. I just started ... 21 years ago."

Woody picked up a baseball, walked into the clubhouse, and tossed it to Aaron Sledd, naked except for a towel around his waist. Without his shirt on, the "cut" Sledd looked like a body builder. "It's not the one you got your 100th RBI on, but it is from the game," said Woody.

"It'll do," said Aaron. "Thanks."

Kojack had one big ice pack taped to his right shoulder and another taped to his elbow. When I congratulated him on the game, he said, "Thanks. After eight consecutive below-average starts, it felt great to be pitching in the dark. In the seventh inning I thought, 'Geez, I'm still out here pitching! Alright!' " Did he know he had a shot at the strike-out record? "You know, I thought I only had about 12 after the eighth inning, but I found out I had 14. That's when I realized I had a shot at the record. It would have been nice to break the record, but I'm happy even to tie it."

I told him that from the beer garden it looked like his curveball had been really fooling the hitters. "No, it was my changeup. I got 11 of the strikeouts with it. It was the nastiest pitch I've ever thrown."

Phill noticed me taking notes as always and said, "Be sure to put in there that I thank the Lord for tonight, that I thank him for everything good I've ever been able to do."

"It'll be my pleasure," I said.

"Applebee's sure is going to taste good tonight!" he said.

My chances to visit every city and ballpark in the league, as I'd hoped to do from the beginning of the season, were running out fast. I decided to hit Evansville on Sunday, the 20th, and then to shoot over (and up) to Springfield the next day. That would leave Johnstown and London as the only league entries I hadn't gotten to, and I was beginning to think that the season would run out before I set foot in either city.

On Friday, the 18th, Max and Schaly started a series in Canton, and since I hadn't watched Max umpire since the 12th in Chillicothe, I made the four and a half hour drive up to Canton to catch Saturday night's game between the Crocodiles and the Dragons. By the time I got inside the ballpark, Dubois County was batting in the top of the second. I watched the rest of the half inning while standing behind the first base dugout at the edge of the wide aisle that separated the lower and the upper decks. After Adam Patterson popped up to third to end the inning, Max took off his mask, turned, and looked up into the stands directly at me, as if he had felt my presence. He tipped his cap, and I waved back at him.

There was a good crowd of 1,311 on hand that was boosted by one of GM Alfredo Portelo's new promotions, Starke County High School Football Weekend. Football players from eight local high schools were sitting in clusters all around Thurman Munson Memorial Stadium. Football is king in Canton, and the rivalry between Canton McKinley and Massillon is one of the most storied in the nation. The Canton McKin-ley–Massillon game is traditionally the last game of the season for the two teams and routinely draws a crowd of 20,000. Alfredo's promotion, which let players wearing their high school football jerseys into the game free, was a shrewd attempt to tap into the sports fan fervor, represented by the McKinley–Massillon game, which independent minor league baseball teams can usually only dream about inspiring.

There was also a buzz around the ballpark about another of Alfredo's brainstorms, a promotion being billed as Super Sunday that was scheduled for August 27. On Super Sunday, Travis Copley was going to play all nine positions during the game; some lucky fans were going to be allowed to take some BP on the field after the game; and, as the main attraction, "Super Joe" Charboneau was going to be activated as a player and get an official at bat against the London Werewolves. As Alfredo told me after the game, the promotion would mark Joe's fourth decade in pro ball as a player; his third decade having come with his participation in the ill-fated Senior Professional Baseball Association. Joe had hit a home run in his final at bat in the Senior League, as it was commonly known; and the sizzle Alfredo was selling for Super Sunday was the $25,000 that one fan would win if Joe managed to hit another home run. Odds are that Charboneau wouldn't homer, but even if he did, the Crocodiles wouldn't have to fork over the money. For a fraction of the $25,000 prize, Alfredo had bought an insurance policy that would pay off if Joe were able to go yard.

Charboneau continued to intrigue and delight me. When I asked Alfredo why Joe had been retained when Dan Massarelli had been fired, he said, "I wanted to keep Joe because of the way he works with the kids. He's hard-working, patient, and professional. Plus, he has a major league air about him that permeates the clubhouse. Joe's such a great guy and a wonderful person that it's beneficial just to have him around the team."

Alfredo could have also mentioned the fact that Charboneau had a knack for keeping everybody loose and the conversation light, if not downright comical. And Joe was the perfect sounding board for good-natured ragging. Everybody felt free to kid Joe, and Joe either gave back as good as he got or deflected the barbs with self-deprecation that made people laugh without ever losing respect for him. In the coaches' office after the game, manager Jeff Isom told us that CBS Sportsline had a story about Joe on the Internet. "It says that Joe's high salary was $38,000," said Isom. "It also says that he was the 'Dennis Rodman of his day.'"

"Where you married to Carmen Electra?" asked Alfredo.

"I was married to her mother," said Joe.

"I'm calling Cindy," said Alfredo.

"Hey, did you know his jock sold for $13,000?" Isom asked Alfredo.

"Joe, you ought to be a rich man if you can sell one of your old jock straps for thirteen grand!" said Alfredo.

"No, no, that's the other Joe Charboneau who's rich," said Joe.

"The 'other Joe Charboneau?'" we all asked.

"Yeah. He's a professional motivational speaker," said Joe. "People ask him all the time about his baseball career, and he says, 'I never played the game.' He's makes a million dollars a year. He doesn't want to be me."

At this point a fifty-ish looking gentleman named Gary Combs who was dressed in a Crocs uniform walked into the room. He was a finish carpenter who'd won Alfredo's 25th Man Contest. He'd gotten to take a few cuts and shag balls during BP and coach first base for an inning or two. When I asked him why he attended Crocodiles' games, he said, "My wife and I go to games all over. We're fans, not fanatics."

I think he was trying to say that he and his wife were fans of baseball in general rather than of any one team in particular, but Charboneau picked up on something else.

"That's an oxymoron," he said. "'Fans' comes from 'fanatics.' Next you'll be telling me about jumbo shrimp. That's a faux paus, at least. Right, Purdue?" Charboneau was referring to Isom, a Boilermaker fan who had been trying to talk Joe into going to the Purdue-Michigan football game with him.

"Joe, where do you come up with this stuff?" Isom said. "You learned something in school, I guess. ... How long did it take you to graduate?"

"Only six years," said Joe.

Canton was still mired in last place in the East Division, but the team had started playing better baseball, under Isom, who had pitched in the Padres' and Pirates' organizations before going into coaching. What accounted for the turn around? "I let them be themselves," Jeff said. "We let them go. If you start telling guys how to play, you take away their game. They bought into what I was doing and started hustling more than what they had been doing the first four or five days I was here. I also try to keep everything professional, so that if they get signed into affiliated ball they won't be in awe. We want them to succeed right away when they get their chance, so we keep it as professional as possible and insist that they play the game the way it's supposed to be played."

Catcher Shaun Argento, a good ballplayer whose 20-game hitting streak had just ended, stuck his head into the room. He was wearing a flapless Atlanta Braves helmet, which he pointed to. "Okay to wear tomorrow?" he asked Isom.

"I don't think so," replied his manager. "Save it for a Braves' game." After Argento left, Isom said, "See what I mean about 'professionalism?'"

Isom had managed in the league before, and even though I had been convinced long ago of Morgan Burkhart's greatness as a Frontier Leaguer, I thought it would be worthwhile to get Jeff's take on the former Roosters slugger. "I didn't have any answers when it came to Morgan Burkhart," he said. "I told my pitchers, 'You're on your own with this guy.' He hit everything ... fastball in, fastball out, curveball low and away, high curve ball ... it didn't matter. And he was just as good from both sides of the plate. He was the Babe Ruth of the Frontier League. Talk to anyone in the league: they've seen him hit at least one home run."

Saturday night's game took almost three hours, but it seemed to fly by, mostly because of the good pitching turned in by starters Dennis Bair and Jamal Gaines. Bair gave up three runs in 6.2 innings, while Jamal shut out Canton on two hits for seven full innings. Dubois County's 3–0 lead looked pretty big going into the bottom of the eighth, considering the way Gaines had been pitching, but Jamal's masterpiece-in-the-making crumbled faster than a sandcastle at high tide. Billy Colome led off with a walk and reached second when second baseman Dennis Pelfrey booted J. D. Coy's potential doubleplay ground ball. After Schuyler Doakes moved the runners up with a sacrifice, Gaines induced Argento to hit a fly ball to right that was too shallow for Colome to tag up on. Even though there were now two outs, I thought the Dragons were playing with fire by not going to their bullpen for a fresh arm. Perhaps because his bullpen had pitched five innings the night before, Fran Riordan did not make any move, which surprised me. I was even more surprised that he left Gaines in after the ever-dangerous Travis Copley singled to right to bring in Colome and send Coy to third. DH Curtis Sapp then doubled over left fielder Dan Horgan's head, and just that quickly the game was tied. All three runs allowed by Gaines were unearned.

At this point Riordan finally brought in Kris Draper, who immediately gave up a single to Gerald Butt to put the Crocodiles up 4–3. Draper loaded the bases on walks but prevented any further damage by grounding out Colome, who'd led off the inning. It didn't really matter, as the Dragons went out 1-2-3 in the top of the ninth with Drew Thomas picking up his league-leading 13th save. Canton's 4–3 comeback win avenged the Dragons' comeback the night before, a game the Crocodiles had led 7–0 before losing 9–8.

I didn't want to conduct, and thankfully I didn't need, a big interview with Jamal Gaines after the game; but I did want to say hello and offer my congratulations on a job well done in the hope that they might make him feel a little better. Jamal remembered me, and he did manage

WHAT KIND OF FUCKN SHOES
MAX "PLIMPTON" GOT ON?

Coy called out at home.

LOOK THOSE PLATE SHOES,
MAX!

a little smile when he saw me. As much as I liked Jamal's pitching, I admired even more his refusal to complain or play the blame game. All he said was "Things happen ... that's all I can say. I'm stunned, and it's disappointing, but all I can control is my pitching."

When I suggested that Dubois County player-manager Fran Riordan might be laboring under a divided focus, Schaly and Max agreed with me. "He should have relieved him sooner," Jim said. "Not only that, he ought to let Marple manage. He's hurt. Marple told him to make the switch."

"He should have relieved him in the seventh inning," said Max, who'd had the best view of Gaines' pitches, besides Dragons catcher Adam Patterson. "For the first six innings he was in a rhythm. He was getting the ball and throwing it, getting the ball and throwing it. Then in the seventh he started backing off the mound between every other pitch. He started thinking too much."

"Yeah. It was a tough one to lose," said Schaly, "but they're all the same to me. ... Although a 3–0 game would have been faster."

Even before Max and Jim got ready to step into the shower, I told them I needed to get on the road so I could get home and get some rest before I got up and headed to Evansville the next day. They had assumed that I'd come up to Canton for two games, and they were surprised that I would not be staying over for Sunday afternoon's game. As they bade me farewell and reminded me to drive carefully, I saw in their faces something that made the drive home a little easier: a recognition that I was willing to sac it up and slog through some late-night, weary-ass driving to get the job done, just as they were.

Tucked against the finger of the Ohio River that sticks up in the Southwestern corner of Indiana, Evansville is what you call a destination city. Since Evansville is a good ten miles south of I-64, the interstate that stretches across the toes of the state, nobody ever passes through the city on the way to someplace else. You have to be going to Evansville to get there.

When Frontier League teams first started going to Evansville in 1995, Evansville was the largest market (250,000) in the league. The nickname of "Otters" was a nod towards Evansville's identity as a river city and a definite upgrade on "River Rats," the moniker of Evansville's professional baseball teams which formerly played in the Class B Three-I (Illinois-Iowa-Indiana) and Class D Central Leagues in the early twentieth century. Evansville's long history in minor league baseball peaked with the Triplets, a Triple-A franchise which was a member of the American Association from 1970 until the team folded after the 1984 season. Strangely, pro baseball in the city then underwent not a downsizing but extinction, for exactly a decade. Helping resuscitate professional baseball in Evansville and then bringing Evansville into the fold was a major coup for Commissioner Bill Lee, as the Otters led the Frontier League in attendance every year for four straight years until newcomer River City took away their crown in 1999.

Besides the city's population and professional baseball heritage, what made Evansville a minor league cherry waiting to be picked was its ballpark, historic Bosse Field; a pretty brick structure with a grand dual-winged entrance, highlighted by fluted brickwork, recessed windows, and art deco-ish ornamentation. Named after Mayor Benjamin Bosse, the ballpark was built in 1915, in the era of the first concrete and steel ballyards, and today it is older than every major league stadium still in use except for Fenway Park and Wrigley Field. The cost to build Bosse Field was either $40,000 or $60,000—both figures are cited in the Otters' yearbook—but at either price, the citizens of Evansville got a bargain. Bosse Field looks its age—so much so that much of *A League of Their Own* was filmed there—but it has grown old so gracefully that it still functions superbly as a great place to watch a ballgame.

By the time I got to Bosse Field on Sunday for the rubber match of

IS THAT A NEW ERA CAP.

Max tries to calm down the Evansville Otters' pitching coach at Chillicothe, while Jim Schaly looks on.

the series between Evansville and Richmond, it was late afternoon and the sun had already begun to sink behind the grandstands, creating a natural theatre for the fans. The diamond, the stage upon which the play would unfold, was brightly lit, while the fans from foul line to foul line sat in complete and welcome shade.

Before either team took infield, I hopped over the low railing onto the field and joined the Roosters, most of whom were standing around idly outside the dugout or sitting on the top step of the dugout with their backs to the diamond. "Hi, guys," I said. "What's new?"

"Jelo won $245,000 at the casino Friday night," somebody said.
"Yeah, sure," I said. For a moment I was little irritated at the smart-alecky reply to my friendly greeting, but when nobody started guffawing or attempting to embellish the fish story, I reconsidered. Woody Sorrell and Mike Zerbe were standing nearby, so I looked towards them for confirmation. "Really?"

They both nodded their heads. "Yeah, he really did," said Woody. "It's been in the newspaper and everything."

"Did he quit the team the next day?" I joked. Looking around, I didn't see Jelovcic anywhere.

"No. And as a matter of fact, he didn't even celebrate much," said Woody. "Some of the guys on the team wanted him to go out and get drunk, but he only had one beer and then he went to bed because he knew he was pitching the next day. We lost the game 3–2 in extra innings, but it wasn't Rich's fault. He went nine innings, didn't give up an earned run, and wound up with a no decision. But he pitched his heart out, and I was really proud of him."

About half way through Sunday's game I learned that Rich's father, Silvio Jelovcic, had flown into Evansville from New York in order to pick up his son's big fat check … for $164,000, which is what was left after taxes were taken out and Rich tipped the dealer $5,000. I found Rich and his dad sitting directly behind home plate, where Rich was timing Phill Kojack's pitches with a radar gun. Kojack was pitching well again. Through the first six innings he gave up only one run and struck out eight. Rich had on khaki shorts, a T-shirt, and his Roosters cap, turned backwards à la Ken Griffey, Jr.; and around his neck he wore a single gold chain … for the time being. From this vantage point, I noticed that the dugouts were extremely close to home plate—something the umpires dearly loved, I was sure—and that the oval shape of the ballpark created lots of foul territory behind first and third bases—something the pitchers did truly love. I also noticed the pitchers in both bullpens sitting, like renegade bleacherites, on platforms built above the billboard fence, that otherwise would have obstructed their view of the game.

Having never set foot in a casino, I was very curious as to exactly how Jelovcic could have won so much money. According to Rich, he hit the jackpot playing Caribbean stud poker; a game which does not permit the discard of unwanted cards in favor of new, hopefully better, cards. In Caribbean poker you play the five cards you are dealt. The dealer at the riverboat Casino Aztar dealt Jelo a royal flush, in hearts. "It costs $10 a hand to play the game," said Rich, "and I was already up a couple of hundred. After I got my first four cards on the next hand and I saw I had a royal flush going, I gave J. T. Engstrom a thumbs up sign. Then when I got the card I needed to finish it, all hell broke loose. It took about an hour to verify everything—they examined the deck and reviewed the video tape—and then they gave me the check. They said there is a one in 650,000 chance of drawing a royal flush."

When I asked Rich what he was planning to do with the money, he said he was going to invest most of it and then forget about it. But first he was going to buy his dream car, a silver M3 model BMW, with the vanity plates RYLFLSH.

Silvio Jelovcic turned out to be an old-school immigrant, the kind who used to be praised for working hard, for assimilating himself and his family into American culture, and, as politically incorrect as it is nowadays to suggest that anybody should be, for being grateful to be a citizen of this country. But Silvio, who'd come to America in 1967 from Croatia, was grateful. "This is a great country, full of opportunity," he said. "I kiss the ground when I come here! Why should I ever leave?"

A city bus driver in Queens, Silvio had worked hard for so long that he was contemplating retirement in January when "our new contract comes up." And, in a story which could be repeated in countless other families, it was through his sons that Mr. and Mrs. Jelovcic adopted as their own the game of baseball, which helped make them feel truly American. "I never knew what baseball was until my oldest sons started playing it," said Mr. Jelovcic. "They played until they were about 15 or 16."

"I'm the one with talent," interjected Rich with a big grin.

"But now, I'm a fanatic about baseball," said Silvio. "And Rich's mother, Maria, she's an even bigger fanatic. She follows the Mets. I used to root for the Yankees, but not so much anymore since they released Rich. You know, Rich loves Richmond, but it's too far from home. My wife, she wishes Rich would play in the Atlantic League. Long Island has a team in that league, the Ducks, and they've drawn 250,000 people the first year. Rich's mother would be at all his games, but the Frontier League is too far to drive."

The Roosters had taken a 2–0 lead in the fourth, the first run driven in by Mike Zerbe's double, but Evansville got one back in the sixth. Brandon Mattingly, no relation to Don Mattingly, the native Evansville hero, led off the bottom of the seventh with a double and tied the game, after a sacrifice bunt, when Otters second baseman John Anderson singled him home. "Phill's losing a little off his fastball," said Jelo, looking up from the radar gun. "He's down to 85–86." Kojack came back to whiff Jose Colon for his ninth strikeout, but Woody Sorrell then went to the bullpen. After walking Dustin Delucchi, Alejandro Bracho K'd Andrew Clements to end the inning and ensure that Kojack would get a no decision and not, possibly, a loss.

When I thought about it, I realized that there were any number of ways that Jelovcic could have gotten his windfall back to New York safely. It really wasn't necessary for his dad to serve as a courier. No, Mr. Jelovcic was in Evansville primarily to celebrate his son's good fortune with him because that's what fathers and sons who are best friends do. "Mr. Jelovcic, I'm curious … who paid for your flight from New York?" I asked.

"You know who," he said, smiling impishly. "Who's richer?"

"When I called home that night it was 1:00 A.M. here, 2:00 A.M. in New York," explained Rich. "My mom answered the phone, and she didn't believe me. She said, 'Rich, have you been drinking?'

"I said, 'Well, yeah, but just one beer, and I am telling you the truth.' She still didn't know whether to believe me or not, so she said, 'Talk to your father when he gets home.'"

"I told her I wanted Dad to book the first flight down here at my expense, and about an hour later my dad called my room. He was really excited and practically shouted, 'Is it true!'

"I said, 'Yeah, calm down. I wouldn't be flying you down here if it wasn't true.'

"That's what I told my wife," said Silvio. "'It can't be a joke … He's never done that before.'"

"Well, Mr. Jelovcic, I'm assuming that Rich will never gamble again," I said. "If it were me, I'd feel as if I'd already used up several lifetime's worth of good luck!"

"Oh, no. We went back to the casino last night—Rich wanted me to see the place—and he played the slot machines," said Silvio.

"Are you kidding me! How you'd do?" I asked Jelovcic.

"I won $1,200," he said.

With the game getting to the point where one pitch could win it or lose it, we quit talking about Rich Jelovcic's lucky streak and focused on the struggle going on before us. Evansville's starter, Cliff Brand, had pitched just as well as Kojack, and in fact he made it through the eighth inning … but just barely. Todd DeGraffenreid led off and hit a shot that Andrew Clements speared up against the left field wall. After Steve Mitrovich walked, Mike Zerbe hit a bomb into dead center. It looked like extra bases for sure, but somehow center fielder Jose Colon caught up with the ball and hauled it in on the warning track, a few feet shy of the center field wall, 415 feet away from home plate. Mitrovich, who'd already passed second, had to retrace his steps and appeared to slide into first safely ahead of the relay. Base umpire Miles Mann didn't see it that way and called Mitro out for an inning-ending double play. This angered Mitrovich, who became incensed when Mann thumbed him out of the game almost as soon as he opened his mouth to complain. Fortunately, Zerbe and first base coach Steve Carver were there to restrain the big catcher and usher him off the field. With Mitrovich disqualified, it suddenly occurred to me to ask, "Who's going to catch now?"

"Keith," said Jelovcic. "Woody talked him into finishing out the season."

"Oh, I see. I guess if he hits another home run, he can always retire again," I joked.

Keith Fout did bat in the game, without homering or retiring, and the Roosters pulled out an extra-inning squeaker, 3–2. Jeff Blitstein pitched two strong innings in relief of Cliff Brand, but Richmond still manufactured the winning run off him in the top of the tenth on a single by Flores, a sacrifice by Borghese, and an error on a Waguespack grounder up the middle. Mr. Dependable, Bobby Chandler, who held Evansville scoreless in the ninth and tenth innings, picked up the win, his third of the year against two defeats. The Roosters had a long bus ride ahead of them—the 594 mile trip between Evansville and London was the third longest in the league—but they left town on a roll, having won eight of their last ten. It wasn't over for them yet, but to catch Evansville, ahead of them by two and half games with nine left to play, they almost needed to run the table.

For my money, the only thing that can compete with a visit to an old ballpark for the first time is an initial visit to a used book store with a good selection of baseball books. If you're a baseball book lover and collector like I am, the excitement offered by the latter can actually be superior to that offered by the former.

Serious bibliophiles don't so much shop as they try to raid the antiquarian book shops they patronize. Like the Blues Brothers, they scour the shelves as if they're "on a mission from God," looking for great books or rare books or simply oddball books in their field of interest that are, they hope, ridiculously underpriced. Collectors arrive at a old book shop they've never visited before with hearts pounding and palms sweating, their adrenaline flowing in anticipation of the thrill of the hunt. They are also nervous that another customer is about to pull off the shelf the very book in all the place they want most, and they're paranoid that if they show too much excitement, or any excitement at all really, at making what collectors call "a find," the shop proprietor will suddenly jack up the price of the book, or worse, refuse to sell it at all! You probably have to be stricken with the disease that author Nicholas A. Basbanes has called "a gentle madness" to understand the feeling of euphoria and sense of accomplishment that a collector gets when he walks out of a used book store with some new additions to his collection.

Whenever I have the time, I try to visit used book stores when I travel. Much to my delight, I discovered that Springfield, Illinois, home of the Springfield Capitals Frontier League team, offers something that is becoming increasingly rare in America: a well-stocked used book store in an easy-to-find downtown location. In that sense, Prairie Archives Booksellers, located conveniently on East Adams, across the street from the Old State Capitol in the heart of historic downtown Springfield, is a civic treasure, as worthy of boasting about as a minor league baseball team.

Abraham Lincoln spent most of his adult life living and lawyering in Springfield, and the city rightfully capitalizes on that heritage by preserving numerous sites associated with Lincoln as tourist attractions. Prairie Archives is also keenly aware of the importance of Lincoln, as the three tall book cases full of Lincoln books near the front door proved. Unfortunately, while the shop had a good number of baseball titles on hand, there were no finds on the National Pastime to be had. On the other hand, the shop did offer some of the quirkiness you would expect to find in such a free-thinking establishment, a series of T-shirts, each imprinted with a quotation purportedly from a famous person, most of whom had a Springfield connection. For instance, one shirt quoted Frank Lloyd Wright, who built a magnificent residence in his famous Prairie Style of architecture in Springfield, as supposedly having said: "I can design a building that would look good even in Springfield." Other quotations and attributions were: "I wouldn't be caught dead in Springfield"—Elvis; "Visiting Springfield was the worst mistake I ever made"— George Custer; "I'd have to be crazy to live in Springfield"—Mary Todd Lincoln; and "They'd have to shoot me to get me back in Springfield"— Abraham Lincoln. I didn't want to read too much into this T-shirt humor, which could have been borne of snobbery or the contempt that is breed by familiarity; but I knew that it was definitely not conceived by the city's Convention & Visitors Bureau, and it made me wonder. Later that night in the press box at Robin Roberts Stadium, I asked the score board operator what it was like to live in Springfield. Her name was Cindy, and she was a salty wench of a woman who pointed out to me the "porno names" on the Caps' roster. "We have Jeremy Cox, Billy Bone, and Tony Harden, and we had Gerald Butt too until we traded him to Canton." Keeping one eye on the televised pre-season NFL game involving her favorite team, the Green Bay Packers, she answered my question by saying, "You can't fart in this town without somebody making a big deal about it. And Springfield is very political. You can't move up in your job unless you know somebody or have a lot of money."

Despite these cautionary signals, my impression of Springfield was that it is a lovely place to live and raise a family. It reminded me, in fact, of Chillicothe and its wholesome, small-town ambience, even though Springfield (105,000) has three times the population of the one-time capitol of Ohio.

Springfield and Chillicothe were connected not only in my ruminations, but also by a history of rivalry in the Frontier League playoffs. Chillicothe had reached the Championship Round of the playoffs three times and lost each time. On two of those occasions (1996, 1998) it was the Capitals who defeated the Paints. The second defeat, which saw the Capitals win the final two games in Chillicothe after the Paints had won the opener in Springfield, had been especially difficult to take and remained a painful scar in the memory of Paints' fans. Although they were nowhere near the playoffs as the 2000 season was coming to a close, the Caps would prove that they were still very capable of dashing the hopes of the Chillicothe Paints.

The Paints came into Monday night's game against the Capitals in a tail spin. They'd just lost two of three at home to River City and four of the last ten to fall into a tie with Richmond at 36–37. Like Richmond, they were now in an almost must-win situation.

The morning had been sunny and warm, but as the Capitals went through their pre-game workouts, the afternoon sky became overcast and hinted at rain. While the Capitals had the field, I waited outside the visiting team's clubhouse in the left field corner where I was able to corner two Paints' players I'd been wanting to interview.

Standing face to face with second baseman Mike Horning, I noticed that his Paints' cap was a shabby, faded old thing with a rumpled crown and perspiration stains around the bill. I'd heard that Horning was the most superstitious player on the team, so I asked if he stayed with the cap out of superstition? "No, it's not so much superstition as the way I play the game," he said. "When you don't have as much talent as other guys, you have to play as hard as you can. My game is scrapping it out every night, and scrappers like me shouldn't have a clean, new-looking hat. ... I feel like if I'm not dirty when the game's over, then I didn't play hard."

"But you are highly superstitious, aren't you?"

"I am to a certain extent," he said. "Like all the other guys, I feel that if something is working, you don't go away from it. But really what I am is an obsessive-compulsive. I have a list of things I do before every at bat and before every pitch, and I always do them exactly the same way. I'm not cocky about it, and I can usually do them so that the other team doesn't even notice. Most of the things I do I do three times; like when I'm on defense, I take three steps back into the outfield grass before every pitch. By the end of the game I wear a path into the grass. ... All

Chillicothe Paints stadium.

the groundskeepers around the league hate me." Horning's obsessive-compulsiveness extended even to his packing. "I check everything three times and zip up my bag, but then I worry that I've forgotten something and I check it again. Byrd usually comes over and checks it for me, or I'd never finish."

We chatted some more about how the season, which had started out so promising for Chillicothe, had turned into such a struggle, and then I asked him about the scoring decision that had been changed at Jamie's behest. "I told Jamie when it happened, 'Jamie, don't make a big deal about it. I'm not upset about it.'

"He said, 'I don't care if you're not upset. I'm upset! You busted your ass just to get to the ball, and you shouldn't get an error for hustling.'

Did Mike think he deserved an error on the play? "I don't worry about scoring decisions," he said. "I'm really not concerned about them. ... But in my mind, I should make that play."

Jason Baker was a devout Christian who, by all accounts, had the complete respect of his teammates. I figured there was only one way that that was possible: instead of preaching about his faith, he tried to live it.

I started off asking him how he'd come to play the violin. He told that me that it was a family thing. Everybody in the family was musically inclined: all six boys—there were no girls—his father, and especially his

mother. Mr. and Mrs. Baker had run a strict household—there was no
TV watching except on special occasions, like baseball games—and the
boys had to practice a string instrument for a half hour every day before
they were allowed to go outside and play. His parents knew what they
were doing though. Jason became accomplished as a violinist, and he
found out later that he was able to make money with his talent. "When
I play on the streets during Christmas, I can make $50–$60 an hour,"
he said. "Last year I went to visit one of my brothers in Baltimore for
Christmas. On the way there I played in Philadelphia and in New York
at Rockefeller Center, and I made $2,000."

When I asked Jason, who had played three years in the Dodgers'
and Expos' minor league systems, how important being able to share
his faith with his teammates was, he said, "It's the main reason I decided
to come back and play one more year, to give testimony to these guys."

Giving testimony was not something he had always been prepared
to do. "I did grow up in a Christian household," he explained, "but my
second year with the Dodgers I really failed, and I didn't know how to
handle it. I broke my hand, had a bad year, drowned my sorrows in drink,
and wound up losing my fiancée over it. I was messed up for a while,
but one of my old coaches at Liberty University, Greg Morhardt, really
helped me. I looked at his life, and I saw that he really lived his faith,
What he said was what he was. I saw that he had a real passion for Christ,
and he encouraged me to read the Bible seriously and to develop a real
relationship with Christ. I did start reading the Bible, and when I did
I saw how God had blessed me in so many ways: with great parents and
family, with a healthy body, with musical talent, and with the opportunity to play professional baseball. When I realized how much God loves
me and everyone else, I started to come to grips with the idea that maybe
His plan was not for me to be a major league player. And instead of a
bitter disappointment, it was a wonderful release to know that my life
was in God's hands. I wasn't worried anymore about what I was going
to do because I thought as long as I live my life to glorify God, he'll open
another door for me that will lead to something just as good as playing
baseball.

"Being a Christian doesn't mean that life is always great, and playing pro baseball is still a challenge. When I don't do well on the field,
when I go 0–4, I'm disappointed. But the bad days don't mean as much
as they used to because I know I'm living for a higher purpose which
is to glorify Christ. So even when things don't go well, I still feel good
about myself."

Since school was back in session in Chillicothe and he wasn't able
to travel with the team, Marty Dunn had asked Jamie Keefe to take over

as acting manager on the team's final road trip of the season. For two and a half hours it looked like Jamie was going to get a win in his managerial debut. Phil Warren got the Paints' offense going in the top of the first by hitting a towering two-run homer that bounced thirty feet into the air after it landed on the Lamphier High School tennis courts behind the left field fence; and Sean Boesch pitched a whale of a game for eight innings, giving up only two runs, both unearned.

The 5–2 lead the Paints took into the bottom of the ninth looked pretty safe, even when reliever Nathan Gardner loaded the bases with two outs. It looked even safer when Gardner got ahead of third baseman Tyson Lindekugel in the count, one and two. I had just enough time before Gardner delivered his next pitch to recall a moment from the week before at McBride Stadium when Don Tincher had lamented the way that Lindekugel "always seems to kill the Roosters."

I knew that Lindekugel had hit the ball well, but when I saw Matt McCay sprinting towards the right-center field gap, I assumed the ballpark was going to hold his drive. It didn't, and when the ball dropped over the fence at the 360 foot mark, the game was suddenly over … or it was going to be over as soon as Lindekugel finished chugging around the bases. Although the startling victory did nothing to change the Capitals' lowly position in the standings, it sent a jolt of joy through the Capitals' players and the Springfield faithful in the grandstands and the press box. "Oh, my god! He did it! He did it!!" shouted Cindy, who was clapping, laughing, and jumping up and down in her excitement. "Oh, look … they're picking him up at home plate!" And, indeed, Lindekugel's teammates had hoisted him off the ground, and they were giving him a hero's ride on their shoulders for having hit a game-ending grand slam when they were one strike away from another uninspired defeat.

I got myself over to the Paints' clubhouse in a hurry, and when I got there Sean Boesch was standing outside on the sidewalk in semi-darkness, with a glazed look on his face as if, against his will, he'd just witnessed a grisly execution. Still in uniform, he had his shirt off and ice packs taped to his right shoulder and elbow. He stood there motionless as Paints' players walked down the sidewalk towards him, turned right, and entered the clubhouse. Presently, Jamie Keefe arrived and, seeing his benumbed pitcher standing there like a zombie, drained of energy and emotion, he made a gesture of affection towards him that was meant to say that he appreciated Sean's valiant effort, wasted though it had turned out to be. Silently, Jamie backed up against the taller Boesch, grabbed the pitcher's left hand, and patted himself over the heart with it. He then spun around and knocked fists with Boesch before turning to his right to enter the clubhouse.

Inside the clubhouse the players undressed, showered, dressed, and packed hurriedly, as if they couldn't wait to get out of the room and out of Robin Roberts Stadium. I didn't dare to speak to anyone, and the total silence was so unnerving I walked outside after a few minutes. When the players started coming out, looking dazed and depressed, they made a U-turn around the building and, walking under the grandstands, headed straight for the Paints' bus idling in the parking lot behind home plate. While the guys merely nodded or mumbled a hello at most, Stephen Byrd stopped for a moment to talk. "How you doing?" he said.

"Better than you guys," I replied.

"We're snake bit," he said. "Anything that can go wrong with this team does go wrong."

I asked him how it had happened. "He threw a splitter. It was supposed to go down and away, but he threw it too hard and it flattened out," he said.

When clubhouse man Aaron Queen came outside, I asked him why Jamie had gone to and stayed with a pitcher who was leading the league in losses. "He didn't have no choice," said Aaron. "Frodsham threw last night ... and he wasn't effective anyway. He gave up a couple of hits and hit a batter. And Woody, he's supposed to be the closer, but ..."

Byrd, Queen, and I joined the stream of Paints quietly leaving the ballpark. When we got near the main gate, we were joined by the Paints' bus driver. "I don't believe that one," I said to him confidentially. "I do!" he said disgustedly.

As I walked over to my van, I passed a husky fellow sitting by himself on a cement curb. Even though he had his head down, I realized when I got near him that it was Nate Gardner. I'd seen a lot of blown leads and crazy endings to ballgames all summer, but nothing to match what had just transpired. This one was a crusher for the Paints, and the player who felt responsible for the disaster was the poor guy sitting on the curb. His physical separation from his teammates on the nearby bus was symbolic, I thought, of the psychological and emotional isolation he felt. I wished that there was something I could say to make him feel better, but I knew, as well as his teammates did, that there were no words that could make him feel not culpable for the loss.

I had come to Springfield still hopeful that the Paints might make the playoffs. I left as hopeless as an atheist.

Driving slowly past Gardner on my way out of the parking lot, I saw him lean backwards, his hands behind him on the ground. He tilted his face towards the heavens and peered into the murky darkness above. As he did, the first rain drops began to fall, too lightly to cleanse the moment of its anguish, too late to save the Paints from a most bitter defeat.

13

"Now That's Entertainment!" The Final Series in Chillicothe

THURSDAY, AUGUST 24TH, and Max and I were back in Richmond, Indiana, for the opening game of the Roosters' last home series of the year. Unless the Roosters made the playoffs, a still possible but unlikely eventuality, the game would be my last of the season at McBride, as I was heading to Jacksonville, Florida, the next morning on a family vacation.

Shortly after Max and I arrived at the ballpark, I bumped into Woody Sorrell coming out of the Richmond clubhouse. Woody accosted me as if he'd been waiting for me to show up. "You need to get in there," he said, pointing towards the clubhouse with a tilt of his head.

As soon as I walked into the room, I knew what was going on, and I was thankful for Woody's tip. The Roosters were holding court, Kangaroo Court.

Kangaroo Court is a player-run activity held universally throughout professional baseball, during which players are tried in mock fashion for transgressions committed both on and off the diamond. Even though Kangaroo Court can be an effective, non-hostile way of maintaining discipline and conveying the message that a player's game performance has been unsatisfactory; it is more often merely a way of having fun and painlessly raising money for a big party at the end of the season.

By the time I got there, court had already been in session for a while. All the players, except for Todd DeGraffenreid who was buck naked, were fully dressed in uniform and sat attentively in front of their lockers, attached to three walls of the room in a "U" formation. At the mouth of the "U" sat four other players, the officers of the Court: Phill Kojack, Keith Fout, Aaron Sledd, and Mike Zerbe. As secretary of the Court, Kojack was the one who recorded in a spiral notebook the various charges made by players against their teammates, and he was the one who formally read each of the charges in court. Phill told me later that the Roosters tried to have court once a week. The fine for a guilty verdict was 50¢. Fines were doubled when a player pleaded innocent but was then found guilty by a vote of the team, and the maximum total of fines per session was $2.00.

Right before I'd come into the room, Bobby Chandler had been "banged" for some transgression and pleaded innocent to the charge. He apparently didn't mount much of a defense because the team unanimously voted him guilty. "That's bullshit!" he said with a big grin on his face, "Bullshit!"

Kojack then moved on to the next case, telling us that (pitcher Matt) "Schweitzer bangs (Alejandro) Bracho for using his glove to warm-up in the bullpen." Bracho pleaded guilty.

Somebody else banged Jelovcic for peeing in the shower. Jelovcic protested—"I was the only one in there," he said—but was found guilty nevertheless.

DeGraffenreid was banged "for sliding into third against London, after tagging at second, on this wimp-ass throw that came looping in from the outfield." The players all laughed at the memory of the play which had occurred the day before in Ontario.

"First of all," said DeGraffenreid who was pleading innocent, "I had my back to the play, so I couldn't see how good the throw was going to be. Second, Nadeau has a hose. I don't know why he made such a bad throw. That's not like him; you all know that. And third, sliding is better than not sliding. It's a hustling play. I don't see how you can convict me for hustling."

I thought DeGraffenreid presented a strong case, but the Roosters proved to be a tough jury and nearly convicted him. The vote was counted twice, and in the end the 12–12 tie was not enough to saddle him with a guilty verdict.

Moments later Ryan Peavey banged DeGraffenreid who pleaded guilty for "peeing towards me in the shower."

Aaron Sledd banged Macky Waguespack for "wrestling with Jelo in my room and knocking over the ice bucket I was using to ice my ankle with and then … picking up an ice cube off the floor and eating it."

This account prompted laughs and groans of disgust and then more laughter when the low-key Waguespack started to offer up a feeble excuse in his thick Cajun accent, something about him being thirsty and the ice cubes being right there while the drinking fountain was way down the hall.

Peavey banged DeGraffenreid, who was beginning to look like a favorite target, for "getting a haircut in Johnstown that makes him look like a twelve-year-old kid." DeGraffenreid pleaded guilty but not before he offered an explanation. "I went to Mastercuts at the mall," he said. "I had no control. ... I knew I was in trouble when the lady came over to my chair. She stunk and had 'Rock 'n Roll' tattooed on her thumb." More laughter from every corner of the room.

Peavey banged rookie Blake Leverett for "asking what channel *Saturday Night Live* was on on a Tuesday night." "I forgot what night it was," said Leverett sheepishly. "Guilty," ruled the officers without waiting for a plea from Leverett.

While the Leverett case was being presented, Rich Jelovcic came up to me and borrowed my pen and a piece of paper from my notebook. He wrote something on the paper and then handed it to Kojack. It was a complaint for the Court, which Phill read immediately. "Jelo bangs DeGraffenreid for being naked during Kangaroo Court," he said. Everybody, including me, laughed and shouted "Guilty!" Todd finally pulled a green towel out of his locker and wrapped it around his waist.

Leverett banged Peavey for "peeing on the elevator"; Chandler banged pitcher Scott Conner for "walking around the clubhouse for 15 minutes asking, 'Have you seen my orange jersey?' when he was wearing it the whole time"; and Chris Lotterhos banged DeGraffenreid for spending a half an hour talking to his former London teammates before a game and for saying he cried when the trade that brought him to Richmond was announced. "I didn't say *I* cried," said DeGraffenreid. "I said, 'Tears were shed ... by fans, host families, whoever.'"

Somebody said, "'Whoever' is you. Guilty!"

"Guilty," agreed the Court officers. This was DeGraffenreid's fourth conviction in my presence which meant that he'd reached the $2.00 limit in fines for the session—if he hadn't reached it even sooner than the last case.

Lotterhos brought the final charge, and he banged Jelo for tipping the dealer $5,000 and not giving his teammates anything. The Roosters had been waiting for this one. "Yeah, yeah!" they said, as almost every hand in the room went up to signal "guilty."

Jelo, slated to start on the mound for Richmond, wasn't buying it. He grabbed his glove, stood up, and barged out of the clubhouse. On his way out he called over his shoulder, "Fuck you guys! She dealt me the cards. You guys didn't."

The rabble of envious Roosters was not appeased and still wanted the nouveau riche Jelovcic to be assessed that symbolic 50¢, but Judge Zerbe asserted his authority and threw the case out.

While I'd been in court, Max and his partner Jon Milesky had been in the umps' dressing room talking about Jon's having worked Dubois County games when the Dragons had been members of the defunct Heartland League. I walked in on them just in time to hear Jon tell Max a story about Sparky, the Dragons' mascot.

"I'd put him up against the Chicken any day," said Milesky. "One day he comes out on the field dressed up like a private detective. He's wearing a fedora, dark sunglasses, and a long trench coat. He looks like Columbo.

"He walks out to the pitcher's mound and sits down. I'm in on the gag, so I walk out to the mound and tell him he's got to get off the field. When I do that he pulls out a sign that says, 'DRAGONS WIN OR ELSE!!!' I tell him to leave again, and he just shows the sign around some more, so I throw him out, like I'm supposed to. He points to the 'OR ELSE!!!' part of the sign in a real defiant manner like he's not going anywhere, so I throw him out again.

"So this time he drops the sign, unbuttons his trench coat, pulls it open real wide, and shows everybody that he has 20 or 30 sticks of dynamite belted around his waist. I never laughed so hard in my life!"

When I was in Cooperstown for the Hall of Fame inductions of Phil Niekro and Tommy LaSorda, I heard LaSorda say, "There's an old saying in baseball: 'You don't want a knuckleballer pitching for you, and you don't want one pitching against you.'" Despite the fact that knuckleballers can be effective—Niekro's Hall of Fame plaque is proof of that—the maxim cited by LaSorda expresses not so much ambivalence towards knuckleball pitchers as it does consistent prejudice against them, whether they are friend or foe. Catchers don't like to catch them; pitching coaches often don't know how to help them; and even when you score plenty of runs off one of them, some of your hitters are going to be messed up for two weeks. The basic problem with the knuckleball is its unpredictability. The knuckleball, when it's working, is as erratic in its movement as a butterfly, and this striven-for chaos of flight goes against the grain of a game where consistency is one of the highest virtues. Things are only worse when the knuckleball is not working. It comes in flatter than three-day-old soda pop and slower than news of a bad report card but is sent back towards cringing infielders like a screaming bottle rocket. As Jim Bouton wrote in *I'm Glad You Didn't Take It Personally*, "When a knuckleball doesn't knuckle, it's not a knuckleball, it's a piece of cake, pound cake."

It's little wonder then that knuckleball pitchers, a disappearing breed in the major leagues, are even more of a rarity in the minor leagues, where the fastball, even when it is not being controlled very well, is king and seen as the surest ticket to the bigs.

The last thing I expected to see in the Frontier League then was a bona fide full-time practitioner of the almost-lost art of flinging the "floater" or "flutterball," as the pitch is sometimes called. But that's what we got when Rich Jelovcic was scratched minutes before game time because some tendonitis prevented him from getting sufficiently loose to start the ballgame. With Jelo on the shelf, Woody Sorrell turned to the Roosters' new secret weapon, a stocky six foot-one inch farm boy named Jason Immekus from Neosho, Missouri.

Immekus had pitched at Crowder Junior College and the University of Washburn at Topeka. It was during his sophomore year that he became predominantly a knuckleball pitcher and joined the fraternity of other knuckleballers, like major leaguers Tim Wakefield and Tom Candiotti, whose Internet websites Immekus visited regularly. A year after graduating he signed with Chillicothe in the spring of 2000 but was released before he faced a live hitter in batting practice. On the way home he stopped in Richmond, just as Freddy Flores had done, and was given a chance to throw a couple of innings during an intra-squad game. Although he impressed the Roosters, especially coach Woody Sorrell, Richmond couldn't find room for him on the roster, so he went home where he worked as the pitching coach at Crowder and as an instructor at the Mickey Owen Baseball School.

He had been out frog gigging with his boss, the head coach at Crowder, when the coach's wife read in the *Kansas City Star* that Woody Sorrell had been named manager of the Richmond Roosters. Remembering that Woody had been in his corner, Immekus called Richmond and left Woody a message: "If somebody goes down and you need another arm for a week or two, please let me be that person." Woody returned the call the next day, and an hour later Immekus was on a Greyhound making the 19-hour bus trip to Richmond.

As Immekus warmed up on the pitcher's mound, Woody and Max shot the bull nearby. After Immekus had thrown about fifteen pitches, Woody said, "Max, I think he's about ready."

"Woody, he gets all the time he needs because it was an injury," said Max.

"Yeah, I know," said Woody, "but he's ready."

"He's only throwing sixty miles an hour!"

"That's about as fast as it's gonna get."

Sixty mph was fast enough. The Johnstown Johnnies were no more familiar with Immekus than Max was, and they didn't get to just watch his knuckleball; they had to try to hit it. The Johnnies made a lot of contact—Immekus recorded just two strikeouts in 7.1 innings—but for most of the night it sounded like they were hitting grapefruits, not baseballs; and they wound up with five hits (four singles and a double) and two runs off the knuckleballer.

When Woody wanted to make a change, after Paul Esposito had singled with one out in the top of the eighth with the Roosters nursing a one-run lead, he stepped out of the dugout, looked down towards the bullpen, and took off his cap, the signal that asked if the pitcher warming up in the bullpen was ready. To answer in the affirmative, the bullpen coach normally takes off his cap. But in this case nobody in the Roosters' bullpen signaled Woody because nobody had been warming up. Woody sent word for Bobby Chandler to heat up, NOW!, and then began a predictable stalling routine. He walked slowly out to the mound where the Roosters' infielders gathered and talked to Immekus as long as Max would let him. He then walked slowly back to the dugout as the infielders returned to their positions. Immekus fidgeted with the resin bag, took forever agreeing with catcher Steve Mitrovich about which pitch to throw first to third baseman David Ferres, and then backed off the rubber when he saw Woody making his second trip of the inning out to the mound; which, according to the rules of professional baseball, required Woody to relieve him.

"Bobby looks like he's ready," said Immekus when Woody climbed the hill.

"Shut up and listen," said Woody. "Ferres is up next. He's hit the ball hard three times against you. If it was anybody else, I'd let you stay in. But I want to tell you something: I think you're a helluva pitcher, and if I'm wearing a uniform anywhere next year, so will you. There will be a spot on my roster for you."

"Are you serious?" Immekus asked.

"Yes, I'm serious," said Woody, "and I'm a man of my word."

Max came over to hurry Woody up, so Immekus handed Woody the baseball and headed off the field. There were only 730 fans on hand, but their mild applause and Woody's praise made Jason feel truly appreciated for his pitching for the first time in a long time. As Immekus stepped over the first base line, Jon Milesky told him, "Good job tonight."

"Beats farming," said Immekus.

Just before he left the mound, Woody handed the baseball to Max and said, "Count to ten and bring in Chandler."

Moments later third baseman Todd DeGraffenreid picked up the resin bag and said, "Hey, Max, what exactly is resin made up?"

"I don't know," said Max, "but I do know you're just trying to distract me from my ten-count, and it's not going to work because I'm up to three ... 'one thousand, four ... one thousand, five ....'"

Max may have felt obligated to usher Chandler into the game in a timely fashion, but the Johnstown hitters were not looking forward to seeing the happy-go-lucky fireballer come jogging across the diamond from the bullpen to the pitcher's mound. They knew that trying to react to Chandler's bullets after having swatted at Immekus' butterflies for seven innings would be tantamount to walking ten miles on a treadmill and then having the thing instantly sped up to an Olympic 100 meter dash pace. Sure enough, Ferres and right fielder Kirk Taylor both struck out swinging to end the eighth, and Bobby then set down the Johnnies 1-2-3 with another strikeout in the ninth to sew up the 4–2 Richmond victory. The save was Chandler's 12th of the year, good for the Roosters' season and career record; and the win, the Roosters' 12th in their last 15 games. I was happy to see the Roosters win the last game of the year I would attend in Richmond and grateful ... that I didn't have to remain, like Max, and Schaly, and their buddies in the profession, dispassionate about the outcome of the game.

As much as I hated leaving Max and the Frontier League again, I had to go down to Florida. We were going down not just to vacation at the beach, but to my parents' 50th wedding anniversary. Nothing could have kept me away from that, and Max understood completely.

This is usually the place where the author waxes eloquently in a father-playing-catch-with-son mode, but it is a road I will travel down only briefly; for neither of my parents were ever big baseball fans. I didn't introduce my parents to baseball, as the Jelovcic boys did their parents, but it was my participation in the sport and my complete obsession with the game as a boy that renewed and sustained their interest in baseball. My dad, John Hubert Shannon, a railroad man devoted to the Catholic faith and his family, actually liked football and basketball better than baseball; but he performed his fatherly baseball duties as well as anyone could have. He drove me to countless practices and games without complaint and, after watching those games and my often ugly performances therein, took me out for an Icee and encouragement, not criticism. His own feelings of self-worth were never on the line in my games. And, although he didn't know much about baseball, he constantly exhorted me to learn control (I wanted to be a pitcher) and stressed that practice was the key to becoming a good ballplayer—pretty damn good advice, whatever one's ambitions are. The first book I ever published was a little chapbook of 27 baseball poems called *The Mantle–Mays Controversy Solved.* It included a somewhat biographical poem that was meant to be a tribute to the way my dad was always there for me, as a catcher to be sure, but more importantly as a father.

Front Yard Pitching

Home from work he would slip off his shoes,
Read the papers, have a smoke and a drink,
All the pleasures life afforded in those years.
And sacrificed more times than not when
Posited against the timid plea, "Will you catch me, Dad?"

Out in the long sandy front yard—grass
Never had a fighting chance—we squared off
Like Old West gunfighters, a hungry, twitching kid
Squinting towards the older hand, resigned, impassive.
The folded hanky inside the mitt was his gesture of respect;
The chair that propped up his catcher's crouch my concession;
The berry bush with prickly leaves looming behind him our academic
     backstop.

I threw myself into every throw, low and hard
Like lengthy punches into his leathery palm,
Smarting with the popping but unyielding to the virulence of agitated
     youth.

All the fastballs that I threw and all the fastballs that he stopped
Came to nothing more than the faster passing of minor league years.
Now in the moments of dead arm time we are back together,
Old battery mates reunited. We read the papers,
Share a smoke and a drink after work,
Enjoying our unworn lawn and other pleasures that life affords.

My mother, the sweetest, kindest person I've ever known, also pitched in. The former Willie Mae Mansfield, she had been an outstanding basketball player in North Carolina at Perquimans High School (the same little country school where Charlie Finley later discovered Jimmy "Catfish" Hunter). Even though baseball wasn't her game, she hit me grounders when nobody else would, and she made me feel that baseball was a topic worthy of adult conversation. As if it were yesterday, I can picture my mother standing over the stove in our kitchen fixing supper after putting in a full day's work at McKesson Drugs and talking to me about what interested me. I remember her asking me, as if she really valued my opinion, what I thought about the chances of the expansion New York Mets and Houston Colt .45s in 1962, their first year of existence. I was eleven years old.

On Monday, August 28th, I cut short the vacation; left Kathy, the kids, and my van at Vilano Beach, Florida, near St. Augustine; and flew back to Cincinnati. Because flights into and out of Cincinnati are so expensive, I actually flew into the Dayton airport, where Max was waiting for me. On our way to Chillicothe for the last two games of the season, Max filled me in on what I had missed. Johnstown had spanked Richmond 13–4 on Friday night, but the Roosters bounced back to sweep a doubleheader on Saturday and take the series (which included a make-up game) three to one. The sweep evened Richmond's record at 40–40 and marked the first time since the end of June that the Roosters had seen .500. Going into Sunday's games, the Roosters and the Paints (39–40) were hanging on by a thread behind Evansville at 42–38. The Paints beat the Roosters in the opener 7–5, virtually eliminating Richmond from the race when Evansville pulled out a 3–2, extra-innings squeaker against River City.

I did all these calculations on my own, as Max never paid much attention to the standings. As usual, his relationship to the games was personal and anecdotal.

The first story he told me involved something dear to his heart: Iron City Beer, everybody's favorite in Johnstown, Pennsylvania, his hometown. "Before the second game in Richmond on Friday night, I ran into Jerry, the guy I told you about who owns Jerry's Lounge, which is right across the street from the ballpark in Johnstown," he said. "I told him, 'If I'da known you were coming to Richmond, I would have asked you to bring me some Iron City Beer.'

"Jerry said, 'I got a case in the trunk of my car. It was supposed to be for Kirk Taylor—he asked me a couple of weeks ago to bring a case of IC Lights over here for this series—but now he don't want it. Says he's decided to quit drinking until after the season.'

"So Jerry gives the case to me, and doesn't even charge me for it. I rang up Kirk in the first inning, and when he was jogging out to right field at the end of the inning I told him, 'Hey, Kirk, maybe you need to start drinking again.'

"He said, 'How'd you know about that?'

"'Because I'm the beneficiary of your going on the wagon. I got the case of IC Light in my trunk! Jerry gave it to me. … Thanks, buddy!'

"'Don't mention it, Max,' he said."

Knuckleballers don't need as much rest as normal pitchers, so Woody Sorrell had no qualms about starting Jason Immekus in the finale between Johnstown and Richmond on Saturday on only two days' rest. The move gave Max his first chance to see the knuckleballer's stuff from the home plate umpire's unique vantage point, wittily described by the title of Lee Gutkind's book about umpires, *The Best Seat in Baseball, But You Have to Stand.* Immekus was on and impressed Max by pitching "six and a third innings of hellacious baseball." When Immekus found himself in a bit of a jam (runners on first and third) only two outs away from throwing a complete game in Saturday's seven-inning nightcap, Woody started out of the Roosters' dugout. As Max recorded the trip to the mound in his notebook, he asked Steve Mitrovich to tell Woody not to do anything until he got out to the mound too. By the time Max joined the conference on the mound, Woody had already signaled to the bullpen for Bobby Chandler. "Woody, why'd you do that!" said Max. "I was going to tell you to leave him in. He's still pitching great—his knuckleball is dropping six to twelve inches—and he can get these next two guys out."

"Now you're trying to manage? ... from behind home plate!" said Woody with a smile.

"Why not?" said Max. "You've been trying to umpire all year from the dugout!"

"Touché," said Woody.

Max's third story, about the game the night before in Chillicothe, wasn't as cute as the first two, and it revolved around the unappreciated antics of Roosters catcher Steve Mitrovich. According to Max, Mitro wanted a couple of pitches thrown early in the game by J.T. Engstrom that Max didn't give the Roosters. In the fourth Mitrovich was hit by one of Rick Blanc's pitches and moved to second on a wild pitch. When Max called a strike on the next batter, Ryan Peavey, Mitrovich showed up Max by holding his hands apart to indicate how far outside he thought the pitch had been. Max saw what Mitrovich did and said to himself, "Wait 'til he gets back here."

When the big catcher came out to warm up Phill Kojack, who'd relieved Engstrom, Max told him, "Hey, Mitro, stop whining or it's gonna be a long night. When you guys were taking three out of four from Johnstown in Richmond, you didn't say a word about those calls, so don't start now. You're getting your ass handed to you now, but you'd better stop crying."

"Sorry, Max," said Steve.

By being two games behind Evansville in the loss column, the Paints had absolutely no margin of error left. If the Paints lost another game, the Otters had only to win one of their three unplayed games to clinch the fourth and final playoff spot (if Evansville clinched on or before the last day of the season, the Otters would not make up their rained out game, nor would the Paints make up their pair of rain outs). Also, if the

Otters won their remaining two scheduled games, they would clinch regardless of what Chillicothe did. The Paints' fate, in other words, was not entirely in their own hands. And so it was perhaps for that reason that neither the fans nor the Paints themselves seemed to be feeling any pressure. The atmosphere at VA Memorial Stadium was not tense at all but was pregnant with expectation; everybody seemed to be as loose and as excited as school kids on the day before summer vacation. Jim Schaly was feeling it too, and he had a sparkle in his eyes as he explained to me before the game that he had a great prank planned. With the cooperation of both teams Jim was going to re-enact the opening of the baseball scene in *Naked Gun*: when the pitcher throws the first pitch of the game right down the cock but Leslie Nielsen, playing a bumbling detective who's never umpired before in his life, doesn't know what to do and takes about half a minute before he finally raises his right arm ever so slowly and timidly guesses, rather than announces, that the pitch is a "Strike???" I laughed hysterically just listening to Jim describe the movie and imagining how much fun it would be to see him and the players perform the re-enactment during a real Frontier League Game. The deal was that Freddy Flores was to take the first pitch of the game, which Jim would call a strike no matter where Stephen Byrd threw it. "Don't get mad if the first pitch is a ball and I call it a strike," Jim had said to Woody Sorrell. "I'll even it up when Chillicothe bats." Flores had asked, "What if I swing at the pitch and get a hit?" Schaly had thought of everything. "I don't care what the result is; if you swing at the pitch I'll call you out for stepping out of the batter's box," he'd said.

In the press box I asked for John Wend's impressions of the game I'd missed the night before. Like most everybody else, John had come to associate me with Max, so his thoughts immediately ran towards the umpiring. "Max had a bad game last night," he said. "Oh, my god, he made some terrible calls. He called a strike on Jason Baker that was unbelievable. Baker never says a word about the umpiring, but he had to say something about that call. I don't know what Max was looking at. Baker was trying to bunt, and the pitch came so far inside it almost took his knee caps off. … Schaly also made a bad call, on the bases. Greg Strickland stole second base in the sixth inning, and I mean he had the base stolen! Blake Leverett tagged him as he was standing up after his slide with his foot already on the base. It was the worst call I've ever seen Schaly make."

On a more positive note, John shared some good news with me: Roger Hanners had recovered enough that he was in the ballpark for the first time since his heart attack and was going to throw out the ceremonial first pitch of the ballgame. "He said it hit him when he got to the gate," John said. "He hadn't realized how much he missed it."

According to John, Roger had visited the team in the Paints' club-house. He started speaking about how much he missed everybody but became choked up and couldn't continue. There was an awkward silence for a few moments; then Jamie Keefe said, "Hey, Roger, what burns your ass?"

"A burning bush about that high," said Roger with a big grin as he held his hand behind his back right below his ass. Everyone laughed at hearing Roger provide the punch line to his favorite joke; and given the perfect exit opportunity, he took it. As he walked past Jamie, he patted him on the shoulder and said, "Thanks for picking me up."

When I asked John about three attractive young women dressed in slinky black dresses and high heels who were roving through the grand-stands, we went from the poignant to the salacious. "They're the Bud Girls," he said. "They're paid to go to events like this and hand out Bud-weiser trinkets: coasters, key chains, beer can insulators. The tall one there, she's horny as hell. I was at a golf tournament, and some guy offered her $5 to pull her dress down and show the top of her tits. She didn't even hesitate. She said, 'They're just tits.'"

About ten minutes before game time, Roger Hanners walked in front of the Paints' dugout, and the cheering started, even before Wend said over the P.A.: "Throwing out the first pitch tonight, a man who needs no introduction ... Roger Hanners!" After Roger delivered the pitch, the entire Chillicothe team came out to greet him and hug him, one by one.

After the crowd settled down, Stephen Byrd waved his cap at Wend, who then sent the starters out to their positions with his introductions. The National Anthem was beautifully played by Jason Baker on his vio-lin, after which Byrd took his final warm-ups to music of a slightly different calibre: the rock 'n roll number "Surfin' Bird" by The Trashmen.

Stephen Byrd's first pitch of the ballgame was a fastball over the heart of the heart. Umpire Jim Schaly made no call or movement what-soever but stood like a statue behind Ben Gerkin, the Paints' catcher. Gerkin froze too, his mitt held out in front of him exactly where he'd caught the pitch. The Roosters' leadoff batter, Freddie Flores, also did not move a muscle for five or six seconds after the pitch had whizzed past him, but then ... ever so slowly, he turned his head backwards until he was staring at Schaly, who still made not the slightest motion or gave any indication that he was even alive. From somewhere in the stands came a single exasperated remonstrance: "COME ON, UMP!" And in the press box, scoreboard operator Dick Whitney practically panicked: "What was it? It was a strike, right? It was right down the middle! ... What's he calling?!"

Schaly waited a few moments more, with the park in absolute silence as if everybody were holding their breath, and then he slowly raised his right arm, cautiously pointed to his right, and meekly said, "Strike?" Immediately, the place went crazy, as if the Paints had just won the ballgame on a ninth-inning home run, and I practically fell off my chair in the press box laughing. The only thing from the movie that was missing in the re-enactment were Nielsen's hot-dogging antics once he warms up to the idea of umpiring: the exaggerated strike calls punctuated by splits, spins, and moon-walking. Thankfully, Schaly knew where to draw the line.

With the game begun in earnest, Flores wound up grounding out to first, pitcher covering. After Jason Borghese singled but was caught stealing, first baseman Macky Waguespack struck out. It was the fifth whiff in a row for Macky, who'd struck out four straight times the night before after beginning the series with a single. The lefthanded swing of the short, stocky Waguespack was pretty, but it definitely had a hole in it; a hole Frontier League pitchers had been exploiting all season.

Mike Horning lead off the bottom of the first for the Paints. When the count ran to one and two on him, Woody Sorrell stepped out of the Roosters' dugout and yelled to Schaly, "Hey, Jim, you said you'd even things up. That first pitch to Horning was a ball!"

"Okay, I'll call the next pitch a strike, no matter what," said Schaly.

"TIME! Whoa! What just a minute!" demanded Horning, as he backed out of the batter's box.

Schaly was just kidding, but Horning decided he wasn't going to take any chances and singled on the next pitch; which brought Greg Strickland to the plate. As Greg settled into the batter's box, Schaly said, "Strick, I hosed you last night."

"Yeah, I know," said Greg. 'Forget about it.'"

Horning was caught stealing, and after the Paints went out without scoring, a couple of water balloons rained down from the grandstand roof and exploded like bombs in the grass near Schaly. "Has anyone seen Chief Crazy Horse?" asked John Wend over the P.A. to big laughs from the crowd. As Bobby Chandler walked past home plate on his way to the first base coaching box, he tossed a baseball to Schaly, who turned and fired it towards the roof in retaliation.

"Boy, Jim's having fun tonight," I said.

"Schaly's really loosened up this year," said Aaron Lemaster. "He used to have no sense of humor ... not on the field, at least. He used to be all business. You couldn't kid around with him. And he'd give Lori Remy, our promotions coordinator, a hard time and tell the people involved in promotions to hurry up and get off the field. But this year he's been great."

In the top of the third the Bud Girls took water bottles out to Schaly and Max. While Schaly, standing near the Paints' on-deck circle with his back to the diamond, took a swig from his bottle, Chief Crazy Horse sneaked up behind him and blasted him with a big Super Soaker squirt gun. An inning later Schaly got a measure of revenge. While Chief Crazy Horse and clubhouse manager Aaron Queen were busy lobbing water balloons into the third base bleachers, Schaly sneaked up behind them, stole a water balloon, and drilled Chief Crazy Horse in the back. Chief Crazy Horse went berserk, flailing his arms around threateningly as if he were swatting at a swarm of bees; but fortunately Aaron grabbed him and was able to prevent him from assaulting the umpire and winding up in the glue factory.

As the hi-jinks between Schaly and Chief Crazy Horse went on, a pretty good game, won 5–4 by the Paints, also unfolded and turned on the bottom of the fifth inning when Chillicothe got three straight run-producing, two-out base hits by Justin Graham, Ben Gerkin, and Chance Melvin, the bottom of the Paints' batting order. In addition to timely hitting, the Paints got good pitching. Byrd gave up all four of Richmond's runs, but only one of them was earned; while Nate Gardner and Woody Fullenkamp held the Roosters hitless over the final three innings. For the suddenly effective-again Fullenkamp, it was his second save in two nights and his fourth in five days.

Just as "Take Me Out to the Ball Game" began to play during the seventh-inning stretch, Paints' GM Bryan Wickline walked onto the field carrying a microphone, and when he reached the waist-high grandstand wall behind home plate, he told Aaron Lemaster to "Cut the music!" Aaron and John Wend looked at each other and said, "Now what? What's he doing?"

After telling the crowd, "I'm gonna need help with this," Wickline asked his girlfriend, Karen Manson, to come onto the field.

As the lovely Karen, a little embarrassed to be in the spotlight but willing, as always, to help out any way she could, made her way towards her boyfriend, Wickline thanked the fans for their support all year long and informed them that the fireworks display scheduled for after the game was being postponed due to technical difficulties and rescheduled for tomorrow night, after the last game of the season. He also announced that everyone in the ballpark would be allowed in free on Tuesday night.

With the perplexed Karen standing gamely next to him, Wickline did not break into song. Instead, he bent over, rolled up his pants leg, and pulled a single red rose out of his sock. Attached prominently to the rose was a diamond engagement ring. "You didn't really think I was going to sing to you, did you?" Wickline said to Karen. Bryan got down on one knee, and proffering the rose and the ring, said, "Will you marry me?" Wickline had not told anyone about his plans for a public proposal, and Karen was shocked to receive it. They'd only met in March and had never discussed getting married. Nevertheless, she pulled him up and gave him a big hug and a kiss, after which the crowd went crazy; ensuring that from then on the seventh-inning stretch would be the favorite part of every ballgame for the future Mrs. Wickline.

After the crowd sang "Take Me Out to the Ball Game" with more spirit than ever, as if they were congratulating Bryan and Karen on their engagement, John Wend told me that Andy Lee had proposed to his girlfriend the night before at the ballpark. Wend was in on that one and rigged the "Lady Paint of the Game" promotion to help out Lee. Normally, the Lady Paint of the Game gets a small bouquet of flowers and a platonic hug from a Paints pitcher, but Kim Ireland got quite a bit more: a marriage proposal and an engagement ring. For the record, she also accepted.

The Paints' win was a fitting conclusion to the night, which had been full of fun and surprises, but it had something of a hollow feeling to it. News of Evansville's victory over River City reached the press box, just minutes after Woody Fullenkamp grounded Jason Borghese out to third to end the game. This meant that a win by Evansville or a loss by Chillicothe tomorrow, either one, would finish the Paints. As soon as Max called Borghese out at first, Queen's rock 'n roll hit about a popular video arcade game, "Another One Bites the Dust," came blaring over the P.A. system. The lyrics of the song were directed towards the vanquished Roosters, but it required no great sense of irony to perceive that they were about to apply equally well to Chillicothe's hopes of finally having a Frontier League championship season.

From the beginning, one of the major problems facing the Frontier League was how to provide housing for its players. The players' salaries were so low that renting apartments was not really a viable option. During the brief existence of the Tri-State Tomahawks in Ashland, Kentucky, Tomahawk players lived in the Sigma Phi Epsilon frat house of Marshall University across the state line in Huntington, West Virginia. The situation was even worse in the early days of the Chillicothe franchise when Paints players stayed in the VA Hospital behind the ballpark. The league would probably not have survived if it had continued to rely on such strange housing arrangements. Fortunately, somebody came up with the concept of having the players live rent-free with each team's best fans. Not only did this arrangement make it possible for the players to survive financially, but it also was guaranteed, with few exceptions, to create lifetime bonds of loyalty between the players and their host families, who invariably treated the players as adopted sons.

On the last day of the 2000 Frontier League season, the Paints publically acknowledged before the game the importance of their host families to the success of the franchise by honoring the baseball moms and dads who'd helped take care of their players all summer. As John Wend called their names over the P.A. system, the host families and their adopted Paints lined up across the infield in front of the pitcher's mound. After John thanked them all on behalf of the organization, he told me, "The players would kill for their host family. Woody and Byrd lived with Bea Beeks and her husband Cliff, and they think so much of her they came in early in the spring so they could lay a new kitchen floor for her. The players would all go over to her house on Sundays, and she would cook all day long for them. She played cards with 'em too. They'd bet big money, and they'd take her money when she lost. But that's the way she wanted it."

Max was going to end the season in the same place he'd started it: behind the plate. Sean Boesch was the starting pitcher for Chillicothe, while Jason Immekus got the ball for Richmond, again on only two days rest. Marty Dunn reminded Stephen Byrd that as the previous day's starting pitcher he was responsible for sitting in the stands behind home plate and keeping a radar gun on the starting pitchers. "Man, I don't need to do that tonight," said Byrd.

"Why not?" said Marty.

"Because Poulsen can tell you if Boesch is losing anything, and their guy doesn't break the speed limit to start with. He only throws 55 miles per hour."

Because nothing is less uncertain than the professional future of an independent minor league baseball player, the season finale had the potential of being the last pro game many of the Roosters and Paints would ever play. Several players knew it would be their last, and the Paints gave final-game sendoffs to Mike Horning and Chance Melvin. Also bowing out was Mike Zerbe, who'd recently announced his retirement. "I always said I'd keep playing as long as it was still fun to go the ballpark," he'd told me. "One day last week I woke up and admitted to myself, 'I don't want to go to the ballpark.' I knew it was time to hang 'em up." No career which fizzles out in mediocrity at the bottom of the minor league food chain is celebrated by historians or memorialized by a bronze statue; but if the player always puts his heart into the effort up to the last pitch of his last game, then he deserves to have somebody there who loves him to help him say goodbye. Mr. and Mrs. Zerbe won't be here, but Max is here, I thought, as John Wend rumbled over the P.A. system: "Ladies and Gentlemen, on your feet for the last time in the 2000 season and cheer for *your* Chillicothe Paints! ... in left field, batting seventh, number 35, Justin Graham; in center field..."

On this last evening of the year at VA Memorial Stadium dull normalcy reigned over the exotic, at least between the lines, as Sean Boesch's fastballs trumped Jason Immekus' knucklers. Immekus uttered what was becoming his trademark exit line, "Beats farming," after only four innings, during which he gave up three of the four runs the Paints would score all night. Boesch went six, while giving up the Roosters' only two runs of the game, and evened his record with the win at 7–7.

In the middle of the third the Paints and Roosters squared off in the Chicken Dance challenge we'd been looking forward to for weeks. The Paints did the usual routine (the beaking, flapping, shimmying, and clapping) during the polka parts of the song, but then let it all hang out during the waltz parts. During the first waltz they did four or five cartwheels each, then lined up for a series of "leap frog" jumps; they started the second waltz by doing synchronized kicks out of a chorus line and capped the number by first huddling, and then tossing Rick Blanc high into the air as if he were a petite high school cheerleader. The crowd, which had Chicken Danced right along with the Paints, went bonkers and gave the bullpenners a standing ovation. The challengers from Richmond, assembled in the grass between the home plate cut-out and the grandstand, paid homage to the Paints by bowing deeply and repeatedly.

After the crowd settled down and the Paints came over from the bullpen to get a closer look at the challengers' act, Bobby Chandler and his cohorts took their turn. With their caps turned backwards, they danced, not to the Chicken Dance song, but to the pop hit of the summer, "Who Let the Dogs Out!" by the Baha Men. Of course, there is not a prescribed routine for the latter song, so the boys from Richmond showed off their free-style night club moves, which were heavily freighted with pelvic thrusting, to the delight of the women in the crowd. The highlight of the number came when pitcher Trae Cary, in performing "The Worm," dove onto the ground and, in a remarkable exhibition of spinal flexibility, undulated himself across the grass like a seal. Towards the end, Chief Crazy Horse rode by on Miner's three-wheeler and squirted the dancing Roosters with his Super-Soaker. When it was over, the crowd roared their appreciation, and the Paints and the Roosters took a deep bow together. Just as the two groups finished shaking hands, Phill Kojack appeared, carrying a tray of drinks for the Paints. In one last fall for the Tripper, he stumbled adroitly, and as he went down he pushed the drinks towards the Paints who scattered out of the way, laughing as they went.

The night before, the Roosters' Macky Waguespack had struck out four out of four times to run his streak of strike outs in consecutive at bats to eight. During his final at bat of the night, after hitting a foul ball that arched back over the grandstand roof, he kissed the barrel of his bat. When Nate Gardner finished him off a couple of pitches later for yet another strikeout, he trudged over to the waist-high fence in front of the visitors' dugout and pounded the railing with his bat. Macky's frustrations continued Tuesday night. He whiffed in the second and again in the fifth, to make it ten K's in a row. On the tenth, Aaron played the theme from "The Twilight Zone."

Macky's streak reminded John of a former Paints player who'd had a similar difficulty. "We had a catcher by the name of Josh Streit," said John. "He struck out the first nine times he batted but came out of it to hit .220. He got a loud hand when he hit a foul ball. He had a cannon for an arm though. Teams would not run on him after they saw him throw."

Waguespack also had a redeeming virtue that offset his propensity for strike outs: his power. He was going to finish the year with 16 home runs, good for second place behind London's Rick Nadeau, who was going to lead the league with 19. The tradeoff of strikeouts for home runs is one most managers are willing to make, and Woody Sorrell was looking forward to Macky being an integral part of the Roosters' offense in 2001. After all, slumps happen to every hitter. Still, a strikeout streak like Macky's could shake the confidence of any hitter. And coming as it did at the end of the season only made it worse, as Macky would have all winter to brood about it and possibly come to doubt his ability to put the bat on the ball.

I was hoping that Macky would break the streak with a home run to give him something positive to hang his wintertime thoughts on. He did bring the streak to an end with a fly ball to left in the seventh, but then he succumbed again to his baseball bad habit, the strikeout, when Woody Fullenkamp came on to face him with two outs in the ninth.

Sean Boesch could have gone longer than six innings, but the Paints had another goal besides winning the ballgame. They wanted to help Andy Lee write his name in the record books a couple of times. Going into the game Andy was tied for the league lead in strikeouts with Johnstown's Takuro Seki. Both pitchers had racked up 124 K's. Andy was also, coincidentally, in a tie for the Paints' season strikeout record with Bob Spears, who'd fanned 124 batters in 1998.

Andy got the job done immediately, striking out Steve Mitrovich to open the seventh inning; and he tacked on another K in the eighth for good measure, to make him the strikeout king among Frontier League pitchers for 2000 and the holder of the Paints' record for strikeouts in a season.

Before the game Chief Crazy Horse had asked Max if he would play along with a gag. Max said he would, but when he asked what the gag was the Paints' mascot wouldn't say. "Just follow my lead," Chief Crazy Horse had said.

It was at the end of the seventh inning when Chief Crazy Horse went to work. Max and Schaly were standing halfway up the first base line engaged in conversation when Chief Crazy Horse started towards them. To pique the interest of the crowd, John Wend said, "Chief Crazy Horse is up to something!"

With every eye in the ballpark on him, Chief Crazy Horse pushed Schaly out of the way, faced Max, and pulled out a homemade sign made out of cardboard. He turned towards the grandstand and showed the crowd the message on the sign. "WILL YOU MARRY ME, PLEASE?" it said. The crowd exploded in laughter.

Chief Crazy Horse then got down on one knee and showed the sign to Max.

After reading the sign, Max nodded enthusiastically. Chief Crazy Horse leapt up; he and Max embraced in a bear hug; and the two of them danced around and around and around in each other's arms, while the crowd continued roaring with glee. When they finished twirling each other around, Chief Crazy Horse presented to his betrothed the best symbol of his affection he could get his hooves on: nothing as cliché as an engagement ring but a new Frontier League baseball. As Chief Crazy Horse proudly strode off the field like a centaur, Aaron played a soundbite of Austin Powers saying, "Oh, behave!" John Wend then summed up the moment perfectly: "Ladies and gentlemen, the third consecutive night that a marriage proposal has been made here at VA Memorial Stadium! ... The home of the Paints is going to become known as 'The House of Love'!!!"

With two outs in the eighth Mike Zerbe came to bat for the last time, against Andy Lee who'd just set his strikeout records the inning before. Mike was hitless in the game; but he had stolen his first base of the season in the second on a botched hit and run, and in the bottom of the seventh, after a long run, he'd made a great, sliding catch in the right field corner of a drive off the bat of Phil Warren. With the count at 2–2, Andy Lee threw a curveball which Zerbe looked over but decided not to swing at. Max hesitated, then rang Zerbe up. Finally, for the first time all season, Zerbe showed his frustration. He snatched off his helmet and with both hands slammed it down to the ground. He then brushed past Max without even looking at him. I felt bad for both of them.

Thankfully, Mike didn't stay mad for long. As he ran off the field

at the end of the eighth inning, the crowd gave him a tremendous hand
when John Wend asked them to congratulate the Paints' old nemesis
for the great career he'd had in the Frontier League. Zerbe stopped at
home plate to see Max, and the two old friends embraced and spoke
briefly. Max then handed something to Zerbe which Mike stuck in his
back pocket without looking at.   RADIO RIC

Right before the ninth inning started, I sat down next to Gary Kitchel
in the visiting team's radio booth. Gary was one of many Frontier League
people I'd become very fond of, and I wanted to say goodbye and thank
you. I also wanted to see Gary's just-completed ballot for the 2000 Frontier League All-Star team, which looked like this:

> Catcher—Steve Mitrovich, Richmond Roosters
> First Base—Fran Riordan, Dubois County Dragons
> Second base—Ryan Moore, River City Rascals
> Third Base—Brian Fuess, River City Rascals
> Shortstop—John Taveras, Dubois County Dragons
> Outfield—Aaron Sledd, Richmond Roosters
>   Rick Nadeau, London Werewolves
>   Kirk Taylor, Johnstown Johnnies
> Starting Pitcher—Ryan Bauer, River City Rascals
> Relief Pitcher—Bobby Chandler, Richmond Roosters
> Manager of the Year—Mike Moore, Johnstown Johnnies
> MVP—Rick Nadeau, London Werewolves.

It was a good ballot, and Gary's home team picks were all legitimate.
It was possible that none of the three Roosters Gary had tabbed for the
honorary team would make it, but Mitro, Sledd, and Chandler had all
had good years. When Gary came back from the commercial break, he
told his listeners back in Richmond: "The Roosters will have a chance
to do what they have failed to do all year ... come from behind in the
ninth to win a ballgame."

As Andy Lee threw his warm-up pitches, John Wend asked the crowd
to give the umpires, Max McLeary and Jim Schaly, a big hand for being
such good sports. The fans did just that, and their appreciative applause
was not diluted in the slightest with the booing and snickering which
the big beer drinkers usually think is de riguer at the mere mention of
the men in blue. Aaron Sledd walked to open the ninth but was erased
when Mitrovich hit into a 5–4–3 doubleplay. In between pitches Wend
recognized a number of people who had made important contributions
to the Paints' season, including the reticent but friendly Harry Chenault. Harry, who always had one cigar in his mouth and several more
in his shirt pocket, ran Chenault Printing which was listed in the *Stable
Report* as a major sponsor of Paints baseball. Chris Hanners had told

me that Harry had done more work than any other single volunteer to fix up VA Memorial Stadium before the Paints' first season. I had seen Harry at every Chillicothe game I attended in 2000—like Bryan Wickline, he always seemed to be walking around from one part of the park to another—but I had no idea just how loyal the man was until I heard Wend say that "Harry has never missed a home game in the eight years of the Paints' existence." Harry may have been a walker, but he always paid attention to the game; and if you spoke to him in the eighth inning about something that had happened in the third, he would not only be able to tell you what had happened, but he'd also be able to give you an intelligent comment about it. So that Woody Fullenkamp could pick up one more save, Marty Dunn brought him in to finish off the Roosters. During the call to the bullpen, Wend gave a final send-off, to the Roosters. "They were good sports this whole series, and we wish them all good luck in the future," he said. With a fireworks display still to come and the bittersweet feeling of the end of summer in the air, the crowd was in a festive mood, and they gave the Roosters, Chillicothe's biggest rivals, a tremendous hand. This reaction was very gracious and sincere, as were John's remarks about everybody he'd thanked and recognized. Still, I couldn't help but think that the applause was the least the Paints' fans could do for the Roosters, since Chillicothe had kicked Richmond's butt all summer. Woody's whiff of Macky Waguespack ended the game and the season and made Chillicothe's final edge in the series over Richmond ten games to two. The last and best hand of the night, a standing ovation, was for the Paints as a team, and it came after the final out when John said, "They didn't make the playoffs, but they didn't quit on you, did they, ladies and gentlemen? ... How about those Paints! They won six of the last seven games."

Evansville completed their sweep of River City by beating the Rascals 2–1 in eleven innings; and so, despite the Paints' win, the Otters clinched the final spot in the playoffs. The final standings of the 2000 Frontier League season looked like this:

East Division	W	L	Pct.	GB	West Division	W	L	Pct.	GB
Johnstown	48	36	.571		River City	46	36	.561	
London	46	37	.554	1.5	Evansville	45	38	.542	1.5
Chillicothe	42	40	.512	5.0	Cook County	38	46	.452	9.0
Richmond	40	43	.482	7.5	Springfield	37	46	.446	9.5
Canton	38	46	.452	10.0	Dubois County	35	47	.427	11

For the fireworks show, the atmosphere at VA Memorial, which had always been most hospitable and light-hearted, became even more relaxed. Kids were welcome to sit in the grass between home plate and the grandstand, and many of the players took seats in the grandstands next to their girlfriends or fiancées. As Marty Dunn got ready to watch the display from his usual vantage point, a folding chair off the corner of the Paints' dugout, one his sons climbed into his lap. Neither team had won any laurels, but the explosion of color, form, and noise over the center field fence that lit up the primeval darkness for twenty minutes seemed like a celebration nevertheless. And why not? The players and the managers and the coaches and the umpires and the non-uniformed people like Bill Lee, Gary Kitchel, John Wend, and Jimmy Miner who had kept the wheels spinning ... they had all spent the summer doing what they loved to do, and they'd done their jobs well. And the fans ... they too had a lot to be thankful for. They'd enjoyed a lot of wholesome, inexpensive entertainment, both athletic and comedic; and even though their beloved Paints hadn't qualified for the playoffs, they knew that, under the leadership of Chris Hanners in whom they had the utmost confidence, another strong Paints' contingent would be back next year to try again.

When the fireworks were over and the grandstands lights were turned back on, the Paints assembled on the field for a presentation of awards. Fifty or so fans stayed around and stood in the main field-level aisle watching, and Max, Schaly, and I walked onto the field near the players.

Marty Dunn didn't use, or need in the sudden stillness of the night, a microphone. Addressing the small crowd he said: "If you knew what these guys went through in the clubhouse with the trainer you'd be very very proud of them."

"We're proud of 'em anyway!" shouted a rotund guy, about thirty, who was holding a seat cushion.

"I want to thank our trainer, Rodger Fleming," Marty continued. "All season long he's been here early and he's stayed late. He's the one who kept the guys together physically and gave us a chance to make the playoffs.

"I say this every summer: There's no better place to spend your summer than Chillicothe, Ohio. This is a great town and a great franchise, and you are great people. I thank God for the opportunity to be here in Chillicothe, and it's no surprise to me that the players on other teams always want to come here because of the community and the great people who live here and support the team."

Everybody, not just the fans, applauded at the sentiments Marty had expressed, and then Marty made the presentations. Andy Lee received the team's Most Valuable Pitcher Award; Mike Horning, the Award for Most Valuable Player. Horning's being voted MVP surprised me, as it's not often that a .252 hitter with no power is honored ahead of three-hundred hitters, such as Greg Strickland, whose .330 tied for fifth-best in the league; Jason Baker, who batted .315 with eight home runs; and Justin Graham, the rookie who hit .312, led the team in triples (5), and finished second in extra-base hits (28). When I saw how affectionately Horning's teammates congratulated him though, I realized that in voting him the Most Valuable Player of the team they had recognized him for being what he had always tried to be: the ultimate gamer. Horning's stats in 2000 weren't impressive, but he'd been a three-year starter, and he was retiring with his name entered prominently into the Paints' record book. He was first in at-bats with 860, first in stolen bases (47), third in hits (229) behind only Scott Pinoni and Mitch House, third in doubles (42), and third in runs (152). Horning even made the Paints' top ten list in home runs and RBI. He was leaving town tied for tenth in homers with eight and in sixth place for RBI with 94. Perhaps, I reasoned later, the Paints' vote had also been a referendum on a career, not just a season. Of course, Schaly didn't see it that way, and he couldn't resist kidding Horning as he walked past us off the field. "What'd you do, Mike?" he said. "Vote for yourself ten times!"

For once, Max was content to leave town without stopping by The Dock, which was fine by me. It had been a long night, and we were all bushed. Besides, Chris Hanners kept the Bud wagon open for awhile, and we drank our fill, on the house, one last time.

For weeks Max had been agonizing over the upcoming playoffs. Now that we knew for certain that the participants would be River City, Evansville, London, and Johnstown, he found himself in a real quandary. Max wanted to umpire the playoffs. He felt honored, entitled, and obligated to work the playoffs, and the managers always asked for him and Schaly. As I well knew by now, Max lived by a code that he'd learned from his father. On numerous occasions he'd told me: "My dad always said, 'You work hard, and you play hard.'" Another component of Max's philosophy coming into play was the belief that you finish what you start; and for him finishing the Frontier League season meant umpiring the playoffs, wherever they might be played, right through the final game of the championship series.

The problem was money, and not so much the actual dollars themselves as what they represented. When plutocrat major league free agents have the gall to say, right after having squeezed another two or three million a year out of their new ballclub, "It wasn't the money but the principle of the thing"; sports fans don't know whether to laugh or throw up. With Max the situation was entirely different. Max had umpired Frontier League games all summer long for not much more money than he could have made working amateur and college games closer to home. He felt that common decency, not to mention baseball tradition, stipulated a sizeable increase in pay for the playoffs; but word through the grapevine was that the pay for the playoffs would be raised only slightly, if at all. Working playoff games in London and Johnstown would be a lot more expensive for Max than doing games in Richmond and Chillicothe; but this practical matter aside, what really hurt Max was the thought that his services were not appreciated. If the league really valued its best umpires, then the owners would put their money where their mouths were. Max was distressed that this apparently wasn't going to happen.

On top of all these other considerations, Max was thinking about Johnstown, his tenacious home town, famous for having survived three devastating floods: a history of perseverance in the face of calamity the residents proudly celebrated by building a Flood Museum. Max obviously loved the place and still felt connected to it. His parents, Wilson and Jeanne, were buried there, and Max still owned the house the three of them had lived in for so many years, the house he rented out to Tom Sullivan, the owner of the Johnnies. Johnstown was the scene of many special memories for Max, none more special than Point Stadium. Max had grown up there, first watching his father officiate football games there and then playing there himself and getting his start as an umpire there before he'd graduated from college. Point Stadium was virtually sacred ground for Max, and if Frontier League playoff games were going to be played there, Max felt compelled to be there too.

We discussed all this Tuesday night on the way home from Chillicothe, and we tentatively decided that, for us, the Frontier League season was over. I explained, or perhaps rationalized, that while the book would be more complete if it contained visits to London and Johnstown, the only two cities I hadn't gotten to during the regular season; it wasn't absolutely crucial for me to see either city, as Max himself not the Frontier League was the focus of the book. As for Max, the idea of driving all the way up to London, Ontario, for a single game and then back down to Johnstown to finish the East Division playoffs for an insultingly-low increase in regular-season pay was an injustice he couldn't bear to withstand. When we parted in the McLeary driveway, once again I found Max apologizing, needlessly: this time for wanting to insist that, as the Bible says, "the laborer is worthy of his hire."

Max and I had talked on the phone almost every morning of the summer, so I wasn't surprised when he called me Wednesday morning. I really wasn't surprised either when I realized that the idea of not finishing what he'd started was driving him crazy. Max had changed his mind,

and although he didn't want to push me into going up to London and
Johnstown, I knew he wanted me to go with him. I said, "Max, if you're
going, then I'm going."

"Atta baby!" he said.

The next day we got an early start on the long drive up I-75. It was
the first time all summer we'd been on the interstate highway that goes
through Cincinnati while stretching from Canada to Naples, Florida,
before crossing through the Everglades and running into a state highway about 30 miles west of Ft. Lauderdale. Somewhere between Cincinnati and Toledo we went over the last night of the regular season in
Chillicothe. I wanted to get Max's reaction to Mike Zerbe's farewell, so
I asked him to tell me about their last encounter on the diamond. Max
said that when Zerbe came running off the field at the end of the eighth
inning, to the tribute from John Wend and the spirited applause of the
crowd, he stopped at home plate to hug Max. "He said, 'It's been a great
run,'" said Max.

"I said, 'Mike, it's been a pleasure. You've been a class act all the
way. Here ... take this home with you. Don't look at it now; wait until
you're on the bus.'"

What Max handed to Zerbe was the Roosters lineup card, on the
back of which Max had recorded Mike's performance inning-by-inning.
"I wrote down his hit and stolen base in the second and the great catch
he made in the seventh," Max said. "It'll make a nice souvenir for him
to remember his career by. At the shop I've got two other lineup cards
I saved for him: one from the last game he ever caught, when he was
with the Kalamazoo Kodiaks, and one from the last game he played in
Richmond. I'll mail them to him later."

"Max, that wasn't a hit in the second inning. It was ruled an error,"
I said. "Zerbe had an o-fer in that game."

"Son of a bitch!" said Max. "They called that an error?"

"Yeah, they did." The second-inning scoring decision put Z's final
at bat, when Max rang him up on a questionable and delayed call, in a
whole different light.

"You know, Max, Gary Kitchel didn't think much of Zerbe as a ballplayer. He loved him as a person, but he'd always say something like,
'Zerbe is the nicest horrible ballplayer in the world.' ... Off the air, of
course. ... He thought Zerbe never hit in the clutch."

Max didn't respond, so I asked him: "Do you agree that Mike didn't
have a very good year?"

"Yeah, but there was a reason for that," Max said. "He was just too
banged up from catching. Zerbe took a lot of punishment catching in
this league, and it eventually just wore him out. You remember I said I
have the lineup card from the last game Zerbe caught? Well, I was the

one who told his manager to take him out. This was when Kalamazoo was in the league, and Andy McCauley was their manager. Zerbe had already been hit by a couple of foul tips in the game, and then he got run over on a play at the plate. I mean he just got hammered, leveled. I called Andy over and told him, 'Hey, Mike was already beat up, and now he's started talking gibberish. You got to get him outta here. I don't want to stand behind him, not when he's in this condition.' Andy laughed, but he took Zerbe out of the game, and Mike never caught again in the Frontier League."

As we made our way north, I engaged in my usual motoring diversion, gazing at every community, small town, and city we passed through with an eye towards spotting where baseball—whether Little League, scholastic, or professional—was played. I'd never seen Ned Skeldon Stadium, home of Toledo's famous Mud Hens, so when we reached the outskirts of the city I asked Max if he'd ever umpired there. I was surprised when he said he hadn't because it seemed as if Max had umpired everywhere, at least everywhere in Ohio and Indiana. We made it into southern Michigan by noon and stopped at a McDonald's for lunch, as our umpire and author per diems were coming out of our own pockets. Max was already having misgivings about having undertaken our final road trip together, but I discovered a good omen: the McDonald's we'd chosen to stop at was decorated in a *Blues Brothers*-fifties music theme. There to greet us by the front door on our way to Big Macs and fries were life-sized statues of our favorite men in black, Jake and Elwood dancing up a storm.

We were going to cross into Canada at Detroit. When we neared the Ambassador Bridge, that connects Detroit and Windsor, Ontario, Max warned me not to joke around with the customs agent who was going to question us, unless I wanted to turn a 30-second interview into a two-hour search of the car and our persons. Accordingly, I bit my tongue when the agent asked if we had any weapons or drugs in the vehicle. The woman asked Max where we were going and what his business there would be. "I'm going to London to umpire the first round of the Frontier League Playoffs," he said.

"And you? Are you going to umpire too?" she said, lowering her head a bit in order to see past Max and get a look at me.

"No, I'm not." I said. "I'm playing Boswell to his Johnson."

"Don't mind him," Max said. "He's an author. You know how goofy they are."

Apparently, Max's explanation was good enough for the agent. "Enjoy your stay," she said, waving us through.

WOOD SORRELL
WAS ASSIST COACH AT CARROLL H.S.
WHEN I UMPED / HEAD COACH AT UD !
BEFORE CURRENT COACH.

The last leg of our trip was a straight shot, in a north-easterly direction, on highway 401 across southern Ontario. I kept staring out of the window, trying to absorb the flat Canadian landscape, which I'd expected to be somehow fundamentally different from the United States. It wasn't. Except that Ontario seemed to be more desolate and more fallow, while every inch of arable land in the U.S. seemed to be under cultivation.

As we drove across Ontario, we talked about the game and the city we were approaching. Although the Werewolves were the defending champs, everybody—Woody Sorrell, Chris Hanners, Bill Lee, Jim Schaly—seemed to think that Johnstown was the class of the league. London ended up only a game and a half behind the Johnnies, but the Werewolves had also finished the season with a four-game losing streak and had gone 3–7 in their last ten. Clearly, London was playing bad baseball at the wrong time of the year. The two playoff participants in the West Division were also teams heading in opposite directions: first place River City having lost their last five in a row; Evansville having won their final three under pressure to edge out Chillicothe for that final league playoff spot. Max agreed with the consensus that Johnstown was the team to beat and that Evansville was the dark horse in the field, but he was really thinking more about London's nightlife than its baseball team. Max told me that London had a bar we had to pay a visit to, a place called The Honest Lawyer.

The name of the pub really tickled Max and inevitably led to some remarks from us both about the legal profession, not all of them charitable. It also reminded me of the two most actionable incidents of Max's umpiring career, and I asked him if he'd thought seriously about suing after the second one. "Andy McCauley said I ought to sue the ass off the company that made the mask. Two of the owners of one of the teams in the Great Lakes League are lawyers, and they said they'd take the case for me for free. But I'm just not the type that likes to sue. ... Besides, I don't know how much I would have gotten even if we'd won a lawsuit. When they heard more of the details, the lawyers said, 'Well, you didn't help yourself by going right back to work the next day.'"

"Yeah, I guess so," I said. "And as painful as the injury was, it's not like it affected your ability to do your job."

"Oh, but it has," Max corrected me. "It's made me flinch. ... Not very often, but on a certain pitch in just the right location, I can't help it: I flinch. And I turn my head a little bit, which is dangerous. So it has affected my ability to do my job, and that really bothers me."

Not once had I noticed Max flinching, which kind of bothered me. I took a good look at him then, as he stared straight ahead through the windshield at the endless sky and empty roadscape ahead of us, and I could see in the fatigue on his face the toll the season had taken on him. We made a pit stop at the next exit, and I offered to drive the rest of the way to London. For the first time all season Max took me up on the offer. Before I'd even gotten comfortable behind the wheel, he had slumped against the passenger door and gone to sleep.

14

Werewolves in London (and Johnstown, PA): The Playoffs

THE OFFICIAL VISITING CLUB HOTEL in London, the Super 8 Motel on York Street, looked fine to me, but Max didn't like it. Mainly, I thought, because it was not practically next door to The Honest Lawyer, as was the centralized hotel on Wellington Street, the London Armories, where the Werewolves had put Max up the previous year.

"Max, this location can't be that bad ... we're still downtown and there's a church across the parking lot," I said.

"Yeah, but look at what's across the street," he said.

The Beef Baron sounded like a restaurant, but upon closer inspection I realized it was a strip joint which had been named by somebody with a penchant for double entendre. "Wow! How convenient for the players. No wonder the visiting teams find it so hard to win in London!" I joked.

Our room at the Super 8, with two double beds, was fine except for one thing, the air conditioning, which is the main thing in August and September. The AC unit in our room switched on immediately and ran hard; it just didn't provide much cold air. Worse, we couldn't open the windows. We'd wanted to get a little rest before the game, but faced with the choice of sweating in a stuffy motel room or at the ballpark, we choose the latter, where the possibility of a cool breeze at least existed.

[handwritten note in margin: ASK FOR ANOTHER ROOM]

359

Labatt Memorial Park, on the west side of town, was only a few miles from our motel. It borders a residential neighborhood called Hyde Park and sits on the banks of the Thames River, both named like many of London's streets and neighborhoods after people, places, and things English, as befitting London's heritage as Britain's earliest Canadian outpost. Facing east, the Park offers past the outfield fence and across the Thames an expansive view of downtown London. We entered the ballpark by driving through the gate of a tall wrought iron fence which surrounds it. Looking straight ahead through the crease between the main grandstand and two roofless sections of bleachers down the first base line, we caught a glimpse of the diamond; turning left, we puttered between girders holding up the main grandstand and reached a large grassy parking lot behind the two roofless sections of bleachers down the third base line. It was the first time I'd ever been in a ballpark that enclosed its parking lot within its walls. An even quirkier feature of the stadium, named after the famous Canadian brewery whose tasty Labatt's Blue I'd found (many times) on tap at The Dock in Chillicothe, was the blue mesh covering that served as the roof over the main grandstand. At first I thought that the mesh roof might be an artistic statement—shades of Cristo again!—but then I decided that it was more likely an economizing tactic. In any event I figured that while it probably offered the fans shade, protection from the rain was almost certainly a different story.

I'd been curious about the Werewolves' home ever since I read references to it in the *Frontier League Directory*. The *Directory* states that the ballpark opened in 1866 and claims (in parentheses) that it is the "oldest facility in the world." For such a claim to be truthful it almost always needs a qualification (or clarification) or two, and in this case my guess was that what might legitimately deserve the title of "oldest in the world" was the site, not the "facility" itself. Delving into my own extensive baseball library, I'd read that London's professional baseball heritage dated all the way back to the formation of the third major league, the short-lived International Association, in 1877; when the London Tecumsehs won the IA's first league championship—Canada's only professional baseball championship until the Toronto Blue Jays won the World Series in 1992 and again in 1993. What I wasn't able to determine was where the Tecumsehs in 1877, as well as amateur and independent professional London clubs prior to 1877, played their home games. Perhaps amateur London ball teams were playing on the site of Labatt Memorial Park in 1866, but no professional team was; as the Cincinnati Red Stockings of 1869 are acknowledged, without challenge, as having been the first completely and overtly professional baseball team.

Regardless of the exact meaning of the phrase used to describe

Labatt Memorial in the *Frontier League Directory*, nobody other than myself was thinking about ancient history. Everybody else was focused on the present and the fact that the Werewolves were staring at their chance to be the first team to win back-to-back Frontier League Cups. The Werewolves immediately blinked.

London manager Andy McCauley started Brian Gillow on the mound, a move which made perfect sense since Gillow had gone 7–1 with a 1.78 ERA during the regular season. He had also been especially tough on Johnstown, going 2–0 against them with a 1.07 ERA and 17 strikeouts versus only two walks. The Johnnies weren't worried about any of this though. They exuded confidence and scored early, often, and easily on the way to a 10–2 victory. Johnstown jumped ahead in the top of the first with a pair of runs that scored on a hit batter and a fielder's choice. With the help of a throwing error by London third baseman Ryan Anholt, they plated another pair in the third; two more in the fourth (after which Gillow retired for the evening); three in the fifth; and a final run in the sixth. By the time the Werewolves drew blood, with single runs in the seventh and eighth, the game was essentially over.

Fortunately for me, in light of the game's turning out to be a blowout, London maintained one of the most entertaining press boxes I'd been in all summer. The tone was set by John Kuhn, the Mike Veeck protégé, who worked as the public address announcer, as well as serving as London's president and general manager. In addition to providing an off-mike comic running commentary, Kuhn interacted with the crowd all night. When he spotted a chunky young guy with a fu-man-chu in the stands, Kuhn said. "Ladies and gentlemen, please welcome sitting in the box seats, fresh off his 19th win of the season, David 'Boomer' Wells! ... Go Blue Jays." The David Wells look-alike actually stood up and took a bow. Later, Kuhn badgered two boys returning from the concession stand into bringing their food up to the press box. "Fans, we now have our pizza and twist-tie bread in the press box," he said as he held the pizza box out the window for all to see. To compensate the kids, he ordered baseballs for them from the concession stand and then announced over the P.A.: "Thank you to the two boys in the box seats on the third base side who brought me their own pizza and twist-tie bread. ... Thanks, guys. ... But I could have done without that big glob of spit you left on the bread." Periodically, throughout the game, we could hear somebody barking like a junk yard dog. Kuhn was highly impressed—"That guy is outstanding!"—and he continually searched for the source of the barking but never could locate the guy.

As disappointing as the Werewolves were on the field, Kuhn was even more disappointed with the attendance at what everyone realized might be London's last home game of the year and with the crowd's

lack of enthusiasm. He also wasn't shy about sharing his feelings. After
the bugle "Charge" over the P.A. in the bottom of the first inning did
not elicit a spirited enough response, he said, "When we play the
'Charge!' music, you're supposed to cheer like you really mean it. Let's
try it again." The crowd did a little better the second time, which Kuhn
acknowledged by saying to them, "Thank you for your support." To us
he said, "Whatever happened to those guys? ... Bartles and James."

Kuhn's mood dampened as the game progressed and the size of the
crowd did not noticeably increase. When the "Charge!" ditty brought
a tepid response in the third as the Werewolves mounted their first
offensive threat of the game, Kuhn actually reproved the fans. "Terrible!" he said. "Try again." This time the crowd's slight improvement
was not good enough. "No sale!" he groused. Kuhn's dissatisfaction
came to a head in the sixth when he told Morris Dalla Costa of *The London Free Press*, in reference to the attendance of 844, "This is just embarrassing ... compared to last year. And you can quote me on that, with
a couple of blanks and an ampersand in front of the 'embarrassing.'"

Moments later the phone rang in the press box, and it was Bill Lee
calling from Evansville to tell Kuhn that in the top of the eighth inning
the Evansville Otters had a 5–1 lead over the River City Rascals in the
first game of the West Division semi-final series.

After the game I eavesdropped on Werewolves pitching coach Bruce
Gray and McCauley talking to the media in front of the London dugout.
"We've been playing ugly for about a week," said Gray. "When the switch
gets turned off, sometimes you can't get it turned back on."

Gray's explanation was an artful admission that he didn't really have
an answer for why London had played so poorly. While the grim McCauley
talked at greater length and more analytically, he didn't have any answers
either and seemed to be trying to convince himself, as much as his listeners, that the Werewolves still had a chance to take the short, best-of-
three series. "Pitching aside," he said, "we have to swing the bats better
... we have to hit with runners in scoring position ... we have to do a
better job of keeping the pressure on them early on.

"When we get down early, we try to hit a ten-run home run. We did
that all season, and you are gonna play in the playoffs the same way you
play in the regular season. What we need to do is to answer the other
team run by run.

"Before the game I thought we were up. I thought we were focused
and very intense. We took a great round of BP and infield. We were up.
Johnstown just brought out their bats tonight.

"Do we have the balls to beat Johnstown and bring it back here for
the finals? Yes. They haven't seen Mark Sheppard, who's going to start
on Saturday, so that's a plus in our favor; and if we win that one, anything

can happen. If we play the way we're capable, we can beat anybody, but we need guttier performances from some guys. ... We're not out of it. We have to execute and do the things we need to do to win. But we've won in Johnstown before, and we can do it again. It won't be easy, but we can do it."

Jamie Blaesing was a left-handed relief pitcher who'd started the season in Richmond. He had come to London as part of the big trade between the Werewolves and the Roosters. Before rejoining Max I stopped by the Werewolves' clubhouse under the third base bleachers and coaxed him into coming out for a few minutes; not just to say hello but in order to get him to tell me about his having been the pitcher who wound up facing Joe Charboneau.

"He was supposed to have batted late in Sunday's game, but we got rained out after seven innings," Jamie said, "so his big at bat was pushed back a day. In Monday night's game I was going to start the bottom of the eighth in relief, and I was a little nervous ... not because I was going to face Charboneau or because the game was on the line—the score was 11–1 in favor of Canton—but because I hadn't pitched in ten days. They've been trying to retain my status as a one-year player for next year by limiting the number of innings I pitch this year.

"Anyway, before I went out to the mound, Bruce Gray, our pitching coach, said that Charboneau was going to be leading off the inning as a pinch hitter, and he told me to throw him fastballs and to try not to walk him.

"The Canton players were all standing on the top step of the dugout, and when he started walking up to the plate the crowd went absolutely crazy. He was kind of smiling on his way up, and when he took his practice swings it looked like he hadn't missed a beat. Somebody later told me that an article in the paper said that he'd been taking BP. The first pitch I threw he took for a called strike. Then I threw a ball. He swung and missed at a pitch in the dirt, and on the next pitch, another fastball, he hit a line drive up the middle. The crowd gave him a standing ovation, and he stayed on the bases and ran. It didn't bother me at all that he got a hit off me. I was just glad to get out of the inning with no runs scored. After I got a little perspective on it, I thought it was actually pretty neat that I got to pitch to him. Afterwards at the hotel my host mom and dad, Del and Pat Gough, who'd made the trip with us to Canton, got him to sign a picture of himself to me. And the next day I got to meet him before the game. A photographer from the Canton paper took my picture with him, and he's going to mail a copy of it to me. The whole thing is something I'll definitely remember for the rest of my life. ... I got to pitch to Joe Charboneau. And although I didn't get him out, he also didn't hit a home run off me."

When I asked Jamie if he'd thought about contacting the insurance company to ask for a piece of the $25,000 he'd saved them by denying Joe a home run, he laughed and said no, the idea had not occurred to him.

After the game we were led to a sports bar called Alibi, which was picked out by Sean Reid, the local guy who'd umped third base. Max, who'd had first base, and Bruce Doane, who'd worked the plate, had nicknamed Reid "The Rookie" because the kid was only 21 years old. Reid, who by his own admission was more of a hockey official than a baseball umpire, had not had any tough plays in the game, but he'd handled himself well. For most of the night Sean sat quietly, sipping beer and working on a pizza he was sharing with his girlfriend, Jade, one of the groundskeepers at Labatt Memorial; but he did have a question for Max.

"What did that mean when you had your hands down by your sides and you were pinching your index fingers and thumbs together?" he asked.

"That's the signal we give when there's only one out to go in the game," said Max, "and it means 'Two six-packs of beer to go!'"

"I thought so," said Sean, "except that in Canada we hold our hands and arms apart like this … one hand at the waist and one at the neck … sort of like the cradle you make for a football handoff, and our signal means we're only one out away from a half barrel of beer."

When Sean and Jade got up from the table to go shoot a game of pool, Bruce said that if Sean was an even better hockey official than he was an umpire then it wouldn't surprise him if Sean made it to the National Hockey League one day. Max gave Sean credit for "sitting here with three old farts trying to learn baseball when he could have gone straight home after the game and gotten laid."

Like Max, Bruce was an American, imported to Ontario for the Frontier League playoffs because Andy McCauley and the Werewolves considered most of the Canadian umpires at their disposal to be incompetent. Although Bruce had umpired in the league during its inaugural season when Lancaster (OH), Newark (OH), and Zanesville (OH) were all in the league along with Chillicothe and later when Kalamazoo joined the league, the playoff game between London and Johnstown was the first Frontier League game he had umpired all summer. To do it he had come up from Grand Rapids, Michigan, where he made $25 an hour working as a waiter in an up-scale steak house he said was "similar to Ruth Crist's." Bruce said he'd gotten into umpiring almost accidentally. "I didn't know what to do with my life, and I'd always loved baseball so my dad said, 'Why don't you go to umpire school?' So I did.

I went to Bill Kinnamon's school, and that's where I met John McSherry who was one of the instructors. As you know, McSherry was the umpire who died on the field in Cincinnati on Opening Day a few years ago. McSherry was a great guy, and everybody loved him. He called me 'Pills' because of Doan's Pills for back pain. At the end of the course, he took me and my girlfriend out to drink beer. He said, 'Pills, you don't know how close you came to being offered a job in rookie ball. Your problem is you don't really give a shit. Go home, drink some beer— I was real skinny back then—and come back next year.' I didn't go back, but six years later I decided to go to a different school, the one run by Harry Wendelstedt. And that was a mistake. You see, there's a lot of jealousy among umpiring schools, and I think that when they found out I'd been to a different school, they didn't like me as much as before. I'd been told I was in the top five in the class, but when it came time to getting hired for a job in pro ball, I slipped all the way to 21, and there were 19 jobs available. So I basically went into college ball.

"Anyway, the place McSherry took us to was a real hole in the wall, a typical umpire bar, but John liked it and everybody there knew him. He ordered two pitchers of beer. One for me and my girlfriend, and one for himself. The waitress only brought two glasses, and I said, 'Don't you want a glass, John?'

"'Hell, no,' he said. He picked up the pitcher with one hand—he had huge hands—and started drinking right out of the pitcher. And he told funny story after funny story. In fact, he's the funniest guy I've ever known. I remember one time towards the end of the umpiring school the students were going to divide into two teams and play a game so that we could practice umpiring under game conditions. We were waiting for McSherry, who was going to manage one of the teams, to show up to start the day. We stood around a while on the field, then here comes ten umpiring students, carrying a couch over their heads, and lying on the couch is McSherry! He's wearing a wild Hawaiian shirt, and he's holding a big fruity drink with a little umbrella in it. They set the couch down on the field, and he managed the whole game from there."

Bruce and Max had never met before the game, but umpiring had given them the instant intimacy and feeling of being united against common enemies and obstacles that people in the same specialized profession acquire naturally. Max was angry that they had been paid $85 for the game. He'd been led to believe that they were going to get $100. The $15 shortage couldn't have meant much (even times three) to the financial fortunes of the Werewolves, but it made a lot of difference to a traveling umpire. Max was so angry that I heard him for the first time bring up a subject I never thought I'd hear him discuss: leading an umpires' boycott of the Frontier League next season.

Bruce was more bothered by the "rats," which is "star" spelled backwards and is what umpires call the players, he explained. "I hate it when the players call me 'Blue,'" he continued. "I have a name. 'Blue' is a color. I'm not a color."

"Jim Schaly, Max's regular partner hates that too," I said.

"They even call us 'Blue' when we wear red shirts!" added Max.

Bruce's main complaint was with the fickleness of the players when the calls don't go their way; an occupational hazard perfectly illustrated by the game he and Max had just umpired. "In the beginning London's catcher, Girod, was a nice guy," Bruce said. "He said, 'How's it going?' … 'Where you from?' … things like that. I've learned that when they do that, you're in for a long night. When we had that play at the plate in the top of the fourth, Girod screamed, 'I got him!'; so I said, 'Tony, when you tagged him he was standing on the plate.'

"He said, 'I wasn't talking to you.'

"'Good. That's fine with me,' I said. I didn't say another word to him all night."

The play that Bruce referred to came when Johnstown's David Ferres lined a single to left with two outs and runners on second and third. Charles Vanrobays scored easily from third, but London left fielder Willie Edwards had a shot at the second runner, Eliott Sarabia. When London catcher Tony Girod could see that Edwards' throw was going to come up short, he moved up the third base line towards it. Sarabia didn't slide, but Girod had to reach backwards to tag him, and Bruce called Sarabia safe. The outrage that came from the crowd was the loudest reaction to an umpire's call I'd heard all summer. It may have been fueled partly by the fact that London had had a runner thrown out at the plate by Johnstown a half inning earlier. Having two plays at the plate in consecutive half innings both go against London probably caused the fans to feel as if the Werewolves were getting "homered" at home by the umpire, but that wasn't the case at all in my opinion.

After Max named his candidates for biggest Dr. Jekyll–Mr. Hyde players in the league, Bruce summed up the umpiring predicament which had made his job that evening more of a pain in the ass than usual. "What's tough is going somewhere where people don't know you. They test you, and you have to prove you know what you're doing, that you can control the game. Then they quit messing with you. But you get tired of always having to prove yourself."

"I couldn't believe how much the crowd got on me tonight, particularly on that play at the plate," he continued. "I think it's because they've had such bad umpiring all summer. I kept hearing this one umpire's name all night … I forget his name, as in, 'You're worse than so-and-so.'" Max knew exactly who the fans had been referring to, and

RATS / STAR — BACKWARDS

I DID NOT know now Till now 11/16 0223

WELL PUT BRUCE

when he said the guy's name, Bruce shouted, "That's it!" and we all had a big laugh about it.

Although I didn't feel like staying out late, I knew that we were going to have to make one more stop; and so, after saying goodbye to Sean and Jade, Max, Bruce, and I found our way to The Honest Lawyer and closed the place.

The next day, Friday, was a travel day. St. Mary's, across the parking lot, did not offer a daily Mass, so I drove the Buick over to Dufferin Avenue in the heart of downtown for the 7:30 Mass at St. Peter's, London's awesome Gothic cathedral which was dedicated in 1885. After Mass I drove around until I found a Tim Horton's, the Canadian doughnut, pastry, and coffee company which had been recently purchased by the Wendy's hamburger chain. I'd been wanting to try a Tim Horton doughnut for some time. After sampling one of their glazed doughnuts, I took one back to Max at the Super 8.

"Here you go, Max," I said handing him the bag. "It's just as I thought: Canadian doughnuts aren't any better than Canadian umpires. There's no comparison between this and a Krispy Kreme, but it'll have to do this morning."

"Thanks," said Max. "By the way, how long have you been going to daily Mass?"

"Ever since I started hanging around with unrepentant hell raisers like you," I joked.

By ten A.M. we were on the road again, making the 412-mile drive from London to Johnstown. Our all-directions route resembled the course of a zig-zagging football player running a kickoff back and forth and up and down the length of the field. We started off in a northeasternly direction on our way to Woodstock, Hamilton, and Burlington; then with Lake Ontario on our left went eastwards across the lower Ontario peninsula to St. Catherines. After driving south to re-enter the good old USA at Buffalo, we headed down Interstate 90 in a southwesternly direction, now with Lake Erie on our right. Just past Erie, Pennsylvania, we caught Interstate 79 and dropped straight down, past Pittsburgh, all the way to I-70 in the southern part of the state. Moving eastward again we stayed on I-70, which merged with the perennially dilapidated Pennsylvania Turnpike (I-76), until we reached state road 219 (right past Somerset). We drove up 219, again in a northeasternly direction, for about 25 miles to where it hooked up with the Johnstown Expressway (about five miles east of downtown) which carried us the rest of the way into Johnstown. This crazy route was the sanest, most direct one available, and Max drove it without once having to look at a map. As we'd done all summer, we reviewed the night before once we got on the highway. I told Max that I'd read in the paper that Evansville had hung on to beat River City 5–2. When I told him about Kuhn's frustration at not being able to locate the canine impersonator, he said that the barking had come out of the Johnstown bullpen. Max didn't know the reliever's name, but he was the only black kid on the Johnnies' roster. I asked Max if The Honest Lawyer the night before had been everything he had remembered it being. The nearly empty bar hadn't seemed like anything special to me; and tired and bored, I'd spent most of the rest of the night feigning interest in the televised Canadian Football League game between Montreal and British Columbia.

"No, it wasn't," he said. "But last year I was in London for the finals, and we went to The Honest Lawyer right after they'd won the league championship. They celebrated all night long, and the place was crawling with good looking women."

"That's quite a difference," I said. "Sometimes, I guess, … you just can't go home again, can you, Max?"

I'd been eating fast food and free hot dogs in Frontier League press boxes all summer. As we neared Johnstown around supper time, I couldn't help thinking about something more substantial. In fact, I was craving a juicy steak and a big salad with lots of blue cheese dressing, and I wanted to eat at a restaurant that was part of a national steak house chain so that there would be no surprises. The problem was I knew Max wanted to eat at a restaurant located on top of Yoder Hill which was part of the famous Johnstown Inclined Plane complex. The Johnstown Inclined Plane, the steepest vehicular incline in the world, was built in 1891 in the aftermath of the Great Johnstown Flood of 1889; the idea being to transport people, horses, and wagons to the safety of the Westmont Borough overlooking downtown Johnstown in the event of a future flood. The Inclined Plane, with the fantastic view it affords of the city and Conemaugh Valley from the summit, was a can't-miss attraction, and there was no way I would miss it. I just didn't want to eat supper at the restaurant there, even though Max had raved many times about the restaurant's onion soup which he'd assured me was out of this world.

"Max, there's gotta be an Outback or Lonestar steak house in Johnstown," I said. "I'm dying for a decent meal. Let's eat supper at one of those places. … I'm buying."

"No! This is my town! I know all the best places to eat," he snapped, settling the question.

Much of the last leg of our drive into downtown Johnstown was literally and figuratively downhill. We passed through neighborhoods of small, poorly maintained houses that had seen better days, and in the heart of downtown there were vacant plants, warehouses, and office buildings. The people of Johnstown had shown great courage and determination in rebuilding the town three times after the devastating floods of 1889, 1936, and 1977, but it was proving to be even tougher to survive the closing of the local steel mills and coal mines, which had always been the backbone of the city's economy. Realizing that its once thriving industrial base was not coming back, the city had switched gears and was well into implementing a plan to make Johnstown a home for high-end technology and heritage-based tourism. In addition to its heroic resilience, the city also manifested a quiet but deep-seated pride in simply being what it perceived itself to be: "Friendly, clean, safe," according to the "Welcome to Johnstown" sign we passed on the way in.

The Johnstown Expressway went right past the hotel, the Town Manor, where the league was putting the umpires up. According to Max, the place had been nicknamed "the Town Manure" by the Johnnies' shortstop, Eliott Sarabia. It was definitely not the best Johnstown had to offer. The plate glass window in the front of the building was cracked, the furniture in the lobby seedy, the carpet threadbare, our bathroom ancient, our mattresses thin and lumpy, and, once again, the air conditioning in our room merely a rumor. Even the wallpaper in the halls betrayed management's hands-off approach towards maintenance, much less renovation. "Max, this is the same stuff we have on the walls in our basement ... the wallpaper that was put up when the house was built in the fifties!" I laughed. Max was again perturbed with the financial arrangements, this time involving the accommodations. The league had not paid for the room, so Max, irritated that he was going to have to get reimbursed, paid for it in cash. Max didn't use a credit card because he didn't have one. "Nobody my age or older has a credit card here," he said, "and whenever they bring in a manager from outside the town to work here, they're always shocked by this. But this is a mill-hunk town. In the old days when the mills and mines were open, you'd get paid on Friday, and after work you'd go to a bar to cash your check because the bars always had lots of cash for that very purpose. You'd drink two beers, go home and hand the rest of the money over to your wife who'd pay the bills, and then you'd eat supper."

The one good thing about our hotel was its location. Everything was right there. Jerry's Lounge, a converted tootsie roll-colored two-story house, was next door on the right. On the left, across the highway and on the other side of the Stony Creek River was the mountainous Yoder Hill and the famous Inclined Plane; while directly across the street was Point Stadium, home of the Johnnies.

Opened in 1926, Point Stadium hosted some of the Pittsburgh Crawfords' and Homestead Grays' Negro League games in the 1930s. It got its name from its location, a wedge-shaped tract of land at the confluence of the Stony Creek and the Little Conemaugh Rivers which come together in the northwest corner of downtown Johnstown to form the Conemaugh River. City founder Joseph Johns (whose German name "Schantz" had been anglicized to "Johns") set aside the plot of land in 1800 for "the town's common and public amusements," but few activities ever took place there, besides occasional baseball games, because the area was so prone to flooding. Between 1881 and 1889 alone Johnstown suffered seven floods of note. And then on May 31, 1889, the most catastrophic flood in the city's history occurred.

Twelve miles above Johnstown a dam across the South Fork of the Little Conemaugh had been built in 1852 in order to provide a reservoir for the Pennsylvania canal. Unprecedented rains caused the dam to burst, unleashing a 37-foot high wall of water that rushed through the valley and down into Johnstown at a speed of 20 m.p.h. It would take a book to recount the almost total destruction of Johnstown and the complete annihilation of seven other towns in the valley which ensued, and in fact numerous books have been written on the subject. Suffice it to say that the devastation of the flood, which killed an estimated tenth of Johnstown's population of 30,000, was unimaginable. Of the thousands of astonishing and heart-breaking details provided by any full account of the tragedy, one of the most remarkable is the fact that the stone railroad bridge at the head of the Point withstood the massive surge of the flood and served as a dam to the four acres of wreckage which piled up in front of it. Unbelievably, this huge island of debris caught fire—coal-burning kitchen stoves in overturned houses ignited fires above the water line all over town—and some people who were saved from drowning by the wreckage in front of the bridge were burned. Weeks later, after the wreckage was removed and the streets were cleared—in some places the debris reached second-story windows—the earth dug from the cellars and streets was dumped at the Point, raising its height five feet. Despite its elevation, the Point was inundated again, by the flood of 1936. Although loss of life this time was negligible, the economic loss was more than $80 million; a loss which prompted the U.S. army corps of engineers to embark on a five-year program to install an $8 million flood-control system. The concrete walls that I saw lining the banks of both rivers were part of that effort, which protected Johnstown from further catastrophic flooding until the city was hit in 1977 with a deluge the National Weather Service characterized as a once-in-a-5,000-to-10,000-year occurrence. In a ten-hour period on July 19–20 11.82 inches of rain fell on the area, causing Johnstown's sewer system and six nearby dams to fail. This time 80 people were killed, and the property damage exceeded $350 million.

When it comes to old ballparks I agree, up to a point, with the view suggested by the title of Philip J. Lowry's seminal book on the subject, *Green Cathedrals.* Baseball parks are not truly sacred in the same sense as churches and perhaps battlefields, but they are undeniably very, very special places where communal and generational bonds, which otherwise might not come to be, are forged and strengthened. Individuals are of course free to reject my rejection of sentimentality in this matter; and, if there is an exception to my view, surely it is Point Stadium which rates one. Far be it from me, I thought, to argue with Max and other Johnstown natives who believe that Point Stadium is a holy place, inexorably connected as it is to the tragic and heroic history of the city. Before we went to dinner Max took me across the street to Point Stadium's newly renovated center field entrance and ticket booth to show me something which meant a great deal to him: two memorial bricks in the walkway that led up to the new ticket booth. The inscription on one said, "'Mac' McLeary, Football Official, 1946–1975." The other said, "Larry McLeary, Baseball Player, And Umpire."

Max and I were the only passengers in the Inclined Plane car when we took our 3,586-foot ride up to the top of Yoder Hill. The roundtrip, souvenir tickets cost $3 each. The view from the restaurant was spectacular ... and sobering, as Max pointed out the path, between two mountains, that the Great Johnstown Flood of 1889 had taken. When it came time to order, Max asked our waitress why he couldn't find the onion soup on the menu. The restaurant was under new management, she explained, and no longer offered onion soup. I'd never seen Max so disappointed, and so we ate in near silence. I'd read in the *Tribune-Democrat* that that evening was the first Friday night of the high school football season in Pennsylvania. Thinking that a visit to his alma mater might cheer Max up, I suggested that we go watch his Richland Rams play host to the Cambria Heights Highlanders. That was our plan until we returned to the Town Manor and Max realized that the annual Johnstown FolkFest was being kicked off that very night in nearby Cambria City, a working-class neighborhood, just north of the Point, that had served as an entry port for many of the immigrants who came to work in Johnstown's steel mills and coal mines in the 19th and early 20th centuries. Max knew that the festival was going to offer lots of great music, ethnic food, and beer; and these attractions, coupled with the likely possibility of his running into some old friends, made the event irresistible to him.

Ten blocks of Chestnut Street were closed off to auto traffic, and we spent hours walking up and down both sides of the street, people watching, and being tantalized by the aromas emanating from the food booths serving Mexican, German, Polish, Chinese, Italian, and Thai dishes. I was astounded to find ten nationality churches, several of them historically important, on this one street; which, much more than the ethnic foods being sold, testified to the true melting-pot character of the neighborhood.

Max never did encounter any old friends, but to his delight we bumped into a group of Johnnies, led by outfielder-coach Kirk Taylor. Congratulations were in order for Taylor, who, according to the morning paper, had been named to the Frontier League All-Star team for 2000. The rest of the team turned out to be: Fran Riordan (Dubois County) 1B, Billy Bone (Springfield) 2B, Brian Fuess (River City) 3B, Geoff McCallum (London) SS, Scott Marple (Dubois County) OF, Rick Nadeau (London) OF, Shaun Argento (Canton) C, Chris Gavriel (London) DH, Ryan Bauer (River City) SP, and Drew Thomas (Canton) RP. Nadeau was named Most Valuable Player; Bauer, Most Valuable Pitcher; and Johnstown's Mike Moore, Manager of the Year. Although I didn't know quite what to make of it, I found it interesting that four of the eleven All-Stars came from the two last place teams, Dubois County and Canton. Evansville, one of the four teams in the playoffs, did not place anybody on the team, nor did Chillicothe or Richmond.

As secure as Max was in his reputation for fairness and professionalism, he'd told me before that it was never a good idea for any umpire to be seen socializing with the members of one team only, and so we parted company with the Johnnies before Max could be accused of hanging out with them. Before we did, I got a chance to clear up an important matter with rookie relief pitcher John Lewter. "Hey, what's the deal with the barking?" I asked.

Lewter, who seemed pleased to be recognized for his unique talent, told me that he barked when things got quiet. "It wakes my team up," he said. Did the Baja Men's song, "Who Let the Dogs Out!," that had been played to death all summer inspire him? No, he'd been barking long before that song became so popular, ever since he pitched in high school back in Frostproof, Florida. Had he ever barked from the mound during a Frontier League game? No, he'd never do that he laughed. I concluded this interview for the ages with one last question on the most crucial point of all: what kind of dog was it?

"A rottweiler," he said proudly.

To get to the festival we had taken a free shuttle van ride from the hotel. To get back we decided to walk. As we headed back towards the Point, Johnstown's abandoned steel mills, which ran for 26 miles, were on our left and on the far side of the Conemaugh. They were the same mills that Max and Max's dad, Wilson, had worked in. Wilson, Max had told me previously, "worked his way up from pushing a broom to assistant to the general manager for safety." It had been decades ago, but Max talked knowledgeably about the business of steelmaking and the work he had done there as if he had just that afternoon removed his detested steel-toed shoes for the weekend. Much is forgotten in any life, but some things you never forget. I could tell without his having to say so that Max was proud of having done the work that once made a man a man in Johnstown. It was also clear that he didn't miss it, even one little bit.

On Saturday we awoke to an overcast and drizzly day. Immediately, we had the same concern we'd had on Opening Day. "I don't care who wins this game tonight, just as long as we don't get rained out," said Max.

Shortly before noon, I left Max at Jerry's and went exploring on foot. I found downtown Johnstown to be clean and safe, as advertised, but because of the weather and its being Saturday I wasn't able to get much of a reading on its friendliness, as I pretty much had the streets to myself. Central Park, the aesthetic heart of the city, was only five blocks away on Main Street. The Park boasted a bust of the town's founder which was erected "by the citizens of German descent of Johnstown June 16, 1913"; a old-fashioned covered wooden bandstand; a memorial to Johnstown's veterans of America's 14 wars, from the Revolutionary War to the Desert Shield/Storm conflicts; and an ornate fountain. This "replacement" fountain was similar in style to the original one, which had been wiped out, along with the entire Park, in a matter of seconds by the Great Flood of 1889.

Evidence, reminders, and commemorations of Johnstown's tragic past were everywhere and inescapable. A block earlier on the corner of Main and Market I had passed City Hall, a handsome structure built in the Richardsonian Romanesque style. Three plaques on the corner of the building indicated the high water marks of the three major floods. The top plaque read "21' May 31, 1889"; the middle one, "17' March 17, 1936"; and the bottom one, "8' 6" July 20, 1977." The original Market House building, which held police and municipal offices, had been completely washed away by the Great Flood of 1889; and the building I stood gaping upwards at in awe was built in 1900.

There were so many of these landmarks around the town that I finally realized, on the way back to Jerry's, that a Johnstown Flood Walking Tour had been organized. What clued me in was Stop #11, a statue of a big black dog that stood as the centerpiece of a small park across the street from City Hall. The plaque explained the significance of the statue known simply as "Morley's Dog": "On May 31, 1889 this post–Civil War cast iron statue was swept away by the flood wave and carried to a pile of wreckage downstream. After being found amidst the debris, it was returned to the front yard of the James Morley mansion which survived the flood on lower Main Street (now the site of Lee Hospital). There it remained until 1903, when it was moved to their son's lawn. In 1944, the statue was donated to the city by Morley heirs." My own little haphazard tour only scratched the surface of painful memories that overlay daily life in Johnstown, PA; but it was enough to confirm my understanding that while the past can't be lived in, in Max's home town the past is most definitely lived with.

In the afternoon Max and I drove out to the suburb of Richland so that he could show me the schools he felt were a legacy to his father's civic-mindedness. When Max was a boy, the area of Richland began growing so fast that there were no schools there for the children to attend. "I got bussed across town to an old miner's school," Max said. "My dad had the vision to see that schools were going to be needed soon, so he got himself on the building committee of the school district and helped oversee construction of the entire system of school buildings, starting with a grade school, then a junior high, and then a high school. He did this as a volunteer; it wasn't his job or anything. ... He had his hands in more shit than the law allowed—that's another Wilson. He'd say that all the time."

"So your dad was kind of a big shot around here, huh?"

"Everybody in Johnstown knew my dad," said Max, "and he always took me with him wherever he went. But he never used his connections to make anything easy for me. I never got any breaks or advantages. As a matter of fact, he went out of his way not to do anything for me."

"Why was that, Max?" I said.

"Because he wanted me to make it on my own, not on his name. He didn't want anybody saying that the reason I was successful was that I was Mac McLeary's son."

When Max and I arrived at the ballpark under threatening skies, Jim Schaly and Chuck Robinson were already there. I was pleased to finally meet Chuck, a pleasant, light-skinned black man, after having heard him frequently mentioned by the story tellers I'd been listening to all summer. Consistent with his assignment to the playoffs, Chuck had just been named Frontier League Umpire of the Year; an honor that for some reason had not yet been bestowed on the man who was almost universally viewed as being the best umpire serving the league: Jim Schaly.

As much as Max loved everything Johnstown, even he had to admit that the umpires' dressing quarters at Point Stadium were the pits. The umpires dressed under the bleachers in the left field corner in a low, cramped room that had all the amenities of a prehistoric cave. As bad as it was, the space didn't even belong entirely to the umps. They shared it with the Stadium's groundskeeper who stored his equipment there. Thus, I was not surprised in the least that the three men left the room as soon as they were dressed and that they preferred to stand around on the field, talking and joking before the game, rather than remain a minute longer than necessary in the claustrophobic, left-over space they were allotted. The place was so much like a dungeon that they had no reservations about leaving their game pay in wads of cash out on a table in the room.

Like the umpires' dressing room, the dimensions of Point Stadium were barely adequate. The distance down the right field line was only 262 feet; the distance down the left field line, a mere 251 feet. In an attempt to correct the latter gross deficiency, a 40-foot high net had been erected above the double-tiered, ad-plastered plywood left field fence, which stood in front of the original, outside brick wall enclosing the ballpark. (To Max the inner plywood fence was an aesthetic abomination.) Anything hit into the net dropped back into the ballpark and was in play; meaning that for a ball to left to count as a home run it had to be hit over or, more precisely, "launched over" the net. Even so, it looked like a ridiculously short poke for a home run in a ballpark used for a professional baseball game; an impression underscored by the fact that there was no need for a warning track because the left fielders played with their backs literally against the wall.

Looks to the contrary, the "Screen Monster" apparently did serve its purpose. I checked the final stats for the 2000 regular season and discovered that, based on team home run totals, Point Stadium was no where near the easiest Frontier League ballpark to homer in. The John-nies finished the season with the second-best team batting average in the league (.290), but their home run total of 55 only tied them for sixth. And true to form, Point Stadium's Little League left field played little role in the outcome of the second game of the 2000 Frontier League semi-final playoff series between the Werewolves and the John-nies.

Thanks to the gutsy pitching of righthander Matt Sheets, Johnstown shut out London 7–0 to close out the series in two straight. Jim Schaly had been impressed with Sheets and predicted that he would beat the Werewolves. That wasn't exactly going out on a limb considering the year that Sheets had put together. He'd finished second in the league

Jim Schaly (left), Johnstown Johnnies manager Mike Moore, and Max.

in ERA (2.50), had won nine games (only one behind league leader Takuro Seki, also of Johnstown), and had pitched a no-hitter against Canton on July 15th.

The game actually started in a slight drizzle and under the lights. The home town crowd stood and began clapping rhythmically as Sheets wound up and delivered the first pitch of the game. When Chuck Robinson called the pitch a ball, they continued clapping. Sheets threw another ball, and the clapping went on, louder. Sheets finally got a called strike on his third pitch to center fielder Dan Wydner; and the crowd, receiving their signal that the game was properly underway—the sound of a bowling alley strike that was blasted over the P.A.—stopped clapping and sat down to enjoy the game.

Up in the Point Stadium press box I listened to Johnstown broadcaster Keith Gearhart do a beautiful job of setting the scene for his listeners. As part of this description he remarked that "Probably the three best umpires in the league are here tonight." Moments later he made another astute observation that would tell the story of the game. After Wydner doubled to right, Sheets walked the next two batters to load the bases, with the heart of the London order coming to bat. That's when Keith said that if Sheets could survive until he found his rhythm, he'd be okay. Just that quickly Sheets proved Keith prophetic. It was obvious from the get-go that Sheets had a live fastball, as the hitters were behind it. After he got league MVP Rick Nadeau on a shallow fly to left (is there any other kind of fly ball to left at Point Stadium, I thought), Sheets started getting his curveball over, and he struck out Chris Gavriel and Willie Edwards to leave the bases full of stranded Werewolves. It took Sheets 31 pitches to get through the first inning.

The Werewolves threatened again in the third inning, as the drizzle began to turn into a bona fide rain. With a runner on first and no outs and the Johnnies leading 1–0, third baseman Ryan Anholt sacrifice bunted. Sheets slipped coming off the mound, and both runners were safe. That brought Nadeau to the plate again, and this time the slugger connected. He knocked one high into the blackness above the stadium lights and out of the park ... but foul, according to Chuck Robinson. The Werewolves, desperate for the cushion and the confidence a three-run homer would have given them, bitterly protested, but to no avail. Before the discouraged runners could return to their bases, Chuck halted play and ordered the groundskeeper to cover the infield.

Forty-five minutes later the game resumed with Nadeau still at bat and runners on first and second. Nadeau struck out, and then Gavriel grounded into a 6–4–3 double play that started with shortstop Eliott Sarabia's nifty snag of a chopper in the hole. From the fourth inning on whenever London batted the top step of the visitors' dugout was lined with anxious Werewolves, over-powered by the feeling that they were quickly running out of outs. After getting out of the third-inning jam, Sheets was never in serious trouble again, and he finished with a complete game six-hitter. Sheets was particularly stingy against the heart of London's batting order, holding Nadeau, Gavriel, and Willie Edwards to a combined 1–12. Over the two games, the trio was a combined 3–24; a dismal performance that was as good as any other explanation for the failure of the Werewolves to advance in the playoffs. As for the "Screen Monster," it turned two fly balls to left, both hit by the Johnnies, into harmless singles. The only home run of the game was a legitimate shot in the bottom of the fourth by the Johnnies' Dan Morse that went about 390 feet. It landed in the Johnstown bullpen just to the right of dead center field and bumped the Johnnies lead to 4–0.

By the time the game ended, the Johnnies knew who they would face in the finals. In the bottom of the eighth we got a report that Evansville had beaten River City 5–3 to sweep the other series.

The Johnnies congratulated each other on the field but rather mildly. Even when the party got underway across the street at Jerry's, it wasn't

BOOK COVER OR PHOTO #9

Max calling a strike.

an all-out celebration, as the players wanted to hold something back until they had won the whole thing. They were obviously taking their cue, as they had all season, from their manager, the even-keeled Mike Moore, who in 1995 had hit the first Frontier League home run by a Johnstown player, when the team was known as the Steal. Moore was happy and proud of his team, but all he said to team owner Tom Sullivan, who was standing by inconspicuously, was "We did it."

"You did it," said Sullivan.

The 2000 Frontier League season was over for Max and me. The finals which would begin in Evansville and conclude in Johnstown would transpire without Max umpiring or me watching. Max and I had done our duty, and we were going home. Before we left Johnstown, however, we had one more stop to make; so at 2:15 A.M. Max, Schaly, and I headed over to Coney Island, a downtown restaurant Max called "the original greasy spoon." When I laughed at the description, Max said, "I'm not kidding. They had the cooking stoves up against the windows, and they were always so greasy you couldn't see in the place. In the flood of 1977 the building that Coney Island was in, which is across the street from where it is now, was the only building that was left standing ... and it was all the grease in the place that saved it. The water just ran off the building because of all the grease!"

Stopping at Coney Island was a tradition for Max and Jim and, judging by the crowd of night owls that was there when we arrived, for many Johnstown residents too. The crowd was noisy, hungry, and impatient. Fortunately, Coney Island had the employees to handle the demand: five tough old ladies who were veterans at dealing with all elements of the public, including the drunk and hung over. Dressed in white uniforms which they somehow kept almost spotless, these ladies handled both their duties and difficult customers with equal aplomb; and I watched in amazement as one of them totaled a large bill merely by counting out loud, while another balanced six chili dogs with all the fixin's on her arm as she prepared them.

The chili dogs looked mighty tempting to me, but Max insisted that I try the special concoction the place was famous for, The Sundowner, which was a cheeseburger with mustard, chili, onions, and fried egg. Schaly, ever the enthusiastic one, insisted that I have two Sundowners, not just one. When they came, I was not bowled over by the taste of the unique sandwich, but I did my best to keep my true opinion about The Sundowner to myself. The last thing I wanted to do was disappoint Max and Jim Schaly, even in such a trivial matter, on our last night of the season together.

The next day Max and I got on the road right after lunch. As we left Johnstown, we passed the Richland cemetery on top of a hill by the highway. "Goodbye, Jeanne. Goodbye, Wilson," Max said.

The ride home was pretty quiet, as we'd about talked ourselves out for a while. When we crossed over into Ohio, we started to get snatches of the Cleveland Browns football game on the radio. The broadcast kept fading in and out, but I heard enough to become irritated by the Browns' announcer who seemed to get overly excited about every little thing in the game. When I voiced my complaint about such announcers to Max, he told me that the announcer he used to hate to listen to was Pittsburgh's Myron Cope.

When I asked him why he'd hated to listen to Cope, he said, "Because he used to rip the officials something terrible."

15

Epilogue:
A Lot to Crow
About in 2001

IN THE FINALS, JOHNSTOWN SPLIT the first two games in Evansville, then won the next two at home to become the Frontier League Champions of 2000. It was the second Frontier League championship for the city, the first having come in 1995 when the team had been known as the Johnstown Steal. I followed the action on the Internet. The league's web-site featured a photo of the joyful Johnnies spraying champagne all over each other in front of the home team dugout at Point Stadium, and I knew that the celebration continued long into the night across the street at Jerry's.

For weeks afterwards Max was still bothered about not having worked the finals. He knew that no one is ultimately indispensable, no matter how much that person might be missed. Still, it hurt him that the idea of the finals being played without him didn't bother anyone enough for that person to make sure that they weren't played without him. He also felt an obligation to do the finals. Max believed with all his heart that he was one of the three best umpires in the league and that only the very best should work the finals. It was typical Max that while he felt he wasn't being treated right, he also felt guilty, felt as if he were letting down the Frontier League. Furthermore, for Max, not working the finals was like sitting through most of a great movie but having to leave the theatre before getting to see the surprise ending.

380

He'd always worked the Frontier League finals, and not working them made him unable to put the season away emotionally. He was nagged by the feeling that he'd left his job unfinished. What made it all even worse was the fact that the finals had been played in his hometown, the tough, hard-nosed, proud community that had helped make him the man he was: Max, the stoic trooper, the gritty survivor, the umpire who got knocked silly but never quit. And not doing the finals felt like quitting.

There was no doubt that the season and especially our last trip had worn Max out. "It took me about a week to recover," he said. "I was so tired I only got out of bed to go lie on the couch."

We stayed in touch over the phone and occasionally got together in person. Max surprised me one night early in the basketball season by showing up at St. Bernard High School to watch my son Mickey play for Landmark Christian Academy. Although he was just a sophomore, the Mick started the varsity game. Landmark took a beating, competitively and physically, and when I disagreed vociferously with one of the officials' calls, Max instinctively came to his defense. "Hey, hey, hey ..." he said disapprovingly, trying to calm me down.

On the first Saturday of February Max and I drove over to Chillicothe for Winterfest 2001, the Paints' annual hot stove league function. Brian Tollberg was to be the guest of honor, and the event was a complete sell-out. To use one of Max's phrases, "it was like old home week," seeing so many people again I'd come to consider real friends.

The place was packed with host family members and representatives from the businesses which are the Paints' most loyal sponsors, and we sat across from Bob and Linda Barlow, who were host family parents and the owners of a major sponsor, Sparkle Cleaners. The Barlows had been Paints fans from the beginning, so I asked them if they had any stories about the early days of the Frontier League. Bob had two stories, both revolving around the poor attendance of the defunct franchises in Parkersburg (WV) and Newark (OH). "I remember that there was always a carnival right outside the ballpark in Parkersburg," he said. "I don't know if it was a permanent part of the city municipal park or a traveling show, but foul balls would fly out of the ballpark and land right in the middle of the rides.

"Anyway, attendance was low, to say the least. There would always be as many Chillicothe fans there as Parkersburg fans. I always buy tickets for split-the-pot. I won twice last year in Chillicothe and took home $480 one time and $430 the other time. I won in Parkersburg, and the take was $30.

"There also weren't very many fans in Newark. The ones who did show up were very clubby, sat all clumped together, in one section. My son, Kory, wound up catching a ton of foul balls because he had no competition. He was walking around holding them in his T-shirt which he had lifted up to form a basket. A Newark batter hit a pop up, and our first baseman, Gabby Angulo, drifted over to the first base stands to try to catch it, but it went into the stands a few rows back. Kory, who was friends with Angulo, got a handle on it and then walked over to Angulo who was still hanging around the railing and said, 'Here, Gabby, you can have it back. I don't need it.'"

Another host mom in attendance was Diane Carnes, who was also a member of the Chillicothe city council and a powerhouse local realtor. Right before we ate, Diane gave the following Invocation:

Dear God,

I thank you tonight for what the Chillicothe Paints organization has brought to our community. I thank you for Chris and Roger Hanners and their vision for this team that has given so much wholesome entertainment to Southern Ohio. I thank you for all of the Paints' players who have been here and the ones who will come in the future. Thank you for all of the host families who make their homes and their hearts open to these young players. In Genesis in your Word you say "In the beginning ..." (the big inning). Each of us faces big innings and no matter what the outcome, in your eyes we are all winners; and even with three strikes against us you don't call us "out," but you show us how to hit a home run even in the worst challenges of our lives. Thank you for being a fair umpire and for never calling our efforts a "foul ball." Thank you that in the game of life you see us all as champions.

For our food, our families, and our country, we give you thanks. Amen.

After dinner the honor of introducing Tollberg went to Roger Hanners, Tollberg's first manager in professional baseball. "I remember Brian Tollberg as a raw-boned young 22-year-old player," Roger said. "He was very humble and a hard worker. He told Chris that he wanted to play, get out, and get ahead; and we were happy with that because that's what we wanted too.

"He had a great curveball and good control. I knew that if he ever got the velocity he needed, he'd be outstanding."

Tollberg himself could not have been more impressive at the podium. He spoke as effortlessly as a politician but with honesty, humility, and gratitude to boot. Above all, he spoke fondly of his time in Chillicothe. His host family had been Tom and Sharon Krieder, who treated him like one of the family in every way. "Tom drove a big combine, and I drove a dump truck behind him," said Tollberg, "and in so doing I learned something about the value of getting dirt under my fingernails." Later, he revealed that he didn't fully appreciate Chillicothe until he got into affiliated ball. "In the affiliated minors I wasn't treated like I was in Chillicothe," he said. "After my first game in Beloit in the Midwest League, I asked how soon after the game the cookout started. They said, 'What cookout? There aren't any cookouts after games here.' So I said, 'You've got to be kidding ... where's the Boosters Club like we had in Chillicothe?!'"

Tollberg knew that everyone present was captivated by the fact that he had overcome million-to-one odds, and so he addressed the question of his own mental attitude towards that predicament. "Making the major leagues is in the back of your mind in high school and college, but you don't let yourself think too much that it could really happen," he said. "Then when you get to Triple-A, you realize: 'I'm only an injury away from the major leagues'—God forbid that anybody gets hurt—but it clicks. You start thinking 'I can make it. I'm as good as those guys up there.' You realize that major leaguers are normal people who are just very good, very consistent at their jobs." He added: "Major league clubs are interested in independent guys because they know they play for the love of the game. They started at the bottom and were willing to work. Guys in independent leagues are playing for the right reasons."

Near the end of his remarks Tollberg related a story about his just-completed rookie season in the big leagues with the San Diego Padres. "It's my first trip into Chicago to play the Cubs. Wrigley Field is packed, and the fans are pounding Budweiser. We'd exhausted our bullpen the night before, so I know I'm gonna be hung out to dry—when I go in, nobody's coming out to relieve me if I get into trouble. So I go out to the bullpen mound, which is right out on the field. I throw one or two warm-up pitches, and then I hear in this real loud voice that can be heard all over the ballpark: 'HEY, TOLLBERG ...'

"I step off the rubber, turn around, and look up in the direction of the voice because I'm thinking, 'Who knows me here? One of my old buddies? Who?'

"And then the guy finishes calling to me by hollering, 'YOU SUCK!'

"I thought, 'All right! I've arrived. The opposition hates me! He's the first guy I'm going to give my autograph to.'"

After Tollberg finished speaking, Paints GM Bryan Wickline presented the pitcher with a framed Paints jersey and announced that his number, #24, was now retired.

During the winter Max's resentment over the Frontier League's pay scale for umpires deepened, and his resolve to lead a strike if necessary hardened. He drafted a letter outlining his demands and asked me to look it over, which I did, making some minor improvements in its wording and rhetoric. The crisis that Max feared would ensue never materialized, and the letter produced every concession, including a bump in pay to $100 for a single game, that he asked for on behalf of himself and his colleagues.

Under the outstanding leadership of "Baseball's Other Bill Lee," the Frontier League continued to enjoy both stability and growth. There were no franchise shifts over the winter, so for the third year in a row the same ten franchises (Canton, Chillicothe, Cook County, Dubois County, Evansville, Johnstown, London, Richmond, River City, and Springfield) were in place. In addition, two new teams joined the league, bringing it within four of what Lee considered to be the optimum number of members (16). The league went back into Kalamazoo (MI), and Andy McCauley returned there to manage the East Division Kings, owned primarily by local auto dealer Bill Wright. The Gateway Grizzlies became the sixth member of the West Division. They were going to be led on the field by two ex–major leaguers, manager Champ Summers and pitching coach Danny Cox; and the franchise's location in Collinsville, Illinois, about a half an hour drive from O'Fallon (MO), promised to make the team bitter rivals with the River City Rascals.

Roger Hanners retired and turned his beloved Paints over to Jamie Keefe, who settled with his wife Kelly in Chillicothe. (In honor of Roger, the Paints also retired his uniform number, #50.) Bruce Gray was promoted from pitching coach to manager in London, and Greg Tagert left Evansville for Dubois County. Fran Riordan, the All-Star first baseman who'd served as the Dragons' player-manager the last half of the 2000 season, surfaced at Richmond as a player-manager for the Roosters. Riordan's hiring was part of a more extensive changing of the guard in Richmond, which saw two local businessmen, Allen Brady and Rob Quigg, purchase 95% ownership of the franchise. John Cate and Duke Ward retained the remaining 5%, and both men were kept on by the new owners: Cate as the Director of Baseball Operations and Duke as a "Business Consultant." Brady and Quigg brought about immediate improvements in several areas; more importantly, they dispelled the cloud of financial instability and the threat of relocation that had hung over the franchise. There was room in Richmond for Riordan because Woody Sorrell, John Cate's hand-picked successor, decided not to return as the Roosters manager. Sorrell was hired as a coach by Andy McCauley and was later promoted to manager when the Kings abruptly fired Andy, who moved on to a job in the Northern League. Although Kalamazoo had a terrible team and finished with the worst record in the league, the city was glad to have the Frontier League back in town, and the Kings were the second best draw in the league at almost 2,500 fans per game.

Not surprisingly, the Roosters and Paints began the season with revamped rosters. This was practically inevitable given the revised Frontier League Player Eligibility Rules that stipulated that each club had to have from 10–12 rookies (depending on the size of the team's roster which could range from a minimum of 22 players to a maximum of 24). Still, a number of familiar faces returned to both teams. Although the Roosters traded Phill Kojack to London and let Bobby Chandler go to Johnstown (where he tacked on enough additional saves to become the Frontier League career leader in the category), Richmond started the season with six hold-over pitchers: Chad Sosebee; J. T. Engstrom; knuckleballer, Jason Immekus; Matt Schweitzer; Rich "Mr. Money Bags" Jelovcic; and Steve Carver. All but Engstrom and Immekus made it through the season. Steve Mitrovich, Blake Leverett, Ryan Peavey, and Key Voshell returned too, and all of them did well, although Peavy and Voshell did not stay in Richmond long. Fran Riordan, who played himself regularly at first base, brought along from Dubois County his best friend, shortstop John Tavares, with whom he'd been playing since their days at Allegheny College. Three other ex–Dragons joined them on the Roosters roster: outfielders Scott Marple and John Schmitz and pitcher Mike McGurk. After brief stints in the Reds' and Cubs' organizations, Aaron Sledd rejoined the Roosters a couple of weeks into the season and came pretty close to performing up to the expectations of Woody Sorrell, who described him as "the best pure hitter in the league, the most dangerous, and the toughest to pitch to." One rookie who became an instant fan favorite was a scrappy infielder from St. Louis named Damon Burkhart. After Voshell signed again with an affiliated club, Burkhart played considerably at second base. His big brother, Morgan, started the year in Triple-A and hit .269 with 25 homers and 62 RBI in 120 games for Pawtucket. In a brief stint with Boston Burkhart struggled (.182 and one home run in 11 games), and the Red Sox released him at the end of the year.

While the Paints lost Stephen Byrd, who signed with Kalamazoo, and Greg Strickland, who was traded to River City for first baseman Darin Kinsolving, Chillicothe returned nine players: pitchers Rick Blanc, Jason Harrison, Sean Boesch, and Woody Fullenkamp; catcher Chris Poulsen; first baseman Phil Warren; and outfielders Matt McCay, Joe Colameco, and Justin Graham. All of them made it through to the end of the season except for Warren. This talented core was supplemented by four key pickups. During the first week of the season Adam Patterson came over from Dubois County, proceeded to tear the cover off the ball, and basically took the starting catcher's job away from the popular Poulsen. Matt Hampton, a big righthander with a blazing fastball out of the University of Washington, proved to be dominating and gave rookie manager

Jamie Keefe, along with Woody Fullenkamp, a pair of hammers out of the bullpen. Second baseman Mike Horning, the team MVP for 2000, was cut during spring tryouts. "The one good thing about Roger retiring is that he didn't have to be the one to cut Horning," said John Wend. With Mike Cervenak still in the Yankees' farm system, the Paints had a giant hole in the middle of their infield, which they plugged by signing shortstop David Dalton and second sacker Kevin Connacher. Both had considerable experience in affiliated ball, Dalton with the Braves and Connacher with the White Sox, and both could do the job with the bat and the leather. "You should have been here to see some of the plays these guys have made ... unbelievable. They're the best double-play combination we've ever had here," Wend told me half way through the season.

General manager Alfredo Portela, manager Jeff Isom, and hitting coach Joe Charboneau all returned to Canton, and together they turned the Crocodiles into a team to be reckoned with. Like everybody else, Max loved to kid around with the witty, good-natured Charboneau, into whose beer he had once dropped his fake eye. One day during the 2001 season Charboneau got off a remark that left Max in stitches. "Hey, Max," asked Joe, "when the grounds crew comes out in the fifth inning to sweep off the bags and rake around the bases, do they bring you a bottle of Windex so you can clean your glass eye?"

Jim Schaly also returned and made his rounds in a brand new car. Schaly was often as head-strong, blustering, and exasperating as ever; but he could be kind and tactful when he wanted to be. He also continued to umpire brilliantly and to prove his worth as a companion, friend, and partner. Early in the season Greg Tagert led the Dubois County Dragons, dressed in new green-and-gold-trimmed uniforms, into Richmond. Jamal Gaines started for the Dragons and became visibly flustered when he could not get Max to call the low strike. Between innings Max consulted with Schaly. "Jim, I called some low pitches strikes in Johnstown, and I didn't want to do that tonight," he confided.

"Five or six of those low pitches Jamal threw looked pretty good," said Schaly softly. "I think you might be overcompensating and squeezing Jamal a little bit. You have to put something like what happened in Johnstown in the back of your mind, not in the front of your mind. Call your game, and you'll do fine."

"Thanks, Jim, I appreciate it," said Max.

As Schaly told me after the game at The Wheel, "He called a great game after that."

Of course, Schaly also continued to be entertaining as hell. Like Max, he never seemed to run out of stories, and he displayed a great memory for details, as evidenced by his account of what in his opinion was the biggest fight in Frontier League history. "The fight took place in a 1994 game between Ohio Valley and Erie in Parkersburg," said Jim, "and the whole thing was the fault of my partner, who did not belong in the league. Jamie H.—I won't use his last name—sent in a resume that was fill of lies. I saw it. It was so untrue it was unbelievable. He said he had experience in pro ball. He didn't. He was over his head from day one. ... He was very passive, and you can't umpire like that in pro ball.

"Joe Yonto was on the plate, I had first, and Jamie had third. It was early in the game, there was one out, and the bases were loaded. Ohio Valley was batting, and Erie was in the field. And Mal Finchman was managing the Erie team.

"There was a sinking line drive hit into left field, so it was Jamie's call. He didn't go 'Safe!' like this or 'Out!' like this ... nothing! The left fielder came up with the ball and threw it to third. The third baseman caught it and stepped on third, thinking it was a doubleplay and the third out. So he rolled the ball to the mound thinking the inning was over. The guy on third ran in and crossed home plate. The guy on second took off for third. Somebody screamed, 'Get the ball! Get the ball!' So the Erie first baseman picked up the ball and tried to go to third with it, but he threw it away.

"In the meantime, the on-deck batter told the guy who scored, 'You didn't tag!' So the guy ran back to tag third, past the guy who was on second who was now coming home. The left fielder had the ball again and threw it to third, but that throw got away too, and the ball rolled again into the middle of the infield. Darrell Fatzinger, who started the play on first, was now rounding third and tried to score, as the pitcher covered home. When Fatzinger reached the plate, he ran over the pitcher, and I mean he floored him. When this happened, both benches emptied. There was utter chaos and fights from bullpen to bullpen.

"A cop came onto the field, and I ordered him to get off the field. He said, 'You can't throw me out!' So I said, 'Maybe not, but I'm worried about your gun. I'm afraid one of the players is going to grab your gun and shoot somebody.' So he did leave.

"After getting rid of the cop, I started looking for my partners. That's the number one rule in a baseball brawl: "Protect your partners." Jamie was nowhere to be found, so I started looking for Yonto. When I found him, he was on the ground with guys tripping over him and falling on top of him. So I yanked him up and actually hugged him so that he didn't get knocked over again. I said, 'Come on, let's go!'

"He said, 'We gotta break this up.'

"I said, 'You're nuts! We're not breaking this up.'

"The fights lasted five minutes, which is a long time because these were real fights, not your typical pushing-and-shoving baseball fights. One of the Erie kids was being held and had his arms pinned behind his back. When one of the Ohio Valley kids saw this, his eyes lit up and I mean he cold cocked him.

"When the brawl finally died down, we got the two managers, Mal and Greg Lemaster, and we told them, 'You get your team in your bull-pen, and you get your team in your bullpen.'

"Jamie said, 'Who we running?'

"I said, 'You shut up.'

"Mal came over and wanted to know how many runs scored. I told him to get down to the bullpen with his team and that we'd let him know. Then I turned back to Jamie and said, 'We got bigger problems. First, did the left fielder make the catch? If he made the catch, then it's easy. The catch is the second out, and the throw to third is the third out. The inning is over, there's no runs. If it's not a catch, it's a lot more trouble, but we can still figure it out. ... Well?'

"Jamie said, 'No, Jim, he did not make the catch.'

"I said, 'Okay. Does the guy on third score? Does his run count?'

"Yonto said, 'I think it does.'

"'Even though he came back onto the field from the on-deck circle and went back to third?'

"'Yeah, his run counts,' said Joe.

"'Okay, that's one run,' I said. 'The guy on second is forced at third. That's the second out, and Fatzinger is the third out, at home, because even though the pitcher got run over he held onto the ball. So it's three outs, one run.'

"After we got all that figured out, we decided who to eject for fight-ing, and we made sure that we got the Ohio Valley kid who cold cocked the Erie kid because the Erie kid was defenseless. Then we brought the managers down. I said, 'Guys, this is not Question & Answer. You listen, I speak, and that'll be the end of it. I don't want any discussion at all. I mean it.' Then I went through the whole play for them: 'Three outs, one run, end of play.'

"Lemaster went, 'Wait, wait ...'

"I said, 'NO! No, no, no. There's no discussion. That's the way it is, and so-and-so is out of the game, and so is so-and-so, and that's it. And, another thing: get control of your teams right now. If your pitcher throws a ball that even comes close to hitting the batter, you're out of this game. I mean it.'

"We finished the game as if we were in church. It was the weirdest play and greatest fight all at the same time."

Schaly also relished telling the tale of the greatest swan song in Fron-tier League history, delivered by Darrell Fatzinger, the same huge Ohio

Valley Redcoats first baseman of the previous story. "Fatzinger was the Babe Ruth of the Frontier League," said Jim; "not because he hit so many home runs, but because he hit a home run in his last at bat in professional baseball and he called his shot. I know he did it because I was there, umpiring the game. He tapped his bat on the plate and then pointed to center field. When he did, the crowd started going nuts. They loved it. He swung and missed at the first pitch and swung so hard that he fell down. He missed the next pitch too and swung so hard that he screwed himself into the ground. The 0–2 pitch came in and CRACK! The ball sailed over the center field fence and bounced off a building across the street. He stood there watching it, with the fans going absolutely crazy, and then he flipped his bat over his shoulder and started trotting around the bases. The first baseman, the second baseman, the shortstop, and the third baseman all gave him high fives as he went around. It was the funniest thing you've ever seen!"

On Monday, July 23, Max got a call from Deanna Beaman, the Roosters' general manager. Deanna told Max that Tim Johnson, one of Max's protégés who was working his rookie season in the Frontier League, had been injured. While standing behind the pitcher's mound, he'd been struck in the head by a vicious line drive off the bat of Fran Riordan. Max immediately dropped what he was doing, got in the Buick, and drove to Richmond. Max took Tim to the hospital, and then returned to McBride Stadium to pick up Tim's gear, pay check, and Jeep. Back at the hospital doctors used six stitches to sew the top of Tim's ear back on, and they needed an additional nine stitches to close a gash on his neck. At first, the thinking was that Tim hadn't been able to pull his head away from the path of the ball fast enough, but later somebody else theorized that he may have actually leaned into the ball by mistake, reacting without having had time to think about which way he should move. In either case, the accident was a sickening and frightening one. Said Franny Riordan: "Max, it was the hardest ball I've ever hit in my life. He didn't have a chance. It scared me to death when I saw him get hit. I thought he was dead. And he would have been killed had that ball hit him in the temple."

By the time Max got Tim home to Cincinnati, it was five o'clock in the morning. Max had too much to do and perhaps he was too keyed up to go to sleep; so he worked at the shop all morning, mowed the grass at home in the afternoon, and drove back to Richmond to umpire that night. Max was scheduled to work the plate, but he was able to talk his partner for the game, Mike Martin, into strapping, in exchange for Max's promising to work Martin's Great Lakes League plate game later in the week. Two days after Tim was nearly killed while umpiring, he was

served with divorce papers, a mere two months after he and his wife had
purchased a home. The cruelty in the timing of such a blow astounded
even Max.

Max himself had an injury-free Frontier League season … almost.
One night we were at The Dock when Tim Johnson's ordeal and the
subject of umpiring injuries in general came up, and Max said: "I always
get injured in Chillicothe, but at least it happens every other year. I'm
safe this year." The next night, in Chillicothe, a foul ball broke the index
finger on his right hand. Thinking about how catchers are taught to keep
their meat hand behind their backs, I asked Max why he'd been resting his hand on his thigh. "Because it's improper to put it behind your
back," he said. A week later in Richmond he was hit by another foul
ball which chipped a bone in his left elbow.

Max's son Marty McLeary made great progress as a pitcher in the
minor leagues during the 2001 season. After going 9–4 with a 3.46 ERA
for Boston's Double-A team in Trenton (NJ) and being selected for the
Double-A All-Star game, Marty was promoted to Triple-A Pawtucket, for
whom he also pitched well after a slow start. When Pawtucket visited
Indianapolis on Friday, July 27, Max went to the game with David Knight
and fellow umpires Jon Milesky and Deron Brown, with whom he'd
worked American Legion games earlier in the day.

A number of Richmonders, including Max's drinking buddy Tom
Arnett, drove over for the game in order to watch Morgan Burkhart play.
They bought their tickets in advance of the game, which turned out to
be a sell-out. Red Sox superstar Nomar Garciaparra had been playing
for Pawtucket while rehabbing an injury; and since Friday night's game
was his last in Triple-A before he returned to the majors, more than
17,000 fans turned out for the game. Max and the friends he drove to
Indianapolis with had to pay $20 each for scalped $7 tickets. The scalper
assured them that the seats were right behind the visiting team's dugout.
They turned out to be in the right field corner, but that was okay with
Max because it put them near Pawtucket's bullpen.

When we talked about the night two days later on the way to Chillicothe for a Sunday afternoon game, Max could not tell me how Burkhart or Garciaparra had done or even which team had won the game.
He only watched the umpires and Marty, who spent the night in the Pawtucket bullpen. Marty, Max told me, was wearing #39, the same number
that Wilson McLeary had always worn on his officiating uniforms.

A few weeks earlier Don Tincher had written a feature story about
Max for the *Richmond Paladium-Item*. During the game at Indianapolis
Max noticed Marty leave the bullpen for a few minutes in order to take
a newspaper into the clubhouse. Tom Arnett, who knew that Max was

going to the game, walked around the ballpark until he found where Max and his friends were sitting. Tom then told Max that it was he who had given Marty the newspaper and that the newspaper was a copy of the *Paladium-Item* that had Tincher's story in it.

When the game was over, Max wanted to visit Marty. Sadly, he was hesitant to do so, out of fear of rejection. Somebody in the group of Richmonders wanted Garciaparra's autograph though, and Max seized on the opportunity to help get it as a pretext for asking for a few moments with his son. "Give me the program and a pen, and I'll see what I can do," he said. A huge crowd of autograph seekers began to dissipate when they were informed that Garciaparra was already on his way to the airport for a flight to Boston. As the crowd thinned out, Max saw the bus driver stowing equipment away in the outside baggage compartments. Screwing up his courage, he went up to him and said, "Do me a favor … ask Marty McLeary if he'll come out for a minute." The bussy returned a few minutes later and told Max that Marty didn't want to come out.

"I wasn't surprised," Max told me on the way to Chillicothe. "He's probably thinking, 'You never wanted to see me before, but now that I've reached Triple-A, all of a sudden, you do.' I can't blame him for thinking that."

I felt terrible for Max and tried to put as positive a spin as possible on things. "Max, did you holler at Marty or wave to him during the game?" I said. No, he hadn't, he told me.

"Well, maybe Marty didn't even know you were there at the game."

"I can't remember if I told the bus driver my name. I don't think I did. … I don't know if Tom told Marty I was there in the ballpark when he gave him the newspaper—I didn't ask him that—but I can't believe that he didn't," Max said.

Even though I'd never met Marty, I was of course rooting that he'd make the major leagues … almost as much as I was praying that Max would somehow find a way to reconcile with him.

A notable promotion to the big leagues that did happen was that of lefthanded relief pitcher Chad Zerbe, who got called up to the San Francisco Giants about half way through the summer. Chad posted a 3–0 record for the Giants with a respectable 3.92 ERA in 27 games and showed that he wasn't at all intimidated at being in the big leagues. In a game between the Giants and the Arizona Diamondbacks, Arizona's star third baseman Matt Williams doubled on a 3–0 pitch with the bases loaded and the D-Backs already ahead 7–0. In retaliation for this supposed breech of baseball etiquette, the next time the veteran Williams came to bat the rookie Zerbe knocked him down, and a brawl between the Giants and D-backs ensued.

Chad's big brother, Mike, remained on my mind. He was back in his hometown of Tampa, Florida, where he was bartending and, as his mother had predicted, coaching, working at a private baseball school giving youngsters individual instruction. On one drive home from Richmond after a long night at McBride and The Wheel, I asked Max if he ever thought about that last pitch to Zerbe. "I think about it once a week," he said ruefully. "It was borderline and could have gone either way. I could have called it a ball, and nobody would have said a thing."

Although the Roosters got off to a slow start (2–5) in 2001, it soon became clear that John Cate and Fran Riordan had put together a good ball club in Richmond. The Roosters evened their record at 12–12 on June 23, never fell under .500 again, and won nine straight in a classic end-of-the-season pennant drive. Losing two of the final three games of the season at home to Chillicothe prevented them from capturing the East Division pennant, but Richmond still finished in second place with the second-best record (49–35) in the league. Joining Chillicothe (51–33) and Richmond in the playoffs were the Canton Crocodiles, who finished two games behind the Roosters with a 47–37 record, and the West Division's lone representative, the first-place Dubois County Dragons whose 48–36 record gave them a two-game edge over runners-up River City (46–38). Ironically, two of the four playoff teams, Canton and Dubois County, were the worst draws in the league, averaging 724 and 597 fans per game, respectively.

In the best-of-three semi-finals, Chillicothe faced Canton, while Richmond squared off against Dubois County. Canton entered the play-offs with the league's two best starting pitchers, statistically speaking: Joe Thomas (9–0, 1.34 ERA) and Matt Baber (8–3, 2.33 ERA). This strength, historically decisive in short series, caused some observers to opine that the Paints were facing the most dangerous team in the play-offs; despite the fact that the Paints had a pair of pretty good starting pitchers themselves: namely, Sean Boesch (8–4) and Rick Blanc. The skinny soft-spoken Blanc, who looked more like a skate-boarder than a professional athlete, had used a mixture of control, savvy, and a sharp slider to fashion a nearly perfect season. After losing his first game of the year, to Richmond, he'd won his final 13 decisions to tie the league record for most wins in a season, held by former Paints' pitcher Brian Scarcello. In the end, what looked as if it would be a low-scoring series turned out to be anything but. Chillicothe won the opener in Canton in a blowout, 12–1; lost the middle game 7–4 at home; and then pulled out a nerve-racking 8–7 victory in extra innings at VA Memorial to take the series.

The Roosters won their semi-final series in a similar fashion. Richmond won the opener at home, lost the second game in Huntingburg, and then won the third game and the series, again at League Stadium. Max umpired all three games of the Richmond-Dubois County series. He strapped for Game Two, and even the losers agreed that he had a great plate game.

Even though the Dragons lost, after the finale on Sunday night, September 2, they partied like champions; first, at Overtime's, the one and only sports bar in tiny downtown Huntingburg, and later, at a greenhouse, out in the sticks, that was owned by one of the Dragons' host families. According to Max, "It was the best time I ever had partying after a Frontier League game. The greenhouse was by a lake, and with the full moon that was out shining over the water, it was a beautiful scene. As soon as I saw the lake, I said to Bill Lee, 'Hey, Bill, how much do you want to bet that I'm in that lake before the night is over!'

"Bill said, 'No, thanks. I'm keeping my money.'

"Bill backed his Ford Explorer up to the shore, opened all the doors, and turned up the radio so that we'd have some party music. After a couple of more beers, I took off my clothes, put them in the back of Bill's car, and then went skinny-dipping with about 15 other people. It was great.

"The finals between Chillicothe and Richmond started two days later in Richmond. Before Game One I was sitting in the dressing room at McBride Stadium with Jim Schaly and Joe Yonto who were going to work the game with me. Bill Lee came into the room, tossed a pair of my underpants to me, and said, 'Here, you left these in the back of my car.'

"Jim jumped up and said to Bill, 'STOP RIGHT THERE! I don't want to hear another word about it!' "

Like Bill Lee, I didn't know quite who to root for in the playoffs, as I'd left bits of my heart in both Richmond and Chillicothe. Bill and I took comfort in knowing that at least one of the franchises would win its first Frontier League championship.

The finals, a best-of-five series, started in Richmond, and the Roosters won both of the games played at McBride, 8–5 and 14–0. Uncharacteristically, the Paints beat themselves, committing four costly errors in each game. Game Two was especially painful to watch, as the Paints fell apart completely in the first inning; allowing ten runs, only three of which were earned. "The biggest inning of the year for Richmond, and what a time for it!" Gary Kitchel told his listeners, when the debacle finally ended. The Paints' self-destruction in the bottom of the first was so devastating to the hopes of their fans and supporters that many of them, unwilling to endure eight more innings of misery, left for Chillicothe shorty afterwards.

Thursday, September 6, was a travel day, so the series resumed in Chillicothe on Friday, with Max on the plate. Max and I drove to Chillicothe separately since he would be staying overnight in a motel with Schaly and Yonto if the Paints won. The crowd, though boisterous, was smaller than I expected and depressed, I was told, by local high school football games also being played in the area. A large and noisy contingent of Roosters' fans made the trip over from Richmond, and they congregated in "the Vatican" near the Roosters' dugout.

Despite their bruised and battered psyches, the Paints, I felt certain, would not give up and would play better baseball at home. I also felt, in all honesty, that they were doomed. The Paints and Roosters may have split their 12 regular season games, but the Roosters now had a huge psychological advantage that dwarfed Chillicothe's home-field advantage.

The Paints scored first in the bottom of the first on a single by Matt McCay and a home run by Darin Kinsolving. When the Roosters immediately answered in the top of the second, tying the score on a single by Raul Cruz, Jr. and a home run by Blake Leverett; I got the unshakable feeling that the purpose of our presence at VA Memorial Stadium was similar to that of Elizabethan theatre-goers at The Globe for the staging of a Shakespearian history: not to see *what* would happen but to see *how* it would happen.

As it turned out, the game revolved around Richmond's Fran Riordan who made the worst mistake a player-manager can make at the worst possible time.

After Chillicothe went ahead 5–2 in the bottom of the fourth inning, the Roosters came back with two in the fifth and two in the sixth. Richmond nursed this 6–5 lead into the bottom of the eighth when they brought on their closer Mike Ziroli, who'd finished the year with a 2.58 ERA and 16 saves (good for a third-place tie in the category). A closer is usually held back until the ninth inning, but the Roosters had a chance to end the series right here, and no one questioned the strategy of bringing in Ziroli an inning early.

After Kinsolving led off the eighth with a single to left, Riordan went to the mound to make sure Ziroli understood how the Roosters were going to defend the sacrifice bunt that the Paints were undoubtedly going to attempt. Pinch-hitting for Justin Graham, Joe Estep did sacrifice, and his bunt down the third base line moved Kinsolving to second and into scoring position. Ziroli retired David Dalton on a fly to left for the second out, and then it happened.

The dangerous Adam Patterson was up next, and Riordan went to the mound, again, to discuss with Ziroli how Patterson should be pitched. Jim Schaly and Joe Yonto immediately called time and jogged towards the center of the diamond, where they told the stunned Riordan that he would have to replace Ziroli. The Frontier League plays by major league rules which stipulate that after a manager or coach's second trip to the mound in the same inning, the pitcher must come out. In the excitement of the moment, Riordan had forgotten that he was not merely *manag,* the Roosters' first baseman. "I worked hard to get this right all year," *also* he said glumly, "and I go and screw it up in this situation."

Even though he'd had nobody warming up in the bullpen, Riordan had no choice but to bring in a new pitcher right off the bench. He turned to Justin Fairbanks, a rookie from Wenatchee, Washington. Fairbanks was a hard thrower and had had a terrific year, posting a 6–1 mark with a 2.56 ERA; but he was not a reliever. He'd appeared in nine regular-season games and started every one of them.

Fairbanks got eight warm-up pitches ... from the mound, not the bullpen ... and half of them either went over catcher Jeremiah Klosterman's head and hit the backstop or bounced in the dirt in front of the plate. Max told me later that he looked at Klosterman and said sympathetically, "Oh, shit!"

Fairbanks' first pitch to Patterson hit the backstop. Kinsolving moved to third and was only another wild pitch from tying the game. Fairbanks missed badly again, but then got a called strike. The count went full, and then Patterson struck out looking. Max told me later, "I don't know what Adam was thinking ... maybe that Fairbanks would throw another one up against the backstop, but it was right down the middle. Not even I could have screwed that one up."

As the Roosters had already used five pitchers (Steve Carver, Matt Schweitzer, Chad Sosebee, Derrick Ellison, and Ziroli) besides Fairbanks, they let him go out for the ninth, after failing to add to their one-run advantage in the top of the inning.

Fairbanks was still, as Gary Kitchel put it, "all over the place" with his pitches, and he walked Andrew See, pinch-hitting for catcher Chris Poulsen, to start the inning. For the fourth inning in a row the Paints had the tying run aboard. Rob Annicelli pinch-ran for See and was immediately advanced to second on a sacrifice bunt by third baseman Vince Cerni. Annicelli went to third on a groundout by Dalton, which brought up Matt McCay with two outs. Fairbanks ran the count even to McCay at 2–2. With Annicelli edging off third, Kitchel nervously reported that "We're ninety feet either from Chillicothe tying up this game or Richmond winning it." McCay swung and missed at Fairbanks' next pitch, a blazing fastball high and outside, but it sailed away from the short Klosterman like a crazy bottle rocket set loose on the Fourth of July. Max shouted, "That's a swing!" and got out of Klosterman's way, as McCay sprinted for first base and Annicelli came charging down the third base line.

After stabbing desperately for the ball, Klosterman turned and flew towards the backstop to retrieve the baseball. Three steps later he pulled up, realized that he'd caught the ball in the webbing of his catcher's mitt, and held up his glove towards Max, who threw a balled fist into the air and shouted: "BATTER'S OUT! BATTER'S OUT!" Suddenly, everyone realized that the game was over. After three previous eliminations, all in the first-round (in '95, '96, and '97), Richmond had its first Frontier League championship.

Moments after the game ended, Bill Lee presented the six-foot-tall championship trophy to the Roosters at home plate, and announced that Jeremiah Klosterman had been voted MVP of the playoffs for batting .556 and playing great defense. As a reward for his performance Klosterman received a brand new catcher's mitt and a check for $200 from the Wilson Sporting Goods Company, which sponsors the Frontier League Championship trophy. The Roosters' celebration commenced immediately thereafter. It started in the visitors' clubhouse and quickly spilled out onto the walkway between the clubhouse and the gate to the field, where the players sprayed each other with champagne. I offered my congratulations to the players I knew best from the year before … Aaron Sledd, Rich Jelovcic, Fran Riordan … and then I sought out the two people I thought the Championship meant the most to: John Cate and Duke Ward. I found them on the field, leaning over the fence that ran down the left field line. They seemed content to share for a while the happiness of the moment with each other exclusively and away from everybody else, who could not even fathom how much of themselves the two men, for seven long years, had put into the effort to make the Roosters champions. Cate seemed almost slap-happy, and when I congratulated him, he said in mock astonishment: "Congratulations? What for? Did something just happen here?!"

I also congratulated Max for having had another great plate game. He was drenched in sweat and obviously drained, both physically and mentally, but in high spirits, nevertheless, now that the short but exhausting Frontier League season was over. "I've never had a finish to a game like that in my life," he mused. "That last pitch was unbelievable. Jeremiah told me, 'Max, I didn't realize I had it.' I didn't either. I was sure it was up against the backstop and that we were going to have a play at the plate to decide the game. … I don't know how he caught that pitch because McCay couldn't have hit it with a Honda hood. … That's a Max, not a Wilson."

In his typically classy fashion Chris Hanners kept open the concession stand in the picnic area down the left field line, and the complimentary beer flowed freely for members and supporters of both teams. Eventually, the crowd in the picnic area began to thin out as the Roosters and their fans headed over to the Dock to party. The team stayed overnight in Chillicothe and returned to Richmond the next day where another celebration took place at McBride Stadium in front of about 500 loyal Roosters fans. Max wanted me to head over to The Dock later with him, Schaly, and Yonto, but I declined to go. I shook hands with the three of them and attributed my haste in departing to a desire to catch up with Rogers Hanners, who was then walking out of the ballpark.

That night before the game I'd gotten the idea to make up two autographed Frontier League baseballs as souvenirs for me and Max. The idea was to get everybody to sign both balls in exactly the same spot, so that the balls would be identical; except for the fact that my ball would have Max's signature on the sweet spot, while his ball would have mine. I'd asked for Max's signature about fifteen minutes after the game ended. He wrote, "Play it to the … Max #9." His hands were shaking when he signed the ball, and of course he apologized for the wavy writing. Nonsense, I told him. As far as I was concerned, the evidence of the adrenaline still flowing through his veins connected the ball to the moment in a wonderfully visceral way and made it that much more special to me.

I was chasing Roger Hanners down because I still needed to get him to sign both of the baseballs.

I caught up with him in the parking lot, right outside the ticket booth. As Roger graciously signed the baseballs, I searched for something consoling to say. The best I could come up with was the cliché uttered so often by the fans of the pre-redemptive Brooklyn Dodgers. "They gave it a good try, Roger … maybe next year," I said.

The sweet old man who was loved by everybody who'd ever had anything to do with the Chillicothe Paints was tired but undefeated by the disappointment. The indomitable spirit of a tough competitor and a winner still burned inside him and was reflected in the words of his reply. "I think Chris is getting tired of hearing that," he said. They were honest, unsparing, combative words, but he was smiling when he said them.

Index

himself umpiring 98; past ejections of Frontier League players 146–48; rated by Chillicothe manager Roger Hanners 93–94; rated by Richmond pitcher Phill Kojack 45–46; remembrance of parents before first pitch of game 34; reprimands Richmond's Steve Mitrovich for showing him up 340; rings up Mike Zerbe in Zerbe's final professional baseball at bat 349; rubbing up baseballs 54–55; signal for rendevouz at The Wheel 33; stopping at Village Pantry pregame ritual 43, 218; umpires home plate during clinching game of 2001 Frontier League Championship series in Chillicothe 394–97; umpires semifinal series of 2001 Frontier League playoffs in Dubois County 393
McLeary, Wilson "Mac" 5, 24, 34, 104, 111, 118–19, 225, 256, 259, 354, 371, 373, 374, 379, 396
McMahon, Pat 309
McMillan, Roy 309–10
McPhee, Bid 49
McSherry, John 365
Medina, Tomas 48, 98
Mellencamp, John Cougar 227
Melvin, Chance 88, 95, 97, 145, 149, 153, 223, 233, 271–72, 282, 284, 286, 307–8, 344, 346
Memmert, Gabe 153, 307
Mendoza, Juan 186
Merrihew, Bob 264–65
Merrihew, Katherine 264–65
Metallica 138
Meurer, Josh 70
Miami Miracle 165
Milesky, Jon 334, 336, 390
Millar, Larry 187

Milwaukee Brewers 137
Mims, Mike 13
Miner, Jim 77, 78, 153, 213, 217, 347, 352
Minnesota Twins 49–50, 193
Mitchell, Kevin 139
Mitrovich, Steve 167, 223, 234, 255, 298, 302, 310–11, 323–24, 340, 348, 350, 385
Mizuno, Takanori 46, 116
Montfort, Jeff 313
Montreal Expos 142, 159, 182, 183, 195
Moore, Kevin 99
Moore, Mike 146, 148, 166, 301, 350, 372, 378
Moore, Ryan 350
Morgan, Joe 248
Morgan, Steve 10–11
Morhardt, Greg 328
Morse, Dan 144, 153, 377
Mosely, Trevor 144, 153
Mulholland, Terry 52
Muro, Roy 176
Murphy, Dale 179
Musselman, Bill 279
Mussina, Mike 138

Nadeau, Rick 35, 203–5, 242, 332, 348, 350, 372, 377
Naked Gun 341
Nass, Connie 156
Neader, Matt 84, 212, 215–16, 225–26
Necciai, Ron 58
New Jersey Jackals 177
New York Giants 180, 197
New York Mets 322, 338
New York Yankees 90–91, 180, 212, 219–20, 257, 300, 302, 322, 386
Newark Bisons 34, 344, 381
Nichols, Brian 172
Niekro, Phil 248, 334
Nielsen, Leslie 341, 343
Nixon, Trot 137
Noodleman, Myron 191
Nuxhall, Joe 35, 49–50, 100

Oakland A's 188
Oceak, Frank 4
O'Donnell, Rosie 156
Ohio Valley Redcoats 12, 140–41, 158, 381, 387–89

Olow, Adam 286
One in a Million: The Ron LeFlore Story 182
O'Neill, John 66
Ott, Mel 197
Oxspring, Chris 179

Paige, Satchel 197
Palladium-Item (Richmond, IN) 115, 127, 221, 256, 297, 390–91
Pallone, Dave 289
Palmer, Jim 248
Pappas, Milt 189
Parkevich, Tom 224
Patek, Freddie 58
Paterno, Joe 21
Patterson, Adam 167, 176–77, 314, 318, 385, 394–95
Paul, Allen 27
Pawtucket Red Sox 40, 385, 390–91
"Peanuts" 249–50
Peavey, Ryan 48, 95, 223, 243, 309, 332–33, 340, 385
Pelfrey, Dennis 285, 317
Perez, Pitulka 251
Perez, Tony 49, 251
Perry, Gaylord 248
Petroskey, Dale 252–53
Pettit, Ryan 213
Pettorini, Tim 8
Phantom of the Opera 194
Philadelphia Eagles 259
Philadelphia Phillies 13, 79–80, 178
Phillips, Murel J. 11
Pierro, Justin 179–80, 183, 185, 186–87, 188, 203–4
Pilger, Mike 153, 168
Pinoni, Scott 79, 141, 237, 267, 353
Pipes, Joey 291
Pittsburgh Crawfords 370
Pittsburgh Pirates 4, 68, 82, 316
Pittsburgh Steelers 227
Pollard, Brandon 142, 179, 183
Portela, Alfredo 51, 57, 67–71, 191, 314–17, 386
Porter, Scott 262
Portland Trailbrazers 62
Portsmouth Explorers 198
Poss, John 59–61, 119
Poulsen, Chris 98, 102,